Thinking about Sexual Harassment

Thinking about Sexual Harassment

A Guide for the Perplexed

MARGARET A. CROUCH

OXFORD
UNIVERSITY PRESS

2001

OXFORD
UNIVERSITY PRESS

Oxford   New York
Athens   Auckland   Bangkok   Bogotá   Buenos Aires   Calcutta
Cape Town   Chennai   Dar es Salaam   Delhi   Florence   Hong Kong   Istanbul
Karachi   Kuala Lumpur   Madrid   Melbourne   Mexico City   Mumbai
Nairobi   Paris   São Paulo   Shanghai   Singapore   Taipei   Tokyo   Toronto   Warsaw

and associated companies in
Berlin   Ibadan

Copyright © 2001 by Margaret A. Crouch

Published by Oxford University Press, Inc.
198 Madison Avenue, New York, New York 10016

Oxford is a registered trademark of Oxford University Press

Library of Congress Cataloging-in-Publication Data
Crouch, Margaret A., 1956–
Thinking about sexual harassment : a guide for the
perplexed / by Margaret A. Crouch.
    p.   cm.
Includes bibliographical references, and index.
ISBN 0-19-514030-3; 0-19-514377-9 (pbk.)
1. Sexual harassment.   I. Title.
HQ1237 .c76   2000
305.3—dc21   00-035965

9 8 7 6 5 4 3 2 1

Printed in the United States of America
on acid-free paper

To Michael,

than whom none . . .

ACKNOWLEDGMENTS

There are many to whom thanks are due. I thank Sandra Peterson, who probably did not realize that when she agreed to be my dissertation advisor, she became my advisor for life. I thank an anonymous reviewer whose comments on an early draft pointed me in the right direction. Thanks to my friends, colleagues, and students who shared their experiences and expertise. Thanks, especially, to Sidney Gendin for his encouragement and advice, to Elizabeth Hackett for lively discussions over lunch, and to Michael Sinclair for his help in obtaining legal materials. The Graduate School of Eastern Michigan University was very generous in its support of this project. I thank Dean Robert Holkeboer for the gift of time. Those who supported my requests for funds include Thomas Regan, Sidney Gendin, Michael Sinclair, Naomi Scheman, and Karen Lindenburg. Thanks to my friends at Skydive Tecumseh for teaching me the true meaning of freedom.

And thanks to Michael Reed for his wisdom and love, and for helping me through this difficult year. I could not have done it without him.

CONTENTS

Thinking about Sexual Harassment

1

INTRODUCTION

It has been more than twenty-five years since feminist activists coined the term "sexual harassment."[1] It has been more than twenty years since a federal court first recognized sexual harassment as actionable under Title VII of the Civil Rights Act of 1964.[2] Today, approximately 40 percent of workplace discrimination lawsuits involve allegations of sexual harassment, and U.S. companies are buying "sexual harassment insurance" to protect themselves.[3] Yet, many of the central questions about the concept of sexual harassment remain unsettled. What is sexual harassment? Or, since there really is no single answer to this question, how should sexual harassment be characterized? What kinds of behavior constitute sexual harassment? Can a six-year-old sexually harass a classmate?[4] Are consensual relationships between students and their professors, or between presidents and their interns, by definition sexually harassing?[5] Why is sexual harassment such a problem in the armed services?[6] Should same-sex harassment be considered illegal sex discrimination?[7] How prevalent is sexual harassment? How harmful is sexual harassment? Can the occurrence of sexual harassment be reduced? Should it be?

These questions are not merely academic. Most people work or go to school in environments governed by sexual harassment laws. Both employers and employees must understand the concept of sexual harassment to avoid violating these laws and to be able to defend themselves if they are harassed. Furthermore, unless there is some degree of consensus about what sexual harassment is and what, if anything, should be done about it, laws against it are unlikely to be accepted as fair. Laws perceived to be unfair are not likely to be effective or to endure.

There are a number of reasons why sexual harassment remains so controversial. First, the term "sexual harassment" is a "term of art."[8] That is, it did not arise naturally, as terms such as "carrot" or "canyon" do. Rather, the term was invented for a particular purpose. Sometimes, invented or stipulated terms are quite precise, but "sexual harassment" was not. The original definition was taken up in judicial decisions and in empirical research and developed in a variety of ways. As I will show, early judicial decisions regarding sexual harassment reached conclusions agreeable to the creators of the concept, but reached those decisions through reasoning that those creators would not condone. Though the concept of sexual harassment has always included the notion that it is an abuse of power that involves gender, there have been many different interpretations of what this means. Because of this, one cannot simply appeal to the "facts" to determine which behaviors fit the category and which do not. There is disagreement about what the relevant "facts" are. People must establish that there are identifiable features of certain behaviors that make it useful to label them sexual harassment. This leaves open the possibility for disagreement about which behaviors, if any, count as sexual harassment.[9]

Second, the controversy surrounding sexual harassment involves political and moral views about the proper relationships between the sexes and the proper role of the law in sexual matters. Such questions are very divisive in the United States. Many believe that there is a "natural" relationship between men and women that is the only proper sexual relationship, and that the law should be kept out of the bedroom, or the "private sphere"—at least when what is going on in that private sphere is consistent with their notions of proper sexual behavior.[10] Others believe that people should be free to develop their sexuality as they see fit, and that the law as it stands interferes with this "right." Still others, such as legal scholar Katharine Franke, argue that gender is enforced by and determined by the law.[11] In her view, this is evident in laws governing appropriate dress for men and women and laws restricting marriage to a man and a woman. It also explains the way in which some courts have decided employment cases involving transgendered people:[12] "The law has been a well-worn tool in the normalization and protection of the signs of sexual differences. By policing the boundaries of proper gender performance in the workplace and in the street, both civil and criminal laws have been invoked to punish gender outlaws, and thereby reinscribe masculinity as belonging to men and femininity as belonging to women."[13] It is difficult to imagine a more vivid contrast in views about sex and the law.

In addition to these disagreements about what constitutes proper sexuality and the role of the law in its enforcement, there are controversies over the role of law in the realms of employment and education. We are currently witnessing a dramatic example of these controversies in the dismantling of affirmative action. Some claim that certain groups require legal protection from discrimination if members of these groups are to enjoy equal opportunity in the workplace and in education. Some of these people hold that protection from sexual harassment is necessary if women, and men who do not meet a particular definition of "masculinity," are to attain equal opportunity. Others argue that employers should be regulated as little as possible, allowing employees to contract individually for conditions of work. If the employees do not want to work under the conditions provided by the employer, they are free to seek work elsewhere. Supporters of this latter view claim that the best arrangement for employers and employees would result if all discrimination laws were revoked.[14] Sexual harassment has been conceived primarily as sex discrimination under the law. Those who oppose employment discrimination laws must, therefore, oppose the notion that sexual harassment should be prohibited under such laws.

Method

My approach in this work rests on the assumption that clarity about concepts is fundamental to responsible deliberation about issues. Thus, getting clear about the concept of sexual harassment should enable us to think more clearly about the legal, moral, empirical, and practical questions about sexual harassment to which we want and need answers. I am not committed to the view that to be genuine, a concept must possess a set of necessary and sufficient conditions—that there must be some property p such that all and only behaviors possessing property p count as sexually harassing behaviors. It seems more likely that behaviors considered to be sexually harassing are related by "family resemblance"—that they share certain features.[15] I am inclined to think that all instances of sexual harassment involve an abuse of power, but not all abuses of power constitute sexual harassment, and the notion of "power" involved may vary so much from instance to instance that it may not be ultimately useful to describe sexual harassment in this way. This shall be taken up in greater detail in chapter 5. In any case, there are plenty of vague, useful concepts in the world for which we do not have necessary and sufficient conditions, so that if it turns out that sexual harassment lacks them, this does not automatically discredit the concept.

It may seem that the clarification of concepts is a rather neutral activity, and that once we get clear on what sexual harassment is, we can move on to the truly controversial issues. However, the clarification of morally and politically loaded concepts such as sexual harassment is anything but neutral. Part of the political struggle taking place in society is over precisely which conception or conceptions of sexual harassment will dominate. As Linda LeMoncheck points out, in many areas of public political debate, the battle over meaning is the battle over which moral and political worldview will prevail, for example,

> debates over abortion and affirmative action are heated precisely because intelligent and well-meaning people cannot agree on what the concepts mean. . . . Indeed, the importance of recognizing these conceptual debates is that each side will fight to put its understanding of the issue on the table and to discredit the conceptual framework of the opposition, since the concepts themselves determine to a large degree the moral and legal evaluations individuals make of them.[16]

What clarifying differing conceptions of sexual harassment can help us to do is to identify which moral, legal, and political concepts are relevant to the differing conceptions, and which moral, legal, and political evaluations determined by these differing conceptions are consistent with our other moral and political beliefs.

In addition to clarity of concepts, clarification of the assumptions that underlie beliefs about sexual harassment is necessary to determining the points of agreement and disagreement in discussions of sexual harassment. The moral and political beliefs mentioned earlier are often unstated in discussions of sexual harassment. To understand the nature of disagreements over sexual harassment, it is necessary to make those assumptions explicit. Only then can we know truly where our disagreements, and our agreements, lie.

Though it is unlikely that clarification of concepts and assumptions alone will enable us to reach agreement about what sexual harassment is and what, if anything, should be done about it, clarification is a necessary step toward any useful public dialogue on the subject. Because of the profundity of the disagreements over the issues involved in sexual harassment, it is unlikely that complete consensus about the nature of sexual harassment and how it should be dealt with is possible. However, it is my belief that we have a better chance of being able to develop policies acceptable to most of us if we try to understand one another's positions. This requires being sensitive to the experiences of those in social positions other than one's own and other than those of the dominant group. One of the causes, and effects, of the attention to sexual harassment is greater sensitivity to power differentials between individuals as individuals and as members of social groups. Understanding these inequalities and the potential for abuse and exploitation that they make possible is necessary for understanding the various positions on sexual harassment. Most of us are members of social groups with power over others, and most of us are members of social groups over whom others have power. Thus, most of us understand, in general, what it means to be vulnerable to exploitation, and what it means to be in a position to exploit. However, the specific workings of power often cannot be understood without effort, especially by those in positions of power. It is not enough simply to take oneself as the paradigm "human being" and reason from that position, as is evident from certain judicial decisions regarding sexual harassment. It was recognition of this that led some male judges to recommend adoption of a reasonable woman standard for deciding cases in which the harassed is a woman.

In the context of sexual harassment, most of the discussion has presumed that the harasser is male and the harassed female, and that the male, at least, is heterosexual. But sexual harassment cannot be understood simply as something that men do to women. Many sexual harassment cases involve race as well as gender. In fact, black women have been at the forefront in bringing sexual harassment claims in both the workplace and in academe.[17] In the wake of the Anita Hill–Clarence Thomas hearings, African Americans have written extensively about what sexual harassment means in the context of the history of race and sex in America, and how viewing sexual harassment solely through the lens of gender distorts that meaning.[18] In addition, most discussions of sexual harassment seem to display a "heterosexual bias."[19] Same-sex harassment is often taken to be modeled on heterosexual male-female harassment. That more men than women do harass seems to be something to which all agree.[20] However, some claim that many more men are harassed than is typically thought, and that the harassers of these men are most often other men.[21] Some of this same-sex harassment is in the form of sexual advances, but much of it is not. Recent scholarly writing on same-sex harassment focuses on the gender of the harassed rather than on their sexuality and has led to a conception of sexual harassment that emphasizes how harassment of people who are seen to deviate from the gendered norm is discriminatory. Vicki Schultz claims that "Title VII was never meant to police sexuality. It was meant to provide people the chance to pursue their life's work on equal terms—free of pressure to conform to prescribed notions of how women and men are supposed to behave in their work roles."[22]

This seems to show that focusing on one kind of case, perhaps the kind of case with which one is most familiar, can lead to a blinkered conception. To guard against this kind of parochialism, many different people's experiences must be sought out. This suggests the need for a kind of democracy in the acquisition of knowledge that takes place before the democratic construction of public policy.[23]

It may be that the disagreements already mentioned, as well as those to follow regarding explanations of sexual harassment, are too fundamental to expect consensus on what sexual harassment is and how it should be treated. However, if we are to make responsible policy, we must first at least understand one another's views. The way the concept of sexual harassment has developed, as well as its connections to other deeply held political and moral beliefs, make understanding difficult. Understanding requires clarity. Clarity will not automatically bring about agreement, but lack of clarity makes any kind of agreement impossible.

This book is designed to be a tool for the use of those who wish to clarify and develop their thinking about sexual harassment. It aims to provide the information necessary for careful, critical thinking about the concept of sexual harassment, and to guide the reader through some of the controversial issues that arise in consideration of the concept. Deliberate reasoning about sexual harassment requires an understanding of the history of the concept. Because the concept is relatively recent, and because its development has taken place mainly in the law and in empirical research, that history is accessible. Part I of this book addresses the history of the concept and its development in the law and empirical studies. The legal history of sexual harassment is crucial to understanding the concept of sexual harassment, because the concept has been largely shaped by the law. In addition, confusions can occur in discussions of sexual harassment when people do not understand the law. Currently, sexual harassment is illegal under certain conditions because it is considered a form of sex discrimination, and some forms of sex discrimination are prohibited by Title VII of the Civil Rights Act of 1964.[24] Empirical studies have also influenced thinking about sexual harassment. Researchers interested in quantifying various elements of sexual harassment—such as its prevalence—have had to construct specific definitions of "sexual harassment." These definitions are then used inappropriately in other contexts. In addition, results of such studies are used in shaping law and policy. Yet, as I will show, many of the most frequently cited studies are seriously flawed. In part I, I trace the construction of the concept of sexual harassment from the first public uses of the term through its definitions in the law, in legal cases, and in empirical research.

Clear thinking about sexual harassment also requires considering issues that arise when one examines the concept of sexual harassment. Part II focuses on some of these issues. Perhaps the most important issue is the definition of sexual harassment: What is sexual harassment? Philosophers have sought to define the concept to make clear just what behaviors should count as sexual harassment. In so doing, they have sought to say what, precisely, is wrong with sexual harassment, that is, what kind of action sexual harassment is such that people think it ought to be prohibited, either morally or legally. A wide range of views on the definition of and harm caused by sexual harassment has been offered, but no definition has been found satisfactory by a majority. Some suggest that this indicates that there is something wrong with the concept of sexual harassment, that it is not a "legitimate" concept.[25]

A set of issues that has arisen within the law usefully illuminates the fault lines between different ways of understanding sexual harassment. These include whether the reasonable woman standard is legitimate, whether same-sex harassment should be considered sex discrimination, and whether sexual harassment should be considered under discrimination law or tort law.[26] Because it helps to highlight assumptions about sexuality and gender in considerations of sexual harassment, I also discuss the relationship between sexual harassment law and the law governing harassment based on race, national origin, disability, religion, and age.

Though I provide my analyses of these issues and present my conclusions, my main goal is to provide information and guidance for those seeking to increase the clarity of their thinking about sexual harassment. In order to begin the task, I think it will be useful to survey briefly the range of explanations of sexual harassment that are abroad in the land. Knowing that these explanations lurk beneath explicit discussions of sexual harassment can help us understand why people say the things they do about sexual harassment. I will use these broad perspectives in the main text to anchor the various views expressed in laws, judicial decisions, and writings about sexual harassment. In the concluding chapter, I will discuss the difficulties with determining which, if any, of these perspectives is most likely to be true.

Perspectives on Sexual Harassment

What do people think sexual harassment is?

Some believe that so-called sexual harassment is simply male-female courtship behavior gone awry. Those who hold this view tend to explain sexual harassment as the result of "misunderstanding" or of "conflict" caused by the differing sexual strategies of women and men. This view has many variations, and adherents of the view cut across political lines. It can be attributed to people with political views as diverse as those held by Phyllis Schlafly, who rails against feminism, and Camille Paglia, who describes herself as a feminist.[27] Warren Farrell, men's rights advocate, and Edmund Wall, an advocate of individual rights, might also be seen as adherents of this view.[28] One of the more recent developments of this view can be found in the writings of so-called evolutionary psychologists, such as Kingsley R. Browne, legal scholar, and David M. Buss, author of *The Evolution of Desire*.[29] These writers develop evolutionary explanations of human behavior which include explanations for why sexual harassment of certain sorts occurs.

Others hold that sexual harassment is one of the ways in which men keep women from competing with them in the economic and political spheres.[30] This perspective also spans a wide range of political positions. While it is characteristic of many feminist views of sexual harassment, including Catharine MacKinnon's and Drucilla Cornell's, some feminists reject it. Camille Paglia, Katie Roiphe, and Naomi Wolf are among those who reject this analysis because they believe that it casts women in the role of "victims" who need state protection against the crudeness of men.[31]

Adherents of these two perspectives on sexual harassment thus place sexual harassment in the context of more general theories that also explain many other phenomena. Both perspectives also take gender to be fundamental in explaining human behavior, though in quite different ways. A third perspective that is necessary for understanding debates about sexual harassment is the liberal perspective. Proponents of this perspective tend to see sexual harassment as behavior by some individuals that unjustly harms other individuals in their place of work (and perhaps elsewhere). On this view, sexual harassment is not intrinsically connected to gender. However, because of contingent gender disparities in our society, men will tend to be the harassers and women the harassed. Advocates of this perspective tend to attribute sexual harassment to misbehaving individuals, rather than to any group-based cause.[32] Again, a range of people with differing political views may be seen to adhere to this perspective. It may be attributed to Schlafly, Farrell, Wall, Paglia, Roiphe, and Wolf.

These three perspectives do not exhaust the ways of understanding sexual harassment, nor, as is clear from what has been said here, are they mutually exclusive.[33] However, they do seem to encompass many of the views people have about sexual harassment.[34] This tripartite division had already been recognized by MacKinnon in her analysis of early judicial decisions in sexual harassment cases. She called them the "natural/biological," the "social," and the "personal."[35] In the early 1980s, Sandra S. Tangri, Martha R. Burt, and Leanor B. Johnson developed a taxonomy of what they termed "models" of sexual harassment.[36] Tangri, Burt, and Johnson described three such "models": the natural/biological model, the sociocultural model, and the organizational model. Although the authors' original characterization of the three models has been justly criticized, they nevertheless correspond roughly to the three perspectives just described.[37]

Some authors have filled out these vague hints of "ways of understanding" sexual harassment so that we can compare them with one another and with available empirical data. One of the most complete accounts of the first perspective, the one that corresponds to Tangri, Burt, and Johnson's "natural/biological" perspective, is that provided by evolutionary psychologists. While not all adherents of the view adopt a biologically based account of human behavior as evolutionary psychologists do, such an account is consistent with the view and makes sense of the claims made by some of those who hold the view. As an example of a fully developed version of the second perspective, corresponding to Tangri, Burt, and Johnson's "sociocultural" perspective, I have chosen to describe Catharine MacKinnon's dominance perspective. According to MacKinnon, sexual harassment is a manifestation of the basic inequality of men and women as "men" and "women" are constructed in our society. She argues that the very meanings of "men" and "women" carry with them the notion that men are dominant and women subordinate. This view is characterized by such principles as: all women are harmed by every act of sexual harassment,[38] and women are harmed by sexual harassment in ways that similarly treated men are not.[39] While not all adherents of the second perspective subscribe to MacKinnon's particular analysis of gender and power, MacKinnon's view has been so important in the development of the concept of sexual harassment that other versions of the perspective are usually developed in reference to her view. Socioculturalists insist that an accurate understanding of sexual harassment requires a gendered analysis that takes into account the ways in which gender involves notions not just of difference but of inequality.[40]

The third perspective is one possible application of liberal political theory to the phenomenon of sexual harassment. Both the liberal perspective and the sociocultural perspective hold that women are more likely to be harassed, and men to be harassers, but they do not agree on how this is to be explained. From the liberal perspective, it is because more men than women are in a position to harass.[41] Sexual harassment is most often seen as a harm to individuals by other individuals. However, some versions of liberal feminism seem to combine a version of the sociocultural perspective with a version of the liberal perspective.

A Natural/Biological Perspective:
Evolutionary Psychology

The evolutionary psychology perspective on sexual harassment is a well-developed version of the natural/biological perspective and can thus serve as an example of that perspective. According to the evolutionary psychology perspective, sexual harassment can be explained in terms of sexual selection. Sexual selection is "the evolution of characteristics because of their reproductive benefits, rather than survival benefits."[42] There are two forms of sexual selection. Some characteristics evolve because they enable an animal to compete with other animals of the same sex for mates. Characteristics such as intelligence and strength evolve because individuals with those characteristics are able to compete for access to mates. Other characteristics evolve because "members of one sex choose a mate based on their preferences for particular qualities in that mate."[43] Mates choose animals with preferred characteristics more often so that their genes, and thus their characteristics, are passed on.

Evolutionary psychology extends the theory of sexual selection to human psychology. Evolutionary psychology seeks to identify evolved psychological mechanisms that explain human behavior. Thus, evolutionary psychology assumes that psychological mechanisms are inherited and that those that enhance survival and reproductive success have been passed on and characterize human beings today: "All of us descend from a long and unbroken line of ancestors who competed successfully for desirable mates, attracted mates who were reproductively valuable, retained mates long enough to reproduce, fended off interested rivals, and solved the problems that could have impeded reproductive success."[44] This means that universal or widespread characteristics must be conducive to survival or reproductive success.[45]

Men and women have evolved different sexual strategies because of their differing roles in reproduction. Different psychological mechanisms—sexual jealousy, preferences, desires, feelings of love, the desire to kill—underlie these sexual strategies. Women are more likely to reproduce successfully if they can attract a mate who is willing to commit to a long-term relationship and provide resources for the woman and the offspring. Men can successfully reproduce either by short-term relationships or by long-term, committed relationships. Though some women also engage in short-term relationships—what is sometimes called "casual sex"—not nearly as many women as men do so. These differences in determinants of reproductive success for men and women produce differing preferences in mates for men and women. Male preferences depend to some extent on whether the man is seeking a short- or a long-term mate. For short-term mates, men are not very selective. They will take just about anyone who is willing. For long-term mates, "Men worldwide want physically attractive, young, and sexually loyal wives who will remain faithful to them until death."[46] Women prefer men possessing characteristics indicative of commitment and resources. This is true for both short-term and long-term mates: "Women's desires in a short-term sex partner strongly resemble their desires in a husband. In both cases, women want someone who is kind, romantic, understanding, exciting, stable, healthy, humorous and generous with his resources."[47] This is because "[a]ll these cues—economic resources, social status, and older age—add up to one thing: the ability of a man to acquire and control resources that women can use for themselves and for their children."[48]

Evolutionary psychology predicts that, since physical attractiveness in both men and women signals health and good genes, both men and women will seek physically attractive mates. However, women should also tend to seek men who will be good providers and protectors, for which physical attractiveness is not a sure sign. And, universally, they do.

These differences in men's and women's psychologies that stem from their respective sexual strategies are bound to produce conflicts between men and women: "The sexual strategies that members of one sex pursue to select, attract, keep, or replace a mate often have the unfortunate consequence of creating a conflict with members of the other sex."[49] One form of sexual conflict is what is called sexual harassment.

According to evolutionary psychology, sexual harassment is a "conflict" between the sexes caused by their differing sexual strategies.[50] Sexual harassment is "typically motivated by the desire for short-term sexual access" to females by males.[51] Evolutionary psychology's interpretation of sexual harassment is said to be supported by empirical data on the "profiles of typical victims, including such features as their sex, age, marital status, and physical attractiveness; their reactions to unwanted sexual advances; and the conditions under which they were harassed."[52] Young, attractive, single, or divorced women are the typical victims of sexual harassment. These are the characteristics of desirable women from the point of view of men who are interested in either short-term or long-term sexual relationships. Women are more likely to have negative reactions to being propositioned, and this is what evolutionary psychology predicts, since women are interested in commitment rather than casual sex. Women are less likely to be upset if the man who makes the sexual offer has high status, which is consistent with evolutionary psychology. And, finally, "[w]omen's reactions to sexual harassment . . . depend heavily on whether the motivation of the harasser is perceived to be sexual or romantic."[53]

Evolutionary psychologists explain some of what is called sexual harassment as the result of "misunderstanding" between the sexes. Because of their interest in causal sex, men "tend to see situations as more sexually oriented than women do."[54] They "tend to perceive sexual interest where women perceive only friendly interest."[55] This can lead to misunderstandings between women and men. According to Browne, "An inevitable consequence of this difference in perceptions is that men sometimes make advances to women who do not welcome them. When this happens in the workplace, it is often labeled 'sexual harassment.'"[56] Men misunderstand women's behavior, seeing sexual interest where none is intended. However, misunderstanding arises from tendencies in women as well: women see behavior as sexually threatening much more readily than men do.

> Because of the substantial fitness costs to a woman who loses control over her choice of a sexual partner and the timing of reproduction, natural selection would favor a woman's cautiousness about sexual coercion. Discomfort should begin well before an overt attempt at physical coercion is made, since by that time it may be too late. As a result, women may perceive a man's behavior as threatening, especially in circumstances where the possibilities of escape are diminished, even if the man does not intend to convey that message.[57]

The empirical evidence of differences between women and men in perception of sexually harassing behavior seems to support this.[58] Women are more likely than men are to consider a particular behavior sexual harassment. The difference between women and men is less for more serious forms of harassment, more for less serious kinds. But the difference persists.[59]

According to evolutionary psychologists, then, the phenomenon of sexual harassment is consistent with the sexual strategies of men (who seek casual sex) and women (who almost always seek commitment), so sexual harassment can be understood as a conflict between different strategies. Notice that this explanation is neutral about whether there is anything *wrong* with sexual harassment. In particular, men are no more to blame for sexual harassment than are women.[60] So-called sexual harassment is simply an effect of psychological mechanisms in men and women that have evolved over millennia.

However, this moral neutrality is only apparent, for evolutionary psychology is also committed to the view that moral values are evolutionary adaptations. Buss suggests, "[t]he values we espouse about sexuality are often manifestations of our evolved mating strategies,"[61] and "taking the long view . . . there is no moral justification for placing a premium on a single strategy within the collective human repertoire."[62] Browne declares that "[i]t should go without saying that the suggestion that sexual harassment is rooted in human psychology is no more an 'endorsement' of sexual harassment than recognition that violent crime has roots in human nature would constitute an endorsement of crime."[63] In general, he acknowledges, "[a] recognition that certain behavioral sex differences have their origins in biology does not in any way answer the question of whether the differences are good and to be fostered by society, or bad and to be suppressed. A large gap may exist between the descriptive *is* and the prescriptive *ought*."[64] However, the biological view is not compatible with every moral and political perspective, and so is not morally and politically neutral, as some of its proponents have claimed.[65]

The moral significance which proponents of the natural/biological perspective sometimes attribute to their explanations can be seen in the tendency of evolutionary psychologists to move from factual explanation to moral justification, while acknowledging that the "facts" do not imply any moral principles. In a recent article on infanticide, Steven Pinker argues that the capacity of mothers to kill their newborns is "understandable" given our evolutionary past.

> Mammals are extreme among animals in the amount of time, energy and food they invest in their young, and humans are extreme among mammals. Parental investment is a limited resource, and mammalian mothers must "decide" whether to allot it to their newborn or to their current and future offspring. If a newborn is sickly, or if its survival is not promising, they may cut their losses and favor the healthiest in the litter or try again later on.[66]

Pinker applies this explanation to the killing of newborns by young women. "We are all descendants of women who made the difficult decisions that allowed them to become grandmothers in that unforgiving world, and we inherited that brain circuitry that led to those decisions. . . . The women who sacrifice their offspring tend to be young, poor, unmarried and socially isolated."[67] In other words, women who secretly kill their newborns are following a strategy that "makes sense" evolutionarily. They are not in a financial or emotional position to rear a child, so they kill it in order to improve their chances for successful reproduction later in life.

Pinker warns that understanding "what would lead a mother to kill her newborn" is not the same as excusing the killing.[68] Yet, he does seem to argue that his explanation of why mothers kill their newborns should mitigate their responsibility and our moral reactions to them. How else do we understand the following?

> The laws of biology . . . are not kind to us as we struggle to make moral sense of the teen-agers' actions. One predicament is that our moral system needs a crisp inauguration of personhood, but the assembly process for Homo sapiens is gradual, piecemeal and uncertain. Another problem is that the emotional circuitry of mothers has evolved to cope with this uncertain process, so the baby killers turn out to be not moral monsters but nice, normal (and sometimes religious) young women.[69]

This belief that biological explanations have significance for morality and legality is found consistently in the writings of evolutionary psychologists.

Browne similarly finds moral significance in biological explanations of sexual harassment. Attributing some instances of alleged sexual harassment to the differing perceptions of men and women, Browne says:

> When a person reasonably receives a message differently from the one that the sender reasonably intended to convey, both subjects are engaging in miscommunication. The ambiguity of cues employed in courtship guarantee that this miscommunication will happen with some frequency, and features of the workplace . . . especially encourage ambiguous conduct that can have multiple interpretations. . . . Unless a presumption against sexual interest (or against men) is adopted, there seems little reason to lay the blame exclusively at the feet of the man. . . . Depending upon the circumstances, either the man or the woman may properly bear the lion's share of responsibility, or they may share it equally.[70]

This is a reasonable position, if, indeed, the behavior is accurately described as miscommunication for which either or both people involved are responsible. But, of course, that is in dispute between the various perspectives on sexual harassment.

Just as the biological perspective is seen to be significant for morality, it is considered significant for politics. The biological explanations for sex differences place constraints on what is possible and desirable politically. Browne, echoing E. O. Wilson,[71] says that "[h]uman nature merely provides a predisposition to behave in particular ways. Social institutions can be constructed to modify behavior, but before such attempts are made the nature of the tradeoff must be assessed."[72] In particular, given that "[t]he sexes are neither biologically nor socially assimilable:"[73] "Consideration of behavioral sex differences is necessary for accurate prediction of the magnitude and duration of the tradeoffs that must be accepted to achieve sexual equality. Accurate estimation is critical since other important values, such as liberty, efficiency, and fairness, are involved in the tradeoff."[74]

Other critics have also considered such theories partisan. Michael Root charges that such theories, like all functional theories, "favor a particular stand on matters of public policy by the way they frame the facts and draw the line between what is fixed and what is variable."[75]

> In evolutionary biology, the functionalist looks to explain the behavior of an individual—for example, that a man invests less time in child care than a woman—by showing that, in his environment, the traits contribute most to the transmission and survival of his genes. The biologist does not consider how, by adapting the environment, the man could invest more time in child care without reducing his fitness or how he could adapt his motivation so that his reproductive fitness has less influence on the time he devotes to child care.
>
> Allowing only the behavior to adapt, the biologist treats the individual's environment and the influence of his genes as fixed. The reproductive fitness of the individual is primary . . . the biologist is committed to a primacy thesis—namely, that the practices of the members of a species are explained by the needs of the members to successfully reproduce themselves. Whatever the needs of the genes, the individual, as if by an invisible hand, moves to serve them. The biologist does not say that this is desirable but presents it as if it were part of the natural order of things and never considers whether the relation between the individual and the genes can be otherwise.[76]

Root's claim is that, "[t]hough there is nothing in the logic that favors a particular conception of the good, there *is* something in the logic that assures that each program will favor some conception of the good over others, in the sense of so framing the facts that other conceptions fall outside and, as a result, seem not to be possible or feasible."[77]

A Sociocultural Perspective:
The Dominance Perspective

The dominance perspective is most completely developed by Catharine MacKinnon. Just as the biological explanation of sexual harassment follows from a broader biology of human nature, MacKinnon's explanation of sexual harassment follows from her theory of feminism.[78] According to MacKinnon, society is divided into two groups, men and women; that is, society is *gendered*. For MacKinnon, gender is a socially constructed category; it is not biological. This means that biology does not determine how people think about sex or gender, nor is biology independent of how we think about it. We decide what biological differences mean socially. This is evident from the fact that, whereas biological sex is a continuum, gender is bipolar.[79] It is part of the meaning of gender that men are dominant and women subordinate. Gender, in this view, is a social hierarchy. Those who subscribe to the natural/biological perspective agree that males and females are different, but they do not claim that males are necessarily superior to females. If males are superior to females in a society, this is incidental to the *meanings* of "male" and "female," or "man" and "woman." For MacKinnon, dominance and subordination are part of the very meanings of those terms.

At the heart of the gender system is sexuality. Sexuality constructs desire. In the gender hierarchy, male dominance and female subordination are eroticized: men desire domination and women desire submission. Male domination and female subordination define heterosexuality, which is also a social construct. According to MacKinnon:

> The feminist theory of power is that sexuality is gendered as gender is sexualized. . . . In other words, feminism is a theory of how the erotization of dominance and submission creates gender, creates woman and man in the social form in which we know them. Thus the sex difference and the dominance-submission dynamic define each other. The erotic is what defines sex as an inequality, hence as meaningful difference. This is . . . the social meaning of sexuality and the distinctly feminist account of gender inequality.[80]

MacKinnon holds that sexual harassment is a manifestation of this gender hierarchy. It is primarily men who harass women. Moreover, while sexual harassment does tend to take place in institutional contexts of hierarchy, such as employer/employee and teacher/student, it also takes place between men and women of the same rank. For MacKinnon, this is evidence of the hierarchy of gender: men dominate women, not just in traditional male hierarchies, but by virtue of their being *men*.

> Sexual harassment has also emerged as a creature of hierarchy. It inhabits what I call hierarchies among men: arrangements in which some men are below other men, as in employer/employee and teacher/student. In workplaces, sexual harassment by supervisors of subordinates is common; in education, by administrators of lower-level administrators, by faculty of students. But it also happens among coworkers, from third parties, even by subordinates in the workplace, men who are women's hierarchical inferiors or peers. Basically, it is done by men to women regardless of relative position on the formal hierarchy.[81]

So, MacKinnon categorizes sexual harassment with what she understands to be other forms of sexual domination of women by men. These include rape, battery, sexual abuse of children, prostitution and pornography.[82] The division of sexual harassment into two categories, quid pro quo and hostile environment, is attributed to MacKinnon.[83]

The Liberal Perspective

The liberal perspective is often more assumed than articulated by its adherents. It has many variants, and people who hold versions of the natural/biological perspective or the sociocultural perspective may also hold a variant of the liberal perspective. The liberal perspective seems to be motivated more by political values, such as freedom and equality, than by adherence to theories about the causes of human behavior. It is the perspective from which Title VII was conceived, though not all its adherents support Title VII.[84] Among those who hold a liberal perspective on sexual harassment are Drucilla Cornell, Ellen Frankel Paul, Barbara Gutek, Camille Paglia, Katie Roiphe, Naomi Wolf, and Michael Crichton.[85] The liberal perspective is not committed to a particular underlying explanation of differences between men and women.

Accounts of sexual harassment from the liberal perspective vary. I shall provide two to illustrate the range of accounts that can be categorized as liberal.

Drucilla Cornell discusses sexual harassment in the context of a larger project concerning "a view of equality that provides us with a new perspective on the relationship of sexual difference to equality and of equality to freedom in the hotly contested issues of abortion, pornography, and sexual harassment."[86] For Cornell, there are three necessary conditions for personhood, or individuation: "(1) bodily integrity, (2) access to symbolic forms sufficient to achieve linguistic skills permitting the differentiation of oneself from others, and (3) the protection of the imaginary domain itself."[87] Sex and sexuality are fundamental to one's personhood. The three "minimum conditions of individuation" just set out "are necessary for the chance of sexual freedom and the possibility of sexual happiness."[88] Legal protection of these conditions is necessary to provide everyone the equal chance to become the person they choose.

Clearly, Cornell values freedom and equality. Her definition of sexual harassment illustrates her concern with the protection of each individual's freedom from the imposition of sexual norms. She describes sexual harassment in the workplace as "the creation and perpetuation of a work environment that imposes sexual shame by reducing individuals to projected stereotypes or objectified fantasies of their sex so as to undermine the social bases of self-respect."[89] Cornell divides sexual harassment into two kinds and claims that there are different harms associated with each. For Cornell, the wrong in quid pro quo harassment—harassment in which an employer demands sexual compliance as a condition of employment—is that it is the "unilateral imposition in a context of unequal power."[90] The wrong in hostile environment sexual harassment—where the conditions of work are themselves discriminatory on the basis of sex—is that it undermines equality in the workplace.[91]

Ellen Frankel Paul provides a different account of sexual harassment. She also provides differing accounts of quid pro quo and hostile environment sexual harassment: "Quid pro quo sexual harassment is morally objectionable and analogous to extortion: the harasser extorts property (i.e., use of the woman's body) through the leverage of fear for her job."[92] Her view of hostile environment harassment encompasses actions that are "objectively injurious rather than subjectively offensive."[93] She does not perceive either form of sexual harassment as inherently gendered. Rather, both involve individuals harming other individuals. She explicitly rejects MacKinnon's view, saying, "This proposal emanates from the 'individual-rights perspective,' which differs markedly from the 'group-rights perspective' MacKinnon endorses. Focusing on individual rights is more compatible with our political and constitutional heritage and more congruent with the 'color-blind' ideal embodied in the Civil Rights Act of 1964."[94] Liberal theory is based on the notion that human beings are autonomous individuals. Each individual is, in principle, equal to every other. This means that each individual deserves equal treatment unless there is some morally relevant reason for treating two individuals differently. Individuals should have the freedom to engage in activities of their choosing as long as they are not harming anyone in doing so. Government exists primarily to protect individuals from one another.

The liberal perspective tends to adhere to some version of the principle of equality, according to which "equals should be treated equally and unequals should be treated unequally, in proportion to their differences."[95] For unequal treatment to be justified, the differences must be relevant to the treatment at issue. This is the perspective that underlies Title VII of the Civil Rights Act of 1964. According to Title VII:

(a) It shall be an unlawful employment practice for an employer —

[1] to fail or refuse to hire or to discharge any individual, or otherwise to discriminate against any individual with respect to his compensation, terms, conditions, or privileges of employment, because of such individual's race, color, religion, sex, or national origin.[96]

However, in the case of sex, an exception to equal treatment in the workplace is built in: the bona fide occupational qualification exception, or BFOQ. Employers are allowed to discriminate against people on the basis of sex if they can show that there is a good business-related reason for doing so. This is consistent with the principle of equality, since it is treating people who are relevantly different unequally.

The relationship of liberal theory to equality is a complex one. While, in the abstract, each individual is equal to every other, in reality, people are not equal. People differ with regard to talents, abilities, and wealth. Some liberal theorists hold that there should be a minimum of government interference in economics, supporting a free market. Others hold that the government should at least ensure equality of opportunity and perhaps even equality of resources.[97] Liberals disagree about what is required to achieve equality of opportunity.

For classical liberals, the ideal state protects civil liberties (for example, property rights, voting rights, freedom of speech, freedom of religion, freedom of association) and, instead of interfering with the free market, simply provides all individuals with an equal opportunity to determine their own accumulations within that market. For welfare liberals, in contrast, the ideal state focuses on economic justice rather than on civil liberties. As this more recent group of liberals sees it, individuals come to the market with differences based on initial advantage, inherent talent, and sheer luck. At times, these differences are so great that some individuals cannot take their fair share of what the market has to offer unless some adjustments are made to offset their liabilities.[98]

Liberalism is committed to no one theory of the good. This means that liberal theory does not dictate what one should desire or value. Liberalism holds that people should be free to determine what they desire for themselves—as Cornell claims here earlier. That is why civil liberties are so important in the liberal state.

Because liberal theory does not have a theory of the good, it is compatible with a wide range of other kinds of theories. For example, some forms of feminism and the natural/biological perspective are compatible with liberal political theory.[99] The biological explanation describes itself as "apolitical," though, as we saw earlier, it does seem to have some political implications. The ideal state of the liberal evolutionary psychologist might not look the same as the ideal state of the liberal feminist, but each is based on liberal theory.

However, liberal accounts of sexual harassment are not compatible with the dominance perspective, though they may be compatible with some sociocultural conceptions of sexual harassment. MacKinnon contrasts her view with what she calls the "differences" approach to inequality, which is consistent with the liberal perspective described here. She contrasts her approach with the differences approach by pointing out that, for the difference approach, gender signifies *difference*, but not *hierarchy*. The differences between the genders are considered to be biological, such as the fact that women become pregnant and men do not. According to the differences approach, inequality arises when people who are relevantly similar are treated differently. Inequality does not arise when people who are relevantly different are treated differently. In fact, the principle of equality requires that they be treated differently. MacKinnon claims that the differences approach conflates equality with sameness.

According to MacKinnon, the effect of combining gender (difference) with the understanding that equality requires that people who are relevantly similar be treated similarly, while those who are relevantly different be treated differently, is that true equality for men and women becomes impossible. Either men and women (who are not the same) will be treated as if they were the same, or they will be treated as if they were different. If men and women are treated as if they were the same, women will lose, since the standard for most positions in society is based on men's lives, and women's lives are not the same as men's lives. Men do not get pregnant and are not responsible for rearing young children. But if women are treated differently from men, then they will also lose, since, again, men are the standard, and women will be seen as demanding unequal protection or consideration. The failure to acknowledge that men are the standard for equality leads the differences approach to reinforce existing inequalities between men and women.

MacKinnon's dominance approach escapes this dilemma by stating at the outset that gender is not just difference but also hierarchy. This means that one cannot simply apply the principle of equality to determine equal treatment. True equality requires that women and men be understood as equal, albeit different, so that their differences are granted equal status. This is not ordinarily done in a liberal view of society.

In summary, there are at least three different perspectives underlying discussions of sexual harassment. These three perspectives have been in existence since the concept of "sexual harassment" was created, and they contribute to the large amount of confusion and disagreement over issues related to sexual harassment. If we could determine which of them was true, or most consistent with the available relevant evidence, much of the controversy surrounding sexual harassment would probably be resolved. However, reaching agreement on whether the natural/biological perspective, the sociocultural perspective, or some liberal perspective is most likely to be true is problematic. There are serious difficulties in trying to compare the three kinds of theories with one another and with the available empirical evidence.

Since our main concern is with social arrangements, we should examine the moral and political values consistent with each theory to see how they coincide with what we think ought to be. Moreover, since we live in a liberal state, we should seek to reach agreement on what should be done, even if we are unable to agree about exactly why. We need not agree on one account of sexual harassment in order to develop public policy that is acceptable to the majority. However, by examining the various perspectives on sexual harassment, we may come closer to agreement.

In my view, the issue of sexual harassment is one symptom of a larger change that is taking place in American society, and in other societies around the world. Traditional views of gender and sexuality are changing, and we are, as a group, struggling to find new ones. Part of the reason for the conflict over sexual harassment is that people are at odds about how they think men and women should be treated in relation to each other.[100] However, changes in views of appropriate behavior for women and men should not surprise us. Scholars have shown that conceptions of sexuality and of relations between the sexes are constantly changing.[101] Perhaps the reason that the changes seem so dramatic and significant to us now is that we are all aware of them due to the effects of mass media. Or perhaps such changes always seem dramatic to those undergoing them.

While it is true that there is still much controversy surrounding sexual harassment, areas of agreement are developing. For example, nearly everyone now agrees that quid pro quo harassment is wrong and should be illegal, though there may be disagreement about how it should be conceived under the law. Quid pro quo ("this for that") sexual harassment is harassment that involves some clear detriment to employment—such as job loss, loss of promotion or demotion—for refusal to comply with sexual demands. As the concept of "hostile environment" sexual harassment developed, the law expanded to include protection from "offensive conduct" as well.[102] This is much more controversial. It is in this area that we must decide what we, as a society, want to do.

Part I

The History of Sexual Harassment

2

THE CONCEPTION OF
SEXUAL HARASSMENT

Before the 1970s

Before the 1970s, the expression "sexual harassment" was not in use; however, behavior of the sort that would later be labeled sexual harassment existed. Evidence for the existence of this behavior is found in documents, narratives, articles, and books about women and work, as well as in legal records. Some scholars have begun examining historical materials for instances of the sorts of behaviors that are now being called sexually harassing, though there is a great deal of work still to be done in this area.[1]

The search for historical evidence of sexually harassing behavior is complicated. It is difficult to know how to interpret evidence from the past, especially when events are described using concepts other than those we wish to use. Complications also arise from the fact that there are differing conceptions of sexual harassment.

For much of U.S. history, women who worked for wages as domestic servants, factory workers, or shop girls were suspected of being sexually disreputable. When Lowell, Massachusetts, was trying to attract young women to work in its factories, it had to counter the perception that factory girls were immoral, a threat to decent family life, and in need of moral supervision by upstanding members of the community.[2] Because of the reputation attributed to working women, if one of them became pregnant by a supervisor or master, her loose morals were blamed, and coercion was not typically suspected.[3] In seventeenth-century America, indentured servants often became pregnant by their employers.[4] This may indicate coercive activity, since indentured servants were largely under the control of their employers—they could not marry or become pregnant or leave their employment without the employer's permission. However, without more information, we cannot determine whether the sexual activity leading to the pregnancy was coerced. Yet, as we shall see, according to some conceptions of sexual harassment, the fact that the servant was so dependent on her employer is sufficient to make the employer's behavior sexual harassment.

In spite of these difficulties of interpretation, there is evidence that coercive sexual activity took place between employers and employees. Such evidence comes from the narratives of the working women themselves, from the cases that became the subject of public concern, and from contemporary books and articles on women and work. One scholar who examined court records of sexual assault in England between 1700 and 1799 found that 29 percent of rape cases in London involved masters and servants.[5] The precise prevalence of coercive sexual behavior is difficult to determine, but a number of the personal accounts of working women suggest that such behavior was fairly common in some employment arrangements,[6] while others suggest that sexual demands in some contexts were rather uncommon.[7]

The experiences of enslaved African women at the hands of white owners, the owners' sons, and overseers, presents in particularly stark terms the dynamic thought by some to underlie all instances of sexual harassment.[8] Under slavery, "[s]lave women were seen as sexual property. . . . Slaves had no legal right to refuse sexual advances from their masters, since legally the concept of raping a slave simply did not exist."[9] When women rejected the advances of their masters, they were often punished severely.[10] Accompanying the sense of entitlement that white men had toward black women was the view that enslaved women were wanton, insatiable seductresses. This made it possible for white men and women to blame the women for men's sexual misconduct, as they did when an enslaved woman managed to bring a white man to court on the charge of rape.[11]

The sexual exploitation of African American women continued after the end of slavery.[12] Women who did domestic work were particularly vulnerable. A personal account of the sort of conduct to which African American women were subjected appeared in an anonymous article in the 1912 issue of *The Independent*: "I remember very well the first and last work place from which I was dismissed. I lost my place because I refused to let the madam's husband kiss me."[13] The outcome of the incident was not only the loss of a job. The African American woman's husband was arrested and fined $25 for confronting the harasser. The woman considered the kind of behavior she faced from her employer common: "I believe that nearly all white men take, and expect to take, undue liberties with their colored female servants—not only fathers, but in many cases sons also. Those servants who rebel against such familiarity must either leave or expect a mighty hard time of it."[14]

The writer's daughter, a nurse, found the same thing in her employment: "The very first week that she started out on her work she was insulted by a white man, and many times since has been improperly approached by other white men."[15] Fannie Barrier Williams wrote in 1904, "I am constantly in receipt of letters from the still unprotected women in the South, begging me to find employment for their daughters . . . to save them from going into the homes of the South as servants as there is nothing to save them from dishonor and degradation."[16]

Women of European ancestry were also subjected to sexual misconduct in their places of work. Dorothy Richardson, a young woman working in New York in the early 1900s, "kept the laundry job until the owner showed an interest in her by making 'some joking remarks of an insulting flattery,' rudely pinching her 'bare arm,' and offering a promotion to the wrapping department. The foreman hinted that this is a proposition, and that since she was a nice girl, she had better leave."[17]

In his 1918 *Instincts in Industry: A Study of Working-Class Psychology*, Ordway Tead referred to the influence of sexuality on industry:

There are industries like the textile, candy, and garment manufacturing where women employed by male foremen or employers are wholly dependent for employment upon the pleasure of the boss. And the power over a girl's destinies which this situation puts into a man's hands can be and has been abused. In New York dress- and waist-shops girls have actually been forced to strike to put a stop to the familiarities of a "superior officer" in the organization. In a small Massachusetts town it was found to be an established practice for the superintendent of a mill to indulge his passions at the expense of any of his girl employees who were at all anxious to hold their jobs. And these cases might be multiplied. Where a man can prey upon girls sufficiently under cover to allow his intimidation to become complete, he can have his way with pitiful ease.[18]

The following is taken from the February 2, 1917, *National Labor Tribune*:

A number of women applied for their leaving certificates on the ground that a man employed also on the night shift had been "rude" to them. Pleading before a tribunal when the chairman and the two assessors were men, this was the way the girls, timid and reluctant to state exactly what had occurred, put their case. The chairman was refusing their applications on the grounds of insufficient evidence when a woman official of the Women's Federation . . . wrote on a slip of paper a brief account of what had really happened, and passed it up to the chairman. He was profoundly shocked, and after some questioning he discovered what the shy and frightened girls had really been subjected to and the case was decided in their favor.[19]

Alice Woodbridge, an activist for working women, claimed that she had been forced to give up a number of otherwise good jobs "because of insulting proposals from employers."[20] And, referring to New York City store clerks in the 1890s, Maud Nathan, another activist, wrote:

Floor-walkers in the old days were veritable tsars; they often ruled with a rod of iron. Only the girls who were "free-and-easy" with them, who consented to lunch or dine with them, who permitted certain liberties were allowed any freedom of action, or felt secure in their positions. . . . A complaint lodged against a floor-walker or against the head of a department—superior officers—was almost invariably followed by dismissal of the one who made the complaint.[21]

There is evidence of coercive sexual behavior all over the world similar to that experienced by women in the United States.[22] Women who worked in factories in England were subjected to sexual misconduct by their supervisors and employers. Friedrich Engels described sexual conduct directed toward factory girls in his *Conditions of the Working Class in England*, published in 1845:

> It will, of course, be appreciated that the girls who work in a factory, even more than girls working in other occupations, find that they have to grant their employers the "jus primae noctis." In this respect, too, the factory owner wields complete power over the persons and charms of the girls working for him. Nine times out of ten, nay, in ninety-nine cases out of a hundred, the threat of dismissal is sufficient to break down the resistance of girls who at the best of times have no strong inducement to chastity. If the factory owner is sufficiently debased—and the Report of the Factories Enquiry Commission recounts several such cases—his factory is also his harem. As far as the girls are concerned the situation is not altered by the fact that not all manufacturers take advantage of their opportunities in this matter.[23]

In Canada, women who worked in factories were harassed by their supervisors.

> In April 1890, the Canadian federal government introduced into the House of Commons an amendment to the criminal law to make it a criminal offense for a person who had a female employed in his factory to seduce her or to use the power that his position gave him to destroy her virtue. The legislation . . . required that the woman be of previously chaste character and under the age of twenty-one, and it only applied to women working in factories, mills, and workshops. Upon conviction the employer was liable to two years' imprisonment. . . . The ultimate vote in the House was to extend the age to thirty and pass the legislation, restricting its coverage to factories, mills, and workshops. The Senate amended the age to twenty-one, and it was enacted in that form. . . . In 1920, this law was amended to apply to women in all forms of employment and only to "girls" (i.e., unmarried women).[24]

Agnes Herrmann, speaking to a congress on the working conditions of female clerks in 1896 in Berlin, said that women clerks were subject to "immoral attacks from numerous superiors."[25]

In the 1930s and 1940s, behaviors that some now consider sexually harassing were considered part of the job for women working in business. A book on business etiquette for women published in 1935 educates young women on what they can expect in the workplace:

> Every young woman with a normal endowment of feminine charm is bound to exert just so much attraction—without any conscious effort

on her part whatsoever. Even when a girl is going quietly along, attending strictly to her own business and not giving a thought to the men in the office—or at least thinking she isn't!—she may become the wholly innocent cause of a situation packed full of dynamite and calling for the wisdom of the serpent to avert a disastrous explosion. . . . It is part of a girl's business training to learn to handle situations of this kind. . . . When it appears that the man has "intentions," honorable or otherwise, the standard technique is to pretend not to see them, or else to continue to act as if they were not serious. The rules of the game for his side provide that he should drop that line at once, without making it necessary for the girl to take up a stand against him.[26]

However, the authors acknowledge that sometimes the recommended strategy does not work. In such cases, the only thing the woman can do is leave.

It does sometimes happen that a man is so far gone in an infatuation that he loses all his control, and his common sense—even his regard for his honor—and behaves like the wicked would-be seducer in a moving picture. And in that case the girl is in a very bad spot indeed. Sometimes there is no alternative but flight. It doesn't happen as often in real life as in "reel" life, but occasionally a girl does have to give up a perfectly good job in order to extricate herself from a situation for which she is entirely blameless.[27]

Women are explicitly warned against complaining to management: "The one thing a girl absolutely cannot do is to carry troubles of this sort to anybody higher up. Unjust? Yes. But that is the way it is. A girl is expected by her employers to be competent to handle matters of this sort for herself, by herself. The front office does not want to be put in the position of having to take sides, to sit in judgment, and, possibly, to risk losing a valuable man or a good customer."[28]

Business was not the only arena in which women encountered unwanted sexual attention. When a strike at the R. J. Reynolds Tobacco plant at Winston-Salem, North Carolina, ended in 1947, the Food, Tobacco, Agricultural, and Allied Workers of America announced that "women in the Reynolds plant could now resist the humiliation of sexual advances by foremen without fear of losing their jobs."[29]

This historical evidence suggests that the use of economic power by employers to obtain sexual access to employees is not new. What is new, then, is how we think about it. Or is it?

One question that arises from an examination of history is whether the concept of sexual harassment adds anything to the nineteenth- and early-twentieth-century concerns for the protection of "feminine virtue." Some claim that the charge of sexual harassment substitutes protection by the federal government for the traditional protection by particular men, such as one's husband, father, or brother.[30] Many contemporary supporters of the notion of sexual harassment do not conceive of the demand for protection from behaviors they consider sexually harassing to be "special protection" for women. One of the major disputes over sexual harassment, both within the feminist community and without it, concerns whether or not at least some of what is being called sexual harassment is just an old concept given a new name. But there is more at stake here than just a name. The question seems to be, Is protection from sexual harassment compatible with equality for men and women? Some claim that equality is not possible in the absence of such protection. Others claim that such protection makes equality impossible.

Camille Paglia admits that there are serious instances of sexual harassment, and that these should be regulated.[31] However, she objects to hostile environment sexual harassment claims.

> The sexual revolution of my Sixties generation broke the ancient codes of decorum that protected respectable ladies from profanation by foul language. We demanded an end to the double standard. What troubles me about the "hostile workplace" category of sexual harassment policy is that women are being returned to their old status of delicate flowers who must be protected from assault by male lechers. It is anti-feminist to ask for special treatment for women.[32]

Patricia Williams illustrates these conflicting views of sexual harassment by juxtaposing two quotations, the first from Catharine MacKinnon, the second from Camille Paglia:

> She said: "Objection to sexual harassment is not a neo-puritan protest."
> She said: "This psychodrama is puritanism reborn."[33]

One of the things we must determine in thinking clearly about sexual harassment is whether calls for regulation of such behavior are calls for the protection of special female virtue. The creators of the concept of sexual harassment certainly deny this.

The Creation of the Concept of Sexual Harassment

Before a particular set of behaviors could be conceptualized as sexual harassment, those behaviors had to be transformed from a "private trouble into a public issue."[34] That is, the notion of sexual harassment carries with it the idea that sexual harassment is a pattern of behavior that can and should be regulated, not simply something that happens to a few people who must handle it on their own. We have seen that behaviors that many now categorize as sexual harassment have occurred historically. However, these behaviors were not seen as part of a larger pattern until the civil rights movements of the 1960s and, in particular, the women's movement. It seems clear that the notion of sexual harassment was modeled on the notion of racial harassment, a form of racial discrimination. Vicki Schultz claims that "[t]he legal concept was created in the context of early race discrimination cases, when judges recognized that Jim Crow systems could be kept alive not just through company acts (such as hiring and firing) but also through company atmospheres that made African-American workers feel different and inferior."[35] It was against this background that the concept of sexual harassment emerged.[36]

The term "sexual harassment" was coined in the 1970s by feminist activists, and their conception of sexual harassment was sociocultural. Lin Farley claims to have discovered the phenomenon of sexual harassment.[37] She reports that the discovery took place in a class on women and work at Cornell University in 1974. As the participants discussed their experiences with work, a pattern emerged: "Each one of us had already quit or been fired from a job at least once because we had been made too uncomfortable by the behavior of men."[38] Farley spoke to many working women and discovered that this pattern was widespread. She does not say just where the term "sexual harassment" came from, only that "[t]he male behavior eventually required a name, and *sexual harassment* seemed to come about as close to symbolizing the problem as the language would permit."[39] Recognition of the problem led to the formation of Working Women United in 1975 to address the issue they labeled "sexual harassment."[40]

The first definitions of "sexual harassment" were formulated by Farley and Working Women United. In order to discover the pervasiveness of sexual harassment, they "distributed the first questionnaire ever devoted solely to the topic of sexual harassment" in May 1975.[41] The definition of sexual harassment used in the survey was: "Any repeated and unwanted sexual comments, looks, suggestions or physical contact that you find objectionable or offensive and causes you discomfort on your job."[42] This definition is nearly equivalent to current legal definitions of "sexual harassment." The notion that sexually harassing behavior is "unwanted" or "unwelcome" has characterized the concept from the beginning.[43] The terms "objectionable" and "offensive" have also been common in interpretations of the concept. Early court cases were concerned with quid pro quo sexual harassment, which involves some clear detriment to employment, such as job loss, loss of promotion, or demotion, for refusal to comply with sexual demands.[44] As the concept of "hostile environment" sexual harassment developed, the law expanded to protect people from "offensive conduct" as well.[45]

In at least three ways, however, this first definition is narrower than later definitions. First, the idea that conduct must be repeated to count as sexual harassment was later revised. It was recognized that some instances of sexual behavior were so severe that one occurrence was sufficient to constitute sexual harassment.[46] Second, the definition seems to limit sexual harassment to *sexuality* harassment. There seems to have been an ambiguity in the term "sexual" from the beginning. Does it refer to "sexuality" or to "gender" or to both? Later conceptions of sexual harassment include gender harassment.[47]

Third, some have insisted that an inequality of power, either institutional or more broadly social, is essential to sexual harassment.[48] However, the definition stated here does not require such an inequality. In this, the definition is consistent with later developments of the concept in the law.[49]

The survey definition is unclear regarding another element of the concept of sexual harassment—what is wrong with it. To read this definition, sexual harassment is "objectionable or offensive" and makes one "uncomfortable"—hardly serious harms, one would think. But it is typical of empirical definitions used in surveys to omit detailed description of the harm that sexual harassment does. For that, one must look to the conceptual definitions.

Farley provides a more conceptual definition in her *Sexual Shakedown*. She characterizes sexual harassment in terms of power and sexuality, showing that she adopts a version of the sociocultural perspective:

> Sexual harassment is best described as unsolicited nonreciprocal male behavior that asserts a woman's sex role over her function as a worker. It can be any or all of the following: staring at, commenting upon, or touching a woman's body; requests for acquiescence in sexual behavior; repeated nonreciprocated propositions for dates; demands for sexual intercourse; and rape. These forms of male behavior frequently rely on superior male status in the culture, sheer numbers, or the threat of higher rank at work to exact compliance or levy penalties for refusal.[50]

It is characteristic of definitions created for empirical research to omit the moral dimension of sexual harassment. But a full understanding of the concept certainly requires an explanation of the harm of sexual harassment such that it should or should not be illegal. Farley believes that "job segregation by sex is to a large degree sustained by male sexual harassment,"[51] and she describes the harm in sexual harassment as "extortion":

> The end result of male sexual harassment of women on the job is the extortion of female subservience at work. As a consequence, the broad range of male aggression brought to bear against working women—which includes, but is not limited to, forced sex either by rape or in exchange for work—cannot be seen as anything more (or less) than the means by which this extortion is effected.
>
> Work is the key element in understanding sexual harassment, because this is the prize men are controlling through their extortion. . . . The consequences of such extortion—being denied work or being forced out of work or being intimidated on the job as a result of male sexual aggression—are at the heart of the problem of sexual harassment.[52]

Thus, Farley conceives of sexual harassment as a widespread pattern of behavior that in part explains, and in part is explained by, male supremacy.

Men impose sexual behavior on women in the context of work because they are in a position to do so, and because it maintains their position of superiority in the workplace.

Catharine MacKinnon's *Sexual Harassment of Working Women*, published in 1979, was a major influence in the construction of the social and legal meaning of sexual harassment.[53] It might with justice be said that everything written on sexual harassment since is a footnote to MacKinnon. Those who agree with her analysis expand on aspects of sexual harassment first identified and described by MacKinnon. Those who disagree with her analysis object to aspects of her analysis.

MacKinnon defines sexual harassment as follows: "Sexual harassment, most broadly defined, refers to the unwanted imposition of sexual requirements in the context of a relationship of unequal power. Central to the concept is the use of power derived from one social sphere to lever benefits or impose deprivations in another."[54] MacKinnon's definition shares with Farley's survey definition the element of "unwantedness"; it also brings to the fore the inequality of power that is evident in Farley's conceptual definition.

Among MacKinnon's contributions to the development of the concept of sexual harassment is the distinction between quid pro quo harassment and hostile environment sexual harassment, a distinction that has become very important in the legal realm. MacKinnon introduced the distinction in *Sexual Harassment:*

> Women's experience of sexual harassment can be divided into two forms which merge at the edges and in the world. The first I term the quid pro quo, in which sexual compliance is exchanged, or proposed to be exchanged, for an employment opportunity. The second arises when sexual harassment is a persistent *condition of work*. . . . In the quid pro quo, the woman must comply sexually or forfeit an employment opportunity. . . . In sexual harassment as a condition of work, the exchange of sex for employment opportunities is less direct.[55]

What MacKinnon calls "sexual harassment as a condition of work" was later termed "hostile environment" sexual harassment (see chapter 3).

Quid pro quo harassment "is defined by the more or less explicit exchange: the woman must comply sexually or forfeit an employment benefit."[56] Employment benefits may include promotions, wage increases, or the retention of the position. As I have said, most people now agree that quid pro quo harassment is unjust and should be illegal, though they might disagree on how to characterize the harassment or on the kind of law that should regulate such behavior. There is more controversy surrounding the injustice of hostile environment sexual harassment.

According to MacKinnon and other adherents of the sociocultural perspective, hostile environment harassment is not different in kind from quid pro quo sexual harassment. Both require a woman to put up with some kind of unequal treatment as a condition of employment: "Note that the distinction is actually two poles of a continuum. A constructive discharge, in which a woman leaves the job because of a constant condition of sexual harassment, is an environmental situation that becomes quid pro quo."[57] For MacKinnon, a woman who is subject to explicit sexual demands from her employer or co-workers and who quits her job because of this is in the same position as a woman who is subject to explicit sexual demands by her employer, refuses them, and is then subject to retaliation of some sort—loss of the job, demotion, et cetera. Moreover, a woman who is subject to unwanted sexual advances of more indirect sorts is in the same position as these women:

> Unwanted sexual advances, made simply because she has a woman's body, can be a daily part of a woman's work life. She may be constantly felt or pinched, visually undressed and stared at, surreptitiously kissed, commented upon, manipulated into being found alone, and generally taken advantage of at work—but never promised or denied anything explicitly connected with her job.[58]

The relevant similarity, on MacKinnon's view, is that the employee is forced to endure this behavior in order to retain her position, and that this amounts to a condition of work to which no one should be subject.

Though MacKinnon and other adherents of the sociocultural perspective see quid pro quo and hostile environment sexual harassment as points on a continuum, those who hold a natural/biological or liberal perspective need not. Those who reject the view that sexual harassment should be conceived of as a form of sex discrimination tend to draw a sharp distinction between quid pro quo and hostile environment sexual harassment, arguing that quid pro quo harassment should be handled under tort law, and that hostile environment sexual harassment should not be illegal at all, or only if an objectively determinable injury results.[59]

MacKinnon's most significant contribution to the development of the meaning of "sexual harassment" is her claim that sexual harassment is sex discrimination, and her working out of this claim in the context of discrimination law. This claim was adopted by the Equal Employment Opportunity Commission and incorporated into their 1980 *Guidelines on Discrimination Because of Sex*, and it has been central to the legal development of the concept.[60] As we shall see in chapter 3, the legal history of the development of the concept of sexual harassment is the history of the courts' acceptance of sexual harassment as sex discrimination.

The development of the conception of sexual harassment as sex discrimination has not been without problems. This is due in part to the differing ways of interpreting the notion of discrimination, described in chapter 1. For socioculturalists, MacKinnon's inequality, or dominance, approach is preferable. However, most judges and government appointees tend to be liberals of one sort or another, and they tend to prefer the differences approach. Whether one adopts the dominance approach or the differences approach determines one's analysis of a case. While sometimes both approaches yield the same result—for instance, the verdict that discrimination has occurred—this is not guaranteed.

After twenty years, however, there is still a good deal of discussion about the kind of law that should regulate sexual harassment. MacKinnon and many others argue that sexual harassment should be considered a form of sex discrimination, in violation of Title VII of the Civil Rights Act. Some have argued sexual harassment *should* be treated under tort law rather than sex discrimination law, using either existing torts, such as invasion of the right to privacy, intentional assault and battery, or intentional infliction of emotional distress, or creating a new tort specifically for sexual harassment.[61] Still others advocate criminal law for some forms of sexual harassment.[62] This controversy is not merely a legal one. It has implications for how we conceptualize sexual harassment.

Tort law concerns person injuries, harms done by one person to another. Its purpose is to compensate the injured party for the harm done to them. According to one account, "Tort liability . . . exists primarily to compensate the injured person by compelling the wrongdoer to pay for the damage he has done."[63] Thus, use of torts—such as "assault and battery, insult, offensive battery, intentional infliction of emotional distress by extreme and outrageous conduct, invasion of privacy"[64]—to litigate sexual harassment claims conceptualizes sexual harassment as behavior offensive to the integrity or sensibilities of an individual. As MacKinnon puts it, "In tort perspective, the injury of sexual harassment would be seen as an injury to the individual person, to personal sexual integrity, with damages extending to the job."[65] Discrimination law, on the other hand, exists to ensure equal opportunity regardless of sex, race, national origin, religion, age, and disability. As such, it is "sensitive to . . . power dynamics" that operate in obstructing equality of opportunity.[66] If the dominant remedy for sexual harassment is tort law, then sexual harassment will be conceived primarily as "personal." Conceiving of sexual harassment in this way tends to undercut the conception of sexual harassment as part of a system of abuses of patriarchal power explicit in many sociocultural conceptions of sexual harassment.[67] Thus, the dispute over which kind of law should govern sexual harassment is a dispute about what sexual harassment *is*. This issue will be discussed in more detail in chapter 6.

As I recount the development of the concept of sexual harassment in the law in chapter 3, the reader should keep in mind that the concept of sexual harassment is not merely a legal concept. Consequently, the development of the legal concept of sexual harassment may be circumscribed in ways that a broader concept is not. From the beginning, sexual harassment in law has been seen by the courts as a particular kind of sex discrimination, so that it has been through the lens of legal conceptions of sex discrimination that the concept has developed. Since sex discrimination under the law is concerned with employment, sexual harassment is conceptualized primarily as a form of employment discrimination under Title VII. However, it need not be. Perhaps sexually harassing behavior should be seen as a wide category, some of which should be illegal in certain contexts, some of which should not. We should not allow the law to dictate our conception of sexual harassment.

In the next chapter, we shall trace the development of the concept of sexual harassment in the law. I shall show how competing conceptions of sexual harassment are evident in the judicial decisions and Equal Employment Opportunity Commission regulations developed from the 1970s through the 1990s.

3

THE LEGAL CONCEPTION
OF SEXUAL HARASSMENT

In chapters 1 and 2, I have discussed sexual harassment only in the context of employment. However, from the beginning, other contexts and relationships were considered similar enough to the employment context to create the conditions for sexual harassment. Perhaps most prominent among these is the academic context, and the relationship between instructors and students. Because the academic environment may involve factors typically absent from workplace environments, I will discuss the development of the concept of sexual harassment in the law in the workplace and in the academy separately. Finally, I will consider some developments of sexual harassment law in countries other than the United States. Though the concept of sexual harassment in these other countries has been influenced by developments in U.S. law, certain differences in the treatment of sexual harassment highlight assumptions underlying our conceptions of sexual harassment.

Workplace Sexual Harassment

The concept of sexual harassment is remarkable for the degree to which the law has influenced its development, and vice versa. This is not surprising, since from the beginning, sexual harassment was viewed not as something that was simply unjust, but as something for which women ought to receive legal redress. When Lin Farley and Working Women United were formulating their conceptions of sexual harassment, they were involved with the case of Carmita Wood, a Cornell employee, who was seeking unemployment benefits for having quit her job because of sexual harassment. As MacKinnon was articulating her concept of sexual harassment, she was arguing that women should receive protection under Title VII of the Civil Rights Act of 1964.

Sex discrimination in employment was prohibited by Title VII of the Civil Rights Act of 1964. The Equal Employment Opportunity Commission (EEOC) was created to administer the act. The most important part of the act for our purposes, section 2000e-2(a)(1), reads:

(a) It shall be an unlawful employment practice for an employer—
(1) to fail or refuse to hire or to discharge any individual, or otherwise to discriminate against any individual with respect to his compensation, terms, conditions, or privileges of employment, because of such individual's race, color, religion, sex, or national origin.[1]

The primary purpose of Title VII was to provide a remedy for discriminatory working conditions so as to provide equal opportunity in employment for everyone. Arbitrary or irrelevant barriers to employment based on membership in the protected categories were to be eliminated.

The category of "sex" was included in the act at the last moment in an effort to defeat the passage of the law.[2] Although more than one-third of complaints filed with the EEOC in the first year of the EEOC's existence involved sex discrimination, there was little attention paid them by the EEOC.[3] Furthermore, "for an eight-year period following its original enactment, there was no legislative history to refine the congressional language."[4] As a result, little guidance was provided the courts by Congress regarding just what the act was intended to prohibit.[5] The activism of feminists and the creation of the National Organization for Women (NOW) helped to change this.[6]

The first influential sex discrimination cases concerned discriminatory policies, such as sex-classified help-wanted advertisements,[7] weight-lifting requirements,[8] height and weight standards applied only to one gender,[9] discriminatory job assignment and transfer,[10] different hours of employment based on gender,[11] "fringe benefits,"[12] discriminating against females because they are married[13] or pregnant,[14] and forbidding employment of married women but not of married men.[15]

The Equal Employment Opportunity Act and Title IX of the Education Amendments Act were approved by Congress in 1972. The former extended the protections of Title VII to federal employees. The latter prohibited sex discrimination at educational institutions receiving federal aid.[16]

It is against this legislative and judicial background that sexual harassment cases were brought forward. But how well did sexual harassment fit this already established legal framework? In the early cases, judges had trouble making sexual harassment fit Title VII sex discrimination legislation and case law. This problem has plagued the development of the concept in the law from the beginning, prompting at least one judge, Robert Bork, to comment on the artificiality of conceiving of sexual harassment as sex discrimination.[17]

Sexual Harassment Is Sex Discrimination

Cases alleging sex discrimination on the basis of sexual harassment began to reach the federal courts in the mid-1970s. All of the cases prior to 1981 involved allegations of what is now considered quid pro quo sexual harassment, though neither expression—"sexual harassment" or "quid pro quo"—was explicitly used. Many of these decisions went against the plaintiffs because judges did not conceive of quid pro quo sexual harassment as sex discrimination. They just could not see how firing or failing to promote someone because they would not have sex with you constituted sex discrimination. It was a personal conflict—unfortunate, but not sex discrimination prohibited by Title VII. The natural/biological and liberal perspectives described in chapter I clearly underlie these judicial decisions.

In some early cases, judges denied that sexual harassment constituted sex discrimination on the grounds that the behavior in question was not "based on sex" in the sense required by Title VII. The first sexual harassment case decided by a federal court was *Barnes v. Train*, decided in 1974.[18] *Barnes* was a quid pro quo case. The plaintiff, Michelle Barnes, an African American woman, claimed that her supervisor had taken retaliatory action against her because she refused his sexual advances, and that this constituted sex discrimination under Title VII.[19] The court clearly did not see Title VII, or the Equal Employment Opportunity Act of 1972, as encompassing such actions. In his opinion, Judge John Lewis Smith, Jr., says explicitly that the "alleged retaliatory actions of plaintiff's supervisor taken because plaintiff refused his request for an 'after hours affair', are not the type of discriminatory conduct contemplated by the 1972 Act."[20] The court argued that the supervisor's behavior did not constitute sex discrimination under Title VII because:

> The substance of plaintiff's complaint is that she was discriminated against, not because she was a woman, but because she refused to engage in a sexual affair with her supervisor. This is a controversy underpinned by the subtleties of an inharmonious personal relationship. Regardless of how inexcusable the conduct of plaintiff's supervisor might have been, it does not evidence an arbitrary barrier to continued employment based on the plaintiff's sex.[21]

Thus, the court saw the relevant class not as "women" but as "persons who refused to engage in a sexual affair with her/his supervisor." While this kind of behavior on the part of the supervisor might be reprehensible, the class of "persons who refused to engage in a sexual affair with his/her supervisor" is not protected under Title VII or by the 1972 Act. The court describes the issue as a "personal" one between the plaintiff and the supervisor, implying that if the relevant class is not "woman" but some unprotected class, then the behavior in question was not appropriately "based on sex." Smith did not think that the supervisor acted as he did toward Barnes because she was a woman, but because she rejected his advances.

Other early decisions agreed that sexually harassing behavior could not be said to be "based on sex," but for reasons other than those given in *Barnes v. Train*.[22] In *Tomkins v. Public Service Electric & Gas*, plaintiff Adrienne Tomkins claimed that a male supervisor asked her to lunch to discuss her prospects with the company. At the lunch, he made sexual advances to her and detained her against her will. When she complained to the company, the company retaliated against her, and fifteen months later she was fired. Judge

Stern, writing the opinion, argued that: "In this instance the supervisor was male and the employee was female. But no immutable principle of psychology compels this alignment of parties. The gender lines might as easily have been reversed, or even not crossed at all. While sexual desire animated the parties, or at least one of them, the gender of each is incidental to the claim of abuse."[23] This kind of argument is typical of a liberal perspective. Stern's interpretation of sex discrimination under Title VII suggests that to count as sex discrimination, it must not be possible to subject both sexes to the treatment in question. As MacKinnon puts it, "An abuse that *can be* visited upon either gender . . . cannot be treatment based on sex."[24] However, it is difficult to know how to interpret this principle. On one interpretation it is obviously inconsistent with the kinds of cases considered to be paradigm discrimination cases. Suppose that women in a company claim that they are receiving lower wages than men who are performing the same work. Surely their claim can be said to be "sex based," even if it is possible to reverse the situation, and men receive lower wages than women. Perhaps Stern means that in this kind of case, because there is only one person who is subject to the behavior, the fact that the plaintiff is a woman is not significant. It could just as easily have happened to a man. This line of reasoning seems to have been quite common in these early decisions, and one can see why people might think that this was not the sort of activity Title VII was intended to prohibit. Stern seems to have believed that this was simply a case of one individual, who happened to be a man, abusing another, who happened to be a woman. In his argument, Stern avers:

> Title VII was enacted in order to remove those artificial barriers to full employment which are based upon unjust and long-encrusted prejudice. Its aim is to make careers open to talents irrespective of race or sex. It is not intended to provide a federal tort remedy for what amounts to physical attack motivated by sexual desire on the part of a supervisor and which happened to occur in a corporate corridor rather than a back alley.[25]

Judge Stern apparently sees the occurrence from the natural/biological perspective, emphasizing that it was motivated primarily by sexual desire. He also seems to believe that the incident can be fully explained without reference to any "unjust and long-encrusted prejudice" against women. He suggests that such activity creates no artificial barrier to full employment for any protected class. However, others, most notably those who hold a sociocultural perspective, disagree. As we saw, they tend to deny that the fact that the defendant was male and the plaintiff female is "incidental" and that such an act involves no "prejudice" against women, and to claim that such behavior does indeed create artificial barriers to women's full employment.

The argument found in *Barnes v. Train*, that the relevant category in quid pro quo cases is not "woman" but "person who refused to engage in an affair with her superior," was used by the defendant in *Williams v. Saxbe*, the first federal court case in which it was argued that sexual harassment *was* properly "based on sex."[26] A female employee alleged that she was subjected to "a continuing pattern and practice of harassment and humiliation" culminating in termination of her employment in retaliation for her refusal of a sexual advance by her supervisor.[27] The court was almost persuaded by the defendant's argument that the behavior complained of did not constitute sex discrimination because the behavior was not appropriately "based on sex." District judge Charles R. Richey summarized the defendant's argument in the opinion.

> They contend that Section 2000e-16(a) sex discrimination may only be found when the policy or practice is applicable to only one of the genders because of the characteristics that are peculiar to one of the genders. When applied to this case, defendants' analysis has produced the argument that since the criteria of "willingness to furnish sexual consideration" could be applied to both men and women, then the class cannot be said to be defined *primarily* by gender and therefore there can be no 2000e-16(a) sex discrimination.[28]

However, Judge Richey did not find this reasoning compelling. He held that "[d]efendants' argument must be rejected because a finding of sex discrimination under Section 2000e-16(a) does not require that the discriminatory policy or practice depend upon a characteristic peculiar to one of the genders."[29] Richey argued that if a person would not have been subjected to the treatment in question "but for her sex," then the treatment in question is "based on sex" in the sense prohibited by Title VII.[30]

Barnes v. Costle, the appeal of *Barnes v. Train*, spoke directly to the issue of "whether the discrimination, in the circumstances described by appellant, was as a matter of law 'based on . . . sex. . . .'"[31] The opinion for the court, by Spottswood W. Robinson III, circuit judge, stated:

> But for her womanhood, from aught that appears, her participation in sexual activity would never have been solicited. To say, then, that she was victimized in her employment simply because she declined the invitation is to ignore the asserted fact that she was invited only because she was a woman subordinate to the inviter in the hierarchy of agency personnel.[32]
>
> In all of these situations, the objectionable employment condition embraced something more than the employee's gender, but the fact remained that gender was also involved to a significant degree. For while some but not all employees of one sex were subjected to the condition, no employee of the opposite sex was affected, and that is the picture here.[33]

Robinson's argument seems to be that the conduct in question—the abolishing of Barnes's job when she refused her supervisor's sexual advances— constituted sex discrimination because Barnes would not have been subjected to the conduct in question if she had not been a woman. This is sufficient, in Robinson's view, to show that the treatment to which she was subjected was "based on sex" in the sense relevant to Title VII protection.

In this early argument for the claim that sexual harassment is "based on sex," then, the proof that the conduct was "based on sex" was located in the sexual motivation of the harasser: sexual desire. The argument that sexual harassment constitutes sex discrimination because the conduct is based on sexual desire goes something like this:

Sexual Desire Argument

1. The plaintiff was propositioned by her male supervisor and then retaliated against because she refused the sexual advance.
2. This implies that the male supervisor sexually desires women.
3. Therefore, if the plaintiff had not been a woman, she would not have been subjected to the proposition and subsequent retaliation.
4. Therefore, "but for" her sex, she would not have been subject to the proposition.
5. Therefore, the conduct was "based on sex" in the sense prohibited by Title VII.

Courts have also linked sexual harassment and sex discrimination in ways that do not rely on the sexual desire of the harasser. Some judges seek the proof that the conduct in question is based on sex in another motivation: animosity toward members of the sex in question. The evidence for this motive seems to be the nature of the conduct: hostility, gender-based epithets, and so on.

Because what might be called the "animosity argument" seems to require inferences from the nature of the conduct, it seems also to rely on what might be called the "sex stereotype argument." This argument comes from early sex discrimination cases. People understood Title VII to prohibit the use of sex stereotypes in employment policies. In *Sprogis v. United Air Lines, Inc.,* for example, the court claimed that, "[i]n forbidding employers to discriminate against individuals because of their sex, Congress intended to strike at the entire spectrum of disparate treatment of men and women resulting from sex stereotypes."[34] According to the "sex stereotype argument," "sexual harassment is treatment based on sex because it is treatment based upon a sex stereotype."[35] One version of the argument, used by the attorneys in *Barnes v. Costle*, seems to be the following:

Sex Stereotype Argument—Quid Pro Quo[36]

1. To condition the work of women on their fulfillment of sex stereotypes is a violation of Title VII.
2. Requiring women to meet the sexual demands of their supervisors in order to retain their positions is conditioning their work on the fulfillment of sex stereotypes of women as "sexual fair game, and passive, willing recipients of their male supervisors."[37]
3. So, quid pro quo sexual harassment is a violation of Title VII.

Judge Richey's reasoning to the same conclusion in *Williams* is somewhat unclear. It seems to be that the retaliatory action in this case constitutes sex discrimination because a condition of employment was imposed upon (one member of) one gender but not the other.[38] This seems a very weak condition and could explain why the court was almost persuaded by the defendant's argument. However, since it was primarily the view set out in *Barnes v. Costle* that influenced later courts, the lack of clarity in the position of the *Williams* court is not crucial. The dominant view thus seems to be that if a person would not have been subjected to the treatment in question "but for her sex," whether because the motivation of the alleged harasser was sexual desire or animosity, then the treatment is "based on sex" in the sense prohibited by Title VII. A version of the argument that omits mention of the motivation is summed up by Michael Vhay: "Since her sex was a significant element behind the invitation, and since refusal of the solicitation prompted retaliation, gender was a substantial factor behind the retaliation, and the harassment constituted a violation of Title VII."[39] This interpretation is referred to as the "but for" test in the 1982 case *Henson v. The City of Dundee*.[40] It exemplifies the approach to sexual harassment as sex discrimination that MacKinnon calls the "differences approach," described in chapter 1. According to the differences approach,

sexual harassment is sex discrimination *per se* because the practice differentially injures one gender-defined group in a sphere—sexuality in employment—in which the treatment of women and men can be compared. Sexuality is universal to women, but not unique to them. All women possess female sexuality, so the attribute in question is a gender characteristic. But men also possess sexuality and could be sexually harassed. When they are not, and women are, unequal treatment by gender is shown. If only men are sexually harassed, that is also arbitrary treatment based on sex, hence sex discrimination. If both sexes are, under this argument the treatment would probably not be considered gender-based, hence not sex discriminatory.[41]

Thus, in order for a practice to constitute sex discrimination, some property characteristic of all members of one sex (and perhaps also members of the opposite sex) is the basis for treatment to which only members of one sex are subject, and that treatment constitutes a detrimental condition of work. As MacKinnon points out, the differences approach is vulnerable to the "bisexual harasser" problem. The bisexual harasser problem seems first to have arisen in *Barnes v. Costle*. In a note, the court says, "In the case of the bisexual superior, the insistence upon sexual favors would not constitute gender discrimination because it would apply to male and female employees alike."[42] Other courts also found occasion to mention this in later decisions, often citing *Barnes v. Costle*.[43] That Title VII did not protect sexual harassment by a bisexual harasser seems to have been seen as an anomalous implication of the developing understanding of sexual harassment as sex discrimination. It was troubling to some, because it seemed strange that, in a particular situation, if only men were sexually harassed, or only women were harassed, the harassed would have protection under Title VII, but none of them would be protected if both genders were harassed. Though this issue was often dismissed as "absurd" or insignificant in a note to a decision, it reveals, as Judge Robert Bork stated, something important about the conception of sexual harassment as sex discrimination. Though some of the reasoning in early court decisions has been ridiculed quite deservedly, there are sometimes important conceptual issues underlying this reasoning. For one thing, it highlights one of the major differences between the sociocultural perspective and some liberal perspectives.

It seems to me that one of the things that the courts are worrying about in raising the possibility of the bisexual harasser is that treating sexual harassment as sex discrimination does not capture all the injustice or harm, or even the most important harm, of sexual harassment. Surely, people harassed by a bisexual harasser suffer injustice just as much as people harassed by heterosexual or homosexual harassers. Should not they also be protected?

One might respond that they have the same access to tort redress that anyone else does. All of the sexually harassed have that option. But, as many who hold that sexual harassment should be prohibited by employment law and not just tort law argue, workplace sexual harassment is unequal treatment in the workplace, and everyone should be able to pursue the same kind of relief—at least all women should be able to. Furthermore, it makes no sense for employers to be held liable for the sexual harassment by heterosexual and homosexual supervisors but not by bisexual supervisors.

MacKinnon acknowledges the position of the courts but argues that the mere possibility of a bisexual harasser should not provide a reason to reject a finding of sex discrimination in a case in which the alleged harasser was not bisexual. MacKinnon points out that, "[a]s a matter of law, no area of discrimination doctrine has ever required that because allegedly discriminatory treatment *could* be leveled equally against another group, when it is leveled against one, the reversed possibility destroys the group referent. Instead, the whole reason that discrimination can be 'arbitrary' is that other groups could be, but are not, so treated."[44] This seems to be true. But what if, as a matter of fact, both women and men were being sexually harassed by the same harasser?

MacKinnon sees the "bisexual problem" as stemming from the "differences approach" of the courts in their interpretation of sex discrimination.

By the logic of the differences argument, if a sexual condition of employment were imposed equally upon both women and men by the same employer, the practice would no longer constitute sex discrimination because it would not be properly based on the gender difference. Title VII, as interpreted, does not concern itself with abuses of human sexuality, only with impermissible differential consequences of the gender distinction in employment.[45]

This suggests that the so-called bisexual problem does not arise only for the analysis of sexual harassment as sex discrimination. It arises for any claim of discrimination from the perspective of the differences approach. In MacKinnon's view, the conclusion to draw from this is that the possibility of a bisexual harasser creates an "affirmative defense," which she terms the "bisexual defense." In a particular case, it could be argued that a plaintiff was not the victim of sex discrimination, even if he or she was harassed, on the grounds that the harasser also harassed members of the opposite sex. However, such a defense would have to be "pleaded and factually proven, not stated coyly, left for guesswork, or raised as a matter of law."[46] This would be consistent with other findings. In *Sprogis v. United Airlines, Inc.*,[47] for example, it was held that forbidding or restricting the employment of married women but not married men was sex discrimination. If the policy had forbidden or restricted employment of all married people, men and women, it would not have constituted sex discrimination.

MacKinnon prefers an approach to sexual harassment as sex discrimination that she calls the "inequality approach," described as part of the dominance perspective in chapter I. This approach begins from the premise that men and women are unequal, not just different. This inequality is not biological, but social. "[D]iscrimination consists in systematic disadvantagement of social groups,"[48] not simply disparate treatment. Thus, the question in determining whether a practice constitutes sex discrimination is does it systematically disadvantage one sex. "Practices which express and reinforce the social inequality of women to men are clear cases of sex-based discrimination on the inequality approach."[49]

MacKinnon argues that from the dominance perspective, sexual harassment means something different for women than it does for men, no matter what the gender of the harasser. It economically disadvantages them in a way that men are not, as a group, disadvantaged.

> Women are sexually harassed by men because they are women, that is, because of the social meaning of female sexuality, here, in the employment context. Three kinds of arguments support and illustrate this position: first, the exchange of sex for survival has historically assured women of economic dependence and inferiority and sexual availability to men. Second, sexual harassment expresses the male sex-role pattern of coercive sexual initiation toward women. Third, women's sexuality largely defines women, so violations of it are abuses of women as women.[50]

Thus, MacKinnon suggests that even if both women and men were to be subject to the sexual harassment of a particular supervisor, the women would have grounds for sex discrimination, while the men would not. This follows from her claim that sexual harassment impacts women differently from men.[51] It would also seem that men should not be protected against sexual harassment by sex discrimination laws at all, or, if they were, it would only be because of the fact that the laws prohibiting sex discrimination apply to both sexes. That is, the harm to which men are subjected when they are sexually harassed is not the same as the harm to which women are subjected when they are sexually harassed. However, it is the harm to which women are subjected that is the reason that sexual harassment should be prohibited as sex discrimination.

MacKinnon's inequality approach has not been the one generally adopted by the courts. This is evident from the fact that the possibility of a bisexual harasser is still considered to be a problem for the analysis of sexual harassment as sex discrimination.[52] This suggests that the analysis of sexual harassment as sex discrimination is problematic for the differences approach, which is the approach most often adopted by liberals. Only if one adopts a sociocultural perspective does the problem of the bisexual harasser appear not to be a problem. Since it is unlikely that the judiciary will adopt a sociocultural approach, the difficulties can be expected to continue. Recently, two federal district courts faced with cases in which a harasser apparently harassed both males and females came to opposite conclusions about whether the harassment could properly be said to be "based on sex." In *Chiapuzio v. BLT Operating Corp.*,[53] the court found that the men and the women were being harassed because of their respective genders and were thus discriminated against because of their sexes, in the sense required by Title VII. However, the court in *Johnson v. Tower Air, Inc.*,[54] determined that the plaintiff, a woman, did not prove that the harassment she suffered was because of her sex. Though the cases are similar, and the courts reached different conclusions, the facts of the cases appear different enough to account for this. Even so, the fact that one of the courts found that the harassment was "based on sex" in the sense relevant to Title VII shows that the bisexual harasser problem is not perceived by all to be a problem.[55] Furthermore, as we shall see later in this chapter, even those adopting versions of the sociocultural approach are coming to believe that men can be and are harmed by sexual harassment in ways similar to the ways in which women are harmed, especially when men are harassed by other men for not measuring up to dominant models of masculinity.

However, it still seems strange that the problem of the bisexual harasser is seen as a problem for the analysis of *sexual harassment* as sex discrimination from the perspective of the differences approach, when the analogous implication for other sorts of practices is not seen as a reason for denying that they constitute discrimination. It suggests that for many of the judges writing the early opinions, and perhaps even today, the wrong of sexual harassment, if any, was not that it was sex discrimination. As MacKinnon pointed out, the possibility of a bisexual harasser did not present a new issue for discrimination law. But many judges did not seem to see the parallel between quid pro quo sexual harassment and other kinds of sex discrimination. Judge Frey cites the *Sprogis* case in his opinion, and then three paragraphs later states, "It would be ludicrous to hold that the sort of activity involved here was contemplated by the Act because to do so would mean that if the conduct complained of was directed equally to males there would be no basis for suit."[56] For many judges, the difference between this kind of case and cases of sexual harassment seemed to be that they did not think that treating married people differently from unmarried people was wrong in itself, whereas they did think that the actions of harassers were wrong in themselves.

Once it was decided that quid pro quo harassment was "based on sex" in the sense prohibited by Title VII, the question became whether the treatment in question constituted a failure or refusal "to hire or to discharge any individual, or otherwise to discriminate against any individual with respect to his compensation, terms, conditions, or privileges of employment." To understand this aspect of the development of the concept of sexual harassment in the law, we must examine the various arguments judges used to support the claim that it does *not*.

One of them, as we saw earlier, is the claim that the conduct later identified as quid pro quo sexual harassment is "personal." This claim is a complex one and can be understood either from the natural/biological perspective or from the liberal perspective.

The claim that the behavior in these early quid pro quo cases is "personal" seems always to have been made as a way of opposing the view that quid pro quo sexual harassment is sex discrimination under Title VII. However, the reasons for denying that the behavior is sex discrimination vary widely.

In *Barnes v. Train*, the context of the remarks suggests that Judge Smith is denying that the conflict involved is anything more than a personal conflict between individuals; one makes a sexual advance toward the other, and the other rebuffs it. This happens all the time, and sometimes, unfortunately, the rebuffed party seeks revenge. It just so happens that in this case, the rebuffed party has the power to affect the employment status of the person who refused his advances, and he does. While this may be wrong, it is not employment discrimination. That is, for the court in this case, the essential characteristic of the case was the relationship not of supervisor to employee, but of rebuffed suitor to possible romantic partner. This understanding of the situation could come from either a natural/biological or a liberal perspective. It emphasizes the "naturalness" of the kind of encounter described and ignores any gendered perspective on the issue.

The judge in *Barnes v. Castle* took up this aspect of the *Barnes v. Train* decision. He did not understand just what the court intended, but he suggested several interpretations, none of which he found cogent.

We . . . note that, in disposing of this case, the District Court referred to it as "a controversy underpinned by the subtleties of an inharmonious personal relationship" . . . we are uncertain as to the reach of the court's observation, and concerned about implications to which it is susceptible.

If the court meant that the conduct attributed to the appellant's supervisor fell outside Title VII because it was a personal escapade rather than an agency project, no support for a summary judgment could be derived therefrom. . . .

If, on the other hand, the court was saying that there was no actionable discrimination because only one employee was victimized, we would strongly disagree. A sex-founded impediment to equal opportunity succumbs to Title VII even though less than all employees of the claimant's gender are affected. . . .[57]

The *Barnes v. Costle* court thus articulates two possible ways of understanding the claim that the conduct in question is "personal." In the first, the concern seems to be that the conduct in question was not a "policy" of the employer but simply the bad behavior of an individual employee. In other words, "personal" is contrasted with "employer policy." In the second, the concern seems to be that only one woman among all the female employees was subjected to the conduct in question. In this case, "personal" is contrasted with "group based." The concern seems to be the same as that exhibited in the arguments about whether quid pro quo sexual harassment is "sex based" in the sense required for it to count as sex discrimination. This has already been discussed. Yet another sense of "personal" concerns the hesitancy of courts to become involved in what they consider to be the regulation of sexual behavior in the workplace, whether for pragmatic or principled reasons. The issues of "policy" and of regulating sexual behavior shall be dealt with in turn.

The claim that quid pro quo sexual harassment is personal behavior on the part of the supervisor, rather than employer policy, concerns employer liability. Employer liability, which may seem to have little to do with the notion of sexual harassment, has been an extremely contentious issue among legal scholars.[58] The subject arises as a consequence of treating sexual harassment as sex discrimination under Title VII, which defines "employer" for the purposes of the act as follows: "The term 'employer' means a person engaged in an industry affecting commerce who has fifteen or more employees for each working day in each of twenty or more calendar weeks in the current or preceding calendar year, and any agent of such a person. . . ."[59] Under Title VII, employers are held responsible for the discriminatory actions of their employees, or agents, when those actions are appropriately related to the employment of the agent. As MacKinnon puts it, "The question for legal doctrine here is what suffices to make actions at or arising out of the workplace into actions *of* the workplace in the sense that these acts can be attributed to the employer."[60] If the actions of supervisor are considered to be the actions of an agent of the employer, then the employer is responsible for the actions of the supervisor. The supervisor is only held responsible secondarily, but by the employer. This has struck many as wrongheaded. In many sexual harassment cases, the employer did not harass; the supervisor did. Yet the employer is held liable as if he or she were responsible for the harassment.

Two arguments for the claim that Title VII applies only to discriminatory employer policies, and that sexual harassment does not constitute an employer policy, are found in *Corne v. Bausch & Lomb, Inc.*[61]

In *Corne v. Bausch & Lomb, Inc.*, plaintiffs Jane Corne and Geneva DeVane claimed that their supervisor, Leon Price, had subjected them to unwanted verbal and physical sexual advances until they finally resigned. In *Corne*, Judge Frey claims that in previous sex discrimination cases, the conduct complained of arose from "company policies" that "apparently" provided some advantage to the employer. After mentioning a series of sex discrimination cases, Frey states:

In all of the above-mentioned cases the discriminatory conduct complained of, arose out of company policies. There was apparently some advantage to, or gain by, the employer from such discriminatory practices. Always such discriminatory practices were employer designed and oriented. In the present case, Mr. Price's conduct appears to be nothing more than a personal proclivity, peculiarity or mannerism. By his alleged sexual advances, Mr. Price was satisfying a personal urge. Certainly no employer policy is here involved; rather than the company being benefited in any way by the conduct of Price, it is obvious it can only be damaged by the very nature of the acts complained of.[62]

Frey's argument here seems to be that Price's behavior does not constitute a company policy or practice for two reasons: (1) Price's behavior was not directed by the employer; no one ordered company supervisors, or Price, to subject female employees to verbal and physical sexual advances until they are forced to resign; (2) Price's actions could not benefit the company, as a policy of the company would presumably do, but only harm it.

The first of these reasons rests on the assumption that in order to constitute an employment policy or practice, a practice must be "directed" by the employer. Though Frey appeals to precedent in support of this assumption, citing sex discrimination cases in which the practice in question was "directed" by the employer, one might wonder just what this means, and whether it should be a criterion for categorizing a practice as a policy. As we shall see, a later court did not agree to this assumption.

The second reason rests on the assumption that no company would sanction policies or practices that were detrimental to it. Frey then claims that Price's actions are detrimental to the company. There are good reasons for thinking that the assumption is false, though the belief that a company is harmed by sexual harassment, and so would not sanction it either explicitly or implicitly, is held by some.

A version of Frey's argument has been offered by certain adherents of the liberal perspective in support of the claim that quid pro quo sexual harassment is not the sort of behavior for which an employer should be held vicariously liable.

The employer's liability for an employee's sins is known as vicarious liability, which is a common feature of law. What makes it a peculiar, indeed a unique, application in the case of sexual harassment is that normally it is only employed when the acts of an employee are intended to serve the business interests of the employer. In the case of sexual harassment, the harassing behavior is not merely orthogonal to the employer's interests, but actually adverse to it.[63]

The argument that sexual harassment by a supervisor is damaging to an employer's business interests is based on a cost-benefit analysis according to which the employer pays for the harasser's activity in "higher turnover rates, greater difficulty in filling positions at otherwise competitive wages, and a less productive working environment."[64] While this may seem compelling in the abstract, reports of various cases of sexual harassment suggest that the cost-benefit analysis by an employer can sometimes yield the highest net benefit on the other side, that of allowing sexual harassment. If the harasser is a highly paid company executive, and the harassed a relatively low-skilled clerical worker, it may be more expensive to replace the executive than a series of clerical workers. A recent case against Lew Lieberbaum and Company brought by seventeen former staff members seems to show that sexual harassment can take place at all levels of a company without its being seen by the company's executives to be detrimental to the company's fortunes.[65] On the other hand, it is possible that employers do not always do what is best for their business interests.

Frey's second argument involves the denial that Price's behavior has any relationship to employment, so that the question of employer policy, and therefore of employer responsibility, does not arise: "there is nothing in the Act which could reasonably be construed to have it apply to 'verbal or physical sexual advances' by another employee, even though he be in a supervisory capacity where such complained of acts or conduct had no relationship to the nature of the employment."[66] Again, it is not clear just what this means. Frey may mean that license to harass female subordinates was not part of Price's job description. However, this is a rather narrow interpretation of "relationship to the nature of the employment." From the point of view of the plaintiffs, the behavior was related to the nature of the employment. They had to put up with Price's behavior if they wanted to continue their employment. It was a condition of their employment. Furthermore, Price was only able to act toward the plaintiffs in the ways that he did because of his position as supervisor.

Yet another variation of the argument that employers should not be held liable for the sexually harassing behavior of their employees appears in *Miller v. Bank of America*.[67] Margaret Miller, an African American woman, was promised by her supervisor that if she would cooperate with him sexually, he would assure her a better job. When she refused, he caused her dismissal. Judge Spencer Williams held that "[t]he issue before the Court is whether Title VII was intended to hold an employer liable for what is essentially the isolated and unauthorized sex misconduct of one employee to another."[68] However, this description begs the question at issue. The behavior in question is described as "isolated and unauthorized sex misconduct," which places it in the category of behavior by an individual that unjustly harms another individual. It is not a practice, much less a policy, since it is isolated. The description ignores the fact that the particular "sexual misconduct"—why it should be considered "misconduct" is left unclear—was possible only because the defendant had the power to influence Miller's promotion or firing. Once the behavior is described as "isolated and unauthorized sex misconduct," it is not possible for the court to find that the employer is liable for the behavior of the supervisor. Williams's argument follows Frey's: "Little can be gleaned from the legislative history of the specific prohibition against sex discrimination. . . . In addition, the great bulk of reported cases, unlike the instant case, concern established company policies that have been found either to violate, or not to violate, the prohibition against sex discrimination."[69]

It was not until *Williams v. Saxbe* that the categorization of quid pro quo sexual harassment as a personal act by one individual against another was successfully rebutted, thus clearing the way for the consideration of quid quo pro sexual harassment as sex discrimination.[70] In *Williams v. Saxbe*, Judge Richey wrote that

> defendants argue that plaintiff has not made out a case of sex discrimination under the Act because the instant case was not the result of a policy or a regulation of the office, but rather, was an isolated personal incident which should not be the concern of the courts and was not the concern of Congress in enacting Title VII . . . whether this case presents a policy or practice of imposing a condition of sexual submission on the female employees of CRS or whether this was a non-employment related personal encounter requires a factual determination. . . . For, if this was a policy or practice of plaintiff's supervisor, then it was the agency's policy or practice, which is prohibited by Title VII.[71]

Richey seems simply to assert what the previous judges denied: that requiring female employees to submit to sex as a condition of their job *may* constitute a policy or practice of a supervisor, and thus of an employer. It depends on the particular facts of the case. Interestingly, Judge Richey notes that "Paragraph 21 of the Complaint alleges that the supervisor's conduct was a policy or practice imposed on the plaintiff and other women similarly situated. This is an essential allegation for presenting a cause of action. Plaintiff's theory has never been that this was merely an isolated personal incident."[72] The assumption here seems be that the sexual conduct of supervisors toward employees in quid pro quo sexual harassment situations *does* concern the "nature of the employment," contrary to Frey, though there is not much argument for this. One can provide an argument without much difficulty, however, for the supervisor is using the power and authority vested in him by virtue of his position to impose conditions on the plaintiff.

The liberal notion that sexual behavior is part of the private sphere, unrelated to the employment context, and so should not be regulated under employment law is evident in a number of the early cases. Judge Frey, in *Corne*, expresses this in his worry that "an outgrowth of holding such activity to be actionable under Title VII would be a potential federal lawsuit every time an employee made amorous or sexually oriented advances toward another. The only sure way an employer could avoid such charges would be to have employees who were asexual."[73] Frey here emphasizes the natural/biological view, expressing the widely held opinion that no sexual behavior should be prohibited under Title VII because the courts would be unable to distinguish ordinary, consensual sexual relationships from allegedly prohibited ones. This worry arises again in *Tomkins*. Judge Stern worried about opening the floodgates to lawsuits because of the inability to distinguish illegitimate sexual advances from legitimate ones. In his argument, he admits what seems to be a crucial premise of the sociocultural view. In response to the EEOC claim that "only sexual advances from a superior to a subordinate under the cloak of the superior's authority would be actionable under Title VII, and then only if such a practice contributed to an employment-related decision," Stern maintains that "plaintiff's theory rests on the proposition, with which this Court concurs, that the power inherent in a position of authority is necessarily coercive. And . . . every sexual advance made by a supervisor would be made under the apparent cloak of that authority. Any subordinate knows that the boss is the boss whether a file folder or a dinner is at issue."[74] This is rather startling, since it seems to admit that all sexual advances by supervisors to subordinates are inherently coercive. It would seem to follow that they are thus illegitimate, and that supervisors ought not to make such advances. Yet, Stern goes on to argue that no such advances should be prohibited by Title VII, because then all of them would be.

> If the plaintiff's view were to prevail, no superior could, prudently, attempt to open a social dialogue with any subordinate of either sex. An invitation to dinner could become an invitation to a federal lawsuit if a once harmonious relationship turned sour at some later time. And if an inebriated approach by a supervisor to a subordinate at the office Christmas party could form the basis of a federal lawsuit for sex discrimination if a promotion or a raise is later denied to the subordinate, we would need 4,000 federal trial judges instead of some 400.[75]

The court seems to realize that behaviors that had previously been accepted in the workplace no longer would be if quid pro quo sexual harassment is considered sex discrimination under Title VII. However, rather than inquire into the possibility that perhaps those were not fair workplace practices, the judge supports the status quo: inebriated supervisors should be able to sexually approach subordinates at office Christmas parties with impunity.

These early opinions seem to show that sexuality in the workplace had not been widely considered or discussed. Judges seem to be using their personal views on sexuality and how it should be treated in the workplace in making their decisions. Hearn and Parkin, writing on sex and the workplace in 1987, remark, "Enter most organisations and you enter a world of sexuality. . . . And yet read the 'mountainous' literature on industrial sociology, organisational sociology, organisation theory, industrial relations and so on, and you would imagine these organisations, so finely analysed, are inhabited by a breed of strange, asexual eunuch figures."[76] What this suggests is that employers and government regulators have perceived the workplace as asexual, that is, they have ignored the sexuality that is present in the workplace. They have wanted whatever sexuality there is to remain "personal," "private," that is, not the business of business or government. The concept of sexual harassment challenges this view.

Another kind of conflict involved in determining the meaning of sexual harassment derives from the ambiguity of the expression "sexuality." Judges in early opinions seemed to focus too much on the fact that the treatment in question involved sexual advances. Sexual advances in themselves were not wrong, they were "natural." So how could they constitute a violation of Title VII? Though the first cases involved conduct that was alleged to be "sexual in nature," it was recognized very early—though perhaps not clearly—that harassment need not be "sexual in nature" to constitute sexual harassment. In *Barnes v. Costle*, the conceptual distinction between harassment "of a sexual nature" and sex discrimination is clearly articulated. In a footnote, Judge Robinson says: "The vitiating sex factor thus stemmed not from the fact that what appellant's superior demanded was sexual activity—which of itself is immaterial—but from the fact that he imposed upon her tenure in her then position a condition which ostensibly he would not have fastened upon a male employee."[77] This might seem odd, given the kinds of conduct that probably come to mind when one hears the term "sexual harassment," but one must remember that in the development of the law prohibiting sexual harassment, sexual harassment had always to be seen as sex discrimination.

This distinction can be understood as stemming from the ambiguity inherent in the term "sex" in "sex discrimination." "Sex" sometimes means "gender," and, as we have seen, many courts have understood it in this way. However, "sex" sometimes means "sexuality." The ambiguity in the case of sexual harassment has been even more prominent. Sexual harassment counts as sex discrimination because it is based on gender (in some sense). But the first cases of sexual harassment, which were quid pro quo, and many subsequent cases, were sexual, as well. Indeed, as we have just seen, it was the fact that the cases involved sexual behavior that convinced some judges that sexual harassment is *not* sex discrimination. On the other hand, it seems that courts who ruled that sexual harassment is sex discrimination considered the "sexual nature" of the conduct a sure sign that the conduct was "based on sex."[78]

This ambiguity, I believe, actually helped sexual harassment to be recognized as a violation of Title VII. Some courts seem to have been so convinced of the wrongness of quid pro quo sexual harassment that they worked to make it constitute a violation of Title VII. Nevertheless, the wrongness that they saw was not necessarily sex discrimination, but morally wrong conduct of a different sort. Several of the courts that denied that quid pro quo harassment constituted sex discrimination under Title VII made it quite clear that they agreed that the behavior was morally reprehensible.[79] It just was not sex discrimination.

Even the EEOC seems to have assumed that sexual harassment had to be sexual. In its 1980 *Guidelines on Sexual Harassment*, the EEOC defined sexual harassment as involving conduct "of a sexual nature" (see the discussion later in the chapter). However, case law has developed in such a way that sexual harassment need not be "sexual" to constitute sex discrimination under Title VII.[80] In fact, the less like a sexual advance the behavior, the more it seems to be sex discrimination.

Hostile Environment Sexual Harassment

In 1980, the Equal Employment Opportunity Commission's *Guidelines on Discrimination Because of Sex* included its first definition of sexual harassment:

> (a) Harassment on the basis of sex is a violation of section 703 of title VII. Unwelcome sexual advances, requests for sexual favors, and other verbal or physical conduct of a sexual nature constitute sexual harassment when (1) submission to such conduct is made either explicitly or implicitly a term or condition of an individual's employment, (2) submission to or rejection of such conduct by an individual is used as the basis for employment decisions affecting such individual, or (3) such conduct has the purpose or effect of unreasonably interfering with an individual's work performance or creating an intimidating, hostile, or offensive working environment.[81]

In the third clause, these *Guidelines* already contained the definition which was to be the most important development in the legal conception of sexual harassment in the 1980s: the notion of "hostile environment" sexual harassment. This is particularly noteworthy, since no court had yet recognized hostile environment sexual harassment as a legitimate cause of action under Title VII.

"Hostile environment" harassment is the term used to refer to what MacKinnon called "conditions of work" harassment (see chapter 2). As we have seen, quid pro quo sexual harassment was considered a violation of Title VII because it "discriminated against an individual with respect to his compensation, terms, conditions, or privileges of employment, because of such individual's . . . sex. . . ." *Bundy v. Jackson*[82] was the first case in which a hostile environment claim was recognized as a violation of Title VII. In *Bundy*, plaintiff Sandra Bundy claimed that she was sexually intimidated by her supervisors. Two of them propositioned her, and when she complained to a third, he also propositioned her, telling her that "'any man in his right mind would want to rape you'."[83] The question before the court was whether "conditions of employment" could be extended to include behavior that did not result in firing, clear failure to promote, and so on, when a sexual advance was rejected. According to the court, "[A]ppellant asks us to extend *Barnes* by holding that an employer violates Title VII merely by subjecting female employees to sexual harassment, even if the employee's resistance to that harassment does not cause the employer to deprive her of any tangible job benefits."[84] The court agreed with Bundy's claim that "'conditions of employment' include the psychological and emotional work environment— that sexually stereotyped insults and demeaning propositions to which she was indisputably subjected and which caused her anxiety and debilitation . . . illegally poisoned the environment."[85] The court acknowledged that it was going beyond what courts had done before, but it took the plunge.[86]

> What remains is the novel question whether the sexual harassment of the sort Bundy suffered amounted by itself to sex discrimination with respect to the 'terms, conditions, or privileges of employment.' Though no court has as yet so held, we believe that an affirmative answer follows ineluctably from numerous cases finding Title VII violations where an employer created or condoned a substantially discriminatory work environment, regardless of whether the complaining employees lost any tangible job benefits as a result of the discrimination.

The recognition of hostile environment sexual harassment as actionable under Title VII had enormous significance for the legal conception of sexual harassment. The paradigm of sexual harassment began to shift from a focus on what some considered "love affairs gone wrong"—the dominant view of the natural/biological perspective—to something less clearly related to sexual attraction. It is also much easier to see hostile environment sexual harassment as sex discrimination by analogy with racial or national origin harassment. Indeed, the court in *Bundy* cited a 1971 racial harassment case, *Rogers v. Equal Employment Opportunity Commission*,[87] in its decision. *Rogers v. Equal Employment Opportunity Commission* involved a Hispanic woman who claimed that she was discriminated against because "by giving discriminatory service to its Hispanic *clients* the firm created a discriminatory work environment for its Hispanic *employees*."[88] The Hispanic woman, Josephine Chavez, did not claim that her employer had deprived her of any tangible employment benefits. Judge J. Skelly Wright, writing for the court in *Bundy*, cites several key passages from the *Rogers* decision, such as the following: "Congress chose neither to enumerate specific discriminatory practices, nor to elucidate in extenso the parameter of such nefarious activities. Rather, it pursued the path of wisdom by being unconstrictive, knowing that constant change is the order of our day and that the seemingly reasonable practices of the present can easily become the injustices of the morrow."[89] Judge Wright quotes from *Rogers* "that 'terms, conditions, or privileges of employment' . . . is an expansive concept which sweeps within its protective ambit the practice of creating a work environment heavily charged with ethnic or racial discrimination. . . . One can readily envision working environments so heavily polluted with discrimination as to destroy completely the emotional and psychological stability of minority group workers. . . ."[90] Judge Wright saw Bundy's claim as covered by the principle enunciated by Judge Goldberg in *Rogers*. The court also refers to EEOC's interpretation of Title VII, which "has consistently held that the statute grants an employee a working environment free of discrimination."[91]

The 1980 EEOC *Guidelines on Sexual Harassment* are referenced in the *Bundy* decision. If the EEOC *Guidelines* were supposed to be based on developments in case law, it is unclear how they could contain "hostile work environment" sexual harassment in the definition, when no court had yet recognized hostile environment sexual harassment as a legitimate cause of action under Title VII.[92] One can surmise that the EEOC reasoned as the court in Bundy did, that in the case of a hostile work environment, the analogies between race and sex were sufficient to warrant similar treatment under Title VII.

Another influential early hostile environment sexual harassment claim was upheld in *Henson v. City of Dundee*.[93] *Henson* uses reasoning similar to that used in *Bundy* to reach the conclusion that a hostile environment "inflicts disparate treatment upon a member of one sex with respect to terms, conditions, or privileges of employment."[94] Judge Vance, writing for the majority in *Henson*, refers to *Rogers* and to *Bundy* in his opinion. The *Henson* decision was very influential because "[t]he court in *Henson* formally listed the elements of what it saw as the prima facie Title VII sexual harassment action, and the majority of sexual harassment decisions since 1982 have adopted the court's approach."[95] According to *Henson*, these elements are:

1. The employee belongs to a protected group.
2. The employee was subject to unwelcome sexual harassment.
3. The harassment complained of was based upon sex.
4. The harassment complained of affected a "term, condition, or privilege" of employment.
5. *Respondeat superior.*[96]

One might wonder why the second element refers to "unwelcome sexual harassment." According to most interpretations of sexual harassment, all sexual harassment is, by definition, unwelcome.[97]

Respondeat superior concerns employer liability. *Henson* made a distinction between employer liability in quid pro quo cases and that in hostile environment cases. "In the classic quid pro quo case an employer is strictly liable for the conduct of its supervisors, while in the work environment case the plaintiff must prove that higher management knew or should have known of the sexual harassment before the employer may be held liable."[98] The reason for this difference in employer liability was said to be that unlike quid pro quo sexual harassment, hostile environment sexual harassment could be perpetrated by people other than supervisors—co-workers, customers, or clients. Such people may not qualify as "agents" of the employer. The court argued that an employer should be held strictly liable for quid pro quo sexual harassment because a supervisor was using the authority vested in him or her in virtue of his or her position as a supervisor. However, the court did not perceive this kind of relationship in hostile environment sexual harassment: even the hostile environment acts of supervisors are not *inherently* affected by their authority. Judge Clark dissented on just this point in *Henson*, arguing that "[c]learly, a supervisor by virtue of his position is enhanced in his ability to create an offensive environment when compared to the janitor, for example. When a supervisor creates such an environment, women employees are not apt to complain for fear of retaliation."[99]

The legitimacy of hostile environment sexual harassment as sex discrimination was confirmed in the first sexual harassment case to be decided by the Supreme Court, *Meritor Savings Bank, FSB v. Vinson.*[100] The case involved Michelle Vinson, who claimed that her supervisor, Sidney Taylor, requested sexual relations over the course of several years, and that she complied out of fear of losing her job. Taylor denied the allegations. The district court held that if any sexual relations had taken place, the "relationship was a voluntary one having nothing to do with her continued employment or her advancement or promotions. . . ."[101] In *Meritor*, the main issues before the court were: (1) whether sexual harassment leading to noneconomic injury could constitute a violation of Title VII, (2) whether conduct with which one voluntarily complied could be "unwelcome," (3) whether evidence about an alleged victim's dress and behavior could be admitted, and (4) whether employers are automatically liable for sexual harassment by supervisors. The court held that: (1) economic injury was not necessary for violation of Title VII, (2) voluntariness does not necessarily imply welcomeness, and (3) evidence of a victim's dress and behavior may be admissible because of its relevance to determining the welcomeness of the alleged conduct. They did not decide between conflicting opinions on point (4).

In support of the first point, the Court argued that "the language of Title VII is not limited to 'economic' or 'tangible' discrimination. The phrase 'terms, conditions, or privileges of employment' evinces a congressional intent 'to strike at the entire spectrum of disparate treatment of men and women' in employment."[102] The Court also cites the EEOC *Guidelines*, which "fully support the view that harassment leading to noneconomic injury can violate Title VII."[103] They claim that the EEOC *Guidelines* are based on "a substantial body of judicial decisions and EEOC precedent holding that Title VII affords employees the right to work in an environment free from discriminatory intimidation, ridicule, and insult,"[104] citing *Rogers v. EEOC* and a number of other decisions in which this principle was applied to harassment based on race, national origin, and religion.[105] In support of the second point, the Court argued that "[t]he correct inquiry is whether respondent by her conduct indicated that the alleged sexual advances were unwelcome, not whether her actual participation in sexual intercourse was voluntary."[106] In other words, the Court did not take voluntariness to be sufficient to prove "welcomeness." Though the Court does not say why they hold this, one might surmise that they were considering that someone might voluntarily undergo unwelcome conduct from fear of loss of employment, as Michelle Vinson claims to have done. In support of the third point, the Court finds that dress and speech are relevant to determining whether sexual advances are welcome. They point to the EEOC *Guidelines*, which state that "the trier of fact must determine the existence of sexual harassment in light of 'the record as a whole' and 'the totality of circumstances,' such as the nature of the sexual advances and the context in which the alleged incidents occurred."[107] They conclude that it is a matter for the district court to determine in the particular case. On the fourth point, the Court did not decide between the competing views: "We . . . decline the parties' invitation to issue a definitive rule on employer liability, but we do agree with the EEOC that Congress wanted courts to look to agency principles for guidance in this area."[108] "Agency principles" concern common-law principles regarding when an employee constitutes an agent of the employer. The EEOC has interpreted the application of these principles to cases of sexual harassment in such a way that employers are not automatically liable for the actions of their supervisors in sexual harassment cases. However, in cases of quid pro quo sexual harassment by a supervisor, an employer will always be held liable.[109] The EEOC states:

> Applying general Title VII principles, an employer . . . is responsible for its acts and those of its agents and supervisory employees with respect to sexual harassment regardless of whether the specific acts complained of were authorized or even forbidden by the employer and regardless of whether the employer knew or should have known of their occurrence. The Commission will examine the circumstances of the particular employment relationship and the job functions performed by the individual in determining whether an individual acts in either a supervisory or agency capacity.[110]

In cases of sexual harassment by co-workers, "an employer is responsible for acts of sexual harassment in the workplace where the employer (or its agents or supervisory employees) knows or should have known of the conduct, unless it can show that it took immediate and appropriate corrective action."[111]

The question of employer liability in hostile environment cases remained in contention until 1998, when the Supreme Court ruled on the issue in two cases: *Burlington Industries, Inc. v. Ellerth*[112] and *Faragher v. City of Boca Raton*.[113] The court ruled that "[a]n employer is subject to vicarious liability to a victimized employee for an actionable hostile environment created by a supervisor with immediate (or successively higher) authority over the employee. When no tangible employment action is taken, a defending employer may raise an affirmative defense to liability or damages, subject to proof by a preponderance of the evidence."[114]

With the *Meritor* case in 1986, the legitimacy of sexual harassment as a claim under Title VII was finally established. It is interesting that the first case before the Supreme Court was a hostile environment case rather than a quid pro quo case, since quid pro quo harassment was the first sexual harassment claim to be recognized in the lower courts. It is also interesting to note that by the end of the 1980s, "sexual harassment" had come to encompass nearly all that the original definitions by activists such as Farley and MacKinnon had included. Recall that Farley included in her definition of sexual harassment: "Sexual harassment is best described as unsolicited nonreciprocal male behavior that asserts a woman's sex role over her function as a worker. It can be any or all of the following: staring at, commenting upon, or touching a woman's body; requests for acquiescence in sexual behavior; repeated nonreciprocated propositions for dates; demands for sexual intercourse; and rape." Any or all of these behaviors had been found to constitute sexual harassment under the law, under certain circumstances. In particular, to state a claim under Title VII, the kinds of behavior that constitute hostile environment sexual harassment must be "sufficiently severe and pervasive 'to alter the conditions of [the victim's] employment and create an abusive working environment.'"[115]

Since *Meritor*, there have been a number of significant developments in sexual harassment law, some of which have affected the legal conception of sexual harassment. Most of these developments have concerned unclear aspects of hostile environment sexual harassment.

One such development concerns the "reasonable woman" standard for sexual harassment.[116] The reasonable woman standard was first mentioned in a dissenting opinion in *Rabidue v. Osceola Refining Co.*, a case alleging hostile environment sexual harassment.[117] The plaintiff, Vivienne Rabidue, claimed that a hostile environment was created by a supervisor named Douglas Henry (who had no supervisory authority over Rabidue) and by other male employees. Henry is described in the majority opinion as "an extremely vulgar and crude individual who customarily made obscene comments about women generally, and, on occasion, directed such obscenities to the plaintiff."[118] Rabidue also complained that male employees displayed in their offices pictures of nude and partially clad women, to which Rabidue and the other female employees were subjected.

Rabidue clearly did consider her work environment to be sexually harassing. However, the plaintiff's own perception cannot be the deciding criterion for determining whether sexual harassment has taken place. This would render any claim by any person an instance of sexual harassment. The standard should not be simply that of the defendant, the person accused, for this would absolve nearly all defendants. The standard should not simply be the perspective of a judge, or even a panel of judges, either. The court thus introduced the concept of the "reasonable person" in an attempt to find an objective standard.

The majority held that

> [t]o accord appropriate protection to both plaintiffs and defendants in a hostile and/or abusive work environment sexual harassment case, the trier of fact, when judging the totality of the circumstances impacting upon the asserted abusive and hostile environment placed in issue by the plaintiff's charges, must adopt the perspective of a reasonable person's reaction to a similar environment under essentially like or similar circumstances.[119]

The court considered the hypothetical reasonable person to be relevant in addressing two issues: (1) whether the conduct alleged would interfere with the work performance of a reasonable person, and (2) whether the conduct complained of would "affect seriously the psychological well-being of that reasonable person under like circumstances."[120] The court further required that the plaintiff prove that she herself had been offended by the conduct and had suffered injury as a result of it.

Using the reasonable person standard, the majority in *Rabidue* found that the environment described did not constitute a hostile environment.

> [T]he record effectively disclosed that Henry's obscenities, although annoying, were not so startling as to have affected seriously the psyches of the plaintiff or other female employees. The evidence did not demonstrate that this single employee's vulgarity substantially affected the totality of the workplace. The sexually oriented poster displays had a de minimis effect on the plaintiff's work environment when considered in the context of a society that condones and publicly features and commercially exploits open displays of written and pictorial erotica at the newsstands, on prime-time television, at the cinema, and in other public places. In sum, Henry's vulgar language, coupled with the sexually oriented posters, did not result in a working environment that could be considered intimidating, hostile, or offensive. . . .[121]

However, some found the reasonable person standard to be inadequate to ensure objectivity. In his opinion, in which he concurred in part and dissented in part, Judge J. Keith argued that the standard should not be a hypothetical "reasonable person," but the *reasonable victim*, which in this case he understood to be the reasonable woman.

> In my view, the reasonable person perspective fails to account for the wide divergence between most women's views of appropriate sexual conduct and those of men. . . . I would have courts adopt the perspective of the reasonable victim which simultaneously allows courts to consider salient sociological differences as well as shield employers from the neurotic complainant. Moreover, unless the outlook of the reasonable woman is adopted, the defendants as well as the courts are permitted to sustain ingrained notions of reasonable behavior fashioned by the offenders, in this case, men.[122]

Thus, Keith seems to be adopting a position closer to the sociocultural perspective. Just because the norm has been discriminatory against women, so that most people are accustomed to it, does not mean that it should continue. In other words, the reasonable person standard supports the status quo. But Title VII may challenge the status quo.

Keith makes this point explicitly in his disagreement with the majority regarding the purpose of Title VII. The majority had agreed with the claim of the district court that "Title VII was not meant to—or can—change" the fact that "in some work environments, humor and language are rough hewn and vulgar. Sexual jokes, sexual conversations and girlie magazines may abound."[123] In their view, Title VII was not "designed to bring about a magical transformation in the social mores of American workers."[124] Keith argues that "Title VII's precise purpose is to prevent such behavior and attitudes from poisoning the work environment of classes protected under the Act. . . . As I believe no woman should be subjected to an environment where her sexual dignity and reasonable sensibilities are visually, verbally or physically assaulted as a matter of prevailing male prerogative, I dissent."[125] In Keith's view, the relevant question was not whether a reasonable *person* would find the conduct in question to interfere with his or her work performance and affect seriously his or her psychological well-being, but whether the reasonable *victim*, in this case, woman, would so find. And using the reasonable woman standard, he found a hostile environment to exist.

The reasonable woman standard was first adopted in the 1991 *Ellison v. Brady* case.[126] One of the main issues in *Ellison* was whether the conduct alleged by the plaintiff, Kerry Ellison, was "severe and pervasive" enough to constitute hostile environment sexual harassment; or, as Judge Beezer put it, "what test should be applied to determine whether conduct is sufficiently severe or pervasive to alter the conditions of employment and create a hostile working environment."[127] The question arose because the district court believed that the alleged harasser's conduct was "isolated and genuinely trivial."[128] The appeals court disagreed, finding that the alleged harasser's conduct "was sufficiently severe and pervasive to alter the conditions of Ellison's employment and create an abusive working environment."[129] In support of their position, they argued that "in evaluating the severity and pervasiveness of sexual harassment, we should focus on the perspective of the victim," arguing, rather oddly, that "[i]f we only examined whether a reasonable person would engage in allegedly harassing conduct, we would run the risk of reinforcing the prevailing level of discrimination. Harassers could continue to harass merely because a particular discriminatory practice was common, and victims of harassment would have no remedy."[130] One might have thought that a reasonable person would not reinforce prevailing levels of discrimination. However, this is just what the *Rabidue* majority seemed to hold. They took themselves to be applying the reasonable person standard and determined that the reasonable person would not be offended by the conduct at Rabidue's place of employment because it was not significantly different from what society condones. Keith stated that "the relevant inquiry at hand is what the reasonable woman would find offensive, not society, which at one point also condoned slavery,"[131] and the *Ellison* court seems to agree. Thus, they chose to take the victim's perspective. But in order to properly appreciate the victim's perspective, they claimed that it was necessary to take into account the differing perspectives of men and women. Thus, they came up with the following "test": "a female plaintiff states a prima facie case of hostile environment sexual harassment when she alleges conduct which a reasonable woman would consider sufficiently severe or pervasive to alter the conditions of employment and create an abusive working environment."[132] This has become known as the reasonable woman standard. It is justified by alleged differences in the perceptions of men and women with regard to sexualized behavior in the workplace. For example, women may perceive an underlying threat of violence in some behaviors that men do not, because women are more vulnerable to sexual assault.[133]

One reason that the reasonable woman standard was so significant in the development of the legal conception of sexual harassment was that it acknowledged something on which socioculturalist feminist activists had insisted from the start: workplace culture was predominantly a male culture, and the standards for acceptable behavior were determined from a male perspective. Women were expected to conform; the culture was not expected to change. However, the reasonable woman standard might also be seen to give support to those who claim that sexual harassment should be understood as protecting female virtues or sensibilities. Which of these understandings one has depends in part on whether one holds the natural/biological perspective, the sociocultural perspective, or a liberal perspective. Most who adopt the sociocultural perspective prefer the reasonable woman standard, while those who adopt the natural/biological perspective do not. Liberals seem to be divided. The arguments for and against the reasonable woman standard are taken up in more detail in chapter 6.

The EEOC had taken a sort of middle path in its guidance on the standard to be used in determining whether conduct is sufficiently severe and pervasive to constitute sexual harassment. In a set of proposed rules published in the *Federal Register* in 1993, the EEOC states that the standard for determining whether harassing conduct is sufficiently severe or pervasive to create a hostile environment is "whether a reasonable person in the same or similar circumstances would find the conduct intimidating, hostile, or abusive."[134] However, this is qualified by the following: "The 'reasonable person' standard includes consideration of the perspective of persons of the alleged victim's race, color, religion, gender, national origin, age, or disability."[135]

Another significant development—or perhaps emphasis—in the legal conception of hostile environment sexual harassment occurred in Justice Ruth Ginsberg's concurring opinion in *Harris v. Forklift Systems, Inc.*,[136] the second sexual harassment case to reach the Supreme Court. One of the issues which arose in the case was "whether conduct, to be actionable as 'abusive work environment' harassment . . . must 'seriously affect [an employee's] psychological well-being' or lead the plaintiff to 'suffe[r] injury.'"[137] The court argued that "[s]o long as the environment would reasonably be perceived, and is perceived, as hostile or abusive . . . there is no need for it also to be psychologically injurious."[138] It is worth remarking that the Supreme Court did not apply the reasonable woman or the reasonable victim standard. However, they did establish that a victim of sexual harassment need not suffer a nervous breakdown before sex discrimination under Title VII can be established. Since sexual harassment is being conceived of as sex discrimination, it does not seem necessary that the harassed individual suffer psychological injury in order to prove that the conduct in question adversely affected her ability to perform her duties. A psychological injury would be one effect of sexually harassing behavior that would interfere with job performance, but it is not the only possible one.

In a concurring opinion, Justice Ruth Ginsburg pointed out that the "critical issue" in sexual harassment cases is "whether members of one sex are exposed to disadvantageous terms or conditions of employment to which members of the other sex are not exposed," and that "the adjudicator's inquiry should center, dominantly, on whether the discriminatory conduct has unreasonably interfered with the plaintiff's work performance."[139] Thus, Ginsburg emphasizes that the issue in sexual harassment law is *sex discrimination in the workplace*, not sexual behavior *per se*.[140] That this point needed making is evidence that the focus of sexual harassment has often been on the sexuality of the conduct rather than on the sex discrimination it causes.

Another important case in the development of the legal conception of sexual harassment was *Robinson v. Jacksonville Shipyards, Inc.*[141] This case marked the first time that pornography in the workplace was considered to be a form of sexual harassment. Robinson worked as a welder in a shipyard, a traditionally male workplace. She argued that pinups (which were described as pornographic), foul language, and insulting remarks constituted a hostile environment. The court adopted the reasonable woman standard and argued that Title VII was designed to eliminate "barrier[s] to the progress of women in the workplace . . . [that convey] the message that they do not belong."[142] *Robinson* extended the scope of hostile environment sexual harassment to include pornography.[143] The defense argued, unsuccessfully, that prohibiting the pinups that had always decorated the workplace violated the First Amendment rights of other workers.[144] Because of *Robinson* and other cases, many have argued that the concept of sexual harassment has come to include expression that is protected by the First Amendment. It is not yet clear how this conflict will be resolved.[145]

An important change in sexual harassment law came as a result of the Civil Rights Act of 1991. Until passage of the 1991 Civil Rights Act, those bringing claims of sexual harassment under Title VII could not sue for compensation or punitive damages. The only remedies available under Title VII were "equitable relief"—such as back pay (in cases where the plaintiff is fired in retaliation or quits because of the harassment), an injunction against the employer to stop the harassing behavior, or reinstatement. The Civil Rights Act of 1991 provided that the plaintiff could seek compensatory or punitive damages—within certain limits—and that if he or she did, either party could demand a trial by jury.[146] Compensatory and punitive damages may be sought in the event of intentional discrimination. The amounts which can be sought are limited according to the number of employees: more than 14 but fewer than 101, $50,000; more than 100 but fewer than 201, $100,000; more than 200 but fewer than 501, $200,000; more than 500, $300,000. Some commentators believe that this changes the nature of sexual harassment law: "The addition of these provisions fundamentally changes the legal model underlying federal discrimination laws. The new Act, in providing for expanded money damages, moves these causes of action away from a format in which the goal is conciliation and improvement of employer-employee relations and toward the more adversarial format of a civil trial for tort damages."[147] Others support the additions because they provide more incentive for sexually harassed employees to pursue claims against their employers. Often, the plaintiff does not want reinstatement because relations are so badly damaged, and it would take a good deal of altruism for a victim of sexual harassment to agree to go through the process of bringing a case against an employer for the sake of future employees.

Another change in the law which some believe has increased the likelihood that people will bring sexual harassment claims was the extension of what is known as the "rape-shield evidence rule" to civil cases. This meant that information about an alleged victim's sexual history was not admissible except under certain circumstances. As was evident in *Meritor*, facts about the plaintiff's clothing and behavior were considered admissible in determining the "welcomeness" of sexual advances. In 1994, the Federal Judicial Conferences extended to civil cases the rule, Federal Rule of Evidence Rule 412, which already held in federal cases. This means that those who bring sexual harassment claims will not have their private lives opened to public scrutiny. Commentators maintain that certain aspects of the plaintiff's behavior are still admissible, but there are limits.[148]

One of the most recent issues to come before the courts is whether same-sex harassment constitutes sex discrimination under Title VII. Most of the sexual harassment cases that have come before the courts have involved male harassers and female harassees. However, Title VII is gender neutral, in the sense that its prohibition against sex discrimination applies both to women and to men.

Wright v. Methodist Youth Servs., Inc., decided in 1981,[149] was the first case in which same-sex sexual harassment was found to be in violation of Title VII. *Wright* was a quid pro quo case involving a man who claimed that another man had made sexual advances to him and then terminated his employment because he would not comply. Subsequently, unwanted sexual advances by homosexual male supervisors have, in some cases, been recognized as discriminatory under Title VII.[150] The argument used to establish that sexual harassment in such cases is sex discrimination is simply a variant of the "sexual desire" argument described earlier.[151] In *Parrish v. Washington International Insurance Co.*,[152] the court reasoned that "if plaintiff complains of unwelcome homosexual advances, the offending conduct is based on the employer's sexual preference and necessarily involved the plaintiff's gender, for an employee of the non-preferred gender would not inspire the same treatment. Thus, unwelcome homosexual advances, like unwelcome heterosexual advances are actionable under Title VII."[153] This kind of reasoning seems to be from a variation of the natural/biological perspective, with its emphasis on sexual desire as the main motivation for harassment. Relying on sexual desire to establish that the plaintiff would not have been subjected to the conduct "but for" his sex, some courts have taken the homosexuality of the perpetrator to be a *necessary* condition for the finding of sex discrimination in same-sex sexual harassment cases.[154]

In cases in which the harasser was not homosexual, courts have found it difficult to make the connection between sexual harassment and sex discrimination. The court in *Hopkins v. Baltimore Gas & Elec. Co.* stated that

> when a male employee seeks to prove that he has been sexually harassed by a person of the same sex, he carries the burden of proving that the harassment was directed against him "because of" his sex. The principal way in which this burden may be met is with proof that

the harasser acted out of sexual attraction to the employee. In McWilliams . . . we noted that a male employee who undertakes to prove sexual harassment directed at him by another male may use evidence of the harasser's homosexuality to demonstrate that the action was directed at him because he is a man.[155]

In the absence of sexual desire, some courts seem to think that the only way of making the connection is by establishing that there is animosity toward the sex being harassed, that an "anti-male" atmosphere has been created. However, some courts have argued that this is not possible when all the employees involved in the harassment are male.

A series of cases in which same-sex harassment was found *not* to be actionable under Title VII commenced with *Goluszek v. Smith*.[156] *Goluszek* was a hostile environment sexual harassment case involving conduct of a sexual nature. It involved a man who was tormented by his fellow heterosexual male workers because they found him insufficiently masculine.[157] The court denied his claim on the grounds that the conduct to which Goluszek was subjected was "not the type of conduct Congress intended to penalize when it enacted Title VII."[158] According to the court:

Goluszek was a male in a male-dominated environment. In fact, . . . every one of the figures in this story was a male. The argument that Goluszek worked in an environment that treated males as inferior consequently is not supported by the record. In fact, Goluszek may have been harassed "because" he is a male, but that harassment was not of a kind which created an anti-male environment in the workplace.[159]

The court that decided *Vandeventer v. Wabash National Corp.*[160] agreed with the court in *Goluszek* that creation of an anti-male environment was necessary for a finding of sexual harassment when all involved are males. They claimed that same-sex harassment among men did not create such an environment because "Title VII is aimed at a gender-biased atmosphere; an atmosphere of oppression by a 'dominant' gender."[161] In another same-sex case, *Garcia v. Elf Atochem North America*,[162] the court referred to *Goluszek* and stated that "harassment by a male supervisor against a male subordinate does not state a claim under Title VII even though the harassment has sexual overtones."[163] *Hopkins v. Baltimore Gas & Elec. Co.*[164] followed *Garcia, Goluszek*, and *Vandeventer* in denying that same-sex harassment constitutes sex discrimination under Title VII. The court reasoned that the alleged harasser "certainly does not despise the entire group, nor does he wish to harm its members, since he is a member himself. . . ."[165]

Thus, in the absence of sexual desire and gender animosity, the courts could find no evidence that the behavior complained of was visited on the plaintiff "because of sex," at least not in the sense intended by Title VII. However, not all courts followed this line of reasoning.[166] One very interesting decision seems to have tried to modify the sex stereotype argument for use in male-male cases. In *Doe v. City of Belleville*,[167] the judge argued that same-sex harassment between heterosexual males is actionable under Title VII.[168]

> When the harasser sets out to harass a female employee using names, threats, and physical contact that are unmistakably gender-based, he ensures that the work environment becomes hostile to her as a woman—in other words, that the workplace is hostile to her 'because of' her sex. Regardless of why the harasser has targeted the woman, her gender has become inextricably intertwined with the harassment. Likewise, when a woman's breasts are grabbed or when her buttocks are pinched, the harassment necessarily is linked to her gender. . . . It would not seem to matter that the harasser might simultaneously be harassing a male co-worker with comparable epithets and comparable physical molestation. When a male employee's testicles are grabbed, his torment might be comparable, but the point is that he experiences that harassment as a man, not just as a worker, and she as a woman. In each case, the victim's gender not only supplies the lexicon of the harassment, it affects how he or she will experience that harassment; and in anything short of a truly unisex society, men's and women's experiences will be different. In that sense, each arguably is the victim of sex discrimination.[169]

The court argues that neither the motive of the harasser nor differential treatment is decisive. The important thing is that the harassment is directed toward the person *as a man* or *as a woman*, that is, *because of his or her gender*. Notice, however, that the court takes the sexual nature of the offending conduct to establish the link between the conduct and the sex of the person. This does not, then, address cases in which the behavior complained of is not sexual in nature.

The *Doe* court shows that it is making use of the "sex stereotype" argument by citing the Supreme Court's decision in *Price Waterhouse v. Hopkins*[170] as precedent for protection against the imposition of gender stereotypes.[171] However, the *Doe* court's understanding of gender stereotypes is very broad.

> Assuming *arguendo* that proof other than the explicit sexual character of the harassment is indeed necessary to establish that same-sex harassment qualifies as sex discrimination, the fact that H. Doe apparently was singled out for this abuse because of the way in which he projected the sexual aspect of his personality (and by that we mean his gender) did not conform to his co-workers' view of appropriate masculine behavior supplies that proof here. The Supreme Court's decision in Price Waterhouse v. Hopkins . . . makes clear that Title VII does not permit an employee to be treated adversely because his or her appearance or conduct does not conform to stereotypical gender roles.[172]

As we shall see, the notion that Title VII protects people from differential treatment based on their "masculinity" or "femininity" is gaining favor among legal scholars.

In addition to the line of argument laid out in *Doe*, there have been a few courts that have found that nonsexual same-sex harassment is actionable under Title VII. In *Quick v. Donaldson Co.*,[173] the Eighth Circuit Court argued that a finding of sexual harassment did not require (1) that the plaintiff be a member of a disadvantaged group, contrary to *Goluszek*; (2) that the conduct be motivated by sexual desire; or (3) that the conduct be of a sexual nature. The court further argued that Quick established his claim that the offending conduct was based on sex by showing that no women were subjected to the behavior in question.[174] Thus, in *Quick*, differential treatment conditions of work seemed sufficient to show that the behavior was "because of sex." This suggests a third argument linking sexual harassment and sex discrimination, the "differential treatment" argument, which exemplifies the differences approach in its purest form:

The Differential Treatment Argument

1. It is a violation of Title VII when "members of one sex are exposed to disadvantageous terms or conditions of employment to which members of the other sex are not exposed."[175]
2. Sexual harassment "differentially injures one gender-defined group in a sphere—sexuality in employment—in which the treatment of women and men can be compared. . . . If only men are sexually harassed, that is also arbitrary treatment based on sex, hence sex discrimination."[176]
3. So, sexual harassment only of men is a violation of Title VII.

Because of the chaos among the lower courts, the Supreme Court in 1998 agreed to rule on whether same-sex harassment is ever actionable under Title VII. They heard the case of Joseph Oncale, a man who worked on an oil rig in the Gulf of Mexico.

Joseph Oncale was employed by Sundowner on an offshore rig from August to November 1991. Oncale filed this Title VII action against Sundowner, John Lyons, his Sundowner supervisor, and Danny Pippen and Brandon Johnson, two Sundowner co-workers, alleging sexual harassment. Oncale alleges that the harassment included Pippen and Johnson restraining him while Lyons placed his penis on Oncale's neck, on one occasion, and on Oncale's arm, on another occasion; threats of homosexual rape by Lyons and Pippen; and the use of force by Lyons to push a bar of soap into Oncale's anus while Pippen restrained Oncale as he was showering on Sundowner premises.[177]

Oncale lost the original case. The decision was appealed in the Fifth District, which felt itself constrained by an earlier decision—*Garcia* and *Giddens v. Shell Oil Co.*[178]—to find in favor of the defendants, because, among other things, "'[h]arassment by a male supervisor against a male subordinate does not state a claim under Title VII even though the harassment has sexual overtones. Title VII addresses gender discrimination.'"[179]

The question at issue for the Supreme Court was "whether workplace harassment can violate Title VII's prohibition against 'discriminat[ion] . . . because of . . . sex' . . . when the harasser and the harassed employee are of the same sex."[180] The Court ruled that same-sex harassment can violate Title VII's prohibition against sex discrimination. Their reasoning was simple. Title VII protects both men and women, and the Supreme Court "has rejected any conclusive presumption that an employer will not discriminate against members of his own race."[181] Thus, by analogy, there is no presumption that males will not discriminate against members of their own sex.

In their argument, the Court addresses the issues of whether (1) a particular motivation (sexual desire) or (2) character of conduct (sexual) is necessary for a finding of sexual harassment. They point out that they have never held that "workplace harassment . . . is automatically discrimination because of sex merely because the words used have sexual content or connotations." Thus, *sexual* behavior is not a sufficient condition for sexual harassment, though it is not clear from this decision whether it is a necessary condition. Furthermore, sexual desire is not a necessary motivation for findings of sexual harassment: "harassing conduct need not be motivated by sexual desire to support an inference of discrimination based on sex."[182] In laying out the conditions for illegal sexual harassment, the Court cites Ginsburg's concurring opinion in *Harris*: "The critical issue . . . is whether members of one sex are exposed to disadvantageous terms or conditions of employment to which members of the other sex are not exposed."[183]

The Supreme Court has thus settled the issue of whether same-sex sexual harassment claims are actionable under Title VII. They have also stated that sexual desire is not a necessary condition for a finding of sexual harassment, and that sexual behavior is not sufficient. In citing Ginsburg's opinion in *Harris*, they seem to focus on the *effect* of the conduct. However, in stating what is not necessary or sufficient, they have only ruled out certain ways in which courts have dismissed claims. They have not done much to help us see how sexual harassment and sex discrimination *should* be linked. We seem still to be left with the question, What does it mean for some kind of behavior to be "because of sex"?

One can see this in the particular case of *Oncale*. The Court ruled that Oncale's claim cannot be dismissed on the grounds that same-sex sexual harassment claims are not actionable under Title VII. But it is still unclear from this and previous Supreme Court rulings whether Oncale was the victim of illegal sexual harassment.

Another way to see that the question of when conduct is "based on sex" in the sense prohibited by Title VII is still open is in consideration of the question of whether Title VII prohibits discrimination based on sexual orientation. Some courts have been quite clear that "sexual orientation" is not a protected category under Title VII. Martha Grevatt is a lesbian Chrysler worker who suffered harassment because of her sexual orientation. Grevatt filed sex discrimination charges with the EEOC. However, "[t]he E.E.O.C. declined to proceed . . . when Chrysler argued successfully that Grevatt was being harassed for being gay and for her political views—neither of which is protected by law—rather than for being female."[184] But if she is being harassed for being lesbian, then surely she meets the "but for" criterion. It is the fact that she is female and sexually desires females that elicits the harassment. If she were male and sexually desired females, she would not elicit harassment.

The Supreme Court settled the legal issue of whether male-on-male harassment could constitute sexual harassment and be prohibited under Title VII in their decision in *Oncale*. In their decision, the Court cited relevant principles previously affirmed by the Court, such as the principle that "Title VII's prohibition of discrimination 'because of . . . sex' protects men as well as women," and "in the related context of racial discrimination in the workplace we have rejected any conclusive presumption that an employer will not discriminate against members of his own race."[185] The Court also cited a case in which "a male employee claimed that his employer discriminated against him because of his sex when it preferred a female employee for promotion. Although we ultimately rejected the claim on other grounds, we did not consider it significant that the supervisor who made that decision was also a man."[186] The Court ultimately concluded, "We see no justification in the statutory language or our precedents for a categorical rule excluding same-sex harassment claims from the coverage of Title VII."[187]

It is difficult to emphasize sufficiently the shifts in the conceptions of sexual harassment and sex discrimination that are taking place as courts find ways of arguing that same-sex harassment constitutes sexual harassment. It is also remarkable that the shifts are taking place so rapidly. A major influence seems to be law review articles published in the past several years which provide ways of arguing that same-sex harassment constitutes sexual harassment understood as sex discrimination. One very important legal scholar in this regard is Katherine Franke. In a series of articles, she has argued that one of the ultimate goals of antidiscrimination law is "to provide all people more options with respect to how they do their gender";[188] such laws should protect a "fundamental right to determine gender independent of biological sex."[189] These arguments are theoretical and controversial and will be discussed in greater detail in chapter 6.

Academic Sexual Harassment

The foregoing section considered the history of the law regarding sexual harassment in the workplace. However, sexual harassment also has been recognized in the context of education. Although some of the same issues arise in the law for workplace harassment and harassment in educational contexts, they are different enough to warrant separate treatment. Of course, workplace harassment can take place in educational contexts. Principals can harass secretaries in their offices, for example. I shall limit my discussion to the kinds of harassment that are covered not by Title VII, but by Title IX. Thus, by "academic sexual harassment," I shall mean harassment that takes place within an academic institution, but in which the relevant relationship between the alleged harasser and the harassed is not one of employment. This includes but is not limited to faculty-student harassment, student-student harassment, and administrator-student harassment.[190]

Title IX of the Education Amendments was approved by Congress in 1972.[191] It reads, in part, "[N]o person in the United States shall, on the basis of sex, be excluded from participation in, be denied the benefits of, or be subjected to discrimination under any educational program or activity receiving Federal financial assistance." As a consequence of this law, educational institutions that receive federal funds must have in place a complaint procedure for victims of sex discrimination.[192] Title IX is enforced by the Office for Civil Rights of the U.S. Department of Education.

Many people are familiar with the impact of Title IX on athletics at high schools and colleges.[193] However, because Title IX addresses all sex discrimination in education, it is also a potential remedy for sexual harassment in such institutions. The first sexual harassment case involving students and faculty, *Alexander v. Yale University*,[194] held that sexual harassment constitutes sex discrimination under Title IX, citing *Barnes v. Costle*. Both students and employees of educational institutions are protected by Title IX.[195]

In general, the development of the law with respect to academic harassment has followed closely that governing workplace harassment. The first case to bring a sexual harassment claim under Title IX was *Alexander v. Yale University*.[196] This was a complex case involving several students and professors. The only claim that was recognized by the court was that of a student who claimed that she received a lower grade in a course than she should have because she rejected the professor's offer to exchange an A for sex. The court saw this as quid pro quo sexual harassment. However, two other claims associated with the case were dismissed. A male faculty member claimed that he was unable to teach in the atmosphere created by harassing professors. Another student claimed that she "suffered distress because of harassing activity directed toward another woman student."[197] The latter two claims may have qualified as hostile environment claims under the 1980 EEOC *Guidelines*. However, at the time these claims were made, no hostile environment claim had yet been upheld. The court dismissed the claim of the second student, saying, "No judicial enforcement of Title IX could properly extend to such imponderables as atmosphere or vicariously experienced wrong."[198]

Not many cases of sexual harassment in the educational context have reached the federal courts since *Alexander*, though they have been occurring with increasing frequency in recent years. Commentators speculate about reasons for the relative lack of early cases. One commentator writing before 1992 suggested that "students had little to gain through Title IX because they could only seek the withdrawal of federal funds from the educational institution, or perhaps an injunction, but not monetary damages."[199] Another suggests that

[f]ew students have brought sexual harassment actions under Title IX, probably for reasons having to do both with the student circumstance and with the nature of the relief that until recently has been available. Students are transient members of the institutional community; they

have little to gain personally by reform. Further, litigation takes a long time; it is not unusual for a student's case to be moot because she graduated before it was heard. Students are also inhibited by the perception that the institution will defend the accused harasser. . . . Until *Franklin v. Gwinnett County Public Schools*, the relief available—the withdrawal of federal funds from the institutions—provided little satisfaction and no financial compensation to a student. . . .[200]

Key issues in Title IX cases have concerned the extension of conceptions developed under Title VII to situations covered by Title IX. Because of the perceived differences between the employment context and the educational context, questions have arisen about the propriety of simply transferring certain conceptions from one context to the other. The relevant differences between the two contexts concern the differences between employer-employee relationships and teacher-student relationships, issues about the ages of harassers and harassed, and issues surrounding academic freedom. In what follows, I focus on those cases that raise issues different from those in workplace cases and thus develop the concept of sexual harassment in distinct ways.

Moire v. Temple University School of Medicine, decided in 1986, was the next federal sexual harassment case brought under Title IX after *Alexander*.[201] The case involved a hostile environment sexual harassment claim brought by a female medical student. The student alleged that "she had been subjected to sexual harassment . . . as a result of which she was given a failing grade in her psychiatry clerkship and not promoted to the fourth year of Temple medical school."[202] Though Moire did not prove her case, the court did recognize hostile environment sexual harassment as actionable under Title IX. In its decision, the court made explicit reference to Title VII, claiming that, "[t]hough the sexual harassment 'doctrine' has generally developed in the context of Title VII, [the EEOC] guidelines seem equally applicable to Title IX."[203]

Several of the cases that have some bearing on the issue of sexual harassment in educational institutions have been brought by university instructors who were penalized for having engaged in sexual relationships with students.[204] None of these cases directly involved Title IX; some do not even involve sexual harassment. They bear on the issue of sexual harassment, however, because they suggest that, in the educational context, the consent of an adult student may not necessarily constitute a defense against a charge of sexual harassment, that is, of unwanted sexual attention.

According to the EEOC definition of sexual harassment, sexual behavior is not sexual harassment unless it is *unwelcome*. Nonconsensual relationships between faculty and students are clearly "unwelcome"; that is, the absence of consent is sufficient to establish unwelcomeness. But what about consensual relationships? Consent to a sexual relationship would seem to show that the relationship *is* welcome and so *is not* sexual harassment. However, some have argued that because of the inherent inequality of students and professors, the consent of a student is not genuine consent.

Louise Fitzgerald defines sexual harassment in such a way that consensual relationships between teachers and their students are impossible.[205] Fitzgerald explains that, according to her definition, "when a formal power differential exists, all sexist and sexual behavior is seen as harassment, since the woman is not considered to be in a position to object, resist, or give fully free consent. . . ."[206] She admits that "[o]ne of the more controversial implications of such a definition is that, within this framework, so-called consensual relationships between persons of formally different statuses (*e.g.*, professor/student) would be, strictly speaking, impossible."[207] Dziech and Weiner present a similar position in their influential *Lecherous Professor*. Dziech and Weiner believe that "true consent demands full equality."[208] They also believe that students and professors are almost never fully equal: "If a professor becomes involved with a student, his standard defense is that she is a consenting adult. Few students are ever, in the strictest sense, consenting adults. A student can never be the genuine equal of a professor insofar as his professional position gives him power over her."[209] The principle that inequality of power problematizes consent is one that is compatible with some versions of the liberal perspective, as well as the sociocultural perspective. However, there is a great deal of disagreement about the extent to which voluntary consent is compromised by different sorts of inequalities. Some socioculturalists, such as MacKinnon, seem to hold that women cannot freely consent to sex with any man because of the fundamental inequality between women and men. Thus, all sex between women and men is coerced. Others seem to hold that only certain kinds of power inequalities are relevant, primarily in contexts where institutional hierarchies give one person significant power over another.

Two 1984 decisions involving university instructors disciplined by their institutions for engaging in sexual relationships with students were seen by commentators as indications that consent may not constitute a defense to sexual harassment in professor-student relationships.[210]

Naragon v. Wharton[211] involved a graduate teaching assistant who had a consensual relationship with a freshman female student for whom she had no direct supervisory responsibilities. The university disciplined Naragon by reappointing her as a graduate assistant whose duties did not include teaching undergraduates. Naragon sued three university administrators to retain her teaching duties. The circuit court agreed with the university that Naragon's behavior was unprofessional, citing in approval several of the university's arguments:

[I]ntimate relationships between teachers and students are unprofessional and likely to be detrimental to the students and to the University.

. . . there may be an adverse effect upon the student and University, and upon the effectiveness of the teacher. . . .

. . . intimacy between a teacher and a student [was] a breach of professional ethics on the part of the teacher, and . . . it undermined the proper position and effectiveness of the teacher because of the perception of other students.

. . . it is an obvious criterion for being a professional teacher to avoid intimate relationships with students.[212]

The fact that the relationship was consensual did not protect Naragon from the interference of the university. The university regarded Naragon as having violated professional rules of conduct.

Korf v. Ball State University[213] involved a tenured professor terminated for "making unwelcomed sexual advances toward" students and "offering good grades contingent upon sexual involvement."[214] Korf claimed that his termination violated his constitutional rights. A university committee found Korf "guilty of unethical conduct because he used his position and influence as a teacher to exploit students for his private advantage."[215]

Korf argued in his defense that "other 'private and consensual' faculty/student sexual relationships had occurred and were presently occurring at Ball State University and that no steps had ever been taken against the faculty members allegedly involved."[216] The court responded that whether or not the activity was "consensual" was not at issue. Korf was not accused of engaging in nonconsensual sexual activity. Rather, he was accused of engaging in "unethical behavior by 'exploiting students for his own private advantage.'"[217] In addition, the court cast doubt on whether or not the sexual activity could truly be considered consensual: "Furthermore, the Committee heard evidence of Dr. Korf's sexual advances towards seven students who refused his advances. One student recounted how he had to be 'very assertive to get away from Dr. Korf's amorous advances'. Such conduct certainly cannot be characterized as consensual sexual activity."[218] In this, the court seems to agree with Fitzgerald and Dziech and Weiner. In its decision, the court said that

> while there is no evidence that the young student Dr. Korf admitted having a sexual relationship with did not consent to engage in sexual activity with him, Dr. Korf's conduct is not to be viewed in the same context as would conduct of an ordinary "person on the street." Rather, it must be judged in the context of the relationship existing between a professor and his students within an academic environment. University professors occupy an important place in our society and have concomitant ethical obligations. . . .[219]

These cases suggest that while there are similarities between employer-employee relationships and teacher-student relationships, there are significant differences. However, they are consistent with the 1986 Supreme Court decision in *Meritor Savings Bank, FSB v. Vinson*.[220] Recall that in *Meritor*, the Court held that conduct with which one voluntarily complied could nevertheless be "unwelcome." Thus, it is possible for someone voluntarily to comply with the request of another to engage in sexual intercourse, and yet for the sexual advance to constitute sexual harassment. This decision has been understood to mean that conduct to which one *consented* could be considered "unwelcome," and, thus, that a charge of sexual harassment could be upheld in consensual relationships.[221]

These cases do not, of course, *prove* that consent would not work as a defense against a charge of sexual harassment against a professor by a student.

However, the influence of these cases on university policies is quite clear. The first university to develop and implement a consensual relationship policy was the University of Iowa, which implemented its policy in 1986. The motivation for the policy seems to have been a desire on the part of many in the university for clear rules regarding appropriate teacher-student relationships.[222] At about this time, recommendations that colleges and universities develop such policies began to appear.[223] The argument seemed to be that campuses that did not adopt such policies might be open to lawsuits.

Some university and college policies state explicitly that the consent of the student is not a defense against sexual harassment. For example, Ohio State University's policy states: "Consensual romantic and sexual relationships between supervisor and employee or between faculty and student are strongly discouraged. In the event of an allegation of sexual harassment, the University will be less sympathetic to a defense based upon consent when the facts establish that a professional power differential existed within the relationship."[224]

In 1992, the Supreme Court declared that sexual harassment was a form of sex discrimination under Title IX in *Franklin v. Gwinnett County Public Schools*.[225] Most agree that with *Gwinnett*, the Supreme Court "appears to signal that the case law developed under Title VII is an appropriate guide as courts develop sexual harassment definitional standards under Title IX."[226] However, some argue that sexual harassment should be understood differently under Title IX because of the issue of consent discussed earlier, and because of the involvement of minors at the elementary and secondary levels.

Stephanie Roth and Carrie Baker argue that in schools, plaintiffs should not have to prove that the harassment is unwelcome. Rather, the presumption should be that the sexual conduct is unwelcome.[227] It should be up to the defendant to prove that the conduct was welcome. This reverses the presumption present in cases of workplace harassment, where it is assumed that sexual conduct is welcomed unless the plaintiff can prove otherwise.

> To require sexual harassment plaintiffs to prove unwelcomeness in their prima facie cases is to assume that sexual conduct between teachers and students is welcome until objections are made. This assumption is not conducive to the creation of an academic environment free from sexual coercion and should not underlie Title IX sexual harassment guidelines.[228]

This seems correct in cases where the victim is a minor. As Roth points out,

> At the elementary and secondary school levels, inappropriate physical contact with and sexual molestation of students is usually characterized as either child abuse or statutory rape, rather than sexual harassment. . . . The fact that such sexual behavior is criminalized reveals society's judgment that such conduct is per se offensive. Thus, under a Title IX analysis, this conduct should be deemed inherently unwelcome or

offensive so that no analytical safeguards need be imposed before categorizing such conduct as actionable sexual harassment.[229]

However, what if the victim is an adult? Roth seems to accept the view that the difference in power between a teacher and an undergraduate student is such that even when the student is an adult, sexual advances toward a student by his or her teacher should be assumed to be unwelcome. Because of the extreme power differential between students and faculty, truly consenting relations between members of these groups may be impossible.[230] Roth seems ambivalent about whether graduate students are able to consent to relationships with professors, though she suggests that the same presumption of unwelcomeness should prevail.[231] Baker does not distinguish between graduate and undergraduate adult students with regard to this issue.[232]

The view that sexual relationships between professors and college or graduate students constitute sexual harassment by definition is opposed by feminist Jane Gallop.[233] According to Gallop, such a conception confuses sexism with sexuality. True sexual harassment is wrong because it disadvantages women in the workplace or in education. But a sexual encounter between a professor and a student need not disadvantage the student with regard to his or her educational opportunities. There are more kinds of power than simply institutional power, and sometimes these kinds of power can balance one another. Gallop argues that sexual harassment has come to refer to the sexualization of professional relationships, regardless of whether this results in discrimination against anyone. But, as she points out, the sexualization of professional relations is not always disadvantageous to women. Gallop warns that when the conception of sexual harassment is divorced from its gendered context, it becomes merely sexual misconduct, or "socially undesirable sexuality."[234]

Gallop points out that the categorization of consensual relationships between students and faculty as sexual harassment disregards entirely the student's desires.

As a feminist, I am well aware of the ways women are often compelled to sexual relations with men by forces that have nothing to do with our desire. And I see that students might be in a similar position with relation to teachers. But, as a feminist, I do not think the solution is to deny women or students the right to consent. Denying women the right to consent reinforces our status as objects rather than desiring subjects. That is why I believe that the question of whether sexual advances are *wanted* is absolutely crucial.[235]

While I do not entirely agree with Gallop's views, I do agree that the Fitzgerald and Dzeich and Weiner perspective is objectionably paternalistic. I think there are reasons other than those having to do with consent for barring sexual relationships between professors and students while those students are in their classes. The potential for conflict of interest is great, as is that for favoritism.[236] Gallop rightly points out how close this kind of paternalism is to harassing behavior itself:

> Prohibition of consensual teacher-student relations is based on the assumption that when a student says yes she really means no. I cannot help but think that this proceeds from the logic according to which when a woman says no she really means yes. The first assumption is protectionist; the second is the very logic of harassment. What harassment and protectionism have in common is precisely a refusal to credit women's desires. Common to both is the assumption that women do not know what we want, that someone else, in a position of greater knowledge and power, knows better.[237]

In 1997, the Office for Civil Rights (OCR) of the Department of Education issued its first guidelines on sexual harassment, "Sexual Harassment Guidance."[238] These guidelines seem to accept Roth and Baker's suggestion that the presumption of unwelcomeness be adopted, at least for younger students. The OCR guidelines reflect the particular issues that have arisen in connection with sexual harassment cases in schools: the ages of those involved and First Amendment rights. According to the guidelines, both quid pro quo and hostile environment sexual harassment are illegal under Title IX. In the context of an educational institution, quid pro quo sexual harassment occurs when "[a] school employee explicitly or implicitly conditions a student's participation in an education program or activity or bases an educational decision on the student's submission to unwelcome sexual advances, requests for sexual favors, or other verbal, nonverbal, or physical conduct of a sexual nature."[239] Hostile environment sexual harassment is defined as "[s]exually harassing conduct (which can include unwelcome sexual advances, requests for sexual favors, and other verbal, nonverbal, or physical conduct of a sexual nature) by an employee, by another student, or by a third party that is sufficiently severe, persistent, or pervasive to limit a student's ability to participate in or benefit from an education program or activity, or to create a hostile or abusive educational environment."[240] The ages of students who are harassed is considered significant, but the OCR provides different rules for different levels of education. "If elementary students are involved, welcomeness will not be an issue: OCR will never view sexual conduct between an adult school employee and an elementary school student as consensual." In the case of secondary school students, "there will be a strong presumption that sexual conduct between an adult school employee and a student is not consensual." The presumption that the behavior is not consensual is in effect for cases involving older secondary students, but "OCR will consider a number of factors in determining whether a school employee's sexual advances or other sexual conduct could be considered welcome." The "Guidance" suggests that the presumption that the conduct is not consensual will not be made for cases involving postsecondary students. Instead, the factors used to determine welcomeness in the case of older secondary students will be used.[241] These factors include:

The nature of the conduct and the relationship of the school employee to the student, including the degree of influence (which could, at least in part, be affected by the student's age), authority, or control the employee has over the student.

Whether the student was legally or practically unable to consent to the sexual conduct in question. . . .[242]

In the case of hostile environment sexual harassment, the conduct must be sufficiently severe, persistent, and pervasive to "limit a student's ability to participate in or benefit from the education program or to create a hostile or abusive educational environment."[243] The reasonable person standard is to be used in determining whether conduct reaches that level. However, the "Guidance" seems not to be quite sure whether the standard of reasonableness should be the reasonable person or the reasonable victim. It suggests that the sex of the victim should be taken into account. [244]

As mentioned previously, issues of First Amendment rights often arise when hostile environment sexual harassment claims are made in educational contexts:

Free speech rights apply in the classroom (e.g., classroom lectures and discussions) and in all other education programs and activities of public schools (e.g., public meetings and speakers on campus; campus debates, school plays and other cultural events; and student newspapers, journals and other publications). In addition, First Amendment rights apply to the speech of students and teachers.[245]

The courts have decided in favor of protecting First Amendment rights against allegations of sexual and racial harassment in classrooms and other educational venues. One well-publicized case involving alleged hostile environment sexual harassment and First Amendment rights is *Silva v. University of New Hampshire*.[246] Silva, a tenured instructor, was fired for allegedly creating a hostile environment for his students. Silva eventually won his case on the grounds that the sexual harassment policy at the university was too subjective.[247]

The complaint against Silva centered on two uses of sexualized language in a course in technical writing. In one, Silva described the activity of "focusing" in writing as follows: "Focus is like sex. You seek a target. You zero in on your subject. You move from side to side. You close in on the subject. You bracket the subject and center on it. Focus connects experience and language. You and the subject become one."[248] The second use of sexualized language was to illustrate the elements of a good definition. Silva took his example from Little Egypt, a belly dancer, who said: "Belly dancing is like jello on a plate with a vibrator under the plate."[249] In explanation of his use of this example, Silva explained: "Little Egypt's definition of belly dancing is classic in its use of concrete differentia and simple metaphor, i.e. the trembling jello equates to the essential movements necessary to the dance. It is unlike the dance but also its very essence."[250] Eight students filed complaints against Silva, six of them on the basis of the classroom remarks, and two on the basis of other alleged utterances made outside the classroom. These included Silva's saying to a student, "How would you like to get an A?"; Silva's remarking to a student on her knees looking through a card catalogue, "It looks like you've had alot of experience or your knees"; an overheard remark from Silva, "I'd like to see that!" when one student told another that she was going to "jump on the computer"; and the remark made to two female students seeking his help on an assignment, "How long have you been together?"[251] A university hearing panel found Silva in violation of the university's sexual harassment policy.

> It is the conclusion of the hearing panel that a reasonable female student would find Professor Silva's comments and his behavior to be offensive, intimidating and contributing to a hostile academic environment. Furthermore, Professor Silva gave the panel no reason to believe that he understood the seriousness of his behavior and the impact it had on the students he was teaching. In addition, Professor Silva stated he would behave in a similar manner in the future.[252]

Silva was suspended and provided with conditions of reinstatement. These included attending counseling for one year at his own expense and a written apology to the students. Silva appealed, and the appeals board reaffirmed the original finding:

> It is the conclusion of the Appeals Board that Professor Silva's repeated and sustained comments and behavior of a sexual and otherwise intrusive nature had the effect of creating a hostile and intimidating academic environment. Furthermore, it is the Board's opinion that as an experienced teacher and professor of communication and language, Professor Silva should have been more sensitive to the effect of his behavior on the students. Unfortunately, Professor Silva gave the Board no reason to believe that he understood the seriousness of his behavior and the impact it had on the students. When the problem was brought to his attention, he tried to defend himself by claiming that the students were immature and in need of better training in the use and interpretation of language.[253]

Silva then filed a lawsuit against the University of New Hampshire, school officials, and the students who brought the complaints. Among other things, he claimed that their conduct violated his First Amendment right to freedom of speech. The court agreed that Silva's First Amendment rights had been violated. Their arguments are puzzling, and at least one commentator has argued that their decision was erroneous.[254] For example, the court claimed that the vibrating-Jello definition was not of a "sexual nature" and so was not proscribed by the University of New Hampshire's sexual harassment policy.

The evidence before the court demonstrates that the belly dancing statement was not "of a sexual nature" . . . but rather that the six complainants who were offended by it were under the mistaken impression that the word "vibrator" necessarily connotes a sexual device. This misunderstanding induced said complainants to regard the focus statement as part of an offensive academic environment.

Because the USNH [University System of New Hampshire] Sexual Harassment Policy does not proscribe verbal conduct not of a sexual nature, Silva's discipline under said policy was erroneous.[255]

The reader can determine whether he or she agrees with the court on this point. The court also argued that the "focus" analogy was protected speech.

[T]he court concludes that the USNH Sexual Harassment Policy as applied to Silva's classroom speech is not reasonably related to the legitimate pedagogical purpose of providing a congenial academic environment because it employs an impermissibly subjective standard that fails to take into account the nation's interest in academic freedom.

Accordingly, the court finds and rules that the application of the USNH Sexual Harassment Policy to Silva's classroom statements violates the First Amendment.[256]

The *Silva* case received a great deal of attention in the press. People were divided over whether Silva's conduct constituted illegal sexual harassment. Another case that was decided in favor of a professor is *Cohen v. San Bernardino Valley College*.[257] *Cohen* involved a composition professor who required students to read and write on controversial subjects such as pornography. A student charged that she had been subjected to a hostile environment in the classroom. The court found in favor of Cohen, arguing that the school's sexual harassment policy was unconstitutionally vague.

This controversy is related to the conflict between hostile environment claims and First Amendment rights discussed in relation to workplace harassment earlier in the chapter. It is not likely to be resolved soon. The OCR "Guidance" briefly addresses First Amendment rights. Two examples are provided, one in which the First Amendment prevails, the other where the sexual harassment claim prevails:

Example 1: In a college level creative writing class, a professor's required reading list includes excerpts from literary classics that contain descriptions of explicit sexual conduct, including scenes that depict women in submissive and demeaning roles. The professor also assigns students to write their own materials, which are read in class. Some of the student essays contain sexually derogatory themes about women. Several female students complain to the Dean of Students that the materials and related classroom discussion have created a sexually hostile environment for women in the class. What must the school do in response?

Answer: Academic discourse in this example is protected by the First Amendment even if it is offensive to individuals. Thus, Title IX would not require the school to discipline the professor or to censor the reading list or related class discussion.

Example 2: A group of male students repeatedly targets a female student for harassment during the bus ride home from school, including making explicit sexual comments about her body, passing around drawings that depict her engaging in sexual conduct, and, on several occasions, attempting to follow her home off the bus. The female student and her parents complain to the principal that the male students' conduct has created a hostile environment for girls on the bus and that they fear for their daughter's safety. What must the school do in response?

Answer: Threatening and intimidating actions targeted at a particular student or group of students, even though they contain elements of speech, are not protected by the First Amendment. The school must take reasonable and appropriate actions against the students, including disciplinary action if necessary, to remedy the hostile environment and prevent future harassment.[258]

Most recent academic sexual harassment cases have involved questions of liability. In *Gebsere et al. v. Lago Vista Indep. School Dist.*,[259] the issue was the proper standard of liability of the school district when a teacher sexually harasses a student. In the decision handed down on June 22, 1998, Justice Sandra Day O'Connor, writing for the majority, stated:

The question in this case is when a school district may be held liable in damages in an implied right of action under Title IX of the Education Amendments of 1972 . . . for the sexual harassment of a student by one of the district's teachers. We conclude that damages may not be recovered in those circumstances unless an official of the school district who, at a minimum, has authority to institute corrective measures on the district's behalf has actual notice of, and is deliberately indifferent to, the teacher's misconduct.[260]

In a dissenting opinion, Judge John Paul Stevens, who was joined by Justices Ruth Ginsberg, David Souter, and Stephen Breyer, argued that "the majority's policy judgment about the appropriate remedy in this case thwarts the purposes of Title IX."[261]

The reason why the common law imposes liability on the principal in such circumstances is the same as the reason why Congress included the prohibition against discrimination on the basis of sex in Title IX: to induce school boards to adopt and enforce practices that will minimize the danger that vulnerable students will be exposed to such odious behavior. The rule that the Court has crafted creates the opposite incentive. As long as school boards can insulate themselves from knowledge about this sort of conduct, they can claim immunity from damages liability.[262]

This decision is puzzling and, as the dissenting opinion points out, conflicts with the EEOC *Guidelines.*

It seems to me that the conception of sexual harassment expanded when it was applied to the academic context. As we have seen, Fitzgerald and Dziech and Weiner find all—or nearly all—relationships between college students and their teachers to be instances of sexual harassment. Would it follow that any sexual relationship between a supervisor and someone he or she supervises is sexual harassment? Their principle that true consent requires absolute equality is ultimately unintelligible, since it renders us unable to distinguish between consensual and nonconsensual relationships. There is a significant difference between the case in which two people mutually agree to a sexual relationship, even if one is the supervisor of the other, and the case in which an employee agrees to a sexual relationship with his or her supervisor only because she believes she must do so to keep her position. In both cases, the employee seems to consent to something, but in one case it is under duress and in the other it is not. Calling both nonconsensual might be acceptable if some other way of distinguishing the two cases were to be made available. The Supreme Court seems to think that the advance by the supervisor is "unwelcome" in one case and welcome in the other. An employer may have other reasons for wanting to discourage romances between employees, whether of the same rank or of different ranks, for reasons similar to those mentioned here in connection with academic relationships: favoritism and conflict of interest.[263]

Perhaps the most dramatic contribution of academic harassment law to the evolving concept of sexual harassment is its expansion to peer harassment.[264] While there may be a parallel to co-worker harassment in the employment context, peer harassment has been discussed primarily as a phenomenon among children. Teasing and bullying that are gender biased have been considered sexual harassment, and schools are put on notice that they are liable for this conduct of students. The phenomenon has caused many to rethink the effects of certain common behaviors of children, while others find categorizing such conduct as sexual harassment outrageous.[265] Socioculturalists and some liberals tend to link gendered harassment by children to the unequal status of women and men in society. They see a continuum from childhood to adulthood, with the gendered harassment that takes place in grade school leading to the social inequality of women and men. Adherents of a natural/biological perspective and other liberals tend to think that what socioculturalists see as sexual harassment is just a form of rude behavior that is distorted when categorized as "gendered."

The issue of students harassing other students, or "peer harassment," came to public awareness when a six-year-old was accused of sexually harassing a classmate by kissing her. The OCR "Guidance" denies that this incident constituted sexual harassment, though it does not provide an argument for this claim. Mention of the case is made in a section describing how age is relevant in determining whether sexual harassment has taken place, but it is not clear why the age of the accused child matters. The incident does not seem sufficiently severe, persistent, or pervasive to qualify as sexual harassment.

Originally, there was resistance to the idea that children could sexually harass other children, and that schools have the responsibility to prevent such harassment. Sexual bullying and teasing have long been accepted as part of being a child. However, opinion has been changing.[266] A number of court cases involving allegations of egregious behavior seem to be sensitizing both adults and children to the prevalence and effects of such behavior. For example, in *Doe v. Petaluma City School Dist.*,[267] a junior high student was subjected to severe harassment by both male and female peers. Eventually, she was driven from the school. Doe sued the school district, claiming that its failure to stop the harassment violated Title IX.[268] Other students have followed suit.[269]

Lower courts have not been consistent in their decisions in cases of alleged peer harassment. "The 5th Circuit held that a school is not liable under Title IX even if it is on notice of peer sexual harassment and it ignores or fails to remedy it, unless it responds differently based on the sex of the alleged victim," in *Rowinsky v. Bryan Independent School District.*[270] The OCR contends that this decision was wrong. In its "Guidance," it states,

[A] school will be liable under Title IX if its students sexually harass other students if (i) a hostile environment exists in the school's programs or activities, (ii) the school knows or should have known of the harassment, and (iii) the school fails to take immediate and appropriate corrective action. . . . Under these circumstances, a school's failure to respond to the existence of a hostile environment within its own programs or activities permits an atmosphere of sexual discrimination to permeate the educational program and results in discrimination prohibited by Title IX. Conversely, if, upon notice of hostile environment harassment, a school takes immediate and appropriate steps to remedy the hostile environment, the school has avoided violating Title IX. Thus, Title IX does not make a school responsible for the actions of harassing students, but rather for its own discrimination in failing to remedy it once the school has notice.[271]

Because of the lack of agreement about the issue, the Supreme Court agreed to hear a case of alleged peer harassment in its 1998-99 term. *Davis v. Monroe County Board of Education*[272] involved fifth-grade students. The issue before the Court was "whether a private damages action may lie against the school board in cases of student-on-student harassment." The majority of the Court found that "it may, but only where the funding recipient acts with deliberate indifference to known acts of harassment in its programs or activities. Moreover, we conclude that such an action will lie only for harassment that is so severe, pervasive, and objectively offensive that it effectively bars the victim's access to an educational opportunity or benefit."[273]

Justice Kennedy dissented, arguing, among other things, that such a finding represented an unjustified intrusion of the federal government into local matters. He was joined in his dissent by Justices Scalia and Thomas. Kennedy raises a number of legal points, some of which have merit. For example, he claims that a school should be held liable only if it had clear and unambiguous notice that it was responsible for preventing sexual harassment among students, and that schools did not have such notice. There does seem to be some question about this.

However, certain of Kennedy's arguments as to why the kind of behavior complained of by Davis does not constitute sexual harassment are remarkably similar to the arguments of early decisions in the development of sexual harassment law under Title VII. For example, Kennedy claims that

> a plaintiff cannot establish a Title IX violation merely by showing that she has been "subjected to discrimination." Rather, a violation of Title IX occurs only if she is "subjected to discrimination under any education program or activity," . . . where "program or activity" is defined as "all of the operations of" a grant recipient. . . . Under the most natural reading of this provision, discrimination violates Title IX only if it is authorized by, or in accordance with, the actions, activities, or policies of the grant recipient.[274]

Kennedy seems to be making an argument analogous to Frey's argument in *Corne v. Bausch & Lomb, Inc.*, that only *policies* of an employer can constitute illegal sex discrimination. Kennedy denies that there is an analogy between co-worker harassment and student-student harassment.

> Analogies to Title VII hostile environment harassment are inapposite, because schools are not workplaces and children are not adults. The norms of the adult workplace that have defined hostile environment sexual harassment . . . are not easily translated to peer relationships in schools, where teenage romantic relationships and dating are a part of everyday life. Analogies to Title IX teacher sexual harassment of students are similarly flawed. A teacher's sexual overtures toward a student are always inappropriate; a teenager's romantic overtures to a classmate (even when persistent and unwelcome) are an inescapable part of adolescence.[275]

These remarks bear a striking resemblance to some of the early decisions in sexual harassment law, such as that in *Barnes v. Train*. The underlying assumption is that the behavior complained of is a romantic overture. However, in many of the cases that have come before the court, "romantic overture" hardly seems the appropriate description of the behavior in question.

The Supreme Court's decision in *Davis* that student-student sexual harassment is discriminatory, and that schools have a responsibility to prevent it, seems appropriate, though some of the dissent's arguments on points of law in *Davis* have merit. Schools are responsible for protecting students from one another, as well as from teachers and staff. Though it may be objected that children are cruel to one another, and that harassment suffered by Davis is not different in kind from nongendered harassment suffered by other students, it should not be forgotten that there is a law against sex discrimination in schools. As long as sexual harassment in the workplace is conceived as sex discrimination, sexual harassment in schools should also be considered such.

Developments outside the United States

While the United States has led the world in recognition of sexual harassment as a phenomenon and in development of the concept of sexual harassment in the law, other countries have been quick to follow. Great Britain, Canada, and Australia have all been involved in the development of the law and theory of sexual harassment. All three tend to follow the United States in interpreting sexual harassment as sex discrimination. However, because of differences in sex discrimination laws and legal administrative structures, there have been differences in the handling of sexual harassment.

In 1992, the International Labour Organization (ILO) published a special issue of their journal, *Conditions of Work*, on sexual harassment.[276] This work represented the results of a survey of twenty-three industrialized nations with regard to whether or not sexual harassment had been recognized, either in legislation or in case law, definitions of sexual harassment, the kinds of laws that might be useable in cases of sexual harassment, liability, sanctions, and remedies, and institutional authorities that either were or might be charged with monitoring sexual harassment in employment.

Of the twenty-three industrialized countries surveyed, only seven had statutes which specifically defined or mentioned the term "sexual harassment" (Australia [federal level and most states], Canada [federal level and a number of provinces], France, New Zealand, Spain, Sweden, and the United States [state level only]). In some countries, the term had been explicitly mentioned and defined by judicial decision (Australia [one state], Canada [some provinces], Ireland, Switzerland, United Kingdom, United States [federal level and some states].) In most other countries, sexual harassment had been defined by implication as an activity in violation of a statute that addressed a subject other than sexual harassment, such as unfair dismissal, tort law, or criminal law.[277] Since this 1992 assessment, a number of countries have specifically addressed sexual harassment in legislation, interpretation of existing laws, and trade agreements. A 1996 survey claimed that "sexual harassment in employment now attracts the full attention of the law."[278]

Since 1976, the various bodies of the European Community (EC) have passed a number of directives and recommendations regarding women and work. Though most of these do not explicitly mention sexual harassment, they paved the way for the 1991 Recommendation by the Commission of the European Communities which directly addresses sexual harassment. Because these directives concerned sex discrimination, sexual harassment has been conceptualized as a form of sex discrimination.[279] However, there are some interesting differences between the European Community and the United States in the conceptualization of both sex discrimination and sexual harassment.

A 1976 EC Council directive "prohibits any form of sex discrimination as regards access to employment, vocational training, promotion and working conditions."[280] A recommendation adopted by the Council of Ministers in 1984 "aims at eliminating inequalities affecting women in working life and at promoting a better balance between the sexes in employment."[281] A resolution adopted by the European Parliament in 1986 addressed violence against women as a barrier to equality for women. A portion of this resolution was devoted to sexual harassment.

The European Parliament . . .
—having regard to the U.N. Convention on the elimination of all forms of discrimination against women . . .
37. Calls on the Commission to conduct a study
(a) estimating the costs incurred by Member States' social security bodies for illness or absence from work due to sexual blackmail at work (psychosomatic disease, neuroses, etc.),
(b) evaluating the relation between drops in productivity in public or private companies where such cases arise and sexual blackmail at work;
38. Whereas sexual harassment can be seen as non-respect of the principle of equal treatment with regard to access to employment and promotion, and working conditions, calls on the Commission to examine national labour and anti-discrimination legislation with a view to determining its applicability to such cases and, in so far as existing legislation may be deemed adequate, to propose a directive to complete existing legislation;
39. Calls on the Council Ministers meeting on the subject of labour legislation to take all the necessary steps to harmonize laws on sexual blackmail at work in the different Member States of the Community and while awaiting this harmonization, calls on national authorities to strive to achieve a legal definition of sexual harassment so that victims of such attacks will have a clearly defined basis on which to lodge complaints; calls also for an investigation of the extent to which national labour legislation provides for sanctions against sexual harassment; to this end calls for complaints bureaux to be set up;
40. Calls on national governments, equal opportunities committees and trade unions to carry out concerted information campaigns to create a proper awareness of the individual rights of all members of the labour force, to highlight the discriminatory nature of sexual harassment and to inform victims of such harassment concerning

courses of action open to them, and calls for this aspect of conduct to be discussed during sex education and social studies classes;

41. Recommends that trade unions should consider that sexual harassment in the workplace shows similar disregard for human dignity as the infringement of equality of opportunity in employment with a view to drawing up strict codes of practice to defend the victims of such harassment and to impose appropriate sanctions on those who exploit the possibilities offered by a working environment to abuse employees or colleagues, based on the definition proposed by the TUC [Trades Union Congress, United Kingdom];

42. Deeply deplores the existence of sexual harassment in professional relationships where the dependent status of women is emphasized as [a] patient in need of professional assistance, for example in the medical and paramedical sectors where the need for professional advice and assistance makes many women feel an increased sense of dependence:

(a) calls on the specialized educational authorities to take account of this dimension in training medical and paramedical personnel so that they are aware of what is unacceptable conduct in such a relationship and make respect for the dignity of their patient a matter of paramount importance;

(b) calls on the health authorities of those Member States where it is not customary to consider whether the presence of a third person should be recommended, if the victim requests it and/or agrees to it;

43. With a view to the protection of the individual wishing to lodge a complaint of sexual harassment, calls for:

—adequate assistance of support groups which would be authorized to lodge a complaint in their own name and on behalf of the person concerned;

—the appointment of "complaints consultants" within the medical and paramedical professional associations to whom complaints could be referred with a view to obtaining advice as to the procedure to be followed.[282]

The text of this resolution clearly conceives of sexual harassment as a problem for *women*, affecting women's equality in the workplace. It also seems to identify sexual harassment with sexual blackmail, or what in the United States is called quid pro quo harassment. The resolution also suggests that sexual harassment, so defined, is an injury to the "dignity" of the victim. This is an expression often used in EC documents. The European Community clearly considers the protection of people's dignity a responsibility of government and labor organizations, and it considers sexual harassment to be a violation of the dignity of a person.

A 1987 report published by the European Commission "found that sexual harassment was a serious problem, but that existing legal remedies were inadequate."[283] A resolution adopted by the Council of Ministers in 1990 on the protection of the dignity of women and men at work included a definition of "sexual harassment."

The Council of European Communities . . .

I. Affirms that conduct of a sexual nature, or other conduct based on sex affecting the dignity of women and men at work, including conduct of superiors and colleagues, constitutes an intolerable violation of the dignity of workers or trainees and is unacceptable if:

(a) such conduct is unwanted, unreasonable and offensive to the recipient;

(b) a person's rejection of, or submission to, such conduct on the part of employers or workers (including superiors or colleagues) is used explicitly or implicitly as a basis for a decision which affects that person's access to vocational training, access to employment, continued employment, promotion, salary or any other employment decisions; and/or

(c) such conduct creates an intimidating, hostile, or humiliating working environment for the recipient. . . .[284]

Such conduct was asserted to be "unacceptable" and, in some cases, to conflict with the 1976 Directive on Equal Treatment.

Finally, in 1991, a recommendation on the protection of the dignity of women and men at work was adopted by the European Commission. The recommendation ordered, in part, that "the Member States take action to promote awareness that conduct of a sexual nature or other conduct based on sex affecting the dignity of women and men at work, including conduct of superiors and colleagues, is unacceptable" under certain specified conditions in accordance with the definition of sexual harassment just stated.[285] Appended to this recommendation was a Code of Practice on measures to combat sexual harassment.[286] The purpose of the Code of Practice is "to give practical guidance to employers, trade unions, and employees on the protection of the dignity of women and men at work." It is designed to "encourage the development and implementation of policies and practices which establish working environments free of sexual harassment and in which women and men respect one another's human integrity."[287] The Code defines sexual harassment and provides examples of unacceptable behaviors. From the perspective of the Code, sexual harassment is primarily a problem of sex discrimination, though the Code mentions that in some Member States, it might also be a criminal offense or a violation of health and safety requirements. Both methods for preventing sexual harassment and procedures for dealing with incidents of sexual harassment are included on the Code of Practice. The recommendation and the Code of Practice were endorsed by the Council of Ministers in a 1991 declaration.[288]

Thus, there is evidence that the European Community has been quite active in raising awareness of sexual harassment among Member States and in developing procedures for its prevention. However, thus far, none of resolutions or recommendations requires Members States to do anything specific about sexual harassment. The European Community is authorized to enact regulations, directives, decisions, recommendations, and opinions. These differ in the degree to which they are binding on Member States.

Regulations are immediately binding on all Member States. They require no subsequent action by Member States to become effective.

A directive requires Member States to which it is addressed to adopt national legislation to effectuate specific objectives. Member States may choose the method adopted to conform with the objectives of a directive. The EC generally uses directives to adopt provisions relating to the single market program or to harmonize Member State legislation in an area of importance to the Community.

Decisions are legally binding on its addressees, which may include specific Member States, institutions, or private parties. The Commission or Council often apply decisions to specific cases whereas regulations and directives apply more broadly to general areas of legislation.

Recommendations and opinions have no binding force. Recommendations set forth, for example, the Commission's or Council's desired course of action in a particular area. Opinions generally express Commission or Council viewpoints on a given topic.[289]

Requiring Member States to act in accordance with demands of the European Community is difficult because of concerns over national autonomy. The European Community approach seems to be to set out broad guidelines, and then to allow each Member State to devise its own way of complying. However, there is no requirement that the Member States comply. This, to some, is a serious weakness of the EC actions on sexual harassment so far.[290]

While the European Community explicitly defines sexual harassment in the context of sex discrimination, there are suggestions of differences between conceptions of sexual harassment in the United States and in the European Community. Particularly striking is the treatment of sexual harassment in resolutions and recommendations "on the protection of the dignity of women and men at work." Discussing sexual harassment in this context suggests that concerns about sex discrimination are part of a larger concern with the conditions of work. This seems not to be the case in the United States, where there is little concern for a worker's dignity. "At-will" employment policies, where employees can be fired without cause and given five minutes to clear their desks while a supervisor observes, are common in the United States.

The concern with the dignity of all workers tends to mitigate the perspective, common in the United States, that the concern with sexual harassment is a concern with *sex*, and thus that those who want to prohibit sexual harassment want to prohibit sex, or to protect vulnerable women from the sexual assaults of men. The focus on sex arises when one considers why *sexual* harassment should be singled out when other forms of harassment are not similarly prohibited. It is true that some harassment on the basis of race, national origin, religion, disability, and age is prohibited by Title VII. However, the prohibition stems from the view that these forms of harassment constitute discrimination on the basis of race, national origin, religion, disability, and age, not because harassment *in general* violates the dignity of a worker.

Perhaps the difference in emphasis between the European Community and the United States regarding sexual harassment should be seen as a de-emphasis on *gender*. The concern with sexual harassment is a subset of the larger concern with the dignity of male and female workers. All forms of harassment should be prohibited, so sexual harassment should be prohibited. This concern is absent from most discussions of sexual harassment in the United States.

While it may seem an insignificant difference, casting the discussion in terms of human dignity points away from the tendency in the United States to describe as "feminine virtue" what is to be protected by prohibiting sexual harassment. Human dignity is something that all human beings share; "feminine virtue" is something that some women are supposed to have, and that men are supposed to protect. When the right to be free from sexual harassment is construed as the right to the protection of "feminine virtue," it is perceived as a "special protection" that women, but not men, require, and therefore either as evidence that women are not equal to men, or as evidence that women seek unequal opportunities. Many people in the United States do not seem to see discrimination against women as an issue of human rights, or of the protection of human dignity. The United States has not ratified the U.N. Convention on the Elimination of All Forms of Discrimination against Women, which was approved by the General Assembly of the United Nations in 1979.[291]

The conception of sexual harassment as a matter of human rights is most compatible with liberal perspectives. Liberals tends to conceive of persons as bearers of rights, and as possessors of certain human rights, regardless of race, gender, nationality, or age. However, among adherents of the liberal perspective, there is much disagreement over just what these rights are and what equality of rights requires. Some believe that equality demands that women and men be treated differently because they are naturally different. It was this view that prevented passage of the Equal Rights Amendment in the United States, and it is this view that in part prevents ratification of the U.N. Convention on the Elimination of All Forms of Discrimination against Women.[292]

The United Nations has also expressed concern over the effects of sexual harassment on equality for women and men. The 1979 U.N. Convention on the Elimination of All Forms of Discrimination against Women "provides . . . that women have the right to the same employment opportunities, including the application of the same criteria for selection in matters of employment, as well as the right to health protection and safe working conditions."[293] The 1985 *Forward-Looking Strategies for the Advancement of Women* contains a specific call for prevention of sexual harassment at work.[294] The Committee on the Elimination of All Forms of Discrimination against Women General Recommendation No. 19 states:

> 22. Equality in employment can be seriously impaired when women are subjected to gender specific violence, such as sexual harassment in the workplace.
> 23. Sexual harassment includes such unwelcome sexually determined behaviour as physical contacts and advances, sexually coloured remarks, showing pornography and sexual demands, whether by words

or actions. Such conduct can be humiliating and may constitute a health and safety problem; it is discriminatory when the woman has reasonable grounds to believe that her objection would disadvantage her in connection with her employment, including recruiting or promotion, or when it creates a hostile working environment. Effective complaints procedures and remedies, including compensation, should be provided. . . .

In light of these comments, the Committee recommends:

1. That States take all legal and other measures which are necessary . . . including . . .

(a) . . . penal sanctions . . . and compensatory provisions to protect women against . . . sexual harassment in the workplace;

(b) preventive measures.[295]

A Draft Declaration on Violence against Women by the Economic and Social Council, Commission on the Status of Women, in March 1992 included sexual harassment as a form of violence against women.[296]

The United Nations's classification of sexual harassment as violence against women seems consistent with the sociocultural perspective. It emphasizes that it is women who are the victims of harassment and that some kind of power is abused in the conduct of sexual harassment. Thus, the United Nations seems to countenance at least two ways of understanding sexual harassment: as a violation of human rights and as a form of violence against women.

A third international organization, the International Labour Organization, has also expressed concern about sexual harassment. Appended to the 1985 International Labour Conference Resolution on Equal Opportunity and Equal Treatment for Men and Women in Employment was a conclusion which included, under the heading "Working conditions and environment": "6. Sexual harassment at the workplace is detrimental to employees' working conditions and to employment and promotion prospects. Policies for the advancement of equality should therefore include measures to combat and prevent sexual harassment."[297] Conclusions adopted at the Meeting of Experts on Special Protective Measures for Women and Equality of Opportunity and Treatment in 1989 included the following: "(15) Personal security of workers (notably sexual harassment and violence arising from work) is a safety and health problem. The need for protection applies to both men and women workers although the nature and degree of such protection may be sex specific."[298] Conclusions adopted by the Tripartite Symposium on Equality of Opportunity and Treatment for Men and Women in Employment in Industrialised Countries included the following:

24. Sexual harassment at the workplace constitutes a major problem. While it can affect men, it is overwhelmingly a problem for women. Its occurrence is a violation of the right to be treated equally; it is detrimental to employees' working conditions and to promotion

prospects; and it discourages women from entering non-traditional occupations. Sexual harassment has also been regarded as a health and safety problem.

25. Measures should be taken by government, employees' and workers' organizations to prevent the occurrence of sexual harassment. Those could include legal methods or redress either through equal opportunity legislation or specific legislation on sexual harassment as well as trade unions' and employers' policies, including guidelines, educational activities, and awareness campaigns at the workplace, a clear statement that sexual harassment is a disciplinary offence, grievance procedures and protection to ensure that the complainant is not retaliated against for making the complaint.[299]

In 1991, a resolution was adopted by the International Labour Conference calling on the ILO "to develop guide-lines, training and information materials on issues that are of specific and major importance to women workers, such as . . . sexual harassment at the workplace."[300]

Perhaps because of its general focus, the ILO tends to see sexual harassment as an issue of work environment. Thus, each of the three international organizations cited here conceives of sexual harassment slightly differently. The European Community emphasizes sex discrimination, the United Nations, violence against women and the violation of human rights, and the ILO, conditions of work. These are not inconsistent conceptions, for all are ultimately concerned with equality of treatment. However, different emphases may result in recommendations for different preventive measures.

Within the broad outlines provided by international organizations, individual countries have addressed sexual harassment in accordance with their individual traditions and legal structures.

Individual Countries

The kinds of law under which sexual harassment has been included in various countries reveal different conceptions sexual harassment. For example, several countries include provisions in their labor laws that protect the morals of employees (Austria, Portugal, Greece). Other countries include provisions for protection of the dignity of employees (see EC recommendation). Both have been interpreted to prohibit sexual harassment in the workplace. The inclusion of sexual harassment as a violation of a worker's morals is particularly interesting given the claim by at least one commentator that European conceptions of sexual harassment are less moralistic than those in the United States.[301] The conception of sexual harassment as a violation of morals seems to support a natural/biological perspective, and to suggest that protection from sexual harassment is protection of feminine virtue. In other words, it seems to come out of traditional concerns about the protection of women from men. This conception is not one that many liberals and socioculturalists would endorse. What does stand out about U.S. attitudes toward sexual harassment in contrast to those of European countries is the desire to punish, and, in particular, to shame, offenders. This, I believe, has to do with distinctive attitudes toward sex in America.[302]

It is beyond the scope of this work to discuss sexual harassment in every country in the world. In what follows, I will provide a sample of approaches in several countries.[303]

Canada   In Canada, sexual harassment, understood as sex discrimination, comes under the jurisdiction of territorial or provincial Human Rights Commissions, which administer a human rights act or code. All such acts or codes forbid sex discrimination. There is also a Canadian Human Rights Code and a commission for its administration. Sex discrimination is prohibited under the human rights legislation of each province and under the federal Canadian Human Rights Act.[304] Since sexual harassment has been recognized as a form of sex discrimination, sexual harassment is prohibited under both provincial and Canadian human rights legislation. Some provinces specifically mention sexual harassment in their codes or acts, and it is mentioned in the current Canadian Human Rights Act. In addition, the Canadian Labour Code prohibits sexual harassment.[305] While this structure seems to foster a perspective on sexual harassment that differs from that adopted in the United States, it limits the recourse of victims of sexual harassment. In Canada, victims of sexual harassment may seek relief only under a human rights statute.[306]

Canada has recognized sexual harassment as a form of sex discrimination since *C. Bell v. The Flaming Steer Steak House Tavern Inc.* in 1980.[307] In 1989, the Canadian Supreme Court found in *Janzen v. Platy Enterprises, Ltd.* that workplace sexual harassment is illegal sex discrimination.[308] The *Janzen* court made reference to the fact that sexual harassment was considered sex discrimination in U.S. law, citing *Meritor*. However, they rejected the distinction between quid pro quo sexual harassment and hostile environment sexual harassment, finding the distinction no longer necessary.[309] In their decision, the *Janzen* court defined sexual harassment as "unwelcome conduct of a sexual nature that detrimentally affects the work environment or leads to adverse job-related consequences for the victims of the harassment."[310] The court described sexual harassment and its harm:

> When sexual harassment occurs in the workplace, it is an abuse of both economic and sexual power. Sexual harassment is a demeaning practice, one that constitutes a profound affront to the dignity of the employees forced to endure it. By requiring an employee to contend with unwelcome sexual actions or explicit sexual demands, sexual harassment in the workplace attacks the dignity and self-respect of the victim both as an employee and as a human being.[311]

Canada has also recognized both female-male harassment and same-sex harassment as constituting sexual harassment.[312]

Clearly, U.S. law has influenced the development of sexual harassment law in Canada.[313] However, Canadian tribunals and courts have been much more willing to recognize sexual harassment as a violation of rights than have U.S. courts. This may be because of their greater willingness to regulate the employment environment. Notice also, in the Canadian court's definition, the emphasis on dignity, similar to that found in U.N. documents and EC recommendations. This seems to come from the Canadian system's inclusion of sex discrimination, and, consequently, sexual harassment, under "human rights," rather than the United States's "protected categories."

A greater willingness to intervene in the employer/employee relationship seems to have made regulation of the workplace with regard to sexual harassment more acceptable to Canadians. They have also been more willing to accept the view that human rights codes can and should be used to change workplace environments that were once all male to ones respectful of females, contrary to the view expressed by the majority in *Rabidue v. Osceola Refining Co.*[314]

There is no justification whatsoever why an environment pre-existing the entrance of women workers should continue to set the contextual norm once women arrive. To accept as a given that a male-dominated workplace will be "rough and coarse"' and that this shall be the standard against which harassment will be judged, entails accepting that existing gender stereotypes will have the weight of law. Canadian standards and expectations in this regard drastically differ from those in the United States. If women are to be encouraged in the workforce, then the old standards of the male-dominated work environment must give way to the emerging new values of equity and respect for women.[315]

In sum, Canada has a developed legal tradition regarding sexual harassment. That tradition has explicitly drawn on U.S. legal decisions and arguments, but, perhaps because of the differing legal structures in Canada and the United States, the resulting legal conception of sexual harassment has been different from that in the United States. Canadian conceptions of sexual harassment seem to come from a liberal perspective, with the emphasis on rights and equality, but to be influenced more by a sociocultural perspective than are prevailing U.S. conceptions.

Great Britain   The treatment of sexual harassment in Great Britain has been complicated by Britain's involvement in the European Community (EC). Labor regulation is one of the most contentious areas of EC negotiations.[316] Different traditions and legal structures must be intertwined to create a universally acceptable set of regulations. However, both the European Community and Britain conceive of sexual harassment as sex discrimination, and as an issue of equality.[317]

The 1975 Sex Discrimination Act (SDA), which is similar to Title VII, is Britain's primary law governing sexual harassment. A provision of the SDA requires that sex discrimination cases be pursued primarily in the industrial tribunal system.[318] In addition, sexual harassment has been found illegal under the Employment Protection Consolidation Act 1978 (EPCA). This act provides protection against unfair dismissal for employees having two years or more of continuous service with their employer. Sexual harassment was established as sex discrimination under the SDA in 1986 in *Porcelli v. Strathclyde Regional Council*.[319] *Porcelli* was a quid pro quo case involving a woman who alleged harassment by co-workers.

The British industrial tribunals are not courts of law. Each tribunal consists of three members: a chairman who is a person qualified in the law, a member appointed by the union, and a member appointed by industry. Each member has an equal vote. Decisions made by the tribunal do not set precedents for courts of law. Points of law that arise in the decisions may be appealed to the Employment Appeal Tribunal, which consists of a High Court judge and two other members. Points of law arising in decisions reached by this latter body may be appealed to the court of appeals.[320]

Britain has an Equal Opportunities Commission (EOC), which was established at the same time as the SDA to enforce the act. The EOC differs from the EEOC in the United States:

> Parliament created the EOC, the counterpart to the United States EEOC, to enforce the law for the protection of the public as opposed to the procedural device of a class action suit available in the American legal system. The EOC consists of eight to fifteen individuals appointed by the Secretary of State. Created with the goals of eradicating discrimination, promoting equality or [*sic*] opportunity between men and women generally, and supervising the implementation of both the SDA and the Equal Pay Act of 1970, the Commission is empowered to issue codes of practice, obtain information, and make recommendations and reports. The Commission's formal investigations . . . may lead to the issuance of an enforceable "non-discrimination notice." . . . Such a notice may require, among other things, that a qualifying individual refrain from the discriminatory conduct, demonstrate compliance with instructions to change the nature of his practices, and provide the relevant parties with notice of such changes. Furthermore, in the case of persistent discrimination, where there is a likelihood that the injury will be repeated, the SDA authorizes the Commission to seek an injunction.[321]

In spite of the similarities between the EOC and the EEOC, the EOC is considered weaker. In particular, unlike the EEOC, the EOC cannot initiate proceedings.

The conception of sexual harassment in British law seems similar to that in U.S. law, although there is no definition of sexual harassment in the law.[322] Both quid pro quo and hostile environment sexual harassment have been found illegal in British law. Both men and women may bring complaints of sexual harassment.

The use of industrial tribunals for deciding most cases emphasizes that sexual harassment is a workplace issue, something to be worked out between parties, rather than something to be decided by the courts. This tends to deemphasize the moralism of much of the discussion of sexual harassment in the United States, and to focus less on blame and punishment of the perpetrator. In a sense, it categorizes sexual harassment as a conflict between workers. This might be seen as supporting a natural/biological perspective, since the emphasis is on resolving the conflict between workers without necessarily ascribing fault. This approach would seem to be congenial to critics of the development of sexual harassment law in the United States who object to the emphasis on faultfinding.[323] However, socioculturalists would probably not find the British approach ideal for this same reason. Without the notion of the alleged harasser's having done something wrong, there is no foothold for an analysis according to which men unfairly use the power granted them by society to control women's labor.

France   The French criminalization of sexual harassment is considered by one commentator to be "[t]he most important development in Europe."[324] France's approach to sexual harassment has been interesting in a number of ways. French people were apparently worried that broad definitions of sexual harassment included ordinary flirting in the office, which they did not want to threaten.[325] As a result, they adopted a narrow definition of sexual harassment, limited to what is elsewhere known as quid pro quo sexual harassment, and, in 1992, effectively made sexual harassment a criminal offense. Quid pro quo sexual harassment is defined in French law as an abuse of authority. The law, which mentions the term "sexual harassment" in the title, but not in the text,[326] defines sexual harassment as "the action of an employer or of a superior in the work hierarchy who, abusing the authority of his position, exercises pressure on an employee with the aim of obtaining favours of a sexual nature on his or her own behalf or on behalf of a third party."[327] It states: "The action of harassing another by using orders or positions by threats or duress to obtain sexual favors by a person who abuses the authority granted by his position may be punishable by a year in prison and a 100,000 Franc fine."[328] In the same year, France adopted changes in the country's Labor Code which address the issue of retaliation for resistance to sexual harassment:

> Any wage earner should not be sanctioned or laid off for having to submit or refusing to submit to actions of sexual harassment by an employer or by his representative or by all persons who abuse the authority given to them by their position through giving orders or uttering threats or imposing will or exercising pressure on the worker for the purpose of obtaining sexual favors or for the benefit of a third party. No worker shall lose salary or a job because of the previous actions.[329]

The effect of these laws is to prohibit quid pro quo sexual harassment, but not hostile environment sexual harassment. This is, evidently, what was intended. Another way in which the French approach differs from that of Canada, the United States, and Great Britain is that co-worker harassment is not prohibited. The existing laws apply only to supervisors. In addition, the scope of the new criminal law is not limited to employment relations.[330] Thus, the French approach to sexual harassment focuses less on gender harassment and more on sexual harassment understood as extortion. This tends to downplay the notion that sexual harassment is sex discrimination.

This approach is consistent with the natural/biological perspective and some varieties of the liberal perspective. The natural/biological perspective would approve of the distinction between true abuses of authority granted by position and the more amorphous power men are said by socioculturalists to possess simply by virtue of being men. Certain versions of the liberal perspective could also countenance this view, though liberals in the United States tend to favor a special sexual harassment tort rather than a criminal law.[331] Socioculturalists might approve of the criminalization of quid pro quo sexual harassment, but they would be more likely to object to the sharp distinction between quid pro quo and hostile environment or conditions of work sexual harassment, since in their view these are on a continuum, and what they have in common is the use of power by men to control women's labor. The French legal treatment of sexual harassment requires no such assumption.

Spain Spain has been quite active in addressing sexual harassment. The Spanish Constitution prohibits discrimination based on sex. In 1989, the Spanish government included provisions against sexual harassment in the Worker's Charter and the Civil Servants Regulations.[332] The Worker's Charter specifies that "[a]n employer must ensure: Respect for a person's privacy and dignity, including protection against verbal or physical insults of a sexual nature."[333] Almost identical language is included in the Civil Servants Regulations. As is evident in this language, Spain has chosen to emphasize sexual harassment as an invasion of privacy.

Spanish law has adopted a different focus—the right of privacy—to provide a firmer legal foundation for banning sexual harassment. According to the broad concept of privacy as self-determination, sexual harassment is clearly a violation of privacy. More specifically, sexual harassment is the imposition of a specific sexual conduct that limits one of the essential personal liberties—sexual liberty.[334]

This does not mean that sexual harassment is not also regarded as sex discrimination. But it is first regarded as an invasion of privacy. This way of thinking about sexual harassment is similar to that recommended by Drucilla Cornell, who takes a liberal perspective.[335] A third way of understanding particularly severe sexual harassment is also possible under Spanish law: as a health and safety issue.[336] This is in keeping with the EC tendency to view sexual harassment as an issue concerning conditions of work. These three approaches seem targeted primarily at hostile environment sexual harassment or gender harassment. However, in 1995, Spain passed a major revision of its penal code. Included in the new code is a specific prohibition of sexual harassment, violation of which can lead to a prison sentence.[337] This new law seems to target quid pro quo sexual harassment.

Spain seems to have four different ways to approach sexual harassment: a violation of privacy, sex discrimination, a health and safety matter, and a criminal offense. However, according to a report on trends in the treatment of sexual harassment, the perception of sexual harassment as a "violation by the employer of safety and health obligations" dominates.[338]

New Zealand   In New Zealand, sexual harassment is prohibited under the country's Employment Contracts Act of 1991 (ECA). The act defines sexual harassment as follows:

> [A]n employee is sexually harassed . . . if that employee's employer or a representative of that employer (a) makes a request of that employee for sexual intercourse, sexual contact, or other form of sexual activity which contains (i) an implied or overt promise of preferential treatment in that employee's employment; or (ii) an implied or overt threat of detrimental treatment in that employee's employment; or (iii) an implied or overt threat about the present or future employment status of that employee; or (b) by (i) the use of words (whether written or spoken) of a sexual nature; or (ii) physical behaviour of a sexual nature, subjects the employee to behaviour which is unwelcome or offensive to that employee (whether or not that is conveyed to the employer or representative) and which is either repeated or of such a significant nature that it has a detrimental effect on that employee's employment, job performance, or job satisfaction.[339]

It is clear from the definition that both quid pro quo and hostile environment sexual harassment are prohibited. However, there is no conceptual relationship between sexual harassment and sex discrimination. Sexual harassment is conceived of as a "personal grievance" on the part of an employee against his or her employer.

In 1993, New Zealand's Human Rights Act was amended to include specifically sexual harassment.

Japan   Japan has lagged behind other industrialized nations in its treatment of sexual harassment. As recently as the late 1980s, there were few resources for Japanese victims of sexual harassment. Sexual harassment was not explicitly prohibited by any existing statute. The Japanese constitution prohibits sex discrimination in "political, economic, or social relations," but not in private employee relations.[340] The country's Equal Employment Opportunity Act prohibits sex discrimination in the private sector but has no enforcement provisions: there are no penalties for those who do not comply, or remedies for those offended against. The landmark case that brought sexual harassment to national consciousness was decided by the Fukuoka District Court in April 1992. Judge Fukuoka used a section of the Civil Code which states that "a person who intentionally or negligently violates the right of another is bound to make compensation for damages arising therefrom."[341] Among the rights protected by Section 709 of the Civil Code are personal rights "to bodily integrity, liberty, honor, life, reputation, and privacy."[342] The judge said explicitly that an employee has a right to a nonhostile work environment. He also ruled that the employer is responsible for preventing hostile work environments.[343] Although the expression "sexual harassment" was never used in the decision, it is understood that the case at issue was a hostile environment sexual harassment case.

Though both quid pro quo and hostile environment sexual harassment have been recognized in Japan, there still is no legal definition of sexual harassment in that country. Neither has it been determined whether sexual harassment is prohibited as sex discrimination.[344]

Recent events both at home and abroad have increased awareness of sexual harassment, or *seku hara*, in Japan, culminating in an "action plan designed to serve as the basis for policies to curb sexual harassment, sexual violence and practices which discriminate against women."[345] The plan called for "the study of laws to prevent sexual harassment" and was to run until the year 2000. News stories on the action plan cited the September 1995 U.N. Conference on Women in Beijing as a stimulus. The conference, which described sexual harassment as a violation of human rights,[346] "called on nations to establish action plans by the end of" 1996.[347] However, in 1996, only a few companies in Japan had sexual harassment policies in place. A government survey of Japanese companies found that 92.5 percent of the 239 companies surveyed had "never taken any measure to prevent sexual harassment."[348]

Japanese companies in London and the United States have had allegations of sexual harassment brought against them. In London, an employee claimed that she had been sexually harassed by a supervisor at Fuji International Finance.[349] The company decided to settle. In the United States, the EEOC filed a class action suit against Mitsubishi Motor Manufacturing of America Inc. in 1996, "accusing it of tolerating 'pervasive' sexual harassment of female workers at its plant in Normal, Illinois."[350] More than 300 women were involved in the suit. As a result, Japanese companies with overseas operations have begun sexual harassment prevention training for their overseas employees.[351] Mitsubishi recently settled its suit for a record $34 million.[352]

One very interesting development in Japan concerns the initiative to reserve certain subway cars for women. It is common for women to be groped and grabbed in subway cars, and, rather than try to stop men, authorities are going to segregate women. This is reminiscent of several tort cases cited by MacKinnon involving the sexual assault of women on railway cars in the late 1800s.[353] It seeks to shield women from the behavior of men rather than to hold men responsible for their inappropriate behavior. This kind of action seems to arise from a natural/biological perspective, according to which such behavior is simply the way in which men's sexuality expresses itself.[354]

Sexual harassment is being recognized and found to be illegal in more and more countries throughout the world. The conceptualization of sexual harassment influences the way in which sexual harassment is fit into existing laws or legal categories, and the way sexual harassment is categorized in the law influences the conceptualization of sexual harassment. We have seen that the European Community categorizes sexual harassment as sex discrimination, as we do in the United States, but that because of certain differences in its treatment of discrimination, there are some different emphases. The European Community emphasizes the dignity of persons. Thus, sexual harassment, while perceived as a problem that particularly affects women, is considered to be a form of conduct that violates the dignity of the person. This places the emphasis on personal dignity and not on feminine virtue. By de-emphasizing gender, the European Community seems to place sexual harassment in the category of behaviors that affect the dignity of women and men.

The United Nations considers sexual harassment to be a violation of human rights and a kind of violence against women. The ILO considers sexual harassment to affect conditions of work, including health and safety, because the organization conceives of sexual harassment as a matter of the personal security of workers.

Individual countries, using their existing legal structures, have considered sexual harassment to be an invasion of privacy, a violation of the health and safety of the worker, sex discrimination, an abuse of power, and a violation of human rights. Many of these approaches seem to avoid the sexual moralism that is evident in early legal decisions in the United States. The emphasis on human rights and work conditions tends to lead away from conceiving of the sexual harasser as a sexual deviant, allowing the focus to turn to the notion of a fair and civil workplace.

It is difficult to draw any firm conclusions about which, if any, of the three perspectives on sexual harassment is most represented in conceptualization of sexual harassment in other countries. As I said earlier in the chapter, emphasis on human rights and personal dignity is compatible with a liberal perspective. The natural/biological perspective seems to be represented in some actions, but, in general, the approaches taken by the European Community and United Nations de-emphasize this perspective.

Perhaps the next area for the development of sexual harassment law concerns countries in which there is no such law, with whom countries that prohibit sexual harassment at home, such as the United States, do business. Trade these days is global, as is labor. What should companies based in the United States and other industrialized nations do for their workers in countries which have no sexual harassment policies? Two possible sources of influence in this area are the United Nations and other nongovernmental organizations.

Some organizations are developing codes for such businesses. For example, the "Maquiladora Standards of Conduct" code is a code of conduct for companies who operate maquiladora factories along the border between the United States and Mexico. This code prohibits sex discrimination, including sexual harassment. The code has been sponsored by the AFL-CIO and interfaith and environmental groups. Only one company had adopted the code by 1994.[355]

Looking at the legal approaches to sexual harassment in countries other than the United States can help us to recognize the tendencies in our legal conceptions of sexual harassment. These tend to be moralistic and to focus on the sexual. As I will suggest in chapter 7, turning away from these elements of sexual harassment toward a consideration of workplace and educational environments might enable us to reach a compromise on how we are going to agree to treat one another.

4

SEXUAL HARASSMENT AND
EMPIRICAL RESEARCH

Empirical studies have been central to the development of our understanding of sexual harassment. The results of such studies have been cited by the courts and in congressional hearings.[1] Empirical research has been used to urge development of policies in workplaces and academic settings and finds its way into nearly everything written on sexual harassment as authors seek to justify their attention to the topic.[2] Empirical data have been used to justify the claims that sexual harassment is widespread, that it happens to women much more often than it does to men, that women's perceptions of sexual conduct are different from men's,[3] and that women who are young, divorced, nonwhite, or single are more likely to be harassed.[4] These research "findings" have, in turn, shaped the concept of sexual harassment. However, many of these studies suffer from serious methodological problems, rendering their results unreliable. In addition, different studies use different definitions of sexual harassment, making comparison between studies problematic. Indeed, the following appeared in a recent critical review of empirical research on sexual harassment: "Several methodological weaknesses were found to be common across much of the published sexual harassment research. Because of these methodological weaknesses, little confidence can be placed in conclusions and little guidance can be offered for future research efforts."[5]

In spite of such critiques of existing research on sexual harassment, people writing on sexual harassment continue uncritically to cite studies found to be problematic in support of their claims.[6] Unfortunately, there seem to be sexual harassment studies to support just about anything one wants to support.

In this chapter, I shall discuss the main criticisms of social scientific research on sexual harassment and provide some examples of still influential studies that are problematic according to these criticisms. I shall also highlight what seem to be sound studies and discuss the conclusions that may be drawn from them. I shall divide the discussion into five sections: general criticisms of research on sexual harassment, a critique of influential studies performed in the United States, reports of studies performed outside the United States, a discussion of some key issues to which empirical data are relevant and what we know about these issues given the results of the empirical studies that have been performed, and the relationship between empirical research on sexual harassment and the three perspectives on sexual harassment introduced in chapter I.

General Criticisms of Research on Sexual Harassment

Social scientists who have surveyed the research on sexual harassment report a wide variety of problems. These include problems with definitions, sampling bias, bias in the reports of respondents, and researcher bias. Since a large number of the studies conducted have been attempts to determine the frequency with which sexual harassment occurs, much of the discussion will focus on these sorts of studies. However, the weaknesses found in such studies are not limited to studies designed to determine the prevalence of sexual harassment.

In order to measure the frequency of sexual harassment, researchers must define sexual harassment in such a way that they can determine, from behavioral evidence, whether or not an instance of sexual harassment has occurred. This is called "operationism": "*Operationism* is simply the idea that concepts in scientific theories must in some way be grounded in, or linked to, observable events that can be measured. Linking the concept to an observable event is the operational definition of the concept and makes the concept public."[7] Providing an operational definition of some concepts is very difficult because the concept is actually defined not by one behavior, but by a set of behaviors. For example, many people have heard of "type-A" behavior, and researchers have been interested in defining it, so that they can determine its association with various other occurrences, such as heart disease. However, "the type A behavior pattern is actually defined by a *set* of subordinate *concepts*: a strong desire to compete, a potential for hostility, time-urgent behavior, an intense drive to accomplish goals, and several others. However, each one of these defining features of the type A behavior pattern . . . is *itself* a concept in need of operational definition."[8] Operational definitions of sexual harassment are of this sort. Sexual harassment is defined in terms of a set of behaviors, and it is *these* behaviors that are described in questionnaires. A good operational definition must be precise, so that it is clear whether a particular observable behavior fits the concept or not.[9]

A major difficulty encountered in interpreting sexual harassment research is that there is no definition upon which all researchers agree.[10] The development of operational definitions for empirical research on sexual harassment has not been systematic.

One might think that the legal definition should be used by all researchers. This would provide a common construct. But, as Lengnick-Hall points out, the legal definition of sexual harassment is not adequate for empirical research. It may be too narrow, since there may be behaviors that a person feels are sexually harassing which do not qualify as illegal sexual harassment. For example, behaviors that appear to be of the sort that are classified as sexual harassment when they are sufficiently severe or pervasive may not be considered illegal sexual harassment when they are isolated or minor. However, we may want to call them sexually harassing nevertheless. More subjective definitions created by researchers or their subjects may seem to be more adequate for the purposes of research, but precisely because they are subjective, it is difficult to draw any meaningful conclusions from studies which make use of them.

The problem of definition makes drawing conclusions about the prevalence of sexual harassment problematic. Many studies designed to measure the rate of sexual harassment rely on definitions of sexual harassment provided by the respondents. For example, a study might ask a respondent "Which of the following have you experienced with male co-workers or supervisors?" and follow this with a list of behaviors such as "Subtle sexual hints and pressures" or "Other forms of sexual harassment."[11] The first behavior listed may not rise to the level of legal sexual harassment, and the second will receive a completely subjective response. Yet, because there is a legal definition of sexual harassment, reports of the results of this sort of survey may be interpreted to mean that everyone who has experienced any of the behaviors in the list has been illegally sexually harassed. According to Lengnick-Hall:

> Most surveys rely on a completely respondent-defined perception of sexual harassment, with little or no direct relationship to the legal definition. The likely impact is to imply a greater percentage of legally proscribed harassment than truly exists in the workplace, thus overstating the potential for employer liability. On the other hand, even reports of subjectively defined sexual harassment (i.e., perceived by the individual) may be misleading as an indicator of the extent of any problem, because reported percentages tell us nothing about the severity or pervasiveness of the harassment.[12]

Arvey and Cavanaugh have also drawn attention to the problem of definition in research for determining the prevalence of sexual harassment.[13] They point out that researchers use very different definitions of sexual harassment in their research. This is well known but, interestingly, does not seem to make people any more cautious in their claims based on such research. In any event, fewer cases will probably be reported if "sexual harassment" is narrowly defined than if it is more widely defined. In addition, researchers often pay little attention to the severity of the behavior labeled. "For example, researchers will combine or sum the number of respondents who indicated that they had experienced jokes of a sexual nature with those who indicated that they had been raped on the job and report the combined total as having experienced sexual harassment."[14]

A second set of methodological problems concerns sampling. This, again, particularly affects surveys used to try to gauge the prevalence of sexual harassment. Such surveys vary dramatically in their estimates of rates of sexual harassment. Some studies have reported that as many as 88 percent of the sample experienced sexual harassment.[15] Others report 44 percent for women and 19 percent for men,[16] and still others report rates as low as 21 percent for women and 9 percent for men.[17] An often cited source of information on sexual harassment in academe is Dziech and Weiner's *Lecherous Professor*.[18] Dziech and Weiner conducted no study of their own, but the result of their survey of the literature is that, no matter how sexual harassment is measured, a consistent "20 to 30 percent of women students report they have been sexually harassed by male faculty during their college years."[19]

Some of the variation in reports of rates of sexual harassment is due to sample bias. Arvey and Cavanaugh report that they "saw serious problems with regard to potential sample selection bias in our review of sexual harassment survey studies. Many survey studies demonstrated considerably low response rates and many used convenience samples. The obvious problem is that individuals who choose to respond may differ considerably from those who do not. . . ."[20] Most of these studies use undergraduates as subjects. But how representative of the adult population of the United States are undergraduates? This question also arises when considering studies designed to determine whether women and men perceive sexual harassment in the same circumstances.

> With one exception, these studies used undergraduate college students as subjects, bringing into question whether they adequately represent a larger population, or whether the findings could be accounted for by an alternate explanation. One study . . . used a sample of 409 employees and found that the sexual harassment perceptions of men and women were very similar. In addition, they used a highly specific, unambiguous, 18-scenario questionnaire, rather than the more typical ambiguous scenario approach. This suggests that less work experience and/or scenario ambiguity are alternate explanations for findings of sex differences in perceptions of sexual harassment.[21]

Sample bias prevents valid generalization of results.

A third set of problems concerns bias in the reports of respondents. Many prevalence surveys rely on self-report methods.[22] However, there are certain biases associated with such methods. Many surveys have been retrospective, that is, they ask the subjects to recall incidents of sexual harassment in the past. This opens the door to memory distortion and bias.[23] Lengnick-Hall points out that, of the studies he examined,

> [a]ll surveys used retrospective self-reports, providing a major source for biased results. Even the U.S. Merit Systems Protection Board . . . asked respondents to report experienced sexual harassment over a previous 2-year period. The use of retrospective self-reports is open to many potential biases that may reduce accurate assessment of sexual harassment. The likely impact of reliance on retrospective self-reporting is to

inflate estimates of harassment compared to other methods. This could result from individuals perceiving incidents that did not take place, or inaccurately reporting incidents that did occur.[24]

Thus, the tendency to use certain sorts of survey techniques with inherent biases casts doubt on the results of such research.

Another problematic feature of sexual harassment studies is researcher bias. This can occur in several different ways. One form of researcher bias occurs when the subjects of the study do not identify themselves as victims of sexual harassment, though the investigators do. Various conclusions, all questionable, have been drawn from such results. An example from Julia T. Wood is typical:

> Compelling evidence that not naming silences victims comes from a recent study in which Brooks and Perot (1991) asked women faculty and graduate students if they had experienced thirty-one situations that meet the legal definition of sexual harassment. While up to 88.8 percent of respondents had suffered at least one, only 2.8 percent of graduate students and 5.6 percent of faculty answered 'yes' to the direct question: Have you ever experienced sexual harassment?[25]

The suggestion is that this shows people's ignorance. But this begs the question. If subjects do not believe that they have been sexually harassed, perhaps it is because they have a different conception of sexual harassment.[26] This raises an issue for feminist researchers, who emphasize respect for the subject of research. When does one listen to the subject, and when not? If, in so many of these studies, people claim to have experienced various phenomena that qualify as legal sexual harassment but deny that they have experienced sexual harassment, then perhaps the legal definition of sexual harassment is defective.

Another sort of researcher bias occurs when the researcher "interprets" the quantitative and qualitative data resulting from a study. This occurs when the researcher goes beyond the data to provide explanations for the data, as a way of supporting a particular theory. Often this is done without the researcher's revealing what that theory is.

An example of this kind of researcher bias appears in a paper on sexual harassment in academe. The study involved a survey of male faculty at a major university in an attempt to examine the characteristics of "harassers." After presenting the quantified data, the researchers included the unsolicited comments that those surveyed had appended to the questionnaire. In both reporting the data and in the discussion of the data, researchers clearly drew on their own interpretations of the data, including the unsolicited anecdotes, to make claims about sexual harassment in academe. In reporting the results of the survey, the researchers state that

> more than 37% of the sample indicated that they had attempted to initiate personal relationships with students (personal relationships were

described as [asking for a date, suggesting you get together for a drink, etc.]). Nearly half of these (40.2%) noted that this behavior was directed exclusively at female students. Over 25% of the sample indicated that they had dated students, while a slightly larger percentage noted that they had engaged in sexual encounters or relationships with students. Eleven percent indicated that they had attempted to stroke, caress or touch female students. *Despite this constellation of behaviors, only one subject reported that he believed he had ever sexually harassed a student.*[27] (My emphasis.)

The bias of the researchers becomes evident in the final sentence of this report, though it is already present in the questionnaire itself. Respondents were told that "a student" included any student enrolled at the university, whether in one of their classes or not. Given this definition, it is highly questionable whether *any* of the behaviors described, without more information, could be said to constitute illegal sexual harassment. Yet, the researchers clearly assume that they do.

The researchers also draw conclusions from the data that show their bias. For example, they report that,

[d]espite the difficulty of drawing firm conclusions from any single study, a few summary comments appear justified. Probably the most dramatic finding is that over 25% of the faculty surveyed admitted to engaging in sexual relationships with students enrolled in their university. Notwithstanding the fact that some of these encounters resulted in personally meaningful, assumedly mutual relationships (e.g., marriage) this seems a rather formidable percentage.[28]

The use of the terms "dramatic" and "formidable" suggests that there is something inherently wrong with such relationships, even when the students are not enrolled in professors' courses. This is highly controversial and requires some sort of argument. Further conclusions are drawn from the anecdotal comments of the respondents, though these were unsystematic and unsolicited:

There appear to be several factors that influence faculty when they evaluate the ethical acceptability of sexual relationships with students: *mutual consent*, the *opportunity to evaluate*, the *status and age of the student*, *outcome*, and whether or not the *student initiated* the relationship. Each of these factors appears to represent a misunderstanding of the power dynamics involved in faculty-student relationships.[29]

One problem with these remarks is that the information on which they are based was not collected in any systematic way. Thus, it seems misleading to include them as though they had as much validity as the quantitative results of the survey. In addition, the claim that the factors listed represent a *misunderstanding* is not something that can be concluded from the remarks themselves, as Fitzgerald and her colleagues admit. To describe them as representing a misunderstanding, rather than, say, a disagreement, is unfair to the respondents. The researchers seem to be using the stray remarks of the respondents to put forward their own perspective.

This completes the general assessment of social scientific research on sexual harassment over the past twenty years. Studies suffer from problems of definition, sampling bias, respondent bias, and researcher bias. Furthermore, people continue to cite studies done in the seventies and early to mideighties, even though awareness of sexual harassment has continued to increase, giving reason for thinking that such survey results might be out of date.

In the next section, I shall discuss several of the most often cited studies and critically evaluate them. Though I will comment on various aspects of the studies, I shall focus on the definitions of sexual harassment used in the studies, showing how they have influenced the development of the concept of sexual harassment.

Critique of Studies Performed in the United States

The first very influential survey of sexual harassment was that conducted by *Redbook* in 1976.[30] This survey seems to have done a great deal to convince people that sexual harassment was a widespread problem for working women. The *Redbook* survey was based on voluntary responses to a questionnaire published in its January 1976 issue. The results were published in its November 1976 issue. Nine thousand women responded to the questionnaire. The majority of the women who responded were married and in their twenties and early thirties, working at white-collar jobs, and earning between $5,000 and $10,000 a year.[31] According to the survey, "nearly 9 out of 10 women report that they have experienced one or more forms of unwanted attention on the job."[32] The questionnaire provided a list, and asked,

Which of the following have you experienced with male co-workers or supervisors? (Circle letters of all answers that apply):

A. Leering or ogling.
B. Sexual remarks or teasing.
C. Subtle sexual hints and pressures.
D. Touching, brushing against, grabbing, pinching.
E. Invitations to a date, with the implication that refusing may count against you.
F. Sexual propositions, with the implication that refusing may count against you.
G. Sexual relations, with the implication that refusing may count against you.
H. Other forms of sexual harassment.
I. No sexual harassment at all.[33]

This list suggests that all of these behaviors, and perhaps others, are to count as sexual harassment. Apparently, the surveyors defined "sexual harassment" as "*unwanted* attention." However, nowhere in the questionnaire is it asked whether the various forms of "attention" were wanted or not. If a woman indicated that she had experienced any of these behaviors, she was counted as having experienced sexual harassment.[34]

The *Redbook* survey was not a carefully designed survey instrument. It was intended to "amass a significant body of information about sexual harassment."[35] It seems to have done that, to some degree. The sample was biased—toward readers of *Redbook* who had a particular interest in responding to the study—so its results cannot be generalized to all women in 1976. The implied definition of "sexual harassment" was too imprecise to allow distinctions between sexual behavior and coercive sexual behavior. Another feature of the *Redbook* definition is that it seems to limit sexual harassment to *sexuality* harassment.[36] All of the specific behaviors listed concern sexuality. There is no measurement of what has come to be known as gender harassment.

Thus, while the *Redbook* survey may show that many women experience sexual conduct at work, it is not clear what conclusions can legitimately be drawn about the prevalence of sexual harassment in the workplace in 1976. The sample is biased toward white-collar women who read *Redbook* and who felt strongly enough about the issue to respond to the survey. It is possible that many more women responded who had experienced the listed behaviors than women who had not, skewing the percentage.

An influential study of sexual harassment on college campuses was carried out by Frank Till for the National Advisory Council of Women's Educational Programs in 1980.[37] "Rather than choose among the myriad, sometimes conflicting definitions of sexual harassment then in use, the Council opted to structure its Call for Information without a definition in hopes of developing a "victim-based" definition from the responses. This approach permitted the problem to define itself and avoided limiting responses to fit any particular bias or ideology."[38]

The definition of "sexual harassment" Till developed from victim responses was: "Academic sexual harassment is the use of authority to emphasize the sexuality or sexual identity of a student in a manner which prevents or impairs that student's full enjoyment of educational benefits, climate, or opportunities."[39] This definition is quite different from the *Redbook* definition, emphasizing as it does what has come to be called "gender harassment" or, simply, sexism. For purposes of data collection, Till created categories of behaviors he believed constituted sexual harassment, and these five categories have been adopted by other researchers.[40] The five categories of behavior constituting sexual harassment are:

1) Generalized sexist remarks or behavior;
2) Inappropriate and offensive, but essentially sanction-free sexual advances;
3) Solicitation of sexual activity or other sex-linked behavior by promise of rewards;

4) Coercion of sexual activity by threat of punishment; and
5) Sexual assaults.[41]

Till considered the five behaviors to have two things in common that placed them within his definition of sexual harassment:

> * Distortion of a formal, sex neutral relationship (e.g., teacher/student, counselor/client) by an unwelcome, nonreciprocal emphasis on the sexuality or sexual identity of the student; and
> * Infliction of harm on the student.[42]

The definition of sexual harassment comes from people who took the initiative to respond to Till's call for information. Thus, like the respondents to the *Redbook* questionnaire, these people were "self-selected." Therefore, as Till admits, nothing can be determined about the actual extent of the phenomena they describe.[43] Furthermore, the definition is not really "victim-generated," since there may be many people who have suffered similar kinds of behavior (are "victims" of them) but who do not consider them sexual harassment, and so do not consider them in the same way the respondents did. The definition Till develops is based on the reports of people who believe they have experienced one or more of the behaviors in the definition *and* who believe that they have been sexually harassed. A definition that better reflects what people on college campuses believe sexual harassment to be should take into account those who do *not* consider some or all of the behaviors listed to be sexual harassment. This definition is biased in favor of those who considered what they experienced to be sexual harassment.

Till considered category 4, which seems to describe quid pro quo sexual harassment, to be the one that best captured the essence of sexual harassment. He states that "[t]his category . . . is at the core of what academic and employment 'sexual harassment' entail: exploitation of a difference in authority to compel a choice between extremely unwelcome alternatives."[44] However, there are problems with Till's definition, and so with the frequency of incidence of sexual harassment he finds using the operational version of the definition. The safe conclusion to draw seems to be that there is sexual behavior in academe, and some of it is considered to be offensive and coercive by the recipients.

Two studies performed by the U.S. Merit Systems Protection Board—one carried out in 1980, and a follow-up, carried out in 1987—are also frequently cited.[45] The authors of the 1980 study considered theirs to be the first "thorough and authoritative study of sexual harassment."[46] The study surveyed more than 20,000 federal employees using a disproportionately stratified sample. The general definition of sexual harassment used in the study was taken from the Office of Personnel Management (OPM) and is as follows: "deliberate or repeated unsolicited verbal comments, gestures, or physical contact of a sexual nature that are considered unwelcome by the recipient."[47] In operationalizing this definition, the authors listed seven behaviors:

a. Actual or attempted rape or sexual assault.
b. Unwanted pressure for sexual favors.
c. Unwanted deliberate touching, leaning over, cornering, or pinching.
d. Unwanted sexually suggestive looks or gestures.
e. Unwanted letters, phone calls, or materials of a sexual nature.
f. Unwanted pressure for dates.
g. Unwanted sexual teasing, jokes, remarks, or questions.[48]

This list of behaviors is an improvement over the list in the *Redbook* survey because "unwanted" is included in the description of harassing behaviors. The people who developed the Merit survey were aware of the difficulty of defining sexual harassment. A survey of the literature on sexual harassment led them to the conclusion that "there has been no common denominator . . . about what behaviors constitute sexual harassment."[49] Their operational definition is derived from the OPM definition, with the addition of item (e).

The researchers were particularly concerned about the definition of sexual harassment because among the questions they were charged to answer were, "What kinds of behavior constitute sexual harassment? Do the attitudes of men and women differ in this regard?" and "To what degree does sexual harassment occur within the Federal workplace? What is the frequency? What are the manifestations?"[50]

To answer the first question, the study asked those surveyed to say whether or not they considered each of the seven behaviors just listed here (except the first) to be sexual harassment.

We found substantial agreement among Federal workers in the way they defined sexual harassment. . . . The majority of women considered all of the six forms of uninvited and unwanted behaviors that were asked about to be sexual harassment, whether initiated by a supervisor or another worker. The majority of men regarded all the forms of behaviors as sexual harassment when initiated by a supervisor but did not consider sexually suggestive looks, gestures, remarks, joking, teasing, or questioning to be harassment when coming from a coworker.[51]

They concluded from this that "the majority of Federal workers considered all of the behaviors listed in the Office of Personnel Management's definition as harassment. Moreover, the form of behavior not included in the OPM definition—"letters and calls"—was behavior about which there was most agreement."[52] The Merit researchers apparently believed that this degree of consensus warranted using the seven categories of behavior to answer the second of the questions they were charged to answer. Their findings regarding the frequency of incidents of sexual harassment were based on respondents' answers to the question whether they had experienced any of the seven behaviors in the past two years. In other words, it was a retrospective study. They found that, "[e]ight in every 20 women (42%), but only 3 in every 20 men (15%), were subjected to harassment on the job over the 2-year period. . . ."[53]

The 1987 follow-up survey used the same definition of sexual harassment as the 1980 survey. This study distributed questionnaires containing many of the same questions as the 1980 survey to 13,000 federal employees, 8,523 of whom responded.[54] The 1987 survey found that more people considered each of the six categories of behavior (omitting the first) to constitute sexual harassment than in the 1980 survey. But perhaps most surprisingly, it found that the frequency of incidents of sexual harassment was nearly identical to that found in the 1980 survey: "In 1987, 42 percent of all women and 14 percent of all men reported they experienced some form of uninvited and unwanted sexual attention. Despite an apparent increase in the level of sensitivity about what behavior may be considered sexual harassment, there has been no significant change since the Board's last survey in 1980 in the percentage of Federal employees who say they have received such uninvited and unwanted attention."[55] The definition used to determine the frequency of sexual harassment was: "If a respondent to the Board's survey stated that he or she had received uninvited or unwanted sexual attention during the preceding 24 months, that was counted as an incident of sexual harassment even though not every incident, if fully investigated, would necessarily meet the legal definition of sexual harassment."[56] This study also used self-reporting for the determination of frequency of sexual harassment among the federal work force, and it recognized the possible weakness in this approach.[57]

Another interesting result from the second survey was that more people considered certain kinds of behavior to constitute sexual harassment. For example, "in 1980, 77 percent of women and 76 percent of men thought that when a supervisor pressures another employee for a date it is harassment. In 1987, 87 percent of women and 81 percent of men believed this behavior on the part of a supervisor is sexual harassment."[58] In the 1987 survey, there was virtual consensus that four of the listed behaviors constituted sexual harassment.

> The 1987 data show that Federal workers solidly believe that four types of behavior—uninvited pressure for sexual favors; pressure for dates; deliberate touching, leaning over, cornering, or pinching; and uninvited letters, telephone calls, or materials of a sexual nature—constitute harassment. There is substantially less agreement among Federal employees about whether the remaining behaviors—uninvited sexually suggestive looks or gestures and uninvited sexual teasing, jokes, remarks or questions—also constitute sexual harassment.[59]

Regarding the particular percentages,

> we find virtual consensus among Federal employees (99 percent for women and 95 percent for men) that uninvited pressure for sexual favors by a supervisor is sexual harassment. It is the behavior that employees most often agreed is sexual harassment, even more so than

in 1980. The next highest percentage (95 percent women, 89 percent men) believed that sexual harassment occurs when a supervisor deliberately touches, leans over, corners, or pinches another employee—and again this represents an increase from the 1980 percentage.[60]

. . .

The percentage of employees who believe that the listed forms of behavior are sexual harassment when initiated by a coworker also increased for all but one of the listed behaviors—uninvited letters, calls, or materials of a sexual nature. In 1980, 65 percent of women and 59 percent of men believed that uninvited pressure for dates by a coworker is sexual harassment. By 1987, those percentages had increased to 76 percent for women and 66 percent for men.[61]

These findings are worth highlighting, since the reasonable woman standard has been justified by the empirical claim that women and men perceive sexual behaviors differently. This claim will be discussed in chapter 6.

In 1994, the Merit Systems Protection Board performed a third study.[62] In this study, 13,200 randomly selected federal employees were surveyed. To the seven categories of behavior used to ascertain the frequency of sexual harassment in the 1980 and 1987 surveys, stalking was added. As in previous surveys, respondents were asked whether they had experienced any of the listed behaviors during the past two years. The numbers of federal employees reporting incidents of sexual harassment increased slightly from 1987: "Some 44 percent of the woment and 19 percent of the men who responded to our survey in 1994 reported have experienced harassing behaviors during the preceding 2 years."[63] Another interesting result of this third study is that even more people than in 1987 consider certain kinds of behavior to constitute sexual harassment: 99 percent of women and 97 percent of men consider uninvited pressure for sexual favors by a supervisor to be sexual harassment; 98 percent of women and 93 percent of men hold that deliberate touching or cornering by a supervisor constitutes sexual harassment. The percentage of people who consider such behavior by co-workers harassing has also increased: 85 percent of women and 76 percent of men believe that uninvited pressure for dates by a co-worker is sexual harassment. In 1987, only 64 percent of women and 47 percent of men considered sexual teasing, jokes and remarks by co-workers to be sexual harassment. In 1994, 77 percent of women and 64 percent of men believed sexual teasing, jokes and remarks to be sexual harassment.[64]

The definitions of sexual harassment used in the Merit studies differ from the legal definitions in at least one significant way. Legal definitions emphasize sexual harassment as sex discrimination, which leads to a de-emphasis on the *sexual* nature of the harassment and an emphasis on its *gendered* nature. The Merit studies' definitions, like that used in the *Redbook* survey, clearly limit sexual harassment to harassment that is *sexual*.

One of the most interesting findings in the Merit studies was that most instances of sexual harassment were perpetrated by *co-workers* rather than supervisors.[65] This is significant because many discussions of sexual harassment assume either that all sexual harassment involves an institutional inequality between perpetrator and victim, or that as a matter of fact, most instances of sexual harassment occur between persons of unequal institutional standing.

The Merit studies are methodologically fairly sound, with the exceptions just noted, and their findings are consistent with those of a number of other studies which also seem sound. The Merit studies are considered to be among the most accurate studies.

Perhaps the greatest weakness of this study, besides its limitation to federal employees, is the fact that the data on incidence of sexual harassment are based on the number of respondents who said they had experienced any of the behaviors in the seven categories. "Thus, the method of identifying victims for this report involved a self-defining process on the part of respondents."[66] In addition, the survey was retrospective, and so it has the weaknesses already mentioned associated with such studies.

The main strengths of the survey include the size of its sample and the sampling technique, which is much more reliable than convenience sampling or self-selecting sampling.

A number of studies of workplace sexual harassment have been carried out by academics. Studies by Gutek[67] and Fitzgerald[68] are often cited.

Gutek's work on the nature and frequency of sexual harassment is summarized in her 1985 book, *Sex and the Workplace*. The data on which the book is based were collected in the summer of 1980.[69] The sample was 1,257 randomly selected working men and women in Los Angeles County.[70] Gutek selected eight categories of behavior that might be considered sexual harassment:[71]

1. sexual comments meant to be complimentary
2. sexual comments meant to be insulting
3. looks and gestures meant to be complimentary
4. looks and gestures meant to be insulting
5. nonsexual touching
6. sexual touching
7. socializing or dating as a requirement of the job
8. sex as a requirement of the job

In her survey, Gutek asked respondents whether they thought each category constituted sexual harassment. More than 90 percent of men and more than 90 percent of women believed that categories 7 and 8 constituted sexual harassment. There was less agreement about the other categories, and divergence between men and women. But more than 50 percent of both sexes believed that categories 6, 2, and 4 constituted sexual harassment. Women were more likely to label each of the categories sexual harassment than were men.[72]

Given the lack of consensus on the definition of sexual harassment, Gutek took three different measurements to try to determine the frequency of sexual harassment in the workplace. She first "assumed all the behaviors listed . . . have the potential of being considered sexual harassment and then could treat everyone who reports any of them as a victim of sexual harassment. This very generous definition undoubtedly overstates the amount of sexual harassment."[73] This first definition seems similar to that used in the *Redbook* study. However, Gutek used two other definitions: "A second way of defining harassment was to label as sexually harassed those people who experience a behavior and consider that class of behavior to be sexual harassment. Yet a third way of assessing the magnitude of sexual harassment was to have an outside rater determine whether each experience was sexual harassment, on the assumption that a person can be harassed and not know it."[74] Thus, Gutek used a variety of ways of understanding what her data showed, since she realized that it was not clear just what they showed. This kind of caution is unusual in sexual harassment research.

According to the second definition of sexual harassment, 37.3 percent of the men and 53.1 percent of the women experienced an incident of sexual harassment sometime in their working lives. Based on further interviews with those reporting incidents of sexual harassment, the outside raters did their own evaluation and found that 21 percent of the women and 9 percent of the men had experienced sexual harassment. Gutek is careful about her conclusions:

> This rather involved attempt to measure harassment suggests the following conservative estimate of the frequency of sexual harassment: Between 21 percent and 53 percent of the women and between 9 percent and 37 percent of the men have been sexually harassed by the opposite sex at least once during their working lives. Because the study involved a representative sample of working men and women in Los Angeles County, these figures probably reflect the experiences of the Los Angeles County work force.[75]

Without some idea of how representative of the total U.S. workforce Los Angeles County is, it is not safe to generalize beyond this population from this study. Gutek does not comment on the likelihood of generalizing from her study. Also, these figures so reported mask the finding that "less serious" sexual harassment was reported much more often than "more serious" sexual harassment. However, in assessing the seriousness of sexual harassment as a problem for women, Gutek again is cautious, finally concluding that it is worth trying to solve the problem of sexual harassment because it would be "relatively easy to solve," though she does not say why she thinks that it would be relatively easy to solve.

> For women, sexual harassment may represent a major workplace problem or a minor annoyance. In comparison to such major issues for women workers as adequate daycare, equal pay, or discrimination in hiring and promotion, sexual harassment is a minor problem. Only 3 percent of the women in the sample said it was a major problem

where they work, and up to half of all working women have not been harassed on the job.

On the other hand, for women who have quit or been fired because they were harassed or for women who have put up with a barrage of comments or unwelcome touching, sexual harassment may represent a much greater personal problem than unequal pay or inadequate fringe benefits. All in all, it is difficult to rank sexual harassment in the list of concerns of working women. . . . It is a problem worthy of attention both because it does affect a large proportion of women and because it appears to be relatively easy to solve.[76]

Gutek's definition is too broad, and without knowing how the raters determined which were "genuine" cases of sexual harassment, it is difficult to know what those figures mean. However, the definition is broad enough to include "gender harassment" that is not explicitly sexual in 2 and 4, although Gutek herself does not distinguish between these in her discussion. The broadness of her definition serves her other purposes, since she is interested in sexual behavior in the workplace *in general*.

Gutek's cautious conclusions seem appropriate for the data on which they are based. Her study appears to be methodologically sound, and the conclusions she draws from it appropriately qualified. Unfortunately, her data are now quite dated. One wishes for a similarly careful study of workplace harassment today.

Louise Fitzgerald has been involved in many sexual harassment studies, most of them concerned with sexual harassment in academe. In 1988, she and her colleagues set out to try to bring order to the chaos that reigned in sexual harassment empirical research. Fitzgerald et al. recognized the difficulty of accurately determining the pervasiveness of sexual harassment from empirical studies as long as all use different instruments in their measurements. Fitzgerald et al. formulated what they call the "Sexual Experiences Questionnaire" (SEQ) in an attempt to produce something that everyone could use. The SEQ was designed "to identify the frequency of various types of harassment."[77]

The questionnaire is modeled on Till's definition of sexual harassment. For the authors' operational definition, behaviors are divided into five categories, with unequal numbers of behaviors listed under each. The categories are:

1. *Gender harassment.* Generalized sexist remarks and behavior designed not necessarily to elicit sexual cooperation, but to convey insulting, degrading, or sexist attitudes about women.
2. *Seductive behavior.* Inappropriate and offensive sexual advances. Although such behavior is unwanted and offensive, there is no penalty explicitly attached to the woman's negative response; nor does this category include sexual bribery.
3. *Sexual bribery.* Solicitation of sexual activity or other sex-linked behavior (e.g., dating) by promise of rewards;

4. *Sexual coercion.* Coercion of sexual activity or other sex-linked behavior by threat of punishment;

5. *Sexual imposition.* Sexual imposition (e.g., attempts to fondle, touch, kiss, or grab) or sexual assault.[78]

Questions were developed for various forms of behavior under these general headings. Questions had the form, "Have you ever been in a situation where a professor or instructor . . . [e.g., made crudely sexual remarks, either publicly in class, or to you privately]?"[79] Responders had the options of choosing "never," "once," or "more than once." The question "Do you believe that you have ever been sexually harassed?" was asked separately, at the end of the questionnaire. Pilot studies were performed with students as respondents.

It has been said that this schema coincides with the legal definition of sexual harassment, but it does not.[80] One element of the EEOC definition that is absent from this definition is "repeated." This is not evident in the questions asked of the students. So, what these survey results show is that there is rather a lot of sexual behavior directed toward women students in academia and toward women in the workplace. This is not surprising. They also show that there is some coercion and some abuse of power. Two pilot studies with students as subjects using the SEQ showed that of one sample, about 50 percent of the women responding answered "once" or "more than once" for at least one of the items in the questionnaire, and of another sample, 76 percent responded positively to at least one item. However, because of the lack of precision in the questions, it does not seem that any reliable rates of frequency of sexual harassment could be derived from use of the SEQ. That is, one cannot conclude that a student was "sexually harassed"—certainly not in the legal sense—simply because that student responded "once" or "more than once" to an item.

For example, question 2–2 asks: "Have you ever been in a situation where a professor or instructor engaged in what you considered seductive behavior toward you (e.g., made flattering or suggestive remarks, asked you for a date, suggested that you 'get together' for a drink, offered you a backrub)?"[81] If a student answers "once" or "more than once" to this question, has the student been sexually harassed? According to this model, yes. But I would say, not necessarily. One must include the circumstances: Was the student in a class of the professor or instructor at the time the offer was made? Was the offer "unwanted"? Did the student think that there would be any penalty for not complying? Was the offer repeated? Question 2–3 asks: "Have you ever been in a situation where you received unwanted sexual attention from a professor or instructor?"[82] Again, a "once" does not seem to imply that sexual harassment has taken place. The question is too vague. Was the attention unwanted because the student simply was not interested, or because it was felt to be threatening? Was the student in the instructor's class at the time, so that some sort of threat was suggested? Was the attention repeated?

Question 2–4 asks: "Have you ever been in a situation where a professor or instructor attempted to establish a romantic sexual relationship with you?"[83] A "once" in response to this question does not necessarily establish sexual harassment, unless you think that every such attempt is wrong. That Fitzgerald does think that such behavior is, by definition, wrong, is shown in the definition she developed after using SEQ:

> Sexual harassment consists of the sexualization of an instrumental relationship through the introduction or imposition of sexist or sexual remarks, requests, or requirements, in the context of a formal power differential. Harassment can also occur where no such formal power differential exists, if the behavior is unwanted by, or offensive to, the woman. Instances of harassment can be classified into the following general categories: gender harassment, seductive behavior, solicitation of sexual activity by promise of reward or threat of punishment, and sexual imposition or assault.[84]

This definition implies that *any* romantic overture by a professor toward a student, unwanted or not, repeated or not, is sexual harassment. It further implies that any unwanted romantic overture by a colleague is also sexual harassment. Furthermore, it contains the very ambiguity between gender and sex that has plagued the concept of sexual harassment from the beginning. The definition implies that a relationship can be "sexualized" by either sexual or sexist behavior. This seems to require that men and women must not acknowledge one another's gender *in any way*. It is not clear that this is possible, much less desirable.

It is the case, however, that Fitzgerald's definition is true to the original socioculturalist, feminist definitions of sexual harassment. Like Farley's and MacKinnon's, it includes the elements of power inequality, which they seemed to think was sufficient but not necessary to sexual harassment, and making the victim a sex object, which they seemed to think was necessary, though perhaps not sufficient for sexual harassment. However, because of the way in which the questions are put, we cannot determine what the results tell us.

Unfortunately, there were not many major studies of sexual harassment in the workplace in the early 1990s. People writing on sexual harassment today continue to cite studies done ten or more years ago. The most significant survey during this period is probably the 1992 study of kindergarten through twelfth-grade students commissioned by the American Association of University Women (AAUW), "Hostile Hallways."[85] This survey is particularly noteworthy because it identified some racial and ethnic categories, showing differences in experiences depending on race and ethnicity. The survey was conducted by Louis Harris and Associates, Inc., a reputable research firm. In February and March 1993, 1,632 African American, white, and Hispanic girls and boys from grades eight to eleven were surveyed. The students were from seventy-nine different public schools across the nation. The sample was selected in such a way that "[t]he findings are projectable to all public school students in the 8th through 11th grades in the United States."[86] The Harris people were very careful to administer the survey in such a way that students would answer truthfully.

The survey itself asked students to respond to specific questions and then to provide comments regarding how they felt about the harassment they had experienced. A list of fourteen different kinds of sexual harassment was developed and used in the survey. The survey defined sexual harassment for the students as follows: "Sexual harassment is *unwanted* and *unwelcome* sexual behavior which interferes with your life. Sexual harassment is not behaviors that you *like* or *want* (for example: wanted kissing, touching, or flirting)."[87] The main question to which students were asked to respond was:

> During your whole school life, how often, if at all, has anyone (this includes students, teachers, other school employees, and anyone else) done the following things to you *when you did not want them to?*

- Made sexual comments, jokes, gestures, or looks.
- Showed, gave, or left you sexual pictures, photographs, illustrations, messages, or notes.
- Wrote sexual messages/graffiti about you on bathroom walls, in locker rooms, etc.
- Spread sexual rumors about you.
- Said you were gay or lesbian.
- Spied on you as you dressed or showered at school.
- Flashed or "mooned" you.
- Touched, grabbed, or pinched you in a sexual way.
- Pulled at your clothing in a sexual way.
- Intentionally brushed against you in a sexual way.
- Pulled your clothing off or down.
- Blocked your way or cornered you in a sexual way.
- Forced you to kiss him/her.
- Forced you to do something sexual, other than kissing.[88]

The options given students for answering this question for each of the listed behaviors were: "often," "occasionally," "rarely," "never," and "not sure." Notice that this is a retrospective survey.

The survey found that many students had experienced one or more of the behaviors listed: "fully 4 out of 5 students (81%) report that they have been the target of some form of sexual harassment during their school lives."[89] This includes 85% of the girls and 76% of the boys surveyed; however, girls reported more frequent experiences than boys. African American boys (81%) were more likely to report harassment than white (75%) or Hispanic (69%) boys, and white girls (87%) were slightly more likely to report harassment than African American girls (84%) or Hispanic girls (82%). Other questions investigated in the survey included who harassed, where students were harassed, and who students went to when they complained about harassment. Most harassment is peer harassment, and high numbers of girls (52%) and boys (66%) admitted having harassed someone. Hallways and classrooms were the main locations in which students were harassed. It was found that students usually tell no adults of their experiences, though many tell friends.

To assess the impact of sexual harassment on students, the surveyors asked students how being harassed made them feel. Some students reported not wanting to go to school, skipping school, and not wanting to talk in class as a result of harassment. Feeling embarrassed, self-consciousness, or upset was also reported. Both boys and girls have felt the impact of harassment, though in different ways.

One of the remarkable aspects of this study is the inclusion of the expression "Said you were gay or lesbian" among the list of harassing behaviors constituting sexual harassment. According to the survey, 17% of those surveyed had been called gay or lesbian when they did not want to be, with 23% of boys and 10% of girls reporting this form of harassment. African American girls and white girls reported this kind of harassment at nearly the same rate (11% compared to 10%), whereas Hispanic girls reported it half as often (5%). All racial and ethnic groups of boys identified reported this form of harassment at the same rate.

Why is this considered a form of sexual harassment that should be considered separately from the other categories under which it might fit—for example, sexual comments, or spreading sexual rumors? "Being Called Gay" is singled out for special comment in a brief published report of the survey results as "The Worst Harassment." The researchers explain:

> Sexual identity is a sensitive issue for adolescents. During this time, being called gay or lesbian is disturbing to a majority of students. Indeed, when students were asked to what degree they would be upset if they were the targets of the 14 different types of sexual harassment outlined in the survey, 86% of all students surveyed said they would be "very upset" if they were called gay or lesbian: 85% of boys and 87% of girls. No other type of harassment—including actual physical abuse—provoked a reaction this strong among boys.[90]

What conclusion we should draw from this explanation is unclear. The researchers and some students considered being called gay or lesbian an insult. Why they should think this an insult is unclear, and that they think it is an insult is disturbing. It would have been interesting to know what percentage of students who were called gay and lesbian when they did not want to be were gay or lesbian. There seems to be an assumption that the subjects of the study are heterosexual. Further studies should be performed to determine whether homosexual students are sexually harassed to a greater degree or in different ways than heterosexual students.

This survey is very carefully done; its sampling methodology seems sound. The definition of sexual harassment is both broad and narrow, when compared to other definitions. It is clearly broader than the legal definition, since no mention is made of the severity or pervasiveness of the conduct. Also, the definition includes the extremely vague expression "interferes with your life." The interference is not limited to the learning environment. The definition is narrower than others in that it seems limited to *sexual* behavior, ignoring gender-based harassment ("Girls can't do math," etc.), unless being called "gay" or "lesbian" is gender harassment.

The surveyors do not say how they arrived at their definition of sexual harassment, or how they came up with their fourteen kinds of behavior, except to say that they had consulted with "experts in the field of sexual harassment."[91] However, given the definition and the kinds of questions asked, what can we conclude?

It seems that we can conclude that there is lot of sexual behavior among thirteen- to eighteen-year-olds, some of it unwanted or unwelcome. If we wish to call that unwanted or unwelcome behavior "sexual harassment," we must keep in mind that not all of it rises to the level of illegal sex discrimination. There is no doubt that some of this behavior is detrimental to the educational experiences of children and to their emotional lives. Children should be protected from harassment that seriously harms them. However, some sexual behavior is probably normal among children, even though some of it is unwanted. Sexual bullying should definitely be curtailed.

We can also conclude that children of different ethnicities or races are affected differently by these so-called sexually harassing behaviors. The researchers highlight the fact that African American girls and boys suffer more harassment and more severe consequences than white or Hispanic students.

> Among harassed girls: 39% of African Americans did not want to attend school, in contrast with 33% of white and 29% of Hispanics. Among harassed boys, the numbers are: 14% of whites, 9% of African Americans, and 8% of Hispanics. . . . Half of all African American boys surveyed (49%) have been intentionally brushed up against in a sexual way. One in 5 African American boys surveyed (22%) have been forced to kiss somes

In addition, African American girls (33%) are more likely to be harassed by adults than are white (25%) or Hispanic girls (17%). These results suggest that we should always include race and ethnicity in studies of sexual harassment so that differences can be determined. As was stated earlier, most studies have not isolated race or ethnicity as a variable, and so not much information is available on such differences among adults experiencing sexual harassment. These differences also suggest that such experiences ought to be considered when educators and administrators are seeking reasons for differences in achievement among different races or ethnicities in schools. The extra burdens that African American girls and boys are carrying, according to this survey, may affect their performance in school.

Christina Hoff Sommers described the findings of the AAUW survey in this way: "Four of five students, male as well as female, reported being harassed. The study does suggest that our schools are the setting for a lot of incivility and even outright violence. It suggests that many kids are erotically overstimulated."[93] However, she does not see these results as evidence of a sexual harassment epidemic in kindergarten through twelfth grade. Sommers also considers the study to undercut any claim that so-called sexual harassment in schools prevents girls from having an "equal opportunity" for education. She plays down the study results, which show that the impact of sexual harassment is more severe for girls than for boys. To the claim that girls are more likely than boys to "want to cut class" as a result of sexually harassing behaviors, she points out, quite rightly, that "*wanting* to cut classes and actually cutting classes are not the same, and the latter effect is just the sort of thing we can check . . . girls should be showing high rates of absenteeism, cutting class, and getting lower grades. In fact, girls have better attendance and earn better grades than boys, and more of them graduate."[94] This is a valid point. However, Sommers does not mention that 24 percent of girls say they did *in fact* skip class because of sexual harassment, whereas only about 8 percent of boys did. While more boys overall may stay away from classes, the reasons for girls and boys doing so may be different.[95] Fewer girls may cut classes if fewer were harassed. In addition, more African American girls and boys may cut class because of harassment. The report of the AAUW survey does not provide the ethnic and racial breakdown for this question.

Children are sometimes cruel to one another. Some of this cruelty takes a sexualized form. We must decide how we are going to teach children to be decent to one another, at least while they are under the care of educational institutions. Sommers and others who object to conceiving of such behavior from a "gendered" perspective seem to assume that sexualized bullying and teasing should not be categorized differently from other sorts of bullying and teasing. But there seems to be some evidence that sexualized bullying and teasing has, until recently, not been seen as serious bullying or teasing at all. Applying the concept of sexual harassment to the behavior of students forces us to think seriously about all such cruelty. Sommers and others seem to want to resist a gendered categorization of cruel behavior, especially when it is joined with the claim that girls are particularly harmed by sexually harassing behavior. Sexual harassment law under Title IX as it is currently understood seems to show a trend toward isolating sexualized behavior.

What are the reasons for differentiating sexualized behavior from other sorts of behavior? The perspective of a socioculturalist and of some liberals might be that girls and boys are differentially impacted by such behavior, so that it is an issue of equality of opportunity. If the educational opportunities of girls are curtailed because of sexual harassment, then we ought to try to eliminate such harassment. If the education of boys and girls is negatively impacted more or less equally because of sexual harassment, then we should still try to eliminate such harassment.

It seems to me that all bullying and harassment, whether sexual or not, should be controlled. This is analogous to the view that harassment of any type should be eliminated in the workplace. There is resistance to this by employers because it forces them to police their workforce and is seen by many as an unwarranted intrusion into their businesses. However, because the victims and perpetrators are often students in educational settings, it should be less controversial to put a stop to all harassment and bullying in schools. Students should be required to respect one another and to act civilly. This will better prepare them for their futures as working adults.

Studies Performed Outside
the United States

The most comprehensive work on research on sexual harassment outside the United States available is Michael Rubenstein's *Dignity of Women at Work: A Report on the Problem of Sexual Harassment in the Member States of the European Communities*, published in 1988. This work focuses on the issue of the rates of sexual harassment in various countries. However, in that work, the results of various surveys in European Community (EC) countries are offered with the caveat that the various studies done in different countries are not directly comparable.[96] The EC has addressed the issue of sexual harassment in its member states, and many of its members have conducted surveys on sexual harassment. However, "[n]o EC-wide comparative studies exist, nor apparently has any researcher examined the prevalence of sexual harassment in each Member State based on similar research methods."[97] Thus, the same problems that plague attempts to determine the prevalence of sexual harassment in the United States are present elsewhere.

The International Labour Organization cites a number of studies in its 1992 "Combating Sexual Harassment at Work."[98] Because little information is provided about the definitions used and the methods of data collection, it is difficult to know how to interpret them. Comparisons of results are problematic.[99] In addition, a number of the studies are quite dated. Because of these difficulties, I shall simply report the results of some studies carried out in countries other than the United States. I shall not include studies with obvious deficiencies, such as clearly unrepresentative samples.

A survey of women carried out in 1986 in Spain found that 84 percent of women questioned had experienced some form of sexual harassment.[100] The study apparently defined sexual harassment broadly, to include the following behaviors: sexual commentaries and jokes (experienced by 84 percent of respondents), sexual looks or gestures (experienced by 55 percent of respondents), pressure for dates for sexual purposes, strong verbal advances (including telephone calls), unwanted touching (experienced by 27 percent of respondents), and attempted sexual intercourse (experienced by 4 percent of respondents).[101] The study also found that "women between 26–30 years old were more likely to be sexually harassed than other age groups," and "[w]omen who were separated, divorced or widowed were not only more likely to be subjected to sexual harassment, but they also experienced the stronger forms of sexual harassment."[102]

A survey of women members of trade unions in Sweden, reported in 1987, found that 17 percent of women who responded had experienced some form of sexual harassment at work. The definition of sexual harassment used included unwelcome verbal comments and unwelcome touching (70 percent of those reporting harassment) and unwelcome requests for sexual favors or sexual relations (nearly one-third of those reporting harassment).[103]

A study carried out by the University of Groningen in the Netherlands and reported in 1986 found that "58 per cent of the women questioned had experienced sexual harassment at work," with verbal harassment being the most common form of harassment reported.[104]

Several small studies have been conducted in the United Kingdom. In 1987, the Labour Research Department found "73 percent of respondents reporting that some form of harassment had taken place in their workplace. The most common types of harassment reported were suggestive remarks or other verbal abuse (48 percent), sexist or patronizing behaviour (45 percent), and unnecessary touching and unwanted contact (34 percent)."[105] It should be noted that this study apparently surveyed all workers, asking them whether they were aware of any harassment in their workplace. Thus, it is possible that a large percentage of workers at one place of work could be referring to the same incident of harassment in answering this question affirmatively. In a 1991 study of their clients carried out for the employment agency Alfred Marks Bureau, "47 percent of women and 14 percent of men stated that they had been sexually harassed. Touching, pinching or grabbing was experienced by 43 percent; suggestive remarks and innuendoes by 41 per cent; direct sexual propositions by 32 percent; being eyed up and suggestive looks by 10 per cent; and personal comments about the body by 6 percent."[106]

Outside of the EC, studies have been conducted in Canada and Japan, among other countries. The Canadian Human Rights Commission conducted a survey of sexual harassment which it published in 1983. The sample consisted of 2,004 women and men. Of these, 49 percent of the women and 33 percent of the men reported that they had experienced some sort of "unwanted sexual attention."[107]

Several studies have been done in Japan. In a study published in May 1996, the Japanese Trade Union Confederation surveyed 1,212 working women and found that 40 percent had encountered sexual harassment more than once.[108] A survey of Kyoto University graduates and female teachers was conducted by Associate Professor Reiko Tanabe in 1996: 1,994 female graduates were surveyed, and 589 of them responded. Of these, 47 percent said they had been sexually harassed at the university; 49.4% of the female teachers surveyed said they had "experienced or heard about sexual harassment at the university."[109] The results of this study are difficult to assess. It is not clear what the female teachers were asked—whether it was "Have you experienced or heard about sexual harassment at the university?" or two separate questions, the results of which are for some reason combined in the report of the findings. The relatively low rate of return among female graduates is also problematic.

Without more information on the composition of samples and the kinds of survey instruments used, not much can be said about the reliability of these surveys. The information available does suggest that they suffer from the same general sorts of weaknesses as studies performed in the United States do. However, it is worth noting that such studies are taking place and being reported, and that definitions of sexual harassment used in the studies are similar to those used in the United States.

What Can We Know about
Sexual Harassment?

Why are there so many empirical studies designed to investigate sexual harassment? One reason is to try to support particular conceptions of sexual harassment, or particular perspectives on sexual harassment, with empirical data. Among the questions for which empirical data are considered relevant are:

- How prevalent is sexual harassment?
- Are more women than men sexually harassed?
- Are all women equally subject to sexual harassment?
- Are perceptions of sexual harassment different for women and men?

In what follows, I shall examine the empirical data available to determine what, if anything, we can know about each of these issues on the basis of those data.

How Prevalent Is Sexual Harassment?

Many of the studies described in the preceding sections seek to provide information about the prevalence of sexual harassment. It should by now be apparent that the prevalence of sexual harassment one finds will depend on one's definition of sexual harassment. The more narrowly one defines sexual harassment, the fewer cases there will be. Thus, as Lengnick-Hall points out, "Despite the variety of samples used and the sheer number of surveys conducted, it is difficult to draw any firm conclusions about the incidence of sexual harassment."[110]

Our attempts to estimate the actual number of instances of sexual harassment are hampered by the absence of any agreed-upon standard definition. Fitzgerald's attempt to create a common operational definition fails because her definition is ideologically skewed in such a way that many will not accept it.

My advice to those interested in knowing the prevalence of sexual harassment is to read with care reports of studies designed to measure the amount of sexual harassment—in other words, each study must be examined to determine what, if anything, one can conclude from it. Determine the operational definition. Examine the characteristics of the sample. Look at the survey questions used to solicit information to ensure that they are unambiguous and precise. Examine the conclusions drawn by the researchers to ensure that they are interpreting the results in an unbiased manner. These are the techniques of critical reasoning. They are our best means of interpreting survey results judiciously.

What the surveys conducted both at educational institutions and in the workplace show is that there is a good deal of sexual behavior between people in these environments. Whether some of it is sexual harassment is another question, the answer to which depends on one's definition of "sexual harassment." Whether some of the behavior is *illegal* sexual harassment is yet another question, and one that is often conflated with the preceding question. For clear thinking, all three question must be distinguished.

The most reliable studies, the three Merit studies and that reported by Gutek, are now becoming dated. The fact that the Merit studies yielded very close numbers—44 percent of women and 19 percent of men—may give us some confidence in those results. However, one must remember that these were retrospective studies and so may be inaccurate because of the problems of such studies, and that not all reported instances of sexual harassment were illegal sexual harassment.

Are More Women than Men Sexually Harassed?

Most researchers and theorists agree that women are more frequently victims of sexual harassment than men. Both the Merit surveys and Gutek's work support this claim. However, there is some disagreement about the extent of the difference, and the explanations for it. Are men less often the targets of what are considered harassing behaviors? Are men simply bothered less by the same behaviors?

One intriguing study seems to show that many more men are sexually harassed than previous studies have shown. The study, conduct by Applied Research Consultants (ARC) in 1989, was commissioned by a university to survey students, staff, and faculty with regard to sexual harassment. The survey instruments were based on Fitzgerald and Shullman's "Sexual Experiences Questionnaire" (SEQ).

> In general, the rates of harassment experiences reported by women paralleled those of previous studies. . . . What was surprising, however, were the rates of harassment experiences reported by men: these were far higher than conventional wisdom led us to expect, often similar to the rates for women. Indeed, the only types of harassment reported twice as often by women than men . . . were sexual seduction . . . and sexual imposition. . . . In several instances, rates were lower for women than men . . . faculty reports of gender harassment . . . graduate and staff reports of sexual bribery . . . and staff reports of sexual threat. . . .[111]

Alan Vaux points out that it is difficult to dismiss these results because "the ARC study employed methods comparable to other studies designed to assess the extent of the problem. . . ."[112] Vaux considers other possible explanations for the surprising result, but none of them are particular to this survey, or to the results for men rather than women. He concludes that the findings should be taken at face value, and that the assumption that many women and few men are harassed should be challenged. He cites other studies that have found narrower sex differences in reports of sexual harassment. One study found little difference among undergraduates,[113] and another found that "women students experience more gender harassment than men, but that both women and men experience the more intense forms of harassment at low or very low rates that are comparable."[114] Vaux also reports that the ARC survey found that "most perpetrators were male, regardless of the target of harassment."[115]

In summary, though the majority of studies consistently show that fewer men suffer the behaviors identified as sexually harassing, not all of the studies do so. Perhaps men and women suffer the most serious forms of harassment in nearly equal numbers, while the less serious forms of sexual harassment are much more common for women. It does seem to be worth questioning the assumption that women suffer sexual harassment to a much greater extent than men. This assumption is so prevalent that in some studies only women are surveyed.[116]

Are All Women Equally Subject to Sexual Harassment?

Claims about who is most likely to be harassed vary with the study. Rubenstein claims that

> the likelihood of being sexually harassed is most closely associated with the perceived vulnerability and financial dependency of the recipient. . . . More specifically, divorced, separated and widowed women, single parents and lesbians, women from ethnic minorities, women working in predominantly male jobs, new entrants to the workforce, and women with irregular employment contracts are among the most likely women to be harassed.[117]

However, different surveys suggest that this is not so, or that there are insufficient data to draw any reliable conclusions.

With regard to who is most likely to be a victim of sexual harassment, the results are contradictory. Findings about women include: that more single than married women experience sexual harassment;[118] that younger women suffer more sexual harassment than do older women;[119] that nonwhite women are more likely than white women to be victims of sexual harassment,[120] and that they are not;[121] that women in low-status jobs report more sexual harassment,[122] and that reports of sexual harassment are evenly distributed among occupations;[123] that more highly educated women were more likely to report incidents of sexual harassment;[124] that women in nontraditional jobs are more likely to be subject to sexual harassment;[125] and that women "[a]re working in a predominantly male environment or have a male as their immediate supervisor."[126] According to one author, research in the mid- to late eighties suggested that "women with low power and status, whether due to lower age, being single or divorced, or being in a marginal position in the organization, are more likely to be harassed."[127]

There are inconsistent findings for men, as well. Some surveys have found that men are more likely to be harassed if they are young,[128] but some have found only a small relationship between a man's age and the likelihood of harassment.[129] Divorced men and men living with a woman are more likely to be harassed.[130] While some surveys found that men who work in offices or who are in clerical or trainee positions, or who work in predominately female work groups or who have female supervisors, are more likely to be harassed; other surveys have not found occupation to be a significant factor, except that managers seem to report more cases of sexual harassment.[131] The 1980 Merit survey found that men were more likely to be victims if they were members of a racial or ethnic minority group.[132] This is consistent with the results of the AAUW survey of children.

The conflicting data readily can be explained by lack of uniformity in samples, survey instruments, and the like. In general, however, it seems that the survey instruments have not been sophisticated enough to provide the sort of precision on the question whether all women are equally subject to sexual harassment that might decide between different perspectives on sexual harassment. For example, if one subscribes to a version of the biological perspective, then one would predict that young, unmarried, attractive women will be the most frequent victims of sexual harassment, consistent with its interpretation of sexual harassment as a manifestation of normal male sexual strategies. Some studies seem to show this. However, Rubenstein interprets these results to mean that it is women who are perceived to be more vulnerable and financially dependent who are targeted—a view more consistent with either the sociocultural or the liberal perspective. Since these two groups of women tend to overlap—not married and financially dependent—it is difficult to use the empirical data to decide between the perspectives. The sociocultural perspective predicts that, in general, more women than men will be subjected to sexually harassing behavior, because sexual harassment is a practice of men to keep women subordinate. MacKinnon, in her 1979 book, says:

> Victimization by the practice of sexual harassment, so far as is currently known, occurs across the lines of age, marital status, physical appearance, race, class, occupation, pay range, and any other factors that distinguish women from each other. Frequency and type of incident may vary with specific vulnerabilities of the woman, or qualities of the job, employer, situation, or workplace, to an extent so far undetermined. To this point, the common denominator is that the perpetrators tend to be men, the victims women.[133]

Thus, the prediction of socioculturalists seems to fit with those of the other two perspectives, though to explain the results differently. This seems to be a case in which empirical data will not decide between the various perspectives. I shall have more to say about this later.

The question whether people of ethnic or racial minorities are more likely to experience sexual harassment is one for which there is insufficient evidence. Most surveys do not ask for the race or ethnicity of the respondent.[134] Some perspectives on sexual harassment, particularly the liberal perspective, predict that members of racial and ethnic minorities will be at greater risk of sexual harassment because they have less social power than members of racial and ethnic majorities. Such claims are made without empirical support.[135] However, the point of making the claims may be to point out that members of racial and ethnic minorities experience unique forms of sexual harassment due to the intersection of race or ethnicity and sex, both in the type of harassment, which often involves racialized sexual epithets,[136] and in the meaning of the harassment, because of the particular histories of racial and ethnic groups in this country.[137]

Are Perceptions of Men and Women Different?

A great deal of research has been done to try to discover whether men and women perceive sexual harassment similarly. Perhaps it would be better to say that data from many studies, some designed for other purposes, have been thought to bear on this issue. This issue is thought to be particularly important because of the reasonable woman standard, to be further discussed in chapter 6.

In 1992, one group of researchers asserted, "There has been ample evidence of differential perceptions of sexual harassment, both in actual cases and in research. One of the most consistent findings in the literature on sexual harassment has been sex differences in perceptions of such incidents, with females often perceiving certain behaviors as more likely to be sexual harassment than do males."[138] However, some researchers claim that the empirical data on this issue is inconclusive. In a survey of such studies, Riggs et al. cite some studies that suggest that women and men agree on what constitutes sexual harassment, and some that suggest that they do not.[139] Another group of researchers cites several studies that seem to show that there are no significant gender differences in assessments of what constitutes more severe sexual harassment such as quid pro quo harassment or sexual coercion.[140] Other studies seem to show that women and men disagree about more "ambiguous" behaviors such as "sexual looks and sexual comments."[141]

A survey of the studies on gendered perception of sexual harassment reveals numerous problems in drawing conclusions about the issue from the data. For example, a study reported in *Psychological Reports* in 1995 under the title "Gender Influence on Perceptions of Hostile Environment Sexual Harassment" concludes that "women rated 'hostile environment' scenarios as more harassing than [did] men."[142] The study presented scenarios of "harassment" to 100 female and 98 male students in introductory psychology classes and asked them to indicate their degree of agreement or disagreement with the claim that the scenario "represented an incident of sexual harassment." Two problems with this study are immediately evident. First, the subjects were predominantly white undergraduate students. This is a rather select group and may not be representative of the general population. Second, the students were asked whether the scenario described an instance of sexual harassment. While it may be true that more women than men indicated that the scenario did describe an instance of sexual harassment, we have no way of knowing what these people thought sexual harassment was. That is, we do not know whether they considered every behavior they thought sexually harassing to be illegal or merely "annoying."[143] It is an unfortunate fact that sexual harassment has come to be, by definition, illegal, when it is not clear that it should be. So perhaps, the women were thinking that sexual harassment includes annoying behavior, and the men were thinking it is limited to illegal behavior, leading them to different conclusions about the described scenarios.

There have been some studies that have not been done on undergraduates. One investigated the influence of gender on juror judgments in sexual harassment cases. The study found that gender influences the outcome of a jury decision when the behaviors in question are "ambiguous," but when the cases were clearly either "innocent or severe," gender influence is "mixed." The result was, "Females . . . were significantly more likely than males . . . to perceive behaviors as offensive when behaviors were labeled ambiguous";[144] females "were significantly more likely than males . . . to vote in favor of the plaintiff" whether the scenarios were ambiguous, innocuous, or severe.[145]

The researchers conclude that "scenarios included as ambiguous . . . were largely examples of gender harassment and seductive behavior, incidents that, according to previous research findings, are likely to be interpreted differently based on one's gender." They agree with another researcher that "unambiguous social norms exist against more severe behaviors, but ambiguity surrounds norms regarding gender harassment and seductive behavior."[146]

This study was more methodologically sound than some of the others, but it still suffers from small sample size. There is also a potential for confusion, since the researchers were testing for more than simply gender influence. They were also interested in how the experience of being the target of sexually harassing behavior influenced one's perception of behaviors. Forty percent of their subjects reported that they had been targets of sexual harassment: 54 percent of Hispanic females, 56 percent of Anglo females, 16 percent of Hispanic males, and 17 percent of Anglo males.[147] They found that "individuals who had been the target of sexual harassment . . . were significantly more likely than those who had not been a target . . . to perceive behaviors labeled ambiguous as more offensive,"[148] and that "[i]ndividuals who had been the target of sexual harassment . . . were significantly more likely to vote for the plaintiff when the scenarios were labeled ambiguous than were those individuals who had not been the target of sexual harassment. . . ."[149] Furthermore, they found that "having been the target of sexual harassment overcomes any gender differences in how a juror would vote when incidents were less clear cut."[150]

The problem is that more women than men reported being targets of sexual harassment, and more women than men considered ambiguous behaviors to be sexual harassment. How do we know that it was not being a target of sexual harassment that determined their perception? It is true that women are more likely than men to report having been sexually harassed. But this seems to produce a circle that is difficult to sort out. Is it gender that causes women both to perceive themselves as targets of sexual harassment and to perceive ambiguous behaviors as sexual harassment, or is it being the target of sexual harassment that causes them to perceive ambiguous behaviors as sexual harassment? Without being able to sort this out, it is not clear how much weight to give the "gender difference" in perception and sympathy for the plaintiff.

Another study that claims to support the view that women and men perceive sexual behaviors differently was designed to test reactions to the EEOC *Guidelines*.[151] "Male and female participants in the study were given one of four possible statements, which varied the form of sexual harassment (physical or verbal) and the consequences of such harassment (economic injury or hostile environment). Participants were then asked to rate the characteristics of the incident in the statement, using a scale. . . . They were also asked to rate the incident on degree of harassment and its potential effects on the victim."[152] The sample consisted of ninety-nine male and ninety-nine female predominantly white undergraduate students enrolled in a psychology course at a midwestern state university. The mean age of these students was 19.56. Each student received a statement based on the EEOC *Guidelines* such as the following: "Person A experiences unwelcome sexual advances or other physical conduct of a sexual nature from Person B. Such conduct involves an expressed or implied condition of employment or is the basis for any employment decision affecting Person A."[153] An experimenter read the statement to the subjects, and for statements including "conditions of employment," four examples were written on the board: performance appraisal, placement, selection, training and development. Students were also given a twenty-two-item questionnaire. Included on the questionnaire were questions concerning "the degree to which the incident represented sexual harassment." Students were also asked to list examples illustrative of the statement.[154]

The results showed that "the physical hostile environment statement was viewed more negatively by females . . . than by males"; "males perceived the physical hostile environment statement less negatively . . . than the verbal hostile environment statement."[155] The researchers concluded that "females rated the statement less favorably than did males, especially when a 'physical' form of behavior with a 'hostile environment' consequence was described."[156] In their discussion of the results, the researchers took these findings to "support the hypothesized sex differences in perceptions of the incident as sexual harassment, with female raters perceiving the incident to be more negative (less favorable), more likely to be considered as sexual harassment, and more likely to have an effect on the victim than did the male subjects."[157]

It should be noted that, since the sample in this study is so small, and since it consists of undergraduate students, no generalization to the U.S. adult population is supported by this study. However, there are other problems, as well. The "statements" developed by the researchers seem to assume a familiarity with legal discourse which many undergraduates may not have. In addition, the vagueness of the statements makes it difficult to know to what the subjects were responding. Subjects had to supply the detail, and they may be supplying very different details. For example, for the statement given, a woman might be thinking of being pinned to a table by her boss who says that she must submit or be fired, whereas a man may be thinking of something less severe. The study seemed not to show gender differences with regard to quid pro quo harassment, however. Hostile environment statements were probably open to even wider interpretation.[158]

What should we say about the claim that women and men have differing perceptions of sexual harassment? The 1987 and 1994 Merit studies suggest that male and female perceptions of sexual harassment are converging, at least about the more serious forms of sexual harassment.[159] Recently, Barbara Gutek and Maureen O'Connor have considered the empirical basis for the claim that "men and women perceive and define sexual harassment differently."[160] They claim that "[i]n general, the finding that women define sexual harassment more broadly and inclusively than men is reliable, but the difference is small, often smaller than intrasex differences, and is affected by a variety of factors, including characteristics of the study itself."[161] Gutek and O'Connor maintain that "most of the research on the definition of sexual harassment . . . has revealed that, compared to men, women are generally more liberal, broad, and inclusive in their definition of sexual harassment"; that "[a]lmost all survey studies have found significant differences between the sexes on at least one category of behavior," but that "[f]ew surveys . . . find that men and women differ in every kind of behavior about which they are asked"; and that "[s]ome studies have not found that men and women differ."[162]

Gutek and O'Connor are cautious, however, and recommend reviewing the research carefully to see just what it allows us to conclude about differences between women and men in perceiving sexual harassment: "How consistent and how large are the sex differences in definition of sexual harassment, under what conditions does the perceptual gap close, and to what extent do the conditions of the research findings parallel a conclusion under which juries are asked to make determinations about sexual harassment?"[163] They first evaluate the consistency and size of the "perceptual gap." They point out that "[m]en and women do not always differ in their evaluation of workplace conduct," but that when they do, "the direction of the differences is consistent; women are somewhat more likely than men to identify behavior as sexual harassment or view behavior as less appropriate."[164] However, the size of the gap is small. They go on to point out that, "especially when the sexual harassment is not severe or the scenario is ambiguous, within-sex variation can be as large or larger than between-sex variation. . . . Only among the most severe behaviors is there consensus among women that sexual harassment has occurred . . . and, under those conditions, men also agree."[165] This seems particularly important to the reasonable woman standard, and it is something not usually mentioned in discussions of the so-called perceptual gap.

The conditions under which the perceptual gap closes are also important to examine. Gutek and O'Connor find that "the perceptual gap is not as great under certain circumstances having to do with (1) the behavior in question, (2) the situation in which the behavior occurs, and (3) the characteristics of the study."[166] First, "[w]hen the harassment is either severe or the behavior is so benign that it clearly is not harassment, the perceptual gap between the sexes closes."[167] Second, "[p]eople who work in sexualized environments . . . may become habituated to it so they define sexual harassment very narrowly around only the most offensive behavior. . . ."[168] Third, "[t]he characteristics of the study (choice of material presented, wording of scenarios and questions) either enhance or decrease the perceptual gap between the sexes. In general, the perceptual gap is more pronounced when the incident described for raters is ambiguous rather than clear."[169] In addition, "[s]ubjects are less likely to label behavior as sexual harassment if they are not asked directly about harassment;" furthermore, the wording of the question is important, since women are more likely than men to label behavior "inappropriate" but do not necessarily consider inappropriate behavior illegal sexual harassment.[170]

Gutek and O'Connor also point out that not all empirical research is relevant to court cases. "We are concerned about the courts using findings from scenario studies that have been designed without regard to their relevance in legal cases. These studies may unwittingly distort the impact of gender on judgments of harassment in actual cases because they often use single incidents of ambiguous behavior . . . rather than patterns of behavior that may be ambiguous, but, on the whole, are more objectionable."[171] Gutek and O'-Connor do not deny that there is a perceptual gap between women and men with regard to sexual harassment. However, they are concerned about "whether the empirical evidence used to demonstrate that gap is sufficiently strong, consistent, and meaningful to justify a sex-based legal standard." They do not think that it does.

> The differences between men and women in definition of sexual harassment are small and most often found in incidents that are atypical of court cases. . . . It may just take a while before we develop a clear consensus on sexual harassment. In the meantime, will the reasonable woman standard help? We think not. We think it would be more useful to explore why women and men differ, rather than to infer that men and women are so different on the issue of sexual harassment as to require different standards of reasonableness. Why not work toward some consensus on what constitutes sexual harassment, rather than assume that the differences that currently exist in men's and women's perceptions are permanent and immutable?[172]

Given the care that Gutek takes in collecting and interpreting data, I believe that her conclusion on this issue can be trusted. There is a gap between women and men in their perceptions that sexual harassment has occurred. The gap disappears for severe forms of sexual harassment and is greater with regard to "ambiguous" behaviors. Whether this degree of difference warrants the reasonable woman standard is another question. It shall be taken up in chapter 6.

Empirical Research and Three Perspectives
on Sexual Harassment

We might think that we could use empirical data to determine which of the three perspectives—natural/biological, sociocultural, or liberal—is most likely to provide the best explanation of sexual harassment. However, this proves to be more difficult than it seems at first sight.

The difficulty in treating perspectives on sexual harassment as competing empirical theories is illustrated in the paper by Tangri, Burt, and Johnson mentioned in chapter 1.[173] Tangri, Burt, and Johnson described three explanatory models derived from the literature on sexual harassment and offered empirical tests of each of the models. They called the models the "the natural/biological model," "the organizational model," and "the sociocultural model." The basic assumptions of each model were described, and empirical predictions were derived from these assumptions. Then, these predictions were tested against the results of the 1980 U.S. Merit Systems Protection Board survey.[174] The authors hoped that the empirical data would support one of the models more than the others.

Tangri, Burt, and Johnson's natural/biological model corresponds roughly to what I have termed the natural/biological perspective on sexual harassment, their sociocultural model to my sociocultural perspective, and the organizational model to my liberal perspective. Thus, we might hope that their study could help us use the empirical data available to decide between these perspectives. Unfortunately, this is not so. Some of the problems have to do with the ways in which Tangri, Burt, and Johnson characterize the three models. But some of the problems have to do with the complex relationship between such models or perspectives and empirical data.

First, the predictions Tangri, Burt, and Johnson derive from their models do not seem to be predictions that proponents of the various perspectives need accept.[175] For example, according to Tangri, Burt, and Johnson, the natural/biological model assumes that "men and women are naturally attracted to each other, . . . both sexes participate in sexually oriented behavior in the workplace, and . . . they like it that way. . . ."[176] From this assumption, the researchers derive the following prediction about likely victims of sexual harassment: "Expected victims should be women or both sexes, and should be similar to their harasser in age, race, and occupational status. If they are truly objects of romantic interest, they should also be unmarried or otherwise 'eligible' as continuing partners, and the only person to whom the harasser directs his attention."[177] To derive this prediction, they also assume that, "[i]f sexual harassment is simply normal mutual sexual attraction, we would expect it to follow well-established patterns for liking and romantic attraction. . . . Male-female pairs should be similar in age, race, and other background characteristics, attitudes and statuses. Further, if asked, both should express interest in and attraction to each other, and no one should want to file a complaint."[178] However, it is unclear why we should make these assumptions, and how they follow from the vague assumption attributed to the natural/biological model. From the assumption that at least some of what is called "sexual harassment" is due to natural attraction between men and women, it does not follow that sexual harassment is "normal mutual sexual attraction." The assumption of mutuality is the problem. If evolutionary psychologists such as Kingsley R. Browne are right, then "natural' attraction between males and females may lead to unwelcome sexual advances, that is, to sexual harassment. The first problem with Tangri, Burt, and Johnson's study, then, is that the different explanatory models are not accurately characterized. This leads to predictions that proponents of these theories need not accept. Thus, if the empirical data do not bear out the predictions, proponents of the natural/biological perspective need not give up their theory.

Another problem arises when the predictions are tested against the data provided by the Merit survey. Tangri, Burt, and Johnson try to differentiate the models sufficiently so that mutually exclusive predictions can be derived from them and tested against the data provided by the Merit survey. While this would not necessarily show that one model was generally correct, as they say, "The evidence we report in this [essay] can, at best, negate some premises of these models and support others, rather than 'proving' that one or another model is the correct view of the world."[179] But it does not do even that. Let us take from the three models what are supposed to be conflicting predictions concerning expected victims. According to Tangri, Burt, and Johnson, the natural/biological model would predict that victims should be women or both sexes, should be similar to harassers in age, race, and occupational status, and should be unmarried or otherwise eligible, and that harassers should target only one person. What they find is that "[n]either the findings on sex of victim nor multiplicity of victims per harasser unequivocally support Model One's interpretation of sexual harassment. However, the relationship to marital status certainly does."[180] This is so, apparently, because the biological/natural model predicts that both men and women will be harassed and that harassers should harass only one person. However, as we saw earlier, neither of these predictions seems to follow from the natural/biological perspective as Browne describes it. In fact, the Browne/Buss natural/biological perspective described in chapter 1 predicts *just what the sociocultural model predicts*: that women should more often be victims, and men who harass should harass any number of women. The survey results support this:

> Men and women are not equally likely to experience sexual harassment. . . . The "normal sexual attraction" version of Model One would suggest attention focused on only one person at a time, rather than indiscriminately spread over whoever is an easy target. Yet only a small minority . . . report that they are unique in suffering the attentions of their harasser. . . .
> Single and divorced women are more likely to be victims than married women. The same pattern holds for men even more strongly.[181]

These findings would seem perfectly consistent with the natural/biological perspective as interpreted by Browne and Buss. More women than men would be victims, since it is men who are seeking partners, and who interpret friend-liness as sexual interest. Some men would harass many women, since they are looking for partners, and not necessarily long-term partners. That single and divorced women would be more likely than married women to be ha-rassed (i.e., to experience unwanted sexual interest) is predicted, since these women would be more likely to be looking for partners (long- or short-term). In fact, Buss claims that "[t]he view that sexual harassment is a product of the evolved sexual strategies of men and women is supported by the profiles of typical victims, including such features as their sex, age, marital status, and physical attractiveness; their reactions to unwanted sexual advances; and the conditions under which they were harassed."[182] He provides evi-dence that "women are generally the victims of sexual harassment and men are the perpetrators";[183] that "victims are disproportionately young, physi-cally attractive, and single"; that "[s]ingle and divorced women are subjected to more sexual harassment than married women"; that women react more negatively to sexual harassment than men; and that the nature of women's reactions to sexual harassment depends on the status of the harasser and the perceived motivation of the harasser.[184]

So, these findings "support" the natural/biological view, in the sense that they are predicted by that view and explainable in its terms. However, these findings also support the sociocultural view. That is, the data do not support one view over the other, because each one can, within its model or perspec-tive, explain the data so that they are consistent with its theory.

According to Tangri, Burt, and Johnson, the organizational model pre-dicts that "[t]he most likely victims are those low in organization power: trainees; temporary or part-time workers; those in low grade or income lev-els; workers on probation, or newcomers such as token women or men, and low status workers who are highly dependent on their job."[185] There is some support for this model in the Merit survey results. Younger workers are more likely to be harassed than older workers, and dependence on a job increases the likelihood of harassment. However, people with more education report more harassment, and income seems not to make a difference in the amount of harassment experienced. This model seems to be least well supported by the data because it focuses on organizational or institutional power rather than on gender as well as power. But this does not help us to distinguish the liberal view from the natural/biological and the sociocultural perspectives, because the liberal view is often formulated in such a way that more women are predicted to be victims of harassment than men.

All three of the perspectives cite empirical data beyond the Merit study in support of their positions. However, the additional empirical evidence does not seem to provide a way of deciding between the perspectives. Many of the studies are methodologically flawed, as we have seen. Yet, even when the data are cleared of prior interpretation as much as is possible, the very same data can be used to support two different perspectives, by being interpreted in two different ways.

Even studies that seem to disconfirm a perspective by showing that pre-dictions based on the perspective do not hold do not necessarily require the elimination of the perspective. One can simply critique the study or offer an alternative explanation of the data. For example, Browne argues that the natural/biological perspective supports the view that a reasonable person standard is meaningless: "At least when it comes to matters of sex and sexuality, there are no 'reasonable persons,' only 'reasonable men' and 'reasonable women.'"[186] He then explores the question whether it makes a difference whether judges adopt a reasonable woman standard or a reasonable person standard:

> Supporting the view that the standard is not important is a recent laboratory study that attempted to measure the effects of selecting between the reasonable person and the reasonable woman standard. Male and female subjects were presented with scenarios drawn from real harassment cases and asked to evaluate them using different standards. Consistent with most other studies, female subjects were more likely to view the scenarios as harassment than the males were. However, the judgments of neither males nor females were affected by whether they were applying a reasonable person or a reasonable woman standard.[187]

This would seem to call into question Browne's claim that there is a difference between the reasonable woman and the reasonable man. However, Browne does not give up his claim. Rather, he considers a number of other possible explanations for this result, some of which were suggested by the researchers themselves:

> [T]he laboratory setting of the research and the use of undergraduate students as subjects could have affected the results. . . .
> . . . men lacked sufficient information concerning 'the reasonable woman's' perceptions about harassment and therefore relied upon their own attitudes.[188]

Browne adds his own suggestion: "[M]en and women were already incorporating their judgments about the perceptions of women into their decision-making. Men may not appreciate the precise feelings and responses experienced by women, but they certainly understand that some things that might appropriately be said or done in front of other men should not be said or done in front of women."[189]

So, the question is, Will empirical data help to decide between the differing views of sexual harassment? From my point of view, the answer is no. All of the perspectives predict that, given current distributions of men and women in positions of power, more men than women will harass. All of them predict that women will be more frequently harassed than men. Thus, all of them are consistent with the most basic findings of such surveys as the Merit survey. If these predictions were not borne out, all would have to go back to the drawing board. But even then, they could probably come up with explanations that would save their theories.

If we cannot point to empirical data to decide between the various perspectives, what can we do? Another way of deciding between these perspectives would be to choose the one that explains the broadest range of the phenomena that have been called "sexually harassing." This would be an application of the general principle that the more phenomena covered by an explanation, the stronger the explanation.[190] It might be thought that to be adequate as explanations of sexual harassment, these perspectives should be able to provide unifying explanations of the various phenomena that have been classified as sexual harassment. Nevertheless, this does not seem to be necessary. Each perspective selectively explains a certain subset of the behaviors that have been classified as sexual harassment, while denying that other behaviors that superficially resemble behaviors in this subset are in fact sexual harassment. Alternatively, they claim that different kinds of behaviors require different kinds of explanations. Drucilla Cornell and Ellen Frankel Paul, both liberals, think that quid pro quo and hostile environment sexual harassment are dissimilar enough to require different explanations. Browne excludes gender harassment from the category of sexual harassment because it is not based on "sexual animus."[191] MacKinnon does not think that harassment of males is the same as harassment of females. All of the perspectives place heterosexual harassment at the center of their analyses, and none of them provides a satisfactory account of the relationship between race and sexual harassment.[192]

We find ourselves in this predicament because the three perspectives on sexual harassment with which we are dealing are related to empirical data in complex ways. Of the three, only the natural/biological perspective bills itself as a scientific theory. The other two are social and political theories. However, all three seek to provide explanations of human behavior. Theories of human behavior always involve values. At least part of the reason that sexual harassment remains so controversial is that people have very different values.

"What we regard as right and wrong greatly influences our assessment of any explanatory theory involved in the interpretation and explanation of human behaviour. . . . Our values provide us with at least some of the criteria for accepting (and for rejecting) explanatory theories."[193] Although values may influence our choice of explanation in any field, explanations involving human behavior are particularly problematic.[194]

[T]he principal reason for disagreement . . . is that explanations of human behaviour almost always involve implicit (and sometimes explicit) value judgments. If some people think that certain kinds of behaviour are immoral they will object to explanations that do not carry condemnation of that behaviour; if they think that certain individuals are morally weak they will reject explanations that do not depend on appeal to that weakness; if they think that an explanation ignores (and *a fortiori* undermines) their values and perhaps, less nobly, their interests, they will find it hard to accept and will seek alternative explanations. Hence the diverse explanations offered for a large number of social and personal events: the outbreak of wars, inflation, road accidents, alcoholism and so on. Nevertheless we do not abandon our search for explanations in human affairs and the hope that there can be some measure of agreement.[195]

Recognition of the relationship between empirical data and perspectives on sexual harassment will not, I think, prevent people from trying to prove or disprove the viability of these perspectives using empirical data. However, we should recognize that we incorporate the perspectives into our understanding of the data, so that most data can be interpreted in such a way that they are consistent with that perspective. If it is not consistent, then the research that gave rise to the data can always be called into question. We have seen that gathering data on sexual harassment is a precarious business.

If we cannot decide between perspectives by using empirical data, then we will have to face the fact that people disagree about sexual harassment—what it is, how prevalent it is, how serious it is, and what we should do about it—at least in part because of deeply held, not entirely empirical beliefs. These include beliefs about women and men and about values. If we cannot be brought to agreement by "facts," then we must reach some other sort of agreement. We must seek a compromise that is morally acceptable to everyone. But, of course, this is true of many political matters.

Part II

Theoretical Issues

5

PHILOSOPHICAL CONCEPTIONS
OF SEXUAL HARASSMENT

> The philosophical analysis of a concept, while by no means
> indifferent to ordinary usage . . . is concerned to give a *rational*
> *account* of such usage. It is concerned, for example, to answer the
> question: What is there about all cases of [sexual harassment]
> that makes us group them under one concept and thus use the
> same word?

In addition to the legal and social scientific conceptions of sexual harassment that have been developed, philosophical conceptions of sexual harassment have been proposed.[1] These conceptions seek to go beyond the constraints imposed by the particular concerns and categories of the law and of empirical research, though they may be made use of in either of these contexts. In particular, philosophical conceptions of sexual harassment typically seek to articulate what it is about sexual harassment that makes those actions that fall under its purview *morally* wrong.[2] Philosophical definitions of sexual harassment commonly claim that sexually harassing conduct is in some way harmful to someone. From a liberal perspective, that a form of behavior harms specific individuals is a reason for regulating that behavior.[3] Since we live in a liberal state, specification of this harm is important in justifying laws that govern sexual harassment. So, the question is, What kind of harm, if any, is caused by sexual harassment, such that we should prevent it by means of the law? Philosophical conceptions of sexual harassment seek to answer this question.

I have selected several theoretical definitions of sexual harassment for analysis. They represent different perspectives on sexual harassment that are circulating in society. I shall explain and evaluate each of them. I will make clear that these definitions are not politically neutral, so that accepting a definition entails accepting a broad theoretical perspective. I shall also argue that each of the definitions is either too narrow, or too broad, or both.[4] In addition, each definition seems to focus on one kind of behavior identified in the law and/or in empirical research as "sexual harassment," and to make the definition adequate to that sort of behavior. This leaves unexplained other sorts of behavior, or at least requires a reconceptualization of this other behavior to allow it to fit the definition. All the definitions seem to assume that sexual harassment should be illegal, though they disagree about the kind of law that should be applied or how it should be applied. Finally, I shall consider the arguments of two philosophers who for different reasons maintain that the concept of sexual harassment is deeply flawed.

The Dominance Perspective

MacKinnon's Conception

Any discussion of conceptions of sexual harassment must begin with Catharine MacKinnon's as it appeared in her 1979 *Sexual Harassment of Working Women*. Her analysis of sexual harassment has been the most influential, whether supported or criticized. MacKinnon defines sexual harassment in such a way that the *harm* of sexual harassment is that it wrongfully discriminates against women. Given this, sexual harassment constitutes sex discrimination under Title VII. Thus, her initial definition was: "Sexual harassment, most broadly defined, refers to the unwanted imposition of sexual requirements in the context of a relationship of unequal power."[5] This very general conception was applied specifically to the workplace. MacKinnon's understanding of sexual harassment incorporated two kinds of inequality and two kinds of oppression: gender and economic.

> Central to the concept is the use of power derived from one social sphere to lever benefits or impose deprivations in another. The major dynamic is best expressed as the reciprocal enforcement of two inequalities. When one is sexual, the other material, the cumulative sanction is particularly potent. American society legitimizes male sexual dominance of women and employer's control of workers, although both forms of dominance have limits and exceptions. Sexual harassment of women in employment is particularly clear when male superiors on the job coercively initiate unwanted sexual advances to women employees; sexual pressures by male co-workers and customers, when condoned or encouraged by employers, might also be included. . . . The material coercion behind the advances may remain implicit in the employer's position to apply it. Or it may be explicitly communicated through, for example, firing for sexual noncompliance or retention conditioned upon continued sexual compliance.[6]

Thus, sexual harassment is most fundamentally a misuse of power. One kind of sexual harassment, the kind that is emphasized in this book, comes at the intersection of two forms of social inequality: male/female and employer/

employee. In the context of employment, "[s]exual harassment at work critically undercuts women's potential for work equality as a means to social equality."[7] This is MacKinnon's response to the question, What kind of harm, if any, is caused by sexual harassment, such that we should prevent it by means of the law. In her view, sexual harassment is caused by the social inequality of women and men, and in turn contributes to that inequality: "[T]he specific injury of sexual harassment arises from the nexus between a sexual demand and the workplace . . . the situations can be seen to include a sexual incident or advance, some form of compliance or rejection, and some employment consequence."[8]

According to MacKinnon, there are two ways of arguing that sexual harassment constitutes sex discrimination, the differences approach and the inequality or, as I have termed it in chapter 1, the dominance approach.

The [differences] approach envisions the sexes as socially as well as biologically *different* from one another, but calls impermissible or "arbitrary" those distinctions or classifications that are found preconceived and/or inaccurate. The [inequality] approach understands the sexes to be not simply socially differentiated but socially *unequal*. In this broader view, all practices which subordinate women to men are prohibited. The differences approach, in its sensitivity to disparity and similarity, can be a useful corrective to sexism; both women and men can be damaged by sexism, although usually it is women who are. The inequality approach, by contrast, sees women's situation as a structural problem of enforced inferiority that needs to be radically altered.[9]

As we have seen, MacKinnon prefers the inequality, or dominance, approach. According to this approach, sexual harassment has a different meaning for women than it does for men. What is perhaps most striking about MacKinnon's conception of sexual harassment is that, given her description of traditional sexual relations between women and men as the sexual dominance of women by men, and given the social realities of the workplace, where workers are dominated by employers, sexual harassment is to be expected. That is, her analysis of inequalities between the sexes and in the workplace *predicts* that sexual harassment will be prevalent. It is not an aberration. Sexual harassment is the manifestation of male sexual dominance over females in the workplace. One commentator describes MacKinnon's view this way:

Sexual harassment . . . is the imposition of a subordinate sex upon women that we know as womanhood itself. Sexual harassment is not then arbitrarily imposed upon women, it is part of their very subordinate identity under the gender hierarchy that characterizes the relationship of heterosexuality. Thus, MacKinnon argues that we should analyze sexual harassment under a theory of inequality that would recognize women's systematic subordination through the imposition upon them of their identity as "fuckees." Her analysis of why sexual harassment is gender discrimination turns on her explanation of why women *cannot* be similarly situated to men for purposes of understanding sexual harassment. Her conclusion is that sexual harassment is at the very heart of the systematic subordination of women.[10]

There are several reasons to favor MacKinnon's definition. One is that it conceptualizes sexual harassment in such a way that its apparent prevalence and intractability are explained. Sexual harassment is what we should expect, since it characterizes heterosexual relationships. Furthermore, MacKinnon's account provides an explanation for why sexual harassment should be conceived of as a form of sex discrimination. Sexual harassment can happen only to women, in her view. What happens to men may look like sexual harassment, but because of the gender hierarchy that puts all men above all women, sexual harassment does not have the same meaning for men it has for women.[11] In her view, sexual harassment places conditions on women's work and educational lives that men do not share. Thus, sexual harassment of women is sex discrimination. Conceiving of sexual harassment as sex discrimination provides a way of seeing all the sorts of sexual harassment as variations of the same fundamental behavior. Sexual taunting and quid pro quo sexual harassment are on a continuum. They are not different kinds of conduct.

Some critics have suggested that MacKinnon's definition be rejected because it is not politic—that is, it is better politically to propound a definition of sexual harassment that does not incorporate controversial assumptions because one is more likely to garner support for the view that sexual harassment is an offense that should be addressed legally. Ellen Frankel Paul contends:

> Incorporating abuse of power into the definition . . . seems unduly limiting. While it mirrors accurately what transpires in the classic quid pro quo situation, it reflects only uneasily hostile environment sexual harassment by co-workers—unless one accepts the added, debatable, and more global assumption that males occupying any position in the workplace enjoy more power than women. If one favored such a claim, arguing for it directly, rather than importing it into the very definition of sexual harassment (thus begging the question and, perhaps, alienating those who might be sympathetic to the complaint but not the assumption), seems desirable.[12]

From a legal and political point of view, Paul's point may be correct—though this criticism of MacKinnon's definition precedes Paul's own ideologically informed argument that sexual harassment is not sex discrimination and is better conceived legally as a harm inflicted by one individual on another (see chapter 6). However, from a philosophical point of view, such a comment is not to the point. How one conceives of sexual harassment, particularly, how one conceives of the *harm* of sexual harassment, will determine the kinds of behaviors one includes as sexual harassment and the kinds of remedies one believes are just, as well as the kinds of changes, both social and political, one thinks required for the eradication of sexual harassment. One must argue directly against MacKinnon's definition if one does not think that it adequately describes the harm of sexual harassment, the kinds of behaviors that should be categorized as sexual harassment, and the changes necessary to eradicate sexual harassment.

Though there are reasons to favor MacKinnon's definition, there are stronger reasons against it. The strongest reasons against MacKinnon's definition are: (1) it rests on problematic assumptions, (2) it is too broad, and (3) it is too narrow.

One implication of MacKinnon's conception of sexual harassment may not be immediately evident. It is that, in this society, *all heterosexual sexual relationships involve sexual harassment.* To see this, one need only go back to the broad definition of sexual harassment as "the unwanted imposition of sexual requirements in the context of a relationship of unequal power." This definition contains no mention of the kind of "unequal power" involved. It can apply to any situation in which sexual requirements are imposed by the powerful on the powerless. According to MacKinnon, in our society, men have sexual dominance over women. Because of this, women are routinely unable freely to consent to sexual relationships with men.[13] MacKinnon usually limits her discussion to economic relationships. But these can include informal arrangements, such as traditional marriages, where economic inequality and sexual inequality are both present. Most fundamentally, however, sexual inequality, the sexual dominance of women by men, combined with the assumption that true consent is not possible in the context of inequality, implies that all heterosexual sexual relationships are sexually harassing.

For some, this implication of MacKinnon's conception of sexual harassment is so clearly false that it reduces the definition to absurdity. However, some sort of argument is required if one wants to avoid begging the question.

The argument can be made that MacKinnon's theoretical equations are just that—equations—and that this makes them absolute and, thus, easily falsifiable. The claim that men have power over women is at the heart of MacKinnon's view. On one interpretation of this claim, every man has power over every woman. This is true by definition, since "woman" and "man" are defined, culturally, in terms of subordination and domination. But when we think about the world, it is evident that not every man has power over every woman. Race, class, ethnicity, nationality, and sexual orientation are just a few of the factors that confound this simple—too simple—equation. There are many vectors of power among peoples of the world. Women of color have been making this argument for years.[14] Some kinds of power may trump others. Some power that a woman has can trump the power a man has by virtue of being a man. And some men do not seem to possess "masculine" power to any degree. Consider men who are thought to be insufficiently masculine. Their "gender harassment" usually begins in grade school and may never cease. In general, MacKinnon's analysis of "power" is underdeveloped. Usually, she equates power and domination: if one person has more power than another, then the first dominates the other. However, people who have examined power describe many uses of power, not all of which are inherently oppressive. Consider the power a parent has over a child, or a teacher over a student. Such power is necessary to enable the child or student to develop.[15]

MacKinnon's binary focus—man/woman, powerful/powerless—is rhetorically effective, but too simple to allow articulations of the complex power relations between human beings in society. Approaches to gender such as those of Franke (see chapters 3 and 6) and Cornell (see the discussion that follows) seem better able to explain the complex relationships between power and gender.[16] They emphasize that gender is not dichotomous and that men as well as women experience dominant conceptions of "masculinity" and "femininity" as coercive.

MacKinnon's definition is both too broad and too narrow. It is too broad because, as we have seen, every heterosexual sexual relationship turns out to constitute sexual harassment. Her description of sexual harassment as "[s]exual pressure imposed on someone who is not in an economic position to refuse it" illustrates this view.[17] Women, in general, are economically subject to men because of their sexual subordination to men, so any sexual initiation on the part of a man toward a woman becomes sexual harassment. However, many women—and men—would deny that this is their experience. They are quite able to distinguish coercive sexual encounters from noncoercive ones. They do not believe that every heterosexual sexual relationship is oppressive, though they believe that some are. MacKinnon can simply claim that such people are victims of false consciousness. However, her grounds for saying this seem to be definitional, and I have already provided reasons for thinking that the absolute claim from which her view follows is problematic. Thus, she must show that individual sexual relationships between women and men are coercive, contrary to their belief, without appeal to the general claim that all such relationships are coercive.

One can also criticize MacKinnon's definition because it is too narrow. Though MacKinnon's definition covers all unwanted sexual behavior addressed to women, it does not provide an analysis of what looks to be similar behavior addressed to men—especially by other men. Sexual bullying and ridicule of the sort discussed by Abrams and Franke seem similar enough to the behaviors experienced by women to suggest a uniform account. MacKinnon seems to have to resort to ad hoc explanations for such conduct. The experiences of gay rights activist Ron Woods at Chrysler should fit the category of sexual harassment—or at least, some closely related category.[18]

Thus, MacKinnon's definition of sexual harassment is problematic for a number of reasons. It rests on problematic assumptions, and it is both too broad and too narrow. One might argue that it cannot be either too broad or too narrow since there really is no standard conception of sexual harassment understood by many with which to compare it. This is a good point, and one that I will bring up again in my discussion of Mane Hajdin's claim that sexual harassment is not a morally significant concept. However, if we are in the process of creating the conception of sexual harassment, we should take into account these consequences of MacKinnon's definition: (1) it categorizes all heterosexual relations as similarly oppressive; (2) it does not allow a similar analysis of the oppressiveness of apparently similar kinds of behavior directed toward women and men. Those who wish to distinguish between morally acceptable heterosexual relationships and morally unacceptable ones should not accept MacKinnon's definition of sexual harassment. Nor should people who believe that dominant conceptions of gender are oppressive to women and men.

MacKinnon's definition of sexual harassment has been extremely influential. Its most salient characteristic is that is conceives of sexual harassment as a social problem rather than as a problem between individuals. That is, sexual harassment is harmful to individual women, and to women in general, because it perpetuates women's social inequality. A more recent conception of sexual harassment, also taking the dominance approach, seeks to articulate and strengthen MacKinnon's conception.

Superson: A Feminist Conception

Anita Superson agrees with MacKinnon that the harm of sexual harassment should be understood primarily as social rather than individual harm.[19] She considers current legal conceptions of sexual harassment to be inadequate and the continued pervasiveness of sexual harassment to be evidence of their inadequacy. Superson argues that sexual harassment, as it is currently defined in the law,

> does not adequately reflect the social nature of [sexual harassment], or the harm it causes all women. As a result, [sexual harassment] comes to be defined in subjective ways. One upshot is that when subjective definitions infuse the case law on [sexual harassment], the more subtle but equally harmful forms of [sexual harassment] do not get counted as [sexual harassment] and thus not afforded legal protection.[20]

To remedy this, Superson proposes a definition of sexual harassment that emphasizes the "group harm" that she alleges results from all forms of sexual harassment. She defines sexual harassment as "any behavior (verbal or physical) caused by a person, A, in the dominant class directed at another, B, in the subjugated class, that expresses and perpetuates the attitude that B or members of B's sex is/are inferior because of their sex, thereby causing harm to either B and/or members of B's sex."[21] Thus, according to Superson, each act of sexual harassment constitutes a group harm, a harm to *all women*. Superson draws an analogy between her conception of sexual harassment and the way racial discrimination is sometimes conceived. Racist ideas expressed in racist speech have been prohibited by a number of national and international charters and declarations on the grounds that dissemination of racist ideas, because of the message of inferiority they carry, harms people. She cites Mari Matsuda's claim that the idea underlying these views is that racist speech "interferes with the rights of subordinated-group members to participate equally in society, maintaining their basic sense of security and worth as human beings."[22] Superson contends that sexual harassment has the same effect on women.

Superson, like MacKinnon, holds that power is at the heart of sexual harassment. Like MacKinnon, she conceives of the oppression of sexual harassment not as one individual having power over another, but in terms of men's power over women. She expresses this in the claim that "[w]hen A sexually harasses B, the comment or behavior is really directed at the group of all women, not just a particular woman. . . ."[23] A particular woman is the target of the behavior simply because she happens to be available. But the "message" of the harassment is for all women. Superson cites examples of such harassment: catcalls on the street, professors who call their female students "chicks," and medical instructors who use *Playboy* pinups in their lectures. Superson concludes: "These and other examples make it clear that [sexual harassment] is not about dislike for a certain person; instead it expresses a person's beliefs about women as a group on the basis of their sex, namely, that they are primarily emotional and bodily beings."[24]

Because "all women" are the target of sexually harassing behavior, "all women" are harmed by such behavior.

> Indeed, when any one woman is in any way sexually harassed, all women are harmed. The group harm [sexual harassment] causes is different from the harm suffered by particular women as individuals: it is often more vague in nature as it is not easily causally tied to any particular incident of harassment. The group harm has to do primarily with the fact that the behavior reflects and reinforces sexist attitudes that women are inferior to men and that they do and ought to occupy certain sex roles.[25]

According to Superson, there are several kinds of harm done to women as a group by sexually harassing behaviors. First, sexual harassment takes away women's autonomy. Harassment determines which roles are appropriate for women and imposes these roles on them. Second, "[t]he belief that [women] are sex objects, caretakers, etc., gets reflected in social and political practices in ways that are unfair to women."[26] Furthermore, "the particular form of stereotyping promotes two myths: (1) that male behavior is normally and naturally predatory, and (2) that females naturally (because they are taken to be primarily bodily and emotional) and even willingly acquiesce despite the appearance of protest."[27] These myths prevent sexually harassing behaviors from being seen as sexist. The first excuses sexually harassing behaviors as simply the expression of "natural" male sexuality. Superson's myth is Browne's and other biologists' truth. Superson claims that "[sexual harassment] has nothing to do with men's sexual desires, nor is it about seduction; instead, it is about oppression of women. Indeed, harassment generally does not lead to sexual satisfaction, but it often gives the harasser a sense of power."[28]

Like MacKinnon, Superson takes it to be a consequence of her conception of sexual harassment that "it is only men who can sexually harass women."

> When a woman engages in the very same behavior harassing men engage in, the underlying message implicit in male-to-female harassment is missing. For example, when a woman scans a man's body, she might be considering him to be a sex object, but all the views about domina-

tion and being relegated to certain sex roles are absent. She cannot remind the man that he is inferior because of his sex, since given the way things are in society, he is not. In general, women cannot harm or degrade men *as a group*, for it is impossible to send the message that one dominates (and so cause group harm) if one does not dominate . . . any bothersome behavior a woman engages in, even though it may be of a sexual nature, does not constitute [sexual harassment] because it lacks the social impact present in male-to-female harassment.[29]

This is simply an implication of her definition of sexual harassment plus the claim that in our society, men as a group dominate women as a group, regardless of individual power relations.

Superson claims that her conception of sexual harassment avoids the problem of subjectivity that plagues current legal conceptions of sexual harassment. According to the EEOC *Guidelines*, sexual harassment is "unwelcome." Thus, to make a claim of sexual harassment, a woman must prove that the behavior to which she objects is "unwelcome." "The criterion of unwelcomeness or annoyance present in these subjective accounts of harassment puts the burden on the victim to establish that she was sexually harassed."[30] The question becomes whether the woman was bothered by the behavior. Superson thinks it is a mistake to make the victim's reaction determinative of whether sexual harassment has taken place. This makes sexual harassment "subjective." Superson's conception makes sexual harassment objective: "what is decisive in determining whether behavior constitutes [sexual harassment] is not whether the victim is bothered, but whether the behavior is an instance of a practice that expresses and perpetuates the attitude that the victim and members of her sex are inferior because of their sex."[31]

Superson points to a number of significant implications of her definition. First, "it reflects the correct way power comes into play in [sexual harassment]."[32] According to Superson's definition, "[t]he one sense in which it is true that the harasser must have power over his victim is that men have power—social, political, and economic—over women as a group." "Defining [sexual harassment] in the objective way I do allows us to see that *this* is the sense in which power exists in [sexual harassment], in *all* its forms."[33] She claims that her conception corrects a deficiency in MacKinnon's conception: it does not rely on the assumption that every man has power over every woman. Rather, it relies on the assumption that the class of men dominates the class of women.

Another implication of Superson's definition is that "it gives the courts a way of distinguishing [sexual harassment] from sexual attraction." She explains:

It can be difficult to make this distinction, since "traditional courtship activities" are often quite sexist and frequently involve behavior that is harassment. The key is to examine the practice the behavior is an instance of. If the behavior reflects the attitude that the victim is inferior because of her sex, then it is [sexual harassment]. Sexual harassment is not about a man's attempting to date a woman who is not interested, as the courts have tended to believe; it is about domination, which might be reflected, of course, in the way a man goes about trying to get a date. My definition allows us to separate cases of [sexual harassment] from genuine sexual attraction by forcing the courts to focus on the social nature of [sexual harassment].[34]

Superson claims that her definition "shifts the burden and the blame off the victim."[35] The victim no longer has to prove that she was bothered by the behavior, or that she did not provoke it. And finally,

defining [sexual harassment] in a subjective way means that the victim herself must come forward and complain. . . . Recognizing [sexual harassment] as a group harm will allow women to come to each other's aid as co-complainers, thereby alleviating the problem of reticence. Even if the person the behavior is directed at does not feel bothered, other women can complain, as they suffer the group harm associated with [sexual harassment].[36]

Superson's definition suffers from many of the same deficiencies as Mac-Kinnon's, with some additional ones: (1) it depends on some disputable facts, (2) it is too broad, and (3) it is too narrow.

Superson claims that "all women" are the targets of each instance of sexually harassing conduct, and that sexual harassment "is not about dislike for a certain person." However, this is questionable. At least some of the time, dislike of a particular person does appear to be the primary motivation for sexually harassing behavior of the sort commonly called "gender harassment," and the use of sexist means for expressing that dislike secondary. These are the sorts of cases forming the group of examples that those who hold the natural/biological perspective consider "nondiscriminatory." In such cases, a person is disliked, and the harasser or harassers choose what they know will be the most distressing means of humiliating the person. In these cases, the target of the insult is not all women, but one particular woman.

Because of the importance of status and dominance in male hierarchies, men are very attentive to signs of weakness in others and correspondingly reluctant to reveal weakness and vulnerability in themselves. Where they see weakness, they may attack. People sensitive to sexually oriented attacks—women and particuarly sensitive men— are likely to be attacked in that way. Potential victims with other sensitivities are likely to be attacked in other ways. This may be vicious and sadistic, but it is not necessarily discrimination.[37]

Now, the natural/biological perspective tends to ignore the reasons that "women and particularly sensitive men" are sensitive to "sexually oriented attacks." However, their way of describing this "weakness" suggests that it is not simply individual, hypersensitive women who are so vulnerable—that there is something social rather than individual that renders women as a group sensitive to such attacks. This would support Superson's claim that such harassment is at least in part drawing on the fact that women can be humiliated or insulted or harmed by such attacks. In this sense, then, it is true that what the harassers say when engaged in certain forms of sexual harassment "applies" to all women. But to say that the harasser is really "directing" the message at all women is simply false. The person may have no such intention, and surely intention is required to attribute "direction" to someone's actions. If Superson means that the message of inferiority is understood by other women and taken to apply to them as well, it is possible. However, she seems not to limit the impact of harassing behavior to those women who hear the remarks or witness the behavior. Also, some kinds of sexist harassment are very individualized and so are probably not taken to apply to all women by those who hear them—for example, sexist behavior that is also racist or based on ethnicity. Women's solidarity with women is not so well developed that women take everything that happens to one of them to happen to all of them— though perhaps they should. Superson may simply be saying that sexually harassing conduct, insofar as it is sexist conduct, perpetuates the sexism in society, thereby contributing to the view that women are inferior to men in certain ways, and so harming women in the ways that such inferiority does harm them. Her analogy between sexual harassment and racist speech, just described, suggests that this is her meaning. Some of her examples also support this interpretation: "a catcall says . . . that he thinks women are at least primarily sex objects and he—because of the power he holds by being in the dominant group—gets to rate them according to how much pleasure they give him. . . ."[38] However, she must demonstrate that all sexually harassing behavior "conveys a message," and this is difficult to do when we are talking about conduct rather than language. In other words, her claims best fit examples of sexually harassing conduct that consists of actual messages, either verbal or pictorial. But can the same be said for quid pro quo harassment?

Superson says that sexual harassment "has nothing to do with men's sexual desires, nor is it about seduction; instead, it is about oppression of women. Indeed, harassment generally does not lead to sexual satisfaction, but it often gives the harasser a sense of power." This is another doubtful claim. Quid pro quo harassment seems often to have something to do with men's desires, to be about seduction, and to lead to sexual satisfaction. Superson has not demonstrated that this appearance is illusory. But admitting that quid pro quo harassment is sometimes about men's sexual desires does not entail that one is committed to the two "myths" that Superson has described, that "male behavior is normally and naturally predatory," and that "females naturally . . . acquiesce." One may admit that some sexual harassment involves sexual desire without excusing quid pro quo harassment as natural and inevitable. One may hold that some men take advantage of their power in one realm to satisfy their desires in another, and that sometimes this is an abuse of power. The second myth suggests that women invite harassment. Superson simply denies this, claiming that "the perpetrator alone is at fault."[39] However, while it may be true that women do not invite sexually harassing behavior, they may invite sexual behavior. What is at issue is when the latter becomes the former. Superson's definition provides no way of determining this, rendering the definition too broad.

Superson recommends her definition on the grounds that it allows for the objective determination of when conduct constitutes sexual harassment and when it does not: "If the behavior reflects the attitude that the victim is inferior because of her sex, then it is [sexual harassment]." But how are we to determine whether behavior reflects the attitude that someone is inferior because of her sex? Superson herself claims that "'traditional courtship activities' are often quite sexist and frequently involve behavior that is harassment." The fact that many Americans continue to engage in such practices and to find nothing wrong with them suggests that there is going to be a great deal of disagreement about what kinds of conduct "reflect the attitude that the victim is inferior because of her sex." Given Superson's understanding of the criterion for determining whether conduct is sexually harassing or not, even if a woman is interested in a man and shows her interest in a relationship with him, if he behaves toward her in a sexist way, he is guilty of sexual harassment *in the sense in which it is illegal under sex discrimination law*. It may even be the case that any man who initiates a sexual relationship with a woman is guilty of sexual harassment since traditionally, men are the sexual initiators because they are dominant in sexual matters, so that the practice of male initiation of sexual relationships may convey the message that women are inferior because of their sex.

Superson's definition is too broad to be used as a legal definition for other reasons. Her definition makes *any* expression of sexist beliefs by men to women illegal. Any behavior that "expresses or perpetuates the attitude" will do. This definition seems to have moved away from quid pro quo cases and nearly to have identified sexual harassment with sexism. In lamenting the inadequacy of current legal definitions of sexual harassment, Superson describes examples of behaviors that are considered sexual harassment under her definition, but that are not currently illegal.

> Victims not protected include the worker who is harassed by a number of different people, the worker who suffers harassment but in small doses, the person who is subjected to a slew of catcalls on her two mile walk to work, the female professor who is subjected to leering from one of her male students, and the woman who does not complain out of fear. The number of cases is huge, and many of them are quite common.[40]

It is not clear that we should want the "victims" of such behaviors to be protected by the law. If we should, Superson has not provided the argument.

There are reasons for thinking that Superson's definition is too narrow. As I argued here, her claims about the social harm of sexual harassment best fits cases of "gender harassment" and catcalls. It is not clear that they fit quid pro quo sexual harassment. In addition, like MacKinnon's definition, Superson's limits sexual harassment to the harassment of women by men. Superson seems not to worry that women sometimes impose themselves on other women, and men on other men. An adequate definition of sexual harassment ought to allow the inclusion of such conduct.

Superson's definition is similar to MacKinnon's and suffers from some of the same deficiencies. It depends on some doubtful claims of fact. It is too broad because it includes behaviors that many reasonable people do not regard as sexual harassment or sex discrimination, or behaviors that should be illegal. It is too narrow because it does not seem to include all cases of quid pro quo harassment and seems to rule out the possibility of sexual harassment of men, or of women by other women.

I turn now to a selection of conceptions of sexual harassment that come from the liberal perspective. Because of the great variety of positions that are included under the liberal perspective, these conceptions differ from one another considerably.

The Liberal Perspective

Hughes and May

John Hughes and Larry May argue that sexual harassment is fundamentally a form of coercion.[41] Sexual harassment is morally wrong because coercion is morally wrong. Hughes and May also consider sexual harassment to be a form of sex discrimination. Allowing the practice of sexual harassment in the workplace discriminates against women: "the harm of harassment is felt beyond the individuals immediately involved because it contributes to a pervasive pattern of discrimination and exploitation based on sex."[42]

Though their analysis seems to support the currently accepted legal analysis of sexual harassment, it exhibits the very bifurcation evident in that analysis.[43] Sexual harassment involves two kinds of harm, at least when the victim is a woman: coercion and discrimination. This raises the question, How are the elements of coercion and discrimination related? In other words, how is the harm to the harassed individual (coercion) related to the harm to other individuals (discrimination)?

Hughes and May define sexual harassment as follows: "The term *sexual harassment* refers to the intimidation of persons in subordinate positions by those holding power and authority over them in order to exact sexual favors that would ordinarily not have been granted."[44] This seems very much like MacKinnon's definition. However, there are significant differences in their interpretation of the definition. These differences become evident when May and Hughes distinguish different kinds of sexual harassment:

(1) Sexual threat: "If you don't provide a sexual benefit, I will punish you by withholding a promotion or a raise that would otherwise be due, or ultimately fire you." (2) Sexual offer: "If you provide a sexual benefit, I will reward you with a promotion or a raise that would otherwise not be due." There are also sexual harassment situations that are merely annoying, but without demonstrable sanction or reward.[45]

May and Hughes's first and second categories seem to be limited to quid pro quo harassment. These are the only kinds of sexual harassment they acknowledge as wrong because they involve coercion. The third category, which they do not number, would seem to include hostile environment harassment, or gender harassment. Behavior in this category is wrong, if it is, because it is discriminatory, not because it is coercive. Thus, their interpretation of sexual harassment differs from MacKinnon's, for she does not treat the two kinds of harassment as different in kind. On their analysis, there is a difference of kind between quid pro quo and other forms of sexual harassment.

Sexual threats are coercive because "they worsen the objective condition the employee finds herself in."[46] A woman who has been sexually threatened by her supervisor is in a worse position than she was before the threat was made. Both her freedom to make choices about her social relationships and the conditions under which her work is evaluated are affected. If the woman gives in to the threat, she may still be coerced into remaining in the relationship, for fear of losing her employment.

Sexual offers are harmful because they change the working environment of the woman in such a way that she is no longer viewed in the same terms as her male co-workers.

> [A] sexual offer disadvantages the woman employee by changing the work environment so that she is viewed by others, and may come to view herself, less in terms of her work and more in terms of her sexual allure. This change, like the threat, makes it unlikely that she can return to the preproposition stage even though she might prefer to do so. Furthermore, to offset her diminished status and to protect against retaliation, a prudent woman would feel that she must accept the offer. Here, sexual offers resemble the coercive threat.[47]

Hughes and May claim that men are not as harmed by sexual offers as women are.

> Men are not similarly harmed by sexual offers because they do not have the same history of sexual exploitation. Men are likely to regard such seductive offers either humorously or as insults to be aggressively combatted, while women have been socialized to be passive rather than combative in such situations. The woman to whom the offer is made becomes less sure of her real abilities by virtue of the proposal itself.[48]

It is not clear whether Hughes and May think that men are not coerced at all by sexual offers, or that sexual offers are less coercive for men. However, in either case, this seems to need further argument. Recent cases of same-sex harassment suggest that many men are very vulnerable to sexual offers, especially young men or men who are relatively powerless because of some other characteristic.

Hughes and May argue that both kinds of sexual harassment, threats and offers, are also discriminatory to women, though not to men. They offer two reasons for this. Each reason analyzes the harm of sex discrimination differently. The first follows the court's argument in *Barnes v. Costle*:

> [Sexual] threats treat women differently than men in employment contexts even though gender is not a relevantly applicable category for making employment-related decisions. The underlying principle here is that like persons should be treated alike. Unless there are relevant differences among persons, it is harmful to disadvantage one particular class of persons. In the normal course of events, male employees are not threatened sexually by employers or supervisors. . . . When persons who are otherwise similarly situated are distinguished on the basis of their sex, and rewards or burdens are apportioned according to these gender-based classifications, illegal sex discrimination has occurred.[49]

This description of the discriminatory nature of sexual threats exhibits MacKinnon's differences approach. It is a straightforward application of the liberal principle of equality. Recall that, according to the liberal perspective, sexual harassment is not intrinsically connected to gender, as it is for proponents of the dominance approach. Women are more often harmed by sexual harassment, however, because of contingent gender disparities in our society.

The second reason that sexual harassment is discriminatory to women is found in the court's reasoning in *Tomkins v. Public Service Gas and Electric Co.*: "Sexual threats also contribute to a pervasive pattern of disadvantaged treatment of women as a group. Under this approach, the harm is not viewed as resulting from the arbitrary and unfair use of gender as a criterion for employment decisions. Rather, emphasis is on the effect the classification has of continuing the subordination of women as a group."[50] This interpretation is not precisely an application of the principle of equality because it is treating women as a group rather than as individuals. Hughes and May call this the "group disadvantage model" of classification: "Under this approach, the harm that results from classification is . . . viewed . . . in terms of whether the effect of the classification of persons is such as to stigmatize or to contribute to the continued subordination of a protected class relative to others in society."[51] This explanation of the discriminatory character of sexual harassment is very close to Superson's account of the harm of sexual harassment.

Hughes and May accept both ways of understanding the harm of discrimination. They acknowledge that there are certain difficulties with each but seem to think that, using both, the deficiencies of each can be lessened. Hughes and May argue that sexual threats such as those involved in the early quid pro quo sexual harassment cases constitute discrimination on the group disadvantage model because

> the burden was imposed on the female employee based on a sex stereotype held by the supervisor and implicitly endorsed by the company when it terminated the complaining employee. It is precisely because a sex stereotype did supply the impetus for the supervisor's classification

that his action injures women as a group, regardless of whether all members of that group are included within the classification. . . . When a company tolerates coercive behavior against one woman, it perpetuates the social convention that a woman's merits are to be measured in terms of her sexual attractiveness and compliance, not in terms of her skills or job performance. Women as a group are injured by the supervisor's conduct. . . . [52]

To summarize, Hughes and May consider sexual harassment to be, at its core, coercion. Sexual threats and, perhaps less obviously, sexual offers both involve coercion because they force a woman into a position less favorable than her position before the threat or offer, and this less favorable position is one she would not have chosen had she had the option. Sexual harassment of women is also discriminatory because it disadvantages women as a group. Men who are sexually threatened are victims of coercion, but not of discrimination. Men to whom sexual offers are made are not coerced as much as women are, and they are not discriminated against.

One benefit of Hughes and May's definition is that behavior directed at men can be counted as sexually harassing, and, unlike MacKinnon's or Superson's definition, the way in which sexual harassment for men is different from that for women is clearly articulated. However, it is not clear why men do not suffer discrimination as a group when one man is sexually threatened. If we think about vulnerable groups of men, it is less clear why such actions are not based on derogatory stereotypes as much as are actions directed toward women, stereotypes that harm men.

Hughes and May's group disadvantage model is articulated in terms of stereotypes. This model is similar to Superson's analysis and suffers from similar difficulties. Like Superson, Hughes and May argue that women as a group are harmed by each sexual threat or offer. Like Superson, they analogize such cases to a supervisor's "use of racial epithets": "Women as a group are injured by the supervisor's conduct, just as blacks as a group would be injured by the supervisor's use of racial epithets against a faction of his black employees."[53] Their argument that a sexual threat or offer disadvantages women as a group depends on the assumption that the supervisor held a derogatory stereotype about women and that the stereotype provided the impetus for the supervisor's classifying the woman threatened. What is that stereotype? The passage cited earlier suggests that the stereotype is that the worth of women in general, and so as employees, "is to be measured in terms of [their] sexual attractiveness and compliance, not in terms of [their] skills or job performance."[54] But how could we determine whether such a stereotype was operative? What does it mean to say that "a sex stereotype did supply the impetus for the supervisor's classification"? Perhaps the stereotype, if there was one, supplying the impetus for the supervisor's action was that employees over whom he has power can be fired at his whim. He fires a man because he perceives him to be a sexual rival. He fires a woman because she will not sleep with him. Why is the latter treated as discriminatory and the former not? The answer would be that the latter disadvantages women as a group, whereas the former does not disadvantage men as a group. However, the reason for this difference is not clear. Like Superson, Hughes and May pass over the possibility, suggested by adherents of the natural/biological perspective, that the motive for a supervisor's threats or offers is sexual desire.

It does seem that coercion is present in the sorts of cases Hughes and May discuss. We have seen this in many accounts of quid pro quo sexual harassment. However, their definition is too narrow, in two ways. First, they do not seem to consider hostile environment sexual harassment to be sexual harassment. This is not surprising, since when they first developed their definition, hostile environment sexual harassment was largely unrecognized. They refer to some sexually harassing behavior as "merely annoying," and by calling such behavior "sexually harassing," they seem to be implying that it is coercive. But they do not analyze the ways in which such behavior is coercive, and by describing it as "merely annoying," they seem to imply that it is not discriminatory, or not discriminatroy enough to warrant legal action. Of course, this is a position that someone might defend; but they do not do so. Secondly, their analysis seems to include only harassment perpetrated by supervisors, omitting co-worker harassment.[55] The reason for this seems to be that only supervisors, persons with the authority to confer or withhold employment-related benefits, have the power to coerce. Yet, co-worker harassment would certainly seem to fit their account of group disadvantage.

Some might argue that Hughes and May's definition of sexual harassment is too broad because it includes sexual offers. Their argument is that sexual offers are similar to sexual threats, but many view such offers—when made to women—as discriminatory toward men, because they treat women and men differently. Hughes and May do not discuss the question whether sexual offers made exclusively to women are discriminatory toward men. They would not see such offers as disadvantaging men as a group, but they might see them as discriminatory on the differences analysis of discrimination. There have been sex discrimination lawsuits brought against employers for "sexual favoritism."[56]

Furthermore, the double analysis of the harm of sexual harassment in terms of both coercion and group disadvantage for women is problematic. Coercion initially seems to be the defining harm of sexual harassment. But how does the coercion fit in the analysis of discrimination? It seems that it does not. That is, the behaviors in question would be discriminatory even if they were not coercive. If coercion is the primary harm of sexual harassment, then it is not clear that considering sexual harassment to be sex discrimination is the best way to address it. Perhaps a better way to say this is: Hughes and May actually provide two analyses of the harm in sexual harassment. Any given act may be coercion, group disadvantage for women, or both. This raises problems for treating all sexual harassment in the same way in the workplace—as sex discrimination. For example, on their analysis, men should not be treated in the same way as women since they suffer only coercion, and not discrimination in addition to it. However, the dominant interpretation of discrimination law is the differences approach, under which women and men must be treated in the same way. Such a two-pronged analysis is necessary for conceptions from a liberal perspective, if one wishes to claim that sexually harassing conduct is wrong and discriminatory.

Hughes and May, in their definition of sexual harassment as coercive, do seem to capture an important element of much sexually harassing behavior. This element is what makes such behavior, in some people's view, a form of extortion.[57] However, as Edmund Wall points out in his critique of this understanding of sexual harassment, discussed in the next section, it does not capture what many think is wrong about other sorts of sexually harassing behavior. Hughes and May focus on sexual threats and sexual offers, which turn out to be very like sexual threats. They categorize as "annoying" certain other forms of behavior that are considered to be sexually harassing. But they do not say how these other forms of behavior are coercive, or, if they are not, how they harm the victims.

Wall: Invasion of Privacy

Edmund Wall's analysis of sexual harassment seems to be the definition most consistent with a natural/biological perspective on sexual harassment, although it is also consistent with certain versions of the liberal perspective. His definition of sexual harassment places at the core an element which has been only implicit in the preceding definitions. In his view, "the mental states of the perpetrator and the victim are the essential defining elements."[58] Wall conceives of sexual harassment as a form of "wrongful communication": "Sexual harassment is described as a form of communication that violates a victim's privacy rights. This interpersonal definition purports to capture the more subtle instances of sexual harassment while circumventing those sexual advances that are not sexually harassing."[59] Thus, Wall wants his conception of sexual harassment to be narrow enough to allow a distinction between morally permissible and morally impermissible sexual advances by men toward women, and to be broad enough to encompass all sexually harassing behavior.

Wall argues that a definition of sexual harassment which takes into account the intentions of both parties to the behavior is adequate. He offers the following:

> Where X is the sexual harasser and Y the victim, the following conditions are offered as the definition of sexual harassment:
> (1) X does not attempt to obtain Y's consent to communicate to Y, X's or someone else's alleged sexual interest in Y.
> (2) X communicated to Y, X's or someone else's alleged sexual interest in Y. X's motive for communicating this is some perceived benefit that he or she expects to obtain through the communication.
> (3) Y does not consent to discuss with X, X's or someone else's alleged sexual interest in Y.
> (4) Y feels emotionally distressed because X did not attempt to obtain Y's consent to this discussion and/or because Y objects to what Y takes to be the offensive content of X's sexual comments.[60]

I take Wall to be providing both necessary and sufficient conditions for sexual harassment in his definition. That is, in order to count as an instance of sexual harassment, an action must meet all four conditions, and any action that meets all four conditions constitutes an instance of sexual harassment.

The first condition, says Wall, is crucial, since it is by not attempting to obtain Y's consent to "a certain type of communication" that X fails "to show respect for Y's rights."[61] "It is the obligation that stems from privacy rights that is ignored. Y's personal behavior and aspirations are protected by Y's privacy rights. The intrusion by X into this moral sphere is what is so objectionable about sexual harassment. If X does not attempt to obtain Y's approval to discuss such private matters, then he or she has not shown Y adequate respect."[62] However, fulfillment of the first condition alone is not sufficient to constitute sexual harassment, since in order to count as harassment, "X's conduct must constitute a rights violation."[63] The second condition supplies this, for "the second condition refers to the fact that X has acted without concern for Y's right to consent to the communication of sexual matters involving Y."[64] Wall contends that X's motive for attempting the communication "always includes some benefit X may obtain from this illegitimate communication."[65]

The third condition is also necessary, since for X to violate Y's rights, Y must not consent to participation in the communication in question. If Y does consent, then the behavior is not sexually harassing. As Wall acknowledges, (3) may seem to make (1) unnecessary. But Wall wants both (1) and (3), to allow for genuine mistakes by alleged harassers.

> Consider the possibility that the second and third conditions are satisfied. For example, X makes a sexual remark about Y to Y without Y's consent. Now suppose that the first condition is not satisfied, that is, suppose that X *did attempt* to obtain Y's consent to make such remarks. Furthermore, suppose that somewhere the communication between X and Y breaks down and X honestly believes he or she has obtained Y's consent to this discussion, when, in fact, he or she has not. In this case, X's intentions and actions being what they are, X does not sexually harass Y. X has shown respect for Y's privacy. Y may *feel* harassed in this case, but there is no offender here. However, after X sees Y's displeasure at the remarks, it is now X's duty to refrain from such remarks, unless, of course, Y later consents to such a discussion.[66]

Wall says that the possibility of genuine miscommunication shows the importance of clear communication.

The fourth condition is necessary because Y's mental state is essential to genuine cases of sexual harassment. According to Wall, "Y must be distressed because X did not attempt to ensure that it was permissible to make sexual comments to Y which involve Y, or because the content of X's sexual comments are offensive in Y's view."[67]

Thus, Wall's analysis includes the notions of wrongful communication, invasion of privacy, and intention. These are important elements in some behaviors considered to be sexual harassment that other definitions do not include. The possibility of genuine misunderstanding should be something for which an adequate conception of sexual harassment allows. Wall's account of how certain behaviors constitute an invasion of privacy well describes certain experiences of sexual harassment. In particular, it seems consistent with an important element of some verbal harassment that MacKinnon points out in her book *Only Words*. [68] MacKinnon suggests that in some cases, words are actions: "To express eroticism is to engage in eroticism, meaning to perform a sex act. To say it is to do it, and to do it is to say it. It is also to do the harm of it and to exacerbate harms surrounding it."[69] Wall may not agree with the argument in the context in which MacKinnon makes these claims. However, MacKinnon's discussion helps to highlight one of the elements of some sexually harassing behavior that Wall's definition captures: by behaving sexually toward one, either verbally or physically, a person can force intimacy or sexuality on one against one's will. MacKinnon pushes this further, by saying that in expressing certain words or gestures, the person can force one to *have sex*.[70]

Thus, Wall's definition accounts well for certain kinds of sexually harassing conduct that Hughes and May's conception, for example, does not. However, Wall's definition is too narrow because of its emphasis on communication. Even more than Superson's and Hughes and May's conceptions, Wall's conception depends on language in a way that renders it inadequate to account for what is wrong with certain types of sexual harassment. To say that sexual harassment is "a form of communication that violates its victim's privacy rights"[71] does not seem to the point in cases of quid pro quo harassment, though this may have taken place. As Hughes and May point out, coercion seems central in these cases. Also, Wall's insistence that whether or not sexual harassment has taken place depends on the intentions of both perpetrator and victim is very problematic, though I agree that it allows him to distinguish between genuine cases of sexual harassment and innocent, but mistaken, behavior. On Wall's view, whether or not a person has committed sexual harassment depends on the intentions and beliefs of the alleged perpetrator.[72] We may ultimately want to adopt such a definition, but we should think carefully about what it means if we do. As we all know, the road to hell is paved with good intentions.

It seems clear that Wall has in mind cases of sexual harassment which might be confused with ordinary "courtship behavior." As I said in chapter I, this is typical of the natural/biological perspective. According to the natural/biological perspective, sexual harassment is primarily a result of misunderstanding. Wall allows that some instances of apparent sexual harassment are not due to misunderstanding. Sometimes people violate the privacy of others intentionally. In such cases, genuine sexual harassment has occurred. To see that the definition is too narrowly focused on a certain kind of case, we can imagine the following sort of case. A supervisor approaches an employee and asks her whether he can communicate his sexual interest in her, because he wants a sexual relationship with her. Suppose that she says no and is denied her next promotion as a result. On many understandings of sexual harassment, this is a classic case of quid pro quo sexual harassment.

The supervisor is retaliating against the woman by denying her employment-related benefits because she has refused him sexual access. However, the case fails to constitute sexual harassment on Wall's definition, because the case fails to meet condition (1). The supervisor did try to obtain Y's consent to communicate his sexual interest in her. Now, suppose that the employee says yes. The supervisor then proceeds to communicate to the employee that if she wants her next promotion, she must have a sexual relationships with him. Again, this seems to be a classic case of quid pro quo sexual harassment. Yet, on Wall's conception, it is not. The case fails to meet conditions (1), (3), and (4).

Though Wall has developed his conception of sexual harassment at least in part in order to allow for a clear distinction between ordinary courtship behavior and sexually harassing conduct, it is not clear that he has done so. Mane Hajdin has argued that many conceptions of sexual harassment, including the one currently in the law, suffer from the "demarcation" problem. That is, it is not possible to distinguish acceptable from unacceptable sexual behavior in the workplace. According to Hajdin, "an individual needs to be able to determine in advance whether the conduct is covered by the definition."[73] However, "often the only way to find out whether someone would find certain conduct of a sexual nature unwelcome and offensive is to ask the person. . . . But here is the catch: asking a person about such matters is itself verbal conduct of a sexual nature that may easily be unwelcome and offensive and thus come under the definition of sexual harassment."[74] One can see how this might occur under Wall's definition. Condition (1) requires that a person, to avoid sexually harassing conduct, attempt to obtain Y's consent to communicate something sexual to Y. But that in itself is sexual. The possibility of an infinite regress looms.

Wall's definition does seem to fit quite well a certain kind of sexual violation. The following explanation fits such cases well:

What is inherently repulsive about sexual harassment is not the possible vulgarity of X's sexual comment or proposal, but X's failure to show respect for Y's rights. It is the obligation that stems from privacy rights that is ignored. Y's personal behavior and aspirations are protected by Y's privacy rights. The intrusion by X into this moral sphere is what is so objectionable about sexual harassment. If X does not attempt to obtain Y's approval to discuss such private matters, then he or she has not shown Y adequate respect.[75]

However, while this may be so in some kinds of cases, it is not what is inherently repulsive in others.

Wall's use of "he or she" in his discussion of sexual harassment indicates that he believes that sexual harassment, as he defines it, is gender neutral (that is, it is not sex discrimination). He does not conceive of sexual harassment as a form of gender discrimination. He clearly distinguishes his conception of sexual harassment from that of Hughes and May when he states that "[s]exual harassment is not necessarily tied to discrimination or coercion."[76] Hughes and May's definition includes both power and sexuality. However, as

I have mentioned previously, and as Wall points out, they seem to leave out co-worker harassment; or, as Wall also says, "May and Hughes would need to demonstrate that social inequities and issues of power are central to all sexual harassment cases before they could say without qualification that sexual harassment is a form of sex discrimination."[77]

It should be evident that each of the different definitions of sexual harassment we have examined seems to fit different kinds of cases, and to account for different aspects of what has been called sexual harassment. Wall's definition seems to account well for a certain kind of hostile environment sexual harassment, and he does provide a way of distinguishing between apparent sexual harassment and real sexual harassment, but it is not clear how helpful the distinction is outside the heads of the people directly involved. Furthermore, he seems to think that there is a "right to privacy" that is fairly straightforward, but in what this right consists is unclear from his discussion.

Cornell: Self-Respect

Some of the definitions we have been examining have been around since the early 1980s. Recently, some new understandings of sexual harassment have been articulated, including some that self-consciously utilize a liberal perspective. Drucilla Cornell provides a definition of sexual harassment in her book *The Imaginary Domain* in the context of a larger project concerning "a view of equality that provides us with a new perspective on the relationship of sexual difference to equality and of equality to freedom in the hotly contested issues of abortion, pornography, and sexual harassment."[78] Cornell sets out what she considers to be the necessary conditions for personhood or, as she puts it, for "individuation." These conditions are "(1) bodily integrity, (2) access to symbolic forms sufficient to achieve linguistic skills permitting the differentiation of oneself from others, and (3) the protection of the imaginary domain itself."[79] For Cornell, one is always in the process of becoming a person, of working through "imposed and assumed personae." Sex and sexuality are fundamental to one's personhood. The "minimum conditions of individuation" she sets out "are necessary for the chance of sexual freedom and the possibility of sexual happiness."[80] Legal protection of these conditions is necessary to provide everyone the equal chance to transform themselves into the person they choose to become.

Central to Cornell's position is the claim that women have been held responsible for men's reactions to them, and that this responsibility has been enforced by law.[81] This is evident in the practice of inquiring into a rape or sexual harassment victim's dress, drinking habits, and sexual history. While the latter two have now been banned from both rape and sexual harassment inquiries, a victim's appearance is still considered to be relevant in determining whether sexual behavior is "welcome." This was stated explicitly in *Meritor*.[82] The claim that women are held responsible for men's reactions to them is used in Cornell's argument that sexual harassment law is not designed to protect women, but to ensure their freedom: "when women demand the space to be sexual in their own way and still be accorded respect for their worthiness as persons, they are demanding the equal chance to seek happiness, not protection."[83]

It is against this background that Cornell provides a reworking of the EEOC definition of sexual harassment:

> [S]exual harassment consists of (a) unilaterally imposed sexual requirements in the context of unequal power, or (b) the creation and perpetuation of a work environment which enforces sexual shame by reducing individuals to stereotypes or objectified fantasies of their "sex" so as to undermine the primary good of their self-respect, or (c) employment-related retaliation against a subordinate employee or, in the case of a university, a student, for a consensually mutually desired sexual relationship.[84]

For Cornell, these three different "routes to claiming sexual harassment . . . stress the importance of the protection of the imaginary domain for the chance of sexual freedom."[85]

Cornell considers clause (a) to be a revision of the legal definition of quid pro quo sexual harassment. She replaces "unwelcome" or "unwanted" with "unilaterally imposed" in the EEOC definition of quid pro quo harassment, and she claims that "[t]he wrong" in quid pro quo sexual harassment, "is in the unilateral imposition in a context of unequal power."[86] Cornell claims several advantages for her revised definition of quid pro quo sexual harassment over the current legal definition. First, "unilaterally imposed," "serves the same purpose as 'unwanted' and 'unwelcome' in directing us to investigate the differences between a desired sexual relationship and one that is not mutual, one that is imposed upon the other party," so nothing is lost.[87] However, it makes clear that the harm involved is failing to respect a woman as an equal human being. This echoes the element of Wall's definition which assumes a right to privacy. Second, "the phrase, 'unilaterally imposed,' would not disallow evidence of mutual involvement in consent but this would be evidence of *mutual* involvement in consent and *not* evidence of how women implicitly invite sex."[88] This would make inquiries into women's attire and general behavior inappropriate when charges of sexual harassment are made. And this would guard against women's being judged according to what Cornell describes as the "psychical fantasy of Woman." Investigation into a woman's general behavior "implicitly incorporates fantasies about women which impose someone else's imaginary upon women's sense of self-worth."[89]

Part (b) of the definition replaces the legal standard of hostile environment sexual harassment. Cornell's definition diverts attention from the question whose perspective represents "objectivity"—the reasonable man or the reasonable woman—to the question of "whether or not the workplace and the contested behavior effectively undermined the social bases of self-respect by enforcing stereotypes or projecting fantasies onto the plaintiff as one unworthy of personhood."[90] This makes the behavior the issue, not the woman's perception of the behavior. Cornell argues that "each one of us should be accorded the primary good of self-respect for ourselves as sexuate beings."[91]

This requires "space for the free play of one's sexual imaginary."[92] Cornell argues that "sexual harassment both enforces sexual shame and does so in a way that effectively undermines any woman's projected self-image of herself as worthy of equal personhood."[93] Cornell contrasts this perspective with the view that prohibitions on hostile environment sexual harassment protect women's virtue. In her view, such prohibitions are not about protection of virtue, but about the defense of freedom. One of the features of this position is that it does not divide women into the reasonable and the unreasonable, and it makes clear why gays and lesbians should be protected from hostile environment abuse by same-sex abusers.[94]

Part (c) of the definition of sexual harassment addresses the kind of behavior regulated by consensual relationship policies at colleges and universities. Cornell says that her formulation focuses on "the wrong of the abuse of power," and she characterizes that wrong as "the inequality in holding women responsible for their sexual behavior in a way that men are not."[95] Clearly, this makes such behavior discriminatory.

For Cornell, the wrong in quid pro quo harassment is the "unilateral imposition in a context of unequal power."[96] The wrong in hostile environment sexual harassment is that it undermines equality in the workplace.[97] The wrong of the third kind of harassment is that it is an abuse of power and treats women unequally. If the wrong in these kinds of behavior is different, why should they all be called sexual harassment? Cornell would probably respond that they are united by their purpose, to curtail people's sexual freedom. However, we might ask whether that is sufficient conceptually to unite them. Are there other sorts of behavior that should also be included in the protection of sexual freedom? And if there is conceptual unity between these behaviors, is sexual harassment the best label for such a concept?

One feature of these definitions is that gender is not essential to sexual harassment. In this, Cornell's definition diverges from MacKinnon's and Superson's, for which gender is essential to the definition of sexual harassment. Cornell's definition points toward an expanded protection of sexual expression, the sort favored by Abrams and Franke. Because of this, many would find her definition too broad. It is unlikely that any would find it too narrow. Both women and men would find protection from such laws. Both are free to develop their sexual selves. All of the kinds of behavior that have been categorized as sexual harassment are covered by the definition.

Like MacKinnon's and Superson's definition, Cornell's rests on a number of problematic assumptions. Her assumptions involve the conditions for personhood and, particularly, for free sexual development. Many people object to sexual harassment law precisely because it challenges the status quo. These people would certainly object to Cornell's definition and its underlying assumptions. Cornell sees herself as articulating the view that women should have what men demand for themselves: "entitlement to their own sexuality as a crucial aspect of their subjectivity."[98] In her view, the behaviors that constitute sexual harassment deny this to women. Women's entitlement to their own sexuality, at this moment in time, requires laws prohibiting sexual harassment.

Cornell's conception, then, is not too narrow but would be regarded as too broad by many, including adherents of the dominance perspective. Perhaps its greatest merit is that it conceives of the prohibition of sexual harassment as necessary for women's equality, yes, but also for their freedom, including their sexual freedom. This is something that is implicit in MacKinnon's conception, with its emphasis on the coercive nature of heterosexual sex. The major fault of Cornell's conception is a certain disunity in the concept of sexual harassment, when different kinds of sexual harassment are conceived as involving different sorts of wrongs. Unity is restored if one accepts Cornell's assumptions that sexual freedom is necessary for personhood, and that these behaviors curtail sexual freedom. The main difficulties for the conception are the controversial assumptions that provide its unity. Many do not want the law's protection of sexual freedom of the sort Cornell says is necessary for personhood.

Cornell's definition seems to emphasize the disparity in the various behaviors that are categorized as sexual harassment. It may be that accepting a definition of the sort she recommends would lead to an abandonment of that concept in favor of a group of concepts classified under the heading of "obstacles to sexual freedom." This may not be a bad idea.

Davis: Sexual Inappropriateness

Breaking apart the category of sexual harassment and giving up the term "sexual harassment" is recommended by Nancy Davis. Davis has written on sexual harassment in academe. She argues that we need to be able to distinguish between different sorts of harassers because different sorts of responses are likely to be effective.

> It is wrong for instructor A to coerce a student into a sexual involvement with the threat of academic reprisal (*quid pro quo*), and it may also be wrong for instructor B to offer academic encouragement to a student in order to have more frequent contact with her and thus more opportunities to initiate a sexual relationship with her. It may be wrong for instructor C to make frequent remarks to female students about how "sexy" they are and wrong for D to use classroom humor that relies on jokes and examples that are demeaning to women. However, though the actions of all four instructors may be wrong, they are not wrong for the same reasons, and the differences may be more significant than the similarities, both with respect to the moral assessment of the instructors' conduct and the design of plans or policies to remedy it. The blanket characterization of all four as sexual harassment conceals and may mislead.[99]

Davis suggests that instructor A is intentionally exploiting students, while B, C, and D may be unwittingly insensitive or confused about their own motivations. She allows that all of these behaviors may be "sexually inappropriate" but says that it is unfair to lump the willful exploiter and the unwittingly insensitive instructor together in the same moral (or legal) category and to treat their misconduct as deserving of the same sorts of sanctions. It is also practically unwise, for the measures that are likely to be effective and appropriate means for eliminating willful exploitation are different from those that serve to eliminate insensitivity.[100]

Davis is more concerned to critique the broad definitions in university sexual harassment policies which are based on the EEOC *Guidelines*. This is an important task: "Because such definitions lump together many different kinds of behaviors, they blur distinctions that may have moral, psychological, and practical relevance."[101] Because people see sexual harassment as involving some sort of sexual offense, if one is charged with sexual harassment, moral opprobrium follows.

I find the analyses of sexual harassment by Cornell and Davis most illuminating. Many of the definitions reviewed here seem to force disparate behaviors under one conception. Cornell and Davis acknowledge that there are significant differences between behaviors that resemble the core sexually harassing behaviors of quid pro quo and hostile environment sexual harassment. However, before I provide my conclusions about conceptions of sexual harassment, I must discuss the view that sexual harassment is not a legitimate concept.

Sexual Harassment Is Not a Legitimate Concept

Some philosophers argue that sexual harassment is not a legitimate concept, or that it is not a "morally significant" concept.[102] These possibilities should be investigated, because they would explain why there are so many flawed definitions of sexual harassment, and why there is so much disagreement about what it is.

F. M. Christensen argues that "the concept of 'sexual harassment' is not a legitimate concept. Its major defects are: "(1) It lumps together serious crimes, minor offenses, and actions that are arguably not wrong at all. (2) What the actions do have in common . . . is irrelevant to what it is about each action that makes it wrong."[103] A legitimate concept, we may infer, is one that properly carves up the world at its joints. This one does not, since it gathers together behaviors that are different in important ways, and that have no significant commonality.

Mane Hajdin's argument that the concept of sexual harassment is morally insignificant is similar to Christensen's argument that the concept is illegitimate. Hajdin agrees with Christensen that there is no single wrong common to all sexually harassing conduct. He further argues that "[t]he distinctions between sexual harassment and other similar kinds of conduct are not morally significant distinctions."[104]

Christensen's first criticism of the concept of sexual harassment is that it encompasses a range of behaviors, some of which are serious wrongs, some of which are less serious wrongs, and some of which are not wrong. A legitimate concept does not do this.

It is true that the behaviors that have been included under the heading sexual harassment have included everything from failed compliments to rape.[105] Rape is a serious injury to a person; unwanted sexual teasing is much less serious. To put them all in one category tends to render the least harmful as serious as the most harmful. Thus, a charge of sexual harassment against a person can take on the moral condemnation associated with rape.[106]

However, this seems to be more a legal problem than a conceptual problem. People are often shocked upon reading *Meritor* because one of the claims is that the supervisor raped Vinson. We think of rape as a criminal offense, not something to be remedied under discrimination law. However, we must consider that different kinds of laws embody different conceptions of the wrong committed, and that it is at least possible that one action—such as rape—could be wrong for different reasons under different conceptions of the action.

Christensen is assuming that a moral concept is legitimate only if the behaviors it encompasses are all of the same degree of wrong, or at least are all wrong. But on the face of it, this is simply false. There are many concepts that encompass such a range of behaviors. Many believe that lying, for example, is a concept of this sort. Some lies are not wrongs, some are less serious wrongs, and some are very serious, indeed. Lies are particularly serious in the context of the law, where lies are sometimes "perjury" and constitute legal wrongs. Another such concept is "homicide." This term encompasses many different kinds of killing, some of which are morally and legally wrong, some of which are not.

However, suppose that we accept Christensen's first criterion for what constitutes a legitimate concept. Is it true that the concept of sexual harassment fails to meet it? I would argue that it has been met by some definitions of the concept of sexual harassment—MacKinnon's concept, for example. According to her conception, all sexually harassing behavior is discriminatory against women, whatever else it might be. This means that it is all wrong and all wrong to the same degree, under at least one way of understanding it. The reason that Christensen does not agree is because of the way that he describes the phenomena usually categorized as sexual harassment. He does not see that these phenomena have anything in common except sex and objectionableness. But he gives us no reason to prefer his description over MacKinnon's. He does argue, however, that sexually harassing behaviors do not constitute sex discrimination. I shall address these arguments later in this chapter.

Christensen's second criticism of the concept of sexual harassment suggests another criterion for a legitimate moral concept: a moral concept is legitimate only if all of the behaviors included under it are wrong for the same reasons. He claims that the concept of sexual harassment does not meet this criterion. In his view, all that the actions called sexual harassment have in common is the fact that they involve "sex" and that they are "objectionable" to someone. His attempt at a definition that captures all of the behaviors considered sexually harassing—"attempted or actual extortion of sexual favors, bodily contact of a sexual nature, and sexual expressions of any kind: jokes, insults, propositions, passing comments, visual displays, facial expressions, etc., etc."—is "[s]omething or other to do with sex that someone or other may find objectionable."[107] However, he claims:

> "[T]he fact that sex is involved has nothing to do with why or whether any of the proscribed actions is wrong. Sexual extortion is heinous because it is extortion, not because it is sexual; unwanted sexual touching is wrong because it is an invasion of personal space, not specifically because it is sexual; sexual insults are objectionable because they are an attempt to harm, not because they are sexual. And simple sexual frankness is not wrong at all.[108]

One could argue, along these lines, that rape is not wrong because it is sexual. But surely rape would not be rape unless it were sexual. Similarly, for those who believe that sexual harassment is a legitimate concept, the sexual element of the behaviors Christensen describes is relevant to their wrong. Take, again, MacKinnon's definition. In a patriarchal culture, heterosexual activity has a particular meaning, so that coercive sexual behavior by men toward women constitutes sex discrimination, whatever else it may constitute. Thus, all behavior classified as sexually harassing behavior is wrong for the same reason.

Christensen creates a category of behavior which he calls "sexual frankness." He does not define it, but it seems to include any kind of "frank sexual talk." It would seem to include most of what has been included in "hostile environment" sexual harassment. An example of sexual frankness is what Clarence Thomas is accused of having said to Anita Hill. Christensen comments: "The fact that a type of behavior as harmless and as natural for human beings as talking about sex would be treated as a crime reveals something deeply perverted in this culture."[109] Christensen argues that "sexual frankness" is not wrong in itself, but that definitions of sexual harassment assume it to be wrong. Christensen admits that sexually frank communication is sometimes wrong. It is wrong when it is used in sexual extortion and in cases in which, "no harm is intended or foreseen but arguably *should* be foreseen, notably, making sexual requests to someone over whom one has supervisory authority: for all the recipient knows, the person having the authority might use it to retaliate for being rejected."[110] In addition, "the use of sexual talk to insult another person"[111] is objectionable, and "unjustifiably hounding someone—over sex or anything else whatever—is certainly objectionable, and those who engage in such behavior must be restrained."[112] But the harm in these cases is not in the sexually frank communication itself: in the first case, it is the intent to cause distress that is wrong, and in the second, it is the hounding that is wrong, not its being "sexual."

I describe "frank sex talk" in order to reveal more of Christensen's position. In his view, the fact that some kind of behavior involves sex is never relevant to its wrongness. In this, he is in disagreement with not only MacKinnon but Wall. Wall seems to hold that communication involving sex requires more privacy than other sorts of communication.

However, should we accept Christensen's second criterion for a legitimate moral concept? We do not, in general, require that legitimate moral concepts be such that all behaviors classified under them be wrong in the same way. Nancy Davis makes this point for the term "homicide": "It is not necessarily incorrect or unreasonable to use one word to refer to a family of behaviors that are wrong for different reasons: *homicide* refers to involuntary manslaughter as well as to first-degree murder, and they are surely wrong for different reasons."[113]

I tend to agree with Christensen that the legal treatment of sexually harassing behaviors is problematic. This is a point that should be acknowledged by supporters of legal redress for sexual harassment. Under some conceptions of sexual harassment, behaviors that are only slightly harmful will be included under the definition. In fact, some definitions used in institutional policies and empirical research are such that not all the behaviors that fit under the definition would constitute sexual harassment in a court of law. This means that there is some sexual harassment that is not harmful enough to qualify for legal remedy. But sexual harassment is often understood to be *by definition* wrong and illegal. This tends to amplify the perceived harm of the less serious instances of sexual harassment, and to classify as *legally* wrong any behavior that is included among sexually harassing behaviors. The association of behaviors labeled "sexual harassment" with sex and harm tends to brand unfairly those accused of, or even found guilty of mild forms of, sexual harassment, ruining their reputations in ways that similar behaviors not involving sex would not.

Christensen thinks that *sexual* harassment is singled out for attention because Americans are antisexual, and because women are thought to require more protection in general than men. He is right to point to the tendency in American culture to intensify the moral tone whenever sexuality is involved. It seems quite clear that judges would never have found that sexual harassment is sex discrimination in those early cases if they had not been appalled by the sexual nature of the offenses. He is also correct that we should look at comparable actions that do not involve sex, to see how we regard them. One of the problems with charges of sexual harassment is the association with sexual perversion or child molestation.[114] Thus, one of the issues that should be addressed in discussing the harm involved in sexual harassment is the gravity of the charge. One has a sneaking suspicion that the fear of being falsely accused, which one writer argues has informed current sexual harassment law, is because the charge is one of *sexual* misconduct.[115] How many men are afraid of being accused of being a bully? But a sexual bully? Carol Smart raises the question of the seriousness of sexual harassment: "if our concern is about the 'use' of women and others as a means to an end, then why do we only seem to become so alarmed about it in a sexual context?"[116] Much of the alarm is from people who do not perceive the context of inequality that some feminists do. This suggests that it is traditional beliefs about male and female sexuality that cause the alarm.

In addition, in considering sexual harassment, one should address the question why *sexual* harassment deserves a kind of attention from the public and the law that is not deemed necessary for other kinds of harassment. As Christensen points out:

> [v]irtually none of the institutions that have created "sexual harass-ment" policies have adopted explicit rules to penalize all the major and minor *non*-sexual ways one person can harm or offend another. The author knows of cases in which co-workers or supervisors have delib-erately made life miserable for someone, forcing the person to quit; also of cases of non-sexual extortion by supervisors. . . . In most institu-tions, except for ethnic and gender discrimination, the larger portion of the many ways in which one person can mistreat or upset another are not in any specific way prohibited. Why single out the sexual ones?
>
> Indeed, why not simply adopt *general* policies of "worksite harass-ment" (or the like), which would automatically cover the sexual variety *as well as* all the other kinds of extortion, assault and offensive expres-sions?[117]

Why not indeed? These are excellent questions and should be addressed by anyone arguing that sexual harassment should be prohibited in the work-place. However, most commentators do not.

Both Christensen and Hajdin argue that the behaviors identified as sexual harassment are not discriminatory toward women. According to Christen-sen, arguments that "sexual frankness" constitutes sex discrimination against women are confused. First, the ambiguity of the term "sex" leads people to think that if something has to do with sex, it is automatically sexist. This is not true because discrimination does not necessarily entail unjust discrimi-nation. Secondly, because many people are only attracted to members of one sex, sexual frankness usually discriminates against one sex—it is directed at members of one sex but not the other. However, as Christensen rightly points out, this kind of discrimination is not in itself wrong.

Hajdin makes a similar argument, though, unlike Christensen, he admits that some hostile environment sexual harassment is illegal sex discrimination. This is because it is "motivated by hostility toward the presence of women, and not men, and because its purpose is to embarrass, humiliate, and intim-idate women, and not men."[118] Thus, Hajdin seems to understand behavior to be sex discrimination when it is motivated by hostility toward one sex and when its purpose is to harm members of that sex.

Hajdin denies that what he calls "offensive sexual advances" and quid pro quo sexual harassment constitute sexual harassment, because they are not motivated by hostility and it is not their purpose to harm women. However, as we have seen, this is controversial. Many would claim that quid pro quo harassment *is* motivated by hostility toward women and that its purpose *is* to harm them.

As we can see, how to describe the phenomena in question in this debate is a major point of contention between those who conceive of sexual harassment as sex discrimination and those who do not. Hajdin seems to be claiming that if the act is intended to lead to sexual interaction, then it is not motivated by hostility but by sexual desire. Since there is nothing wrong with discriminating based on one's sexual desire, then it is not wrongful discrimination on the basis of sex. However, one could argue that these are not mutually exclusive motivations. When a male supervisor threatens a female employee with harm in order to obtain sexual favors, hostility or at least indifference toward women seems to be part of the motivation. People who engage in such behavior tend to hold the female sex in low regard. Women exist for their use. It is true that the supervisor may also feel this way about other men. But unless the supervisor acts on this feeling, it is unclear whether this is relevant.

Hajdin might respond that the purpose of the supervisor's conduct in cases of quid pro quo harassment is not to humiliate, embarrass, or otherwise harm the employee; rather, the supervisor wants a sexual relationships with the employee. Since this is not wrong, then discrimination on the basis of sex is still not wrongful sex discrimination. Again, one could respond that the supervisor does intend to harm the employee. He intends to intimidate her, and to take away her freedom to make choices about her job and her sexual activity. This is what many feminists, such as MacKinnon and Superson, would claim.

Hajdin's debating partner, Linda LeMoncheck, emphasizes that the dispute over sexual harassment is a dispute over how certain sorts of behavior will be described in moral and legal discourse.[119] It is clear that whether one considers quid pro quo sexual harassment to be sex discrimination will depend on how one describes the behavior in question. The main political dispute lies here. A part of the struggle concerns whose experiences will be taken as definitive.

Christensen's main argument against treating sexual frankness as discriminatory is a critique of the argument that sexual frankness confines women to her traditional sex role:

> Traditionally, women in this culture were limited to the roles of sex partner and mother. . . . What seems to have happened since the rise of feminism is that the roles women were traditionally *allowed* have been aversively associated, in the minds of some, with those they were *denied*. Consequently, calling attention to sexuality seems to these individuals to devalue women's other roles—notably, that of productive worker.[120]

Christensen points out that the proper response to this problem is not to deny the sexuality of women, but to acknowledge that women and men are full human beings, sexual and productive. This sounds similar to Cornell, and thinking about this superficial similarity can help to highlight the assumptions of Christensen's response. He claims that allowing "sexual frankness" is the way to treat everyone as fully human. Cornell argues that such frankness— by which I take it Christensen means talk that is not insulting or bullying or otherwise objectionable—under current circumstances will impose the fantasies of men on women and subject women to shame and curtailment of freedom. Women and men do not engage in "sex talk" equally in the workplace, and it is difficult to see how this can change under the current circumstances, where if a woman talks about sex publicly, she is seen as having given up her freedom to say no to any man. While Christensen's suggestion might be ideal, it ignores present realities.

Christensen also denies that sexual extortion—also known as quid pro quo harassment—is discriminatory toward women. His argument is that "the fact that a given offender victimizes members of only one sex is not part of what *makes* the actions wrong."[121] There is something correct about this argument. As Christensen points out, if the fact he states were to render sexual extortion wrong, then every crime would be discriminatory, since not everyone is victimized. However, what is left out of Christensen's characterization of the "offense" is the factual claim that motivated people like Lin Farley to invent "sexual harassment." Many women had to quit jobs or put up with sexual impositions to keep their jobs. Not nearly as many men have had to do so. Christensen characterizes the aspect of the extortion that is relevant to discrimination in such a way that the "crime" is between two individuals, and it is incidental that women tend to be the victims. I admit that this is not the way that sex discrimination is established by law, and I also admit that the arguments seeking to fit quid pro quo sexual harassment into the sex discrimination analysis strike me as artificial. As Christensen points out, "[T]he fact that most sexual harassment involves the 'discrimination' of being heterosexual or homosexual is not grounds for calling it sexist."[122] However, I take it that those arguing for the use of Title VII and Title IX to address sexual extortion acknowledge this.[123]

The primary point of disagreement between Christensen and those whose definitions we have examined—perhaps with the exception of Wall—seems to be whether sex in our culture has the same meaning for women and men. Christensen assumes that it does or should, and the others say it does not but should. Their major disagreement is over how to get to the position that it does. Christensen thinks that this happens by eliminating legal and moral differences in treatment. Others think this merely reinforces the status quo. They claim that we must use the law to bring women to a position of equality with men in the sexual realm. In part, this is an empirical claim. How we could determine who is right without actually trying the two approaches is unclear, however. What we now seem to do is base some law on one approach, and some on the other. This ensures that both remain in the running.

Many of those who oppose Christensen and Hajdin would claim that what those actions considered sexual harassment have in common is a particular combination of sex and power—coercion in the context of sex—or a particular kind of invasion of privacy. They claim that what instances of sexual harassment have in common is that they are expressions of and manifestations of inequality. Christensen and Hajdin's inability to find a common "wrong" in sexual harassment stems from their denial that the kinds of behaviors collected under the heading "sexual harassment" have anything significant in common. All they can see is that they have "sex" in common. And that is not morally significant, in their view. In other words, they beg the question.

Considering Hajdin and Christensen's view and then the others examined here is like putting on two different sets of spectacles which enhance certain features of the landscape while diminishing the rest. Proponents of the concept of sexual harassment emphasize the commonality of the behaviors identified as sexual harassment, while playing down the similarities between those behaviors and other behaviors. Christensen and Hajdin downplay the similarities between behaviors identified as sexual harassment and focus on the similarities between the behaviors identified as sexual harassment and other behaviors that are not considered to be sexual harassment. Christensen focuses on talking, and Hajdin on sexual advances. Both play down the significance of *gender*.[124] This is an abstract approach, and it is this very abstraction that allows Christensen and Hajdin to ignore what other theorists claim is inequality between the genders.

In summary, Christensen and Hajdin raise some important issues for those who seek to define sexual harassment. Their questions help to specify what such a definition must do. To meet the objections, any responsible analysis of sexual harassment should clearly differentiate between a moral (or conceptual) definition of sexual harassment and the legal definition of sexual harassment. The boundaries of the moral definition should be clear, so that no behaviors resembling sexual harassment but not morally wrong should be included in the definition. The moral definition should be clearly differentiated from the legal definition: It is not required that all instances of a moral wrong also be illegal. Nor is it necessary that there be only one approach to a moral wrong under the law.

Conclusion

The problem with all these definitions of sexual harassment seems to be that everyone has got a piece of the truth. That is why each has some appeal. But none seems to provide an adequate definition for all of the kinds of behavior that have been considered. This does not necessarily imply that a definition is wrong; but it should suggest to us that perhaps these behaviors are not similar enough to fit under one category.

Christensen and Hajdin's discussions highlight the difficulties in conceptualizing sexual harassment as a single concept, and in conceiving of sexual harassment as sex discrimination.

In my view, Cornell's approach may be the sort of approach that is necessary if all of the behaviors that are now considered sexually harassing are to be included in the concept. I am thinking, in particular, of the recent Supreme Court decision that same-sex harassment constitutes sexual harassment. Cornell has provided a wider justification for finding quid pro quo, hostile environment, and certain other behaviors wrong. However, this justification is so broad that one starts to lose the glue that holds together those behaviors originally identified as sexually harassing. The label no longer seems to fit. Perhaps this is pointing the way to the post–sexual harassment society, where the kinds of rights to self-determination articulated by Cornell and others are legally protected. The question then becomes, Does the country want to protect individual gender development to the extent this implies?

The problem is that there are so many different kinds of behavior that are collected under the concept sexual harassment. Feminists such as MacKinnon and Superson do not see this as a problem because they subcribe to underlying theories that render these behaviors similar enough to warrant treating them as similar. Biologists see these behaviors as having similar causes (male sexual strategies), but they distinguish between those that are (unacceptably) coercive and those that are not. But we are discussing what we should do in a liberal state, so it seems that we should be as neutral as we can between competing ideals of the good. We should not inscribe either of the views into law. However, if we circumscribe actionable sexual harassment according to what feminists and biologists agree are wrong actions, we will favor the biologists. Those actions they believe are wrong will be illegal, and those they do not consider wrong will not be. Feminists will have some of the actions they believe are wrong be illegal, but many they think are wrong will not be illegal. How are we to reconcile these positions?

The legal definition of sexual harassment, as it stands, is surely both too wide and too narrow. It is too wide because it counts as sexual harassment any "unwanted sexual advance." This would seem to include invitations offered by well-meaning people to anyone who is not interested. We seem to have a law against sexual initiation, unless the recipient desires the initiation. But, as many have pointed out, how does one know whether such an initiation is wanted?

There have been studies purporting to show that men perceive sexual interest in women's behavior when women intend friendliness. If this is true, then there will be many unwanted sexual advances, not through malice, but because men think that their advances are desired. Simply making such advances illegal does not appropriately address the problem. Perhaps teaching boys, from a young age, that not every smile is a sexual come-on would be more appropriate.

6

LEGAL ISSUES

In this chapter, I shall address several issues in sexual harassment law that are controversial and that help to explain some of the controversy surrounding sexual harassment in general. The issues, to be addressed consecutively, are (1) whether sexual harassment should be considered sex discrimination under Title VII, (2) whether the so-called reasonable woman standard should be adopted (3) whether same-sex harassment is sex discrimination, and (4) whether other forms of harassment should be conceptualized in the same way as sexual harassment.

Sexual Harassment and the Law

As I have emphasized throughout this work, the concept of sexual harassment has been developed on the assumption that it should be illegal. This is why, from the start, sexual harassment was conceived as a legal wrong—either extortion, or sex discrimination, or an invasion of the right to privacy. It is important to recognize, however, that a definition of sexual harassment need not entail its illegality. Even if one agrees that some or all of the behaviors that have been designated sexual harassment are morally wrong or cause inequality, it does not follow that they should be considered legally wrong. One might hold that some of the behaviors should be illegal, but not all. If what is desired is the cessation of such behaviors, then we must consider whether the instrument of the law is the best means to this end.

Ours is a liberal society, in the sense that our governmental institutions are based on liberal political theory. Liberal theory values liberty, or freedom, first. In our society, this is often seen in terms of a right to do what we desire unless what we are doing harms others. The idea that our behavior can justifiably be proscribed if it harms others has been called "the harm principle."

According to this principle, "A person's liberty may be restricted to prevent physical or psychic injury to other specific individuals; likewise, a person's liberty may be restricted to prevent impairment or destruction of institutional practices and regulatory systems that are in the public interest."[1] Other reasons for prohibiting behavior have been advanced, but most can be seen as variations of the harm principle. As we saw in chapter 5, most people who argue that sexual harassment should be prohibited couch their arguments in terms of the harm done to the victims of sexual harassment, or to women in general. They argue that sexual harassment should be illegal because it unjustifiably harms its victims. However, some are skeptical about whether the law can be used to prevent sexual harassment, because they doubt whether the law can effect meaningful social change.[2] Even MacKinnon acknowledges that laws crafted by women to address harms suffered by women may end up harming women.[3] In addition, those who agree that sexual harassment should be illegal do not agree on whether tort law or discrimination law is best suited to its regulation.[4]

Whether sexual harassment should be illegal, and if so, in what sense, remains controversial. The issues considered below examine aspects of these controversies.

Discrimination Law or Tort Law?

In the approximately twenty years since the concept of sexual harassment was created, most people have come to agree that quid pro quo sexual harassment is wrong and should be illegal. Many also agree that the more severe forms of behaviors included under the term "hostile environment sexual harassment" should be illegal. However, there is still a good deal of disagreement about the kind of law that should regulate sexual harassment. MacKinnon and others argue that sexual harassment should be considered a form of sex discrimination, in violation of Title VII of the Civil Rights Act. However, until passage of the 1991 Civil Rights Act, those bringing claims of sexual harassment under Title VII could not sue for compensation or punitive damages. The only remedies available under Title VII were "equitable relief"—such as back pay (in cases where the plaintiff is fired in retaliation or quits because of the harassment), an injunction against the employer to stop the harassing behavior, or reinstatement. In order to receive compensation or punitive damages, people sued under tort laws such as invasion of the right to privacy, intentional assault and battery, and intentional infliction of emotional distress. Some have argued that sexual harassment *should* be treated under tort law, rather than under sex discrimination law, either using existing torts,[5] or creating a new tort specifically for sexual harassment.[6] Still others advocate criminal law for some forms of sexual harassment.[7]

This dispute may sound arcane, but there are two general issues that are important for understanding the sexual harassment controversy. The first is that whether sexual harassment is litigated primarily under tort law or under discrimination law determines how sexual harassment is conceptualized in the law. The second concerns access to the law for victims of sexually harassing behavior.

Tort law concerns personal injuries, harms done by one person to another. Its purpose is to compensate the injured party for the harm done to them. According to one account, "Tort liability . . . exists primarily to compensate the injured person by compelling the wrongdoer to pay for the damage he has done."[8] Thus, use of torts—such as "assault and battery, insult, offensive battery, intentional infliction of emotional distress by extreme and outrageous conduct, invasion of privacy"[9]—to litigate sexual harassment claims conceptualizes sexual harassment as behavior offensive to the integrity or sensibilities of an individual.[10] Discrimination law, on the other hand, exists to ensure equal opportunity regardless of sex, race, national origin, religion, age, or disability. As such, it is "sensitive to . . . power dynamics" that operate in obstructing equality of opportunity.[11] If the dominant remedy for sexual harassment is tort law, then sexual harassment will be conceived of primarily as "personal." Conceiving of sexual harassment in this way tends to undercut the conception of sexual harassment as part of a system of abuses of patriarchal power explicit in many feminist conceptions of sexual harassment.[12] Thus, the dispute over which kind of law should govern sexual harassment is a dispute about what sexual harassment *is*.

The definitions we examined in chapter 5 fit rather neatly in either the sex discrimination group or the tort group. This is not surprising, since, as I remarked there, these definitions were created with an eye toward the law. The definitions offered by MacKinnon, Superson, Hughes and May, and Cornell conceptualize sexual harassment as sex discrimination. Wall's is a definition that lends itself to a tort interpretation. The first two of the broad perspectives discussed in chapter 1 also fit quite well into these groups. Browne suggests that there is no "sexual harassment" that qualifies as sex discrimination, so any illegal behavior would be a criminal act or a violation of tort law. The dominance perspective would favor the view that sexual harassment is sex discrimination. Only sex discrimination law is concerned with ensuring the equality of groups, which is central to the dominance perspective. Proponents of liberal perspectives might support sex discrimination or tort law, depending on the kind of liberalism they espouse. As we shall see, libertarians tend to support the use of torts, while more egalitarian liberals support the use of sex discrimination law. Some advocate the use of both sex discrimination law and tort law, because they believe that both are needed to capture the full character of the harm of sexual harassment.[13]

We have seen that MacKinnon considers sexual harassment to be sex discrimination. Because of her more general theory of the sexual subordination of women to men, conceiving of sexual harassment as primarily a violation of tort law is inadequate.

> "[T]ort is conceptually inadequate to the problem of sexual harassment to the extent that it rips injuries to women's sexuality out of the context of women's social circumstances as a whole. In particular, short of

developing a new tort for sexual harassment as such, the tort approach misses the nexus between women's sexuality and women's employment, the system of reciprocal sanctions which, to women as gender, become cumulative. In tort perspective, the injury of sexual harassment would be seen as an injury to the individual person, to personal sexual integrity, with damages extending to the job. Alternatively, sexual harassment could be seen as an injury to an individual interest in employment, with damages extending to the emotional harm [attendant to the sexual invasion as well as to the loss of employment.] The approach tends to pose the necessity to decide whether sexual harassment is essentially an injury to the person, to sexual integrity and feelings, with pendent damages to the job, or whether it is essentially an injury to the job, with damages extending to the person. Since it is both, either one omits the social dynamics that systematically place women in these positions, that may coerce consent, that interpenetrate sexuality and employment to women's detriment because they are women.[14]

MacKinnon holds that the distinctive character of those behaviors she believes should be classified as sexual harassment is that they are a result of and a cause of gender inequality. Classifying sexual harassment as a form of sex discrimination captures this; conceiving of sexually harassing behaviors as violations of torts does not. If sexual threats, unwanted sexual advances, and unwanted sexual touching are all considered to be forms sex discrimination, one tends to consider them violations of equality, harms that one sex inflicts on another. However, if sexual threats are considered intentional infliction of emotional distress, unwanted sexual advances are considered invasions of privacy, and unwanted sexual touching is considered battery, one tends to see them as kinds of invasions of privacy, inflictions of distress, and battery, but with nothing common among them. They are simply some among the many wicked things that individuals do to other individuals.[15]

Those who favor a tort interpretation of sexually harassing behaviors sometimes do so because they oppose all employment discrimination law. One of the most eloquent advocates of this position is Richard Epstein. Epstein opposes Title VII because he believes the costs of enforcement outweigh the benefits. In his view, laws prohibiting discrimination against groups threaten the fundamental principles of "individual autonomy and freedom of association": "Their negation through modern civil rights law has led to a dangerous form of government coercion that in the end threatens to do more than strangle the operation of labor and employment markets. The modern civil rights laws are a new form of imperialism that threatens the political liberty and intellectual freedom of us all."[16] In general, Epstein believes that "discrimination by private parties are not wrongs requiring state intervention or correction" and that "the norms of ordinary contract law are adequate to deal with the problems that arise in the employment context." However, "[s]exual harassment is an entirely different matter. Contractual principles play a leading role, and significant common law tort liability for both individual and firm would, and should, remain even if the antidiscrimination laws were erased from the statute books tomorrow. With harassment cases, the elimination of the antidiscrimination law does not return us to a world of properly functioning competitive markets."[17]

Epstein emphasizes the conceptual difference between the tort approach and the sex discrimination approach: "Does Title VII offer a regime for regulating sexual harassment better than its common law alternative? The analytical contrast between the two systems is stark. Title VII stresses the harasser's motive, while the common law ties liability to the use or threat of force that results in emotional distress to its victim."[18] Epstein opts for use of torts, and he seems to think that existing torts are sufficient. Besides his general objections to Title VII, he considers the tort approach superior to the sex discrimination approach in the case of sexual harassment because it does not face the problem of the bisexual harasser, and because it allows women and men to be protected equally. Of course, MacKinnon and other advocates of the dominance approach do not think that men need the degree of protection that women do, so this reasoning would not be persuasive to them.

Other advocates of a tort approach to sexual harassment recommend that a special tort of sexual harassment be legislated. Most seem to advocate a new tort because they believe that neither existing sex discrimination law nor existing tort law adequately compensates the victim of sexual harassment.[19] This tort is targeted at quid pro quo sexual harassment. Ellen Frankel Paul argues that

> [q]uid pro quo sexual harassment is morally objectionable and analogous to extortion: The harasser extorts property (i.e., use of the woman's body) through the leverage of fear for her job. The victim of such behavior should have legal recourse, but serious reservations can be held about rectifying these injustices through the blunt instrument of Title VII. In egregious cases, the victim is left less than whole (for back pay will not compensate her for ancillary losses), and no prospect [sic] for punitive damages are offered to deter would-be harassers.[20]

This is no longer true, since the passage of the Civil Rights Act of 1991. Victims of discrimination are now able to sue for punitive and compensatory damages. However, as I stated in chapter 3, the amounts are limited, according to the number of employees.[21] Paul may not believe these limited amounts to be sufficient. However, even if this change in the law did meet this objection to the use of Title VII for sexual harassment cases, she has a further objection.

> Even more distressing about Title VII is the fact that the primary target of litigation is not the actual harasser, but rather the employer. This places a double burden on the company. The employer is swindled by the supervisor because he spent his time pursuing sexual gratification and thereby impairing the efficiency of the workplace by mismanaging his subordinates, and the employer must endure lengthy and expensive litigation, pay damages, and suffer loss to its reputation. It would

be fairer to both the company and the victim to treat sexual harassment as a tort—that is, as a private wrong or injury for which the court can assess damages. Employers should be held vicariously liable only when they know of an employee's behavior and do not try to redress it.[22]

This objection introduces the subject of employer liability, which has been an extremely contentious issue among legal scholars.[23] It is not necessary for our purposes to engage in that debate. However, Paul's point is important to consider. Treating sexual harassment as sex discrimination under Title VII holds the employer responsible for the actions of the harassers, in cases in which the employers are not the harassers themselves. The harasser is only held responsible secondarily, and not by the law. This has struck many as unfair. The employer did not harass; the employee did. Yet the employer is treated as if he or she did.

Whether holding the employer liable is perceived as unfair depends on one's conception of sexual harassment. If, like MacKinnon, one conceives of sexual harassment as a group-based problem, as a form of discrimination, then this may not be objectionable. Employers are charged with maintaining nondiscriminatory environments for their employees. If an employee is discriminating against someone, the employer has the responsibility to stop it. More broadly, the employer has a responsibility to act so as prevent such discrimination in the first place by making it clear to all employees that discrimination will not be tolerated and by punishing those who discriminate. However, if one conceives of sexual harassment not as group based, but in terms of individuals, this is likely to seem wrongheaded. The person who performed the harmful act—and especially, the person who *benefited* from the act—should be held responsible, should *pay* for the harm; and the person who performed the harmful act and benefited from it is the harasser. The employer might be seen to have harmed the victim in an extenuated way—by not protecting the victim from the harasser—but the employer does not benefit from the harassment. In fact, the employer suffers harm. That something like this underlies Paul's objection is suggested by her inclusion of the remark that employers suffer a "double burden." Some have argued that the fact that the employer is harmed by the harassing employee suggests that market forces do, if allowed, eventually eliminate much sexual harassment without any interference by the government.[24]

Paul's sexual harassment tort would apply to both quid pro quo and some of what has been termed hostile environment sexual harassment. She suggests that

[o]nly instances above a certain threshold of egregiousness or outrageousness would be actionable. In other words, the behavior that the plaintiff found offensive would also have to be offensive to the proverbial "reasonable man" of the tort law. That is, the behavior would have to be objectively injurious rather than merely subjectively offensive. The defendant would be the actual harasser not the company, unless it knew about the problem and failed to act.[25]

It is unclear how this differs from the current interpretation of Title VII in cases of hostile environment sexual harassment, except for the fact that it is the harasser that is the primary target rather than the employer.

Paul objects to MacKinnon's definition of sexual harassment on the grounds that it includes abuse of power in the very definition of sexual harassment.

> While it mirrors accurately what transpires in the classic quid pro quo situation, it reflects only uneasily hostile environment sexual harassment by co-workers—unless one accepts the added, debatable, and more global assumption that males occupying any position in the workplace enjoy more power than women. . . . I prefer a neutral definition of sexual harassment to MacKinnon's, which injects an ideological bias against men and the capitalist marketplace.[26]

Thus, she seems to reject the assumption of male dominance central to the dominance perspective. This is reinforced by her argument against the notion that "sexual harassment is essentially a group injury."[27] According to Paul, quid pro quo sexual harassment is not a group injury because it lacks "an essential attribute of discrimination: that is, that *any* member of the scorned group will trigger the response of the person who practices discrimination."[28] She claims that the quid pro quo harasser acts only on someone he finds sexually attractive, not on all women. Paul argues that hostile environment sexual harassment fails to count as discrimination for similar reasons. Usually, it is *individuals* who are singled out for harassment, not every woman employee. Furthermore, she points out, there are difficulties with making the Title VII analysis of sex discrimination fit same-sex harassment.

> Discrimination . . . is harming someone or denying someone a benefit because that person is a member of a group that the discriminator despises. What the harasser is really doing is *preferring* or *selecting* some one member of his gender for sexual attention, however unwelcome that attention may be to its object. He certainly does not despise the entire group, nor does he wish to harm its members, since he is a member himself and finds others of the group sexually attractive. . . . Homosexual sexual harassment . . . raises the large issue of whether it makes sense to characterize the archetypical case of male to female harassment as discrimination, rather than as a preference, albeit misguided and objectionable.[29]

These concerns are those of courts confronting same-sex harassment, as we saw in chapter 3. However, Paul sees them as reflecting back on the original analysis of sexual harassment as sex discrimination. They do suggest that certain of these analyses are problematic.

Paul's recommended sexual harassment tort would allow behaviors others have wanted to classify as sexual harassment to be grouped together, thereby emphasizing that they have a common element. However, that common feature for Paul differs from that for MacKinnon. Paul supports an "individualist" approach, one that "stresses the victim's rights to privacy, to freedom from physical assault or the threat of it, and to freedom from the infliction of severe emotional distress."[30] The tort approach is consistent with this perspective. She argues that her approach "would also place all similar behavior under the same theoretical umbrella."

> Sexually offensive behavior occurs in settings other than the work-place—in universities, housing, and ordinary social situations of all sorts. When such behavior becomes egregious, plaintiffs should have a remedy, and a tort would allow courts to treat all sexual harassment alike. Moreover, a new state tort of sexual harassment, created by judicial construction or legislative craftsmanship, would be preferable to the doctrinal and theoretical confusion that the sexual-harassment-as-sexual-discrimination theory has engendered.[31]

Thus, what all instances of sexual harassment have in common is that they are "sexual," "offensive," and "egregious."

The tort itself would resemble the tort of intentional infliction of emotional distress, which distinguishes between "mere insults, indignities, threats, annoyances, petty oppression, or other trivialities,"[32] and behavior that causes emotional distress "so severe that no reasonable man could be expected to endure it."[33]

> Liability has been found only where the conduct has been so outrageous in character, and so extreme in degree, as to go beyond all possible bounds of decency, and to be regarded as atrocious, and utterly intolerable in a civilized community. Generally, the case is one in which the recitation of the facts to an average member of the community would arouse his resentment against the actor, and lead him to exclaim, "Outrageous."[34]

In addition, the behavior in question must be reckless or intentional. Paul's tort is:

(1) Sexual harassment is comprised of
  (a) unwelcome sexual propositions incorporating overt or implicit threats of reprisal, and/or
  (b) other sexual overtures or conduct so persistent and offensive that a reasonable person when apprised of the conduct would find it extreme and outrageous.
(2) To be held liable, the harasser must have acted either intentionally or recklessly and the victim must have suffered, thereby, economic detriment and/or extreme emotional distress.

(...) the employment context

(... the employer is liable when the plaintiff had notified an appropriate
official of the company (or himself the alleged harasser) of the offensive conduct and the employer failed to take good faith action to
forestall future incidents.

(... the employer is liable also when he should have known of the offending conduct [that is, when he failed to provide an appropriate
...... against the abuse].

This tort is supposed to include both quid pro quo and hostile environment
sexual harassment in its definition of sexual harassment and would use the
reasonable person standard for determining whether hostile environment sexual harassment had occurred.

(One major difference between this tort and MacKinnon's Title VII analysis
is that the definition of hostile environment sexual harassment is narrower. It
makes no mention of the gender of the harassed and harasser, or of their sexual orientation. No formal relationship between the harassed and the harasser
(such as employer-employee) is necessary; the law applies anywhere that offensive
sexual behavior may exist.

The last point made by Paul is significant. It essentially omits any mention of inequality
between the parties involved in an instance of harassment, a sexual harassment tort is warranted, he argues, Paul advocates the creation of a sexual
harassment tort to be used in addition to existing discrimination and tort laws.
His proposal includes the notion of "abuse of power." To establish a prima facie case
of sexual harassment, the following conditions would have to be fulfilled:

(1) A sought to participate in a special activity (e.g., tenancy, school, or work).
(2) B harassed A.
(3) B's harassment unreasonably harmed A.
(4) B holds a position with respect to the special activity that creates a duty
for B towards people in A's position.[36]

Thus, how we decide to treat sexual harassment under the law is important
for how we think about sexual harassment. Both group-based and individu-
alistic approaches are consistent with a broad, liberal perspective. Besides these
conceptual issues, there are what might be called external reasons for prefer-
ring one sort of approach over another.

One significant factor is that when someone files a suit under Title VII, the
government pays for it, not the individual on whose behalf the suit is filed.
This is not the case with state torts. This means that torts are available only
to those who can afford them. Also, the burden of proof on the complainant is
heavier in a tort case than in a discrimination case.[37] In addition, under tort
law, there is "no administrative mechanism to preserve confidentiality, protect against retaliation, seek conciliation, or encourage the company to make
changes. Also, consider that filing a lawsuit it usually an inflammatory act—
likely to jeopardize your job status and aggravate your working relationship

with your employer."[38] Therefore, bringing charges against one's employer would be feasible only if one did not intend to continue one's employment with the concern.

I have been comparing two approaches—tort and sex discrimination—but there may be others. Anita Bernstein suggests that we look to the Europeans for suggestions.[39] She claims that in the United States, there are currently two paradigms for treating sexual harassment: (1) as sex discrimination and (2) as rude behavior. The remedy for (1) is Title VII, and the remedy for (2) is tort law. But this may be a false dilemma. She suggests a third approach. It is to consider sexual harassment as a form of "detrimental workplace conditions."

According to Bernstein, Europeans are more skeptical than are Americans of the ability to bring about social change through civil litigation.[40]

> While Americans see the problem of sexual harassment as either wrongful private conduct between two people or as sex discrimination, Europeans have shaped it as a problem of workers, and sited the problem in the workplace. In the United States, sexual harassment is a legal wrong; in Europe—with the exception of extreme situations that amount to blackmail or physical violence—sexual harassment is atmosphere, conditions, an obstruction, or trouble, with very little blame from the law.[41]

While Bernstein does not advocate exchanging the American approach for the European approach as she describes it, she does suggest that we reconceive sexual harassment as "detrimental workplace conditions" and use litigation to remedy it.

While some European countries have conceived of sexual harassment as sex discrimination, as discussed in chapter 3, it remains true that, "[i]n most EC countries, sexual harassment cannot be the basis for criminal prosecution or private civil actions for damages . . . the idea that sexual harassment constitutes a legal wrong is not widely shared in Europe."[42] According to Bernstein, this is because, "[m]ore than any other country, the United States associates individual rights with private-law remedies. . . . The array of private-law remedies available—at least in theory—is wider in the U.S. than anywhere else."[43]

As we saw in chapter 3, responses to sexual harassment are circumscribed by the European Community. Bernstein argues that Europeans "describe sexual harassment as a danger to health and safety in the workplace," and that this conception works well within the constraints of the Community, since "working conditions have always been regarded as part of the economic policy that justified the formation of the Community."[44] She suggests that controversy among the Member States over what should be done to prevent discrimination can be sidestepped by focusing on health and safety. Bernstein points out that there is research by both Americans and Europeans to support the claim that sexual harassment can cause physical and emotional harm.

Bernstein raises the question of why Americans have not adopted this approach to sexual harassment.

The answer lies in the tension between viewing sexual harassment as a discrete wrong amenable to civil litigation and viewing it as an instance of collective harm, with neither victims nor wrongdoers sharply defined. A wrongful-conduct approach dominates the entire perception of sexual harassment. When sexual harassment is seen as a legal wrong, tort concepts predominate and the concept of workplace hazard becomes harder to keep in mind.[45]

Viewing sexual harassment as a workplace hazard has several potential advantages. One is that such a view relates sexual harassment to the "rights of workers in general." Such a conception focuses on human rights, on the right of every person, and thus every worker, to be treated with dignity. Also, in Europe, this way of conceiving of sexual harassment has led to the development of a variety of ways of treating sexual harassment in the workplace. These methods aim at preventing or stopping harassment, rather than at finding who is at fault. For example, some Europeans distinguish between formal and informal ways of resolving sexual harassment complaints.

> "[A]n informal method refrains from trying to judge the validity of the complaint of harassment, whereas a formal method points toward the goal of determining fault. An employee who wants only that the harassment stop and who has no interest in official blame would prefer an informal approach to a formal one. Such a preference is likely to be found in cases where a fault-based inquisition has not yet caused the employee to suffer, or where the objectionable conduct is not quite outrageous."[46]

In addition, the greater strength of trade unions in some European countries has meant that labor agreements can be used to address sexual harassment. As Bernstein points out, union involvement in remedying sexual harassment "would offer little to an American worker, who typically is not a member of a union and can be terminated without cause."[47] However, it would be possible for unions in the United States to do more to prevent sexual harassment than they currently do.

Bernstein ultimately recommends that we conceive of sexual harassment as "detrimental workplace conditions, to be cured by devices other than litigation."[48] She emphasizes that this is not intended to replace existing remedies for sexual harassment, but to provide additional remedies for sexual harassment.

There are thus several large questions before us (1) Is the law the best way to prevent sexual harassment? (2) If so, which kind of law, or combination of kinds of laws, is most likely to bring this about? Advocates of both the tort approach and the sex discrimination approach claim that their approach will be most likely to bring about the desired outcome. Of course, the outcomes they desire seem to be different. As we have seen, some supporters of the sex discrimination approach desire radical changes in the workplace, for example, the elimination of *any* sexual behavior. Advocates of the tort approach, such as Paul, do not think this end desirable. Paul wants an end to what she considers to be the "most egregious" examples of quid pro quo and hostile environment sexual harassment. (3) If the law is not the best way of preventing sexual harassment, what ought we to do? These questions shall be taken up in chapter 7. But first, we must address several other legal issues.

The Reasonable Woman Standard

One of the most controversial elements of sexual harassment law in recent years has been the question of the standard to be used in assessing whether hostile environment sexual harassment has occurred. It has been customary for courts in harassment cases to adopt a reasonable person standard as an objective standard. The notion of the reasonable person standard is borrowed from tort law.[49]

However, as we saw in chapter 3, in *Ellison v. Brady*, the court argued that adopting such a standard was unfair. The court claimed that because women and men experience sexual behavior differently, the standard used to determine whether harassment has occurred should be the perspective of the "reasonable victim." Because in sexual harassment cases, the victim is usually a woman, this has become known as the reasonable woman standard. Some commentators distinguish between the reasonable woman standard and the reasonable victim standard, so that the issue of which standard to use in sexual harassment cases involves three possible standards.[50] I shall treat the reasonable woman standard and the reasonable victim standard as variations of the same standard in what follows.

The reasonableness standard becomes relevant in hostile environment sexual harassment cases in seeking to prove one of the elements of a prima facie case: "For sexual harassment to be actionable, it must be sufficiently severe or pervasive to 'alter the conditions of [the victim's] employment and create an abusive working environment.'"[51] The question is how can it be determined whether the behavior in question is severe and pervasive enough to alter the conditions of employment.[52] And what standard should be used? It should not simply be that the plaintiff, the alleged victim, claims that her conditions of work have been altered by severe and pervasive behavior, though the Supreme Court has made this a necessary condition for satisfaction of this element of hostile environment cases.[53] This would render any such claim by any person an instance of sexual harassment. The standard should not be simply that of the defendant, the person accused, for this would absolve nearly all defendants. The standard should not simply be the perspective of a judge, or even a panel of judges, either. It is clear from some of the early decisions discussed in chapter 3 that judges sometimes simply use their own perspectives, with apparently unfair results.

The standard used to determine whether an abusive environment exists should take into account the perspective of the victim, of the defendant, of the judges themselves, and of society as a whole—to a certain extent. And this is where things begin to get tricky. Conceiving of sexual harassment as sex discrimination seems to require a departure from the status quo. This is evident in the disagreement between the majority and Judge Keith in *Rabidue*.

Recall that the majority in *Rabidue* declared: "It must never be forgotten that Title VII is the federal court mainstay in the struggle for equal employment opportunity for the female workers of America. But it is quite different to claim that Title VII was designed to bring about a magical transformation in the social mores of American workers."[54] Judge Keith's dissenting opinion challenged this claim: "[U]nless the outlook of the reasonable woman is adopted, the defendants as well as the courts are permitted to sustain ingrained notions of reasonable behavior fashioned by the offenders, in this case, men."[55] Keith believed that the reasonable person standard did not represent an objective viewpoint. Rather, it represented the viewpoint of those who had, until quite recently, had the power to determine appropriate workplace behavior. It does not represent the viewpoint of those who have had to suffer the consequences of this "appropriate workplace behavior"—having to leave a position, being fired in retaliation for rejecting advances, having to suffer an abusive work environment. The reasonable person standard only represents what society finds socially acceptable if society is limited to those in power.

The claim that sexual harassment—particularly hostile environment sexual harassment—is illegal under Title VII poses a challenge to prevailing norms of appropriate workplace behavior. If, as Keith seems to claim, the reasonable person standard represents the view of "society," and it is the standard adopted, we can expect sexual harassment case law to lag behind changes in social perceptions of appropriate workplace behavior, rather than to cause these changes. Keith suggests that fairness requires that the standard used to determine whether hostile environment sexual harassment has occurred must take into account the perspective of those whose voices have not, until now, been taken into account in determining appropriate workplace behavior.

Whether or not the courts should promote social change is a question over which there is much disagreement. Actual courts seem to disagree, since they have not been consistent in their choice of standard in deciding hostile environment sexual harassment cases. "Within the First Circuit, confusion abounds regarding the appropriate perspective to apply in evaluating harassing conduct. One court has applied a 'two perspective standard.' . . . Another has adopted a 'reasonable person' standard. . . . And yet a third has addressed harassing behavior from the standpoint of the particular plaintiff."[56]

Where did the idea of a reasonable woman standard come from? Was it created from nothing? Prior to its appearance in *Ellison*, the reasonable woman standard was already in use in certain torts and self-defense cases.[57] In 1984, a Note appeared in which the author argued that a "reasonable woman" standard should be adopted in hostile environment sexual harassment cases.[58] Judge Keith referred to this Note in his dissenting opinion in *Rabidue v. Osceola Refining Co.*[59]

At least one commentator has argued that the urgency of a clear, uniform standard for judging whether hostile environment sexual harassment has taken placed increased after the Supreme Court's decision in *Harris v. Forklift Systems, Inc.*[60] In *Harris*, the Supreme Court ruled that psychological injury was not necessary for a finding of hostile environment sexual harassment. However, this meant that courts could no longer use the criterion of whether psychological injury had resulted from a behavior to determine the severity of the behavior.

> [T]he abrogation of an injury element in hostile environment claims makes the clarification of the standard for determining hostility of critical importance. An injury requirement for hostile environment liability provided some certainty to employers as well as individual offenders. Gauging the culpability of one's conduct is much easier if actual injury to the victim is necessary to make the conduct legally prohibited. Also, incidents severe enough to cause actual injury to a victim would be much more likely to come to the attention of an employer than conduct that is not likely to cause actual injury. The Court's recognition that requiring injury to the victim would subvert the goals of Title VII creates a greater degree of uncertainty in the workplace with regard to the type of conduct necessary to cause liability.[61]

Most commentators seem to agree that *Harris* did not give a definitive answer to the question of whether the standard should be the reasonable person or the reasonable woman.[62] Some see *Harris* as silent on this issue. Others interpret *Harris* to imply that "reasonable person" can include features of the actual claimant, such as sex or race.[63] Thus, to this day, there is uncertainty about what standard should be used in judging hostile environment sexual harassment cases.

In order to determine what standard should be used, we must inquire just what the reasonable person standard means. We can begin trying to get clear on this by looking at the historical development of the standard. The use of the standard begins in cases involving negligence.

> One of the earliest reported uses of the reasonable man standard occurred in a 19th century British case, Vaughan v. Menlove, 132 Eng. Rep. 490 (1837). In that case, the court stated that "[i]nstead . . . of saying that the liability for negligence should be coextensive with the judgment of each individual . . . we ought rather to adhere to the rule which requires in all cases a regard to caution such as a man of ordinary prudence would observe." . . . The reasonableness test, as it has developed, is intended to reflect changing social mores as well as to present an objective standard that imposes the same behavior on everyone, thereby limiting arbitrary or politically based decision-making by judges.[64]

Over time, the reasonable person standard has come to mean one of two things: "(i) an ideal, albeit not perfect, person whose behavior served as an objective measure against which to judge our actions and (ii) an average or typical person possessing all of the shortcomings and weaknesses tolerated by the community."[65] Commentators claim that it is the second interpretation that has become the primary meaning of the standard. It is this second interpretation that is used to define the reasonable woman standard: "[T]hose courts that have moved to the 'reasonable woman' standard intend it to describe average or typical women—women who react differently to situations than do most men but who, at the same time, are neither hypersensitive to nor unoffended by men's workplace behavior."[66] Thus, the reasonable woman is one who is average, in some sense—not too sensitive, but not insensitive, either—in her reactions to workplace behavior. However, this seems to be a purely descriptive interpretation of the reasonable woman, focusing as it does on the way a reasonable woman *does* behave. This impression is strengthened by the common use of empirical data to support the view that reasonable women and reasonable men perceive certain conduct differently. However, the origins of the reasonable person standard make it clear that the standard is also prescriptive, or normative. It includes societal views about how a reasonable person *should* react or behave. It follows that the reasonable woman standard is also normative.

Focusing on the normative aspect of the reasonable person and reasonable woman standards suggests that we do not need a reasonable woman standard—that the reasonable person standard is adequate if we acknowledge that such a standard must change with the changing mores of society. The dispute between the majority and Judge Keith in *Rabidue* can be interpreted as a clash about what it is to be a reasonable person in the United States in the 1990s. People have interpreted Keith's response to mean that we should jettison the reasonable person standard and replace it with a reasonable woman or reasonable man standard. One argument for the reasonable woman standard, based on *Rabidue*, seems to go like this:

1. The court in case *x* used a reasonable person standard (or an unstated standard) in determining whether sexual harassment occurred.
2. This court did not find that sexual harassment occurred.
3. But sexual harassment did occur.
4. So, the reasonable person standard should not be used when determining whether sexual harassment has occurred.[67]

However, this argument is faulty. There are many cases in which a reasonable person standard (or an unstated standard) was used and the result was considered just by those who think the outcome in *Rabidue* was unjust. Thus, it is hasty to conclude that it is the reasonable person standard that is at fault.

However, this is not the only possible way of interpreting Keith—or, if he has since agreed with the predominant interpretation—it is not the only possible way of thinking about what went wrong in *Rabidue*. An alternative is to understand the majority in *Rabidue* to have used an obsolete version of the reasonable man standard when they should have used a genuine reasonable person standard. Judge Keith can be seen as pointing out that a reasonable person standard would take into account that not all persons are male, not all persons are unaffected by vulgarity, and so on. I say an obsolete version of the reasonable man standard was used because it seems to me that the circumstances described in *Rabidue* would have been seen as abusive by many people, not just women. The same can be said of some of the other cases in which the reasonable person standard was used and the plaintiff did not prevail.[68] Rather than throw out the reasonable person standard because it gave the wrong verdict, we should retain it and refine it with knowledge of what is viewed as abusive by different people, and of what people want and have a right to expect in their work environment.

Still another way of viewing *Rabidue* is as a misapplication of the reasonable person standard. The judges simply used their own, rather restricted perspectives in deciding the case, taking their opinions to represent the reasonable person. The application of a standard can be wrong, even if the standard itself is not inherently flawed.

Sometimes the issue of the reasonable woman standard is presented as if it could be settled by empirical research. If women and men really do perceive sexual and other behaviors differently, we should have different standards; if not, we should not. Arguments in favor of the reasonable woman standard usually do depend in part on empirical data on male and female perceptions of behaviors. But, as we saw in chapter 4, these data are inconclusive; and, as I argued in chapter 1, empirical data are subject to manipulation. Given this, proponents of the competing views seems to be driven by deeper, more global perspectives. Ironically, it turns out that both those who hold a natural/biological perspective and those who hold the sociocultural perspective tend to support use of the reasonable woman standard.

Kingsley Browne argues that male and female sexual strategies are so different that they produce differing perceptions of behavior, and that these differing perceptions must be acknowledged if the law is to be fair.

> If a biological perspective can contribute anything to sexual harassment policy, it must be the insight that a "reasonable person" standard is meaningless. At least when it comes to matters of sex and sexuality, there are no "reasonable persons," only "reasonable men" and "reasonable women." The different and discrete sexual natures of men and women cannot be blended into a one-size-fits-all "human sexual nature"; sex must be specified in order to make the concept intelligible.[69]

To support his claim, Browne seeks to refute Gutek and O'Connor's claim that the empirical data on male-female differences in perception do not support use of a reasonable woman standard. He also raises the possibility that which standard is adopted may have no effect on the outcome of cases, and he urges more empirical study to determine whether or not this is the case.

Adherents of a sociocultural perspective, such as MacKinnon, would seem to favor the reasonable woman standard, but McKinnon herself does not.[70] It is clear, however, that many who adopt her perspective do. One of the best arguments for employing a reasonable woman standard is articulated by philosopher Debra DeBruin.[71] DeBruin argues that justice requires that courts adopt the reasonable woman standard when determining whether hostile environment sexual harassment has taken place because the reasonable *person* standard is actually the reasonable *man* standard. In other words, simply changing the word "man" to "person" does not change the standard from a male standard to a genderless one. Because males dominate in our society, their "identity and experience serve as the characterization or standard of what it is to be a person." So, applying a reasonable person standard amounts to applying a reasonable *man* standard. This is significant because in matters of sex, men and women have different perspectives, and they sometimes disagree about whether sexual harassment has occurred or not. DeBruin refers to empirical studies to support this claim. In particular, there is evidence that a woman sometimes feels justifiably threatened by behavior that, at most, shocks a man.[72]

There are both conceptual and practical issues in DeBruin's argument. The conceptual issues include her claim that "person" in a male-dominated society means "man," so that the "reasonable person" is really a "reasonable man." I find this argument somewhat persuasive; however, I think that it was more true twenty or thirty years ago than it is today. The civil rights movement and the women's movement challenge this assumption in their claim that opportunities should be open to everyone, not just to certain groups of Americans. In the years since Title VII was enacted, we have seen a deepening of our collective understanding of the extent to which opportunities are not equal. Many beliefs that would have seemed unreasonable to the reasonable man of thirty years ago are now seen as wholly reasonable— which is not to say that there is not a great deal of disagreement.

This brings us to the more practical elements of DeBruin's argument. She claims that, because "person" means "man," and because in the context of sexual harassment, there is a relevant difference between women and men, it is unfair to women to adopt a reasonable man as the standard for determining whether hostile environment sexual harassment has occurred. I claim that the truth of the claim that "person" means "man" has changed, and that it is less true than it once was. We have seen evidence that the gap between women and men in perceiving the existence of sexual harassment has narrowed. DeBruin ends her paper with the comment that, "at least at this point in our history, embracing a gender-neutral ideal of justice damns us to the perpetuation of gender oppression."[73] This suggests that DeBruin's argument is ultimately a practical one. The question at issue is which approach is most likely to bring about the changes in the workplace—and in society at large—that will bring about equality for women and men (if that is what is desired). DeBruin and others seem to believe that adoption of the reasonable woman standard is necessary to bring about a more egalitarian society. I disagree. I do not think it is necessary, nor do I think it is sufficient.

I do not think it is necessary because, as I said earlier, I believe that there are ways of bringing about the kinds of changes that DeBruin desires without adopting such a standard. DeBruin herself seems almost to recognize this when she takes up the notion of reasonableness that the reasonable woman standard requires. This cannot be the average woman since such a woman would probably have imbibed the same sexist culture as the average man and may think that women simply must put up with what DeBruin considers sexual harassment.[74] Nor can the reasonable woman be simply any woman since this would mean that if one woman found behavior harassing, it would be. This would lead to behaviors that should not be considered harassing being categorized as harassing. DeBruin suggests that

> an acceptable account of reasonableness must be based on an adequate understanding of what it is like to be a woman in this society. . . . [I]nformation about how gender affects our lives is crucial if we are to determine whether it is reasonable to judge that certain treatment is severe and pervasive enough to create an intimidating, hostile or offensive environment, and thus is hostile-environment sexual harassment.[75]

However, it seems to me that if we were to develop the notion of a reasonable person in this way, we would not need judges to adopt the reasonable woman standard in sexual harassment cases. The particular information about what it is to be a woman in this society—to be, in fact, particularly vulnerable to sexual violence—would be available to judges. The kinds of behavior that are problematic because of these facts could be codified, as DeBruin suggests: "[O]ur sexual harassment regulations should codify guidelines for making . . . judgments. These guidelines should be as specific as possible—including specific types of behavior that it is reasonable to classify as sexual harassment."[76] If this were to be done, it is not clear why adoption of the reasonable woman standard would be necessary.

My view on the reasonable woman standard is consistent with that of legal scholar Kathryn Abrams. Abrams argues that we should use a reconceived notion of a reasonable person: the reasonable person "interpreted to mean not the average person, but the person enlightened concerning the barriers to women's equality in the workplace."[77] Abrams describes four kinds of information about women that would be necessary for judges and juries to make informed decisions: (1) [i]nformation about "barriers that women have faced, and continue to face, in the workplace"; (2) "the role of sexualized treatment in thwarting women in the workplace"; (3) "effects on the work lives of women" of sexual harassment; and (4) "information about the responses of women workers to harassment."[78] Katherine Franke describes the virtues of this standard.

> Abrams' new standard has the additional advantage of being more likely to provoke the transformation of workplace norms rather than merely critique them from a woman's perspective—whatever that might be. This standard embodies a progressive normative bias absent from existing sexual harassment doctrine. At best, the reasonable woman standard imposes liability on men who simply "don't get it," while at the same time building into the law the notion that men and women "get" sexual conduct differently: reasonable men and reasonable women, in a sense, agree to disagree about the meaning of sexual conduct in the workplace. Abrams' new standard, on the other hand, substitutes a gender neutral normative standard for what is reasonable conduct in the workplace—harassers have to "get with it."[79]

I do not think adoption of the reasonable woman standard is sufficient to bring about equality of opportunity because I think that without the other kinds of activities that are bringing about change, such as the efforts of activists and writers, the reasonable woman standard will become the very thing that many fear it already is: a capitulation to people who claim that women are fragile and just need more protection than men. Adoption of the reasonable person standard does not guarantee outcomes with which one agrees, nor does adoption of a reasonable woman standard. Without education, people will not know how to apply the standard. But if people need to learn to apply the standard by seeing what things are like from another's point of view, why cannot we simply change the reasonable person standard to include these points of view?

DeBruin responds to the argument that adoption of a reasonable woman standard will simply reinforce harmful gender stereotypes. She calls that argument the "Entrenching Sexism Objection." She takes as her target a version of the argument from *Radke v. Everett*.

> Although well intended, a gender-conscious standard could reintrench the very sexist attitudes it is attempting to counter. The belief that women are entitled to a separate legal standard merely reinforces, and perhaps originates from, the stereotypic notion that first justified subordinating women in the workplace. Courts utilizing the reasonable woman standard pour into the standard stereotypic assumptions of women which infer women are sensitive, fragile, and in need of a more protective standard. Such paternalism degrades women and is repugnant to the very ideals of equality that the [civil rights] act is intended to protect.[80]

DeBruin argues that the reasonable woman standard, contrary to this argument, provides equal protection for men and women—it protects each from behaviors that harm them, though these behaviors may not be identical. She makes the important point that this is only seen as paternalism if the traditional male point of view is adopted: *real* harm is what *men* think is harmful. What men do not think is harmful is not really harmful. If women think it is, they are being overly sensitive.

I do not disagree with DeBruin's response to this argument. However, my point is that we should only adopt the reasonable woman standard if it is either necessary or sufficient for ensuring equal opportunities for women in the workplace, and that it is neither. It is certainly not sufficient, and DeBruin seems to realize this, since she calls for explicit guidelines on what constitutes harassment, enlightened judges, and educational programs, as well as for adoption of the reasonable woman standard.

However, if everything else that DeBruin recommends were implemented, the adoption of the reasonable woman standard would be otiose. So, my disagreement with DeBruin concerns the necessity of the reasonable woman standard, since we agree that the adoption of the reasonable woman standard is not sufficient to deal adequately with sexual harassment.

Additional reasons have been offered for not adopting the reasonable woman standard. Some have argued that the reasonable woman standard requires that men be judged according to a standard of behavior which they are "unable to understand or appreciate fully."[81] "Undoubtedly, the most troubling question is whether it is proper or fair to impose liability, including potential liability for substantial money damages on men (and on their employers) for well-intentioned behavior that they do not realize is illegal or offensive."[82] This is a genuine worry of men in the academy and in the workplace. As such, it should be taken seriously. If the reasonable woman standard *does* require that men act in accordance with standards of behavior they are unable to understand fully, clearly it would be unfair to adopt it. However, on most understandings of the reasonable woman standard, men are not required to do this. This objection makes several erroneous assumptions. It seems to assume that unless men can have the *same* experiences as women, men will be unable to distinguish between harassing and nonharassing behaviors. Men cannot have the same experiences as women; so, men cannot distinguish between harassing and nonharassing behaviors. There are two ways of criticizing this argument. It is not necessary that someone have the same experience as another person to understand that person's perspective. Listening to people and reading what they write can provide insight into another person's reality. Empathy and imagination may be required, but most of us have those capacities. We must, of course, be willing to exercise them. We must also be willing to entertain the idea that our feelings and reactions are not the only possible legitimate ones. It may also be true that men *can* have the same experiences as women, or at least very similar ones, in many areas of life, including those relevant to sexual harassment. Many boys are the victims of sexual abuse by adults, and many others are bullied and ridiculed about their sexuality as they are growing up, and even as adults. Perhaps these are not the harassers, perhaps they are. We do not know the relationship between child sexual abuse and sexual harassment of others. However, not all men harass, and many of these fully understand the meaning of such behavior, whether because they can identify with victims of harassment because of experiences of their own, or because they have sufficient imagination to do so.

However, the worry raised by Davis, Browne, and Wall over genuinely unintentional behaviors that are considered harassment should be addressed.[83] Miscommunication certainly does occur, and it is most likely to occur in those ambiguous cases over which women and men tend to disagree. It is difficult to determine a person's true intention, but that is a general difficulty, not one peculiar to the issue of sexual harassment. Again, it is in the kinds of cases over which there is disagreement that intention is most difficult to determine. Both Browne and Wall seem to think that in cases of miscommunication, men are being asked to bear an unfair burden. Both think that much of the current treatment of sexual harassment, both in the courts and in writings on the subject, ignores women's role in miscommunication.

Recall Wall's definition of sexual harassment. He tries to capture the notion of "unwanted sexual advances" by saying that sexual harassment occurs when X does not attempt to obtain Y's consent to communicate sexual interest to Y but communicates that interest anyway (if certain other conditions are also satisfied).

> [S]uppose that somewhere the communication between X and Y breaks down and X honestly believes he or she has obtained Y's consent to this discussion, when, in fact, he or she has not. In this case, X's intentions and actions being what they are, X does not sexually harass Y. X has shown respect for Y's privacy. Y may certainly *feel* harassed in this case, but there is no offender here. However, after X sees Y's displeasure at the remarks, it is now X's duty to refrain from such remarks, unless, of course, Y later consents to such a discussion.[84]

As Wall rightly points out, the way to avoid such misunderstandings is to practice clear communication. People must make their desires clear to one another. He provides an example: "when someone wishes not to discuss an individual's sexual interest in them, it would be foolish for them to make flirting glances at this individual. Such gestures may mislead the individual to conclude that they consent to this communication."[85] Without making a point of it, Wall seems here to be distributing the responsibility for misunderstandings between the parcipants of the sort that may appear to be sexual harassment but are not, on his view.

Browne takes up a similar line: "When sex differences in perspective lead to miscommunication, who, if anyone, is to blame? The usual answer in the sexual harassment literature is that it is the man who is responsible; after all, he has made a sexual advance that was 'unwelcome.'"[86] Browne points out that the source of misunderstanding can come from the woman. The man might think that the woman is welcoming sexual attention by her clothing or makeup, that she is sending "signals," whether intended or unintended. Because of this, it is unjust to simply place the blame on men.

> If men sometimes engage in sexually oriented conduct or speech that a reasonable woman might perceive as threatening even though no threat was intended, the problem could be characterized as either a misperception on the part of the woman or insensitivity on the part of the man concerning the effect of the signals he is sending. By the same token, if women sometimes engage in conduct that a reasonable man might perceive to be inviting even though no invitation was intended, the problem could be characterized as either a misperception on the part of the man or an insensitivity on the part of the woman concerning the signals she is sending. In both cases, however, the usual analysis deems the miscommunication the fault of the man, without explanation of why, if men are held responsible for threats they did not intend, women should not be responsible for invitations they did not intend.[87]

Though this is stated somewhat contentiously, it addresses an important issue. Men are being asked to change their behavior, but women are not being asked to change theirs. One response would be to point out that the men who are being asked to change their behavior have done something wrong, while the women have done nothing wrong. But this is to beg the question at issue. The controversy is over whether behaviors in the gray zone—flirtation, sexual teasing, sexual jokes, sexual comments, and the like—should be considered illegal sexual harassment. Though I disagree with Browne's framing of the issue, I do agree that both women and men need to change their behaviors. This has not been sufficiently emphasized in most writing on sexual harassment.

In the context of the discussion of the reasonable woman standard, I agree with Browne that its adoption seems to place an unfair burden on men. However, I do not agree with the stronger claim, that it requires men to do the impossible—adhere to a standard they cannot understand.

Another argument against adoption of the reasonable woman standard takes the form of a reductio ad absurdum. Some argue that if the reasonable victim approach is adopted, understood as the reasonable woman when the issue is sex, there is no reason not to adopt the appropriate category for other protected classes:

> Title VII bars discriminatory behavior based not only on sex, but also based on race, color, religion, or national origin. If the courts are to apply a "reasonable woman" standard in sexual harassment cases, does this suggest that a "reasonable victim" standard will apply in other hostile environment cases? We see no basis for refusing to extend the reasoning in Ellison and similar sexual discrimination cases to causes of action involving other classes protected under Title VII. . . . [88]

Particularizing the "reasonable x" has been done in a case of racial harassment, *Harris v. International Paper Co.*[89] In *Harris*, the judge adopted a "reasonable black person" standard, using the analogy to the reasonable woman standard.[90]

> To give full force to . . . [the] recognition of the differing perspectives which exist in our society, the standard for assessing the unwelcomeness and pervasiveness of conduct and speech must be founded on a fair concern for the different social experiences of men and women in the case of sexual harassment, and of white Americans, and black Americans in the case of racial harassment. . . . [I]nstances of racial violence . . . which might appear to white observers as mere "pranks" are, to black observers, evidence of threatening, pervasive attitudes closely tied with racial jokes, comments or nonviolent conduct which white observers are more likely to dismiss as non-threatening isolated incidents. . . . Since the concern of Title VII and the MHRA [Maine Human Rights Act] is to redress the effects of conduct and speech on their victims, the fact finder must "walk a mile in the victim's shoes" to understand these effects and how they should be remedied. In sum, the appropriate standard to be applied in this hostile environment is that of a reasonable black person.[91]

A non–Title VII case involving religious rights adopted a "reasonable non-adherent" standard.[92] In a case involving claims of both sexual and racial harassment, *Stingley v. Arizona*,[93] the court claimed that the proper standard was the "reasonable black woman": "[t]he proper perspective from which to evaluate the hostility of the environment is the 'reasonable person of the same gender and race or color' standard."[94] The possibility that this particularizing of the standard could extend to all protected classes has led some commentators to reject the reasonable woman standard.[95] Others point to it as a problem that must be faced if the standard is adopted.

> If consistency rules in those courts that adopt the "reasonable woman" standard, we see no way for them to avoid adopting similar standards in cases involving race, color, religion, or national origin. To say the least, this presents serious concerns for corporate officials who must comply with Title VII in future years as increasing numbers of women and racial, ethnic, and religious minorities enter the job market. Tailoring the workplace to avoid offending "reasonable Haitians," "reasonable blacks," "reasonable Asians," "reasonable Rastafarians," "reasonable Muslims," as well as "reasonable women," may prove to be an insuperable task.[96]

The tone of this suggests that this is intended as a reductio ad absurdum. However, others welcome the application of particularized standards to protected classes.[97]

I do not think it is absurd to extend the particularity of the reasonable victim standard on the basis of group characteristics other than sex. I do think that the listing of combinations of national origin, race, sex, age, and disability shows that there is something wrong with the approach. For one thing, most judges do not know what a reasonable Muslim female perspective is. However, this is not a reason to retreat to some vague reasonable man standard. Sensitivity to the situations of people of protected classes should be a part of every judge's education. Since membership in these classes changes, continuing education is needed. But if judges were to become more sensitive to people from groups other than their own, a "reasonable x" standard would not be needed. The experiences of all people should be incorporated into the reasonable person standard, not just one's own experiences.[98]

The suggested extension of the reasonable victim standard does show a problem with the adoption of a reasonable woman standard that has influenced feminist scholars who previously endorsed the reasonable woman standard to change their minds.[99] What is the *common* experience of a woman? Which woman is the *reasonable* woman? How do race, class, religion, and national origin influence the experiences of women? Also, as we saw in chapter 3, same-sex harassment cases can involve harassment of men who are seen as not properly masculine. Use of a reasonable man standard will not help here, because some conceptions of the reasonable men might be more masculine, though many would say that the man is being harassed because of his sex, and that it is negatively affecting his working conditions.

While a reasonable woman standard could help women in some respects, a reasonable man standard could hamper male plaintiffs because the implementation of such a subjective review would invoke all of the traditional notions of manhood. As a result, a man could lose a suit because his response to the sexual harassment was not close enough to the response of a reasonable man, i.e., the traditionally sexually receptive man. A man would lose under the reasonable man theory versus the reasonable person theory because a "hypersensitive" response would be unreasonable under the dictates of his patriarchal gender. In contrast, it would be reasonable (and traditionally accepted) for a woman to be "hypersensitive" to sexual harassment, so she would have a greater chance of prevailing with the reasonable woman standard. Tradition becomes the male plaintiff's nemesis, however. [100]

It seems that the shift of some feminist writers from advocates of the reasonable woman standard to advocates of some reconstructed reasonable person standard is prompted at least in part by a wider view of the victims of sexual harassment. Franke, for example, argues that if we look at the causes of sexual harassment of women, we will see that it has to do with the policing of a gender-sex partnering duo—the insistence that biological males be masculine and biological females be feminine. But if this is considered to be discriminatory, then other instances of such regulation, such as harassing men who are not considered to be masculine or heterosexual enough, should also be considered discriminatory. This expansion of the concept of sexual harassment may not be one to which everyone agrees. But it does tend to make sexual harassment more clearly everyone's problem, and not just women's.

Katherine Franke cites Kathryn Abrams's recommendation for an "enlightened reasonable person" standard with approval, noting that it does not go far enough to protect the right to "do gender" as one wishes:

> [T]o the extent that Abrams' standard demands only that reasonable people be enlightened with respect to the barriers to women's equality in the workplace, it demands too little. Title VII should enlighten the underlying causes of women's inequality, which include the sexual harassment of men who deviate from a hetero-patriarchal script. Thus, I urge that we take Abrams' standard one step further, and demand that reasonable people be educated in and sensitive to the ways in which sexism can and does limit workplace options for all persons, male or female. [101]

It seems that even if one accepts the arguments that women and men have been socialized differently—or are inherently different—so that women, but not men, tend to view certain behaviors as threatening or demeaning, it does not follow that the reasonable woman standard should be adopted. Adopting this standard seems to require an additional premise: men are incapable of coming to see which types of behavior *are* threatening and demeaning to women. But if men are so incapable, then there is no hope, since charging them with sexual harassment and disciplining them will not teach them what is harassing. In discussing the necessity of a reasonable woman standard, commentators often seem to forget that it was a male judge who first articulated the standard (Keith in *Rabidue*) and that both female and male judges have adopted the reasonable woman standard and the reasonable person standard for hostile environment cases.

If men are truly unable to understand which behaviors compromise women's equality, the only alternative would seem to be to prohibit *all* sexual behavior in the workplace—and this is what some recommend. This would, in effect, ban sexual expression of any kind in the workplace. But why should we do this? There is nothing wrong with sexuality. The burden would seem to be on those who want it banned from the workplace to show that there is something wrong with it. I do not think they have done so.

One commentator has argued that sexual conduct should be banned from the workplace because it has no positive business value. This is an example of placing the onus on those who would allow sexual behavior in the workplace to prove that it should be allowed. However, unless it can be proved that it seriously harms people, any kind of behavior that the employer condones should be allowed in the workplace.

> The existence of the unwelcomeness requirement suggests that "welcome" sexual conduct has some value in the workplace, so that the law is required to distinguish between the two forms of conduct. But why should the law tolerate any sexual conduct in the workplace? What redeeming value does such conduct have that the law should go to such lengths to protect that conduct? While good working relationships between supervisors and subordinates and between coworkers are conducive to their employer's interests, the existence of even consensual intimate relationships is not likely to result in good working relationships. Moreover, the hundreds of published sexual harassment cases should inform employers that the existence of sexual banter and sexual posters in the workplace does nothing to enhance the working atmosphere for many, if not most, employees. Surely the law has no interest in bending over backwards to preserve the right of sexist or mean-spirited employees to engage in behavior that almost everyone recognizes is inappropriate for the workplace.[102]

This seems to dismiss the evidence that many people want sexuality not to be banned from the workplace. As more and more women work, the workplace is a source of romantic partners. It is difficult to see how this kind of interaction could take place if sexual conduct were banned from the workplace, if romantic relationships were prohibited among employees.

Short of banning all sexuality from the workplace, we should place our hope in education. Enormous changes have already taken place with regard to men's perceptions of the effects of sexual behavior on women in the workplace. The 1987 and 1994 Merit Surveys show a growing consensus among men and women about what is harassing behavior and what is not. Some recent national polls report very little difference in the perceptions of men and women today.[103] With regard to those items which women seem more prone to see as harassing than men, serious discussions need to take place to determine whether they *should* be treated as harassing, and whether they should be illegal. Most men, being well-intentioned, will not engage in them if women say they are harassing or offensive. But those who do can be ostracized or educated by the group. Men can learn to see which behaviors are threatening to women and which are demeaning. Such claims are not based on "intuition." They are based on reason. Martha Chamallas emphasizes this point in describing her idea of a reasonable woman: "the hypothetical reasonable woman is the woman who is able to offer a reasoned account of how the sexual conduct challenged in the lawsuit functions to deprive women of equal employment opportunities."[104] Reasons can be used to rationally persuade, rather than to force.

Many seem to misunderstand the reasonable person standard. If a heterosexual male alleges harassment by a homosexual male, and the typical heterosexual male is homophobic, does the reasonable victim standard require us to consider the perspective of a homophobic, heterosexual male as the reasonable victim? Surely not. This suggests that the reasonable person standard is a construct which embodies what we, as a society, have decided is reasonable behavior. It is *this* that is at issue at this moment in time. Adoption of a reasonable woman standard does not solve *this* problem. We still must decide, as a society, which kinds of behavior people may seek legal remedy for, and which they must handle on their own. The reasonable person should not rely solely on his or her intuitions or first thoughts in making a decision. The reasonable person should realize that his or her experiences are parochial. He or she looks for arguments, evidence of what other people experience, and tries to make a fair judgment based on both personal experience and the claims of others. To insist on the reasonable woman standard suggests that women will simply consult their intuitions, and men will consult women. Surely this is not reasonable.

Same-Sex Harassment

Most of the sexual harassment cases that have come before the courts have been cases in which men were the harassers and women the harassed. Those who originally conceived of sexual harassment as sex discrimination had such cases in mind. However, Title VII is gender neutral in the sense that its prohibition of sex discrimination applies both to discrimination against women and to discrimination against men. There have been some cases in which women have allegedly harassed men, men harassed men, and women harassed women.[105] The number of sexual harassment cases filed with the EEOC by men has been increasing, but it was only 10 percent of all such cases in 1994.[106] Men usually lose cases in which they allege harassment by a woman.[107] However, some men have received very large amounts of money when the decision went in their favor.[108]

Since the late 1970s, sexual harassment has been illegal under Title VII of the 1964 Civil Rights Act. This is because sexual harassment is considered to be a form of sex discrimination. However, as I showed in chapter 3, the reasons for categorizing sexual harassment as sex discrimination have never been clear. Legal scholars and judges continue to struggle to say just why sexual harassment should be considered a form of sex discrimination prohibited under Title VII (or why it should not). As we saw in chapter 3, this issue is highlighted in cases of same-sex sexual harassment—that is, cases in which the alleged harasser is of the same sex as the alleged harassee. In these cases, the assumptions underlying the claim that sexual harassment constitutes illegal sex discrimination are laid bare.[109]

In chapter 3, I laid out three arguments that have been used by the courts to connect sexual harassment and sex discrimination: the sexual desire argument, the sex stereotype argument, and the differential treatment argument. In this section, I shall discuss the contributions of legal scholars to this debate. The theoretical debate over whether same-sex harassment constitutes sex discrimination is interesting for the light it sheds on the very different perspectives that underlie the more general question of whether sexual harassment constitutes sex discrimination under Title VII.[110]

Predictably, legal scholars disagree about whether same-sex harassment should be treated in the same way as different-sex harassment, and their arguments for why sexual harassment constitutes sex discrimination—when it does—vary. I will survey some representative theorists who seek to show that at least some sexually harassing behavior is also illegal sex discrimination and compare them by showing the implications of their views for whether Joseph Oncale, the plaintiff in the case in which the Supreme Court ruled that same-sex harassment can constitute sex discrimination under Title VII, was a victim of sex discrimination under Title VII. I shall also discuss whether harassment based on sexual orientation constitutes sex discrimination under each theory.

Many legal scholars subscribe to a version of the differences approach described in chapter 3. Kara Gross holds that the purpose of Title VII is to eliminate gender inequality. She argues that different-sex and same-sex harassment should be treated in the same way because both perpetuate gender inequality:

> Title VII's provision prohibiting sex discrimination was enacted to eliminate gender inequality in the workplace by ensuring that employment decisions are based on individual merit and not on the gender of the employee. Therefore, gender-based decisions motivated either by the employee's sex (male or female) or by stereotypes associated with the individual's sex (masculine or feminine) violate Title VII's mandate of workplace equality. Similarly, harassment of an individual because of the individual's sex or because of the individual's failure to conform to preconceived gender roles violates Title VII because such harassment perpetuates gender inequality. The threshold question in determining Title VII violations is whether the harassment is gender-based. Therefore, it should make no difference whether the harasser and the victim are the same gender, provided that the harassment occurs because of the employee's gender.[111]

Gross's argument very clearly makes use of two of the ways of linking sexual harassment and sex discrimination discussed in chapter 3: sexual desire and sex stereotypes. In her view, there should be no difference in the application of Title VII to different-sex and same-sex cases of sexual harassment.

Gross would find for Oncale, because the kind of treatment to which he was subject was "because of sex," involving, as it did, behavior of an explicitly sexual nature.[112] However, it is not clear why the sexual nature of behavior should be sufficient to render it discriminatory—unless she is assuming that *any* conduct that acknowledges alleged differences between the sexes is sex discriminatory. And I think she is making this assumption. This would indicate a reliance on the "differential treatment argument." It should be noted that alleging that any sex difference is a stereotype involves a denial that there are any *true* general differences between males and females, something with which many Americans would not agree.[113]

According to Gross, harassment based on sexual orientation constitutes sex discrimination, since heterosexuality is clearly part of the stereotype associated with gender, and she says that "harassment of an individual because of the individual's . . . failure to conform to preconceived gender roles violates Title VII because such harassment perpetuates gender inequality."[114]

I take Gross to be articulating the position of the Supreme Court. Though they have not been as explicit as Gross is, the direction of their decisions suggests that they would agree that any conduct based on sex may rise to the level of prohibited sex discrimination if it is severe enough to alter the conditions of a person's employment. "[T]he statute does not reach genuine but innocuous differences in ways men and women routinely interact with members of the same sex and of the opposite sex. The prohibition of harassment on the basis of sex requires neither asexuality nor androgyny in the workplace; it forbids only behavior so objectively offensive as to alter the 'conditions' of the victim's employment."[115] The major alternative to the differences approach is Catharine MacKinnon's inequality or dominance approach. According to the dominance approach, sex discrimination is not only *differential* treatment but also *unequal* treatment. As we have seen, MacKinnon defines sexual harassment as "the unwanted imposition of sexual requirements in the context of a relationship of unequal power."[116] Thus, sexual harassment is most fundamentally a misuse of *power*, not of a matter of *difference*. MacKinnon sees sexual harassment as arising out of the general social inequality of women and men, and as contributing to this inequality. In the context of employment, "[s]exual harassment at work critically undercuts women's potential for work equality as a means to social equality."[117] She contrasts the approach with the differences approach: "The [differences] approach envisions the sexes as socially as well as biologically *different* from one another, but calls impermissible or 'arbitrary' those distinctions or classifications that are found preconceived and/or inaccurate. The [inequality] approach understands the sexes to be not simply socially differentiated but socially *unequal*. "[118] In MacKinnon's view, sexual harassment can happen only to women. What happens to men may look like sexual harassment, but because of the gender hierarchy that puts all men above all women, sexual harassment does not have the same meaning—or effect—for men that it has for women.[119] In her view, sexual harassment places conditions on women's work lives that men do not share. Thus, sexual harassment of women, but not of men, is sex discrimination.

Furthermore, MacKinnon's account links the "group harm" that sex discrimination effects with the individual harm that members of the group suffer. Individual acts of sexual harassment serve to reinforce the subordination of women to men. Therefore, all women are harmed by each incident of sexual harassment.

The implications of this analysis for sexual harassment are clear: sexual harassment has a different meaning, and a different effect, for women than it has for men. For men, unwanted sexual advances are not part of a larger social understanding that men are sexually accessible to men, or are sex objects for men or women. Nor is gender hostility, designed to keep women in their place, the same when practiced between men. The meaning of sexual harassment, both quid pro quo and hostile environment, is different for men and for women. Ideally, the law should recognize this.

Some legal scholars who follow MacKinnon have argued that same-sex sexual harassment does not constitute sex discrimination and so is not prohibited by Title VII. Susan Woodhouse claims:

> The motivation behind recognizing sexual harassment as a form of discrimination under Title VII is that, commonly, the harassment based on sex is a result of the struggle between those in power. This struggle has in the past been mostly between men and women or other races that worked for them. Combined with this motivation is the additional effect that a person who sexually harasses another inflicts an injury on the entire gender by harassing an individual.
>
> Same-gender sexual harassment, however, does not result in the same type of injury as would occur between males and females. The harassment is not a result of a power struggle between members of the same gender. Persons of the same gender usually do not suffer from the same imbalance of power that is present between males and females.[120]

Woodhouse confines her argument to same-sex cases. However, the reasons she offers for why same-sex harassment is not sex discrimination under Title VII would support the claim that *no* sexual harassment claims by men should be actionable under Title VII. Contrary to Gross, Woodhouse claims that prohibition of same-sex harassment does not further the goals of Title VII.[121] She recommends that same-sex complaints be brought under existing tort laws. Thus, Oncale would not have a claim under Title VII. What about harassment based on sexual orientation?

Many who follow MacKinnon's dominance approach want to include some harassed men among people protected by Title VII. These are men who fail to meet the accepted norms for masculinity, and this would include men who are harassed because of their sexual orientation.

Some adherents of the dominance approach have argued that men who are harassed because they are not "masculine" enough are protected from discrimination by Title VII because they are, in effect, "honorary women." Martha Challamas and Mary Anne Case argue that men who are harassed because they are considered to be "effeminate" or not sufficiently masculine are harassed because of their similarity to women.[122]

Katherine Franke argues that both the differences approach and the dominance approach are too narrow. However, because of her inadequate characterizations of the two positions, her own view very much resembles Gross's.

In Franke's view, sexual harassment is

> a tool or instrument of gender regulation. It is a practice, grounded and undertaken in the service of hetero-patriarchal norms. These norms, regulatory, constitutive, and punitive in nature, produce gendered subjects: feminine women as sex objects and masculine men as sex subjects. On this account, sexual harassment is sex discrimination precisely because its use and effect police hetero-patriarchal gender norms in the workplace.[123]

Franke argues that we have a fundamental right to sexual identity, and that we should be protected from gender harassment aimed at people who do not fit "normal" models of femininity and masculinity. Franke claims that one of the ultimate goals of antidiscrimination law is "to provide all people more options with respect to how they do their gender;"[124] and that such laws should protect a "fundamental right to determine gender independent of biological sex."[125]

On Franke's view, some, but not all, cases of same-sex sexual harassment constitute sex discrimination. The test is whether the harassment performs the regulatory function described earlier. Thus, male-on-male quid pro quo cases would not constitute sex discriminatory harassment because they perform no policing or regulating of gender norms. However, Franke suggests that men who are the victims of such behavior should go straight for sex discrimination: they are being treated differently than women because of their sex, and so they could get protection under Title VII. Male-on-male hostile environment sexual harassment involving sexual horseplay would not constitute sex discrimination simply because it involved sexual conduct. Sexual conduct in itself does not constitute sex discrimination. In order to constitute prohibited sexual harassment, male-on-male hostile environment sexual harassment would have to involve the punishment of a man for not performing his gender properly. She takes *Goluszek* to be the paradigm case of such punishment.

What would she say about Oncale? It is difficult to say. Insofar as Oncale was targeted because he was not considered sufficiently masculine, he would have a claim under her interpretation. There is some evidence that this is what was going on. Harassment for sexual orientation would definitely constitute a violation of Title VII in her scheme.

The only court of which I am aware that has put forward a theory similar to Franke's is that in *Doe*. Recall that the court claimed:

Assuming arguendo that proof other than the explicit sexual character of the harassment is indeed necessary to establish that same-sex harassment qualifies as sex discrimination, the fact that H. Doe apparently was singled out for this abuse because the way in which he projected the sexual aspect of his personality (and by that we mean his gender) did not conform to his co-workers' view of appropriate masculine behavior supplies that proof here. The Supreme Court's decision in Price Waterhouse v. Hopkins . . . makes clear that Title VII does not permit an employee to be treated adversely because his or her appearance or conduct does not conform to stereotypical gender roles.[126]

While I am sympathetic to this view, I do not think that there is at this time widespread consensus that people have a fundamental right to "do" their gender as they see fit. Nor do I think that most people understand antidiscrimination laws the way Franke does. This does not mean that we may not come to understand the purpose of antidiscrimination laws as Franke does.

While there may be some theoretical differences between Gross's and Franke's understandings of sexual harassment, both would find for Oncale and would include sexual harassment based on sexual orientation actionable under Title VII. Gross's concern for people who are harassed because they violate gender stereotypes is mirrored in Franke's concern with the policing and regulating of masculinity and femininity. This does seem to be the way the courts are moving, though they are not there yet.

This discussion of same-sex sexual harassment has examined only cases involving male-male harassment. Some of the reasons for denying that such cases can constitute sex discrimination apply only to cases in which the harassee is male. There are not many female-female cases of sexual harassment in case law, and legal scholars rarely discuss such cases. Both Gross and Woodhouse say that their analyses apply equally to male-male harassment and female-female harassment.[127]

After surveying the arguments used to connect sexual harassment and sex discrimination, I must conclude that the arguments against allowing same-sex sexual harassment claims under Title VII are not justified. The main argument comes from the dominance approach and involves the assumption that only members of "vulnerable groups" or subordinated groups should be protected. Though the courts for the most part adhere to the differences approach, some decisions have shown elements of the dominance approach. The chain of cases discussed in chapter 3, starting with *Goluszek*, speaks of Title VII's purpose as protecting "vulnerable groups" and excludes men from those groups.[128]

Title VII was not originally designed to protect men from discrimination, but this does not mean that it should not protect them. As the Supreme Court said in *Oncale*, "[M]ale-on-male sexual harassment in the workplace was assuredly not the principal evil Congress was concerned with when it enacted Title VII. But statutory prohibitions often go beyond the principal evil to cover reasonably comparable evils, and it is ultimately the provisions of our laws rather than the principal concern of our legislators by which we are governed."[129] They might have pointed out that Congress did not have sexual harassment in mind at all when they enacted Title VII.

The Supreme Court settled the legal issue of whether male-on-male harassment could constitute sexual harassment and is prohibited under Title VII in its decision in *Oncale*. The Court ultimately concluded, "We see no justification in the statutory language or our precedents for a categorical rule excluding same-sex harassment claims from the coverage of Title VII."[130] Their conclusion is based on law. But it accords with my understanding of sexual harassment and sex discrimination, also.

Other Forms of Harassment

Title VII includes prohibition against discrimination on the grounds of race, sex, religion, and national origin. More recent legislation prohibits discrimination on the grounds of age and disability.[131] In addition, Title IX prohibits discrimination based on race, sex, religion, and national origin in educational institutions.[132] In principle, harassment on the basis of any of these categories is actionable. If harassment is to be found on the basis of any protected category other than sex, it would most likely be similar to hostile environment sexual harassment rather than quid pro quo.

The relationship between sexual harassment and other forms of harassment seems to be mutually influential. The 1980 EEOC *Guidelines* were justified on the grounds that they brought sexual harassment law more into line with the law in other areas of discriminatory harassment.[133] Later, harassment law in these other areas seemed to follow the lead of sexual harassment law. In addition, developments in Title VII harassment law influenced development in Title IX.[134] However, there has not been nearly as much attention paid to harassment based on race, national origin, religion, or age as has been paid to sexual harassment.[135] One would think there would be, and that issues raised in relation to sexual harassment cases would have their analogues in cases involving other sorts of harassment. But this does not seem to be the case.

In 1993, the *Federal Register* published for comment the suggestion that other forms of harassment be treated more like *gender* harassment, which the EEOC distinguished from *sexual* harassment.

> The Equal Employment Opportunity Commission is issuing Guidelines covering harassment that is based upon race, color, religion, gender (excluding harassment that is sexual in nature, which is covered by the Commission's Guidelines on Discrimination Because of Sex), national origin, age, or disability. The Commission has determined that it would be useful to have consolidated guidelines that set forth the standards for determining whether conduct in the workplace constitutes illegal harassment under the various antidiscrimination statutes.[136]

The issue of religious harassment caused the greatest outcry.[137] "'Religious harassment' is a dangerous concept. It can be used as a club by disgruntled employees. The proposed guidelines prohibit free expressions. . . . They turn the private workplace into an extension of the public sphere. They impose impossible burdens on employers."[138] This raises an interesting set of questions. Is sexual harassment analogous to other forms of harassment? If so, should they be treated more like sexual harassment? Or should sexual harassment be treated more like they are? If sexual harassment is not like other forms of harassment, why is it not?

How one answers these questions will depend, in part, on one's general perspective. Both the natural/biological perspective and the dominance perspective consider sexual harassment to be a special case. It is unlikely that they would extend their analyses to other sorts of harassment, though they would undoubtedly provide some sort of modified analysis. The liberal perspective could allow a general conception of workplace harassment. In what follows, I shall discuss the relationship of sexual harassment to other forms of harassment as they are developing in the law.

Racial Harassment   It is clear that the concept of sexual harassment was in part formed by analogy with racial and national origin harassment. In her 1979 book, where she argues that sexual harassment is prohibited by Title VII, MacKinnon often makes reference to the use of Title VII to prohibit racial harassment.

> [T]he law with respect to racial discrimination is well developed and instructive. Personal insults or intimidation having a racial basis or referent have repeatedly been found to be discriminatory by the EEOC. An atmosphere that creates psychological strain and emotional distress because of race-based treatment is likewise a violation of Title VII. . . . Insult, pressure, or intimidation having gender as its basis or referent should be equally proscribed.[139]

In addition, sex discrimination law was modeled on race discrimination law.[140] However, from the start, certain perceived differences between sex discrimination and racial discrimination prevented simply applying legal strategies used in racial discrimination decisions to sex discrimination.

There is no doubt that the hostile environment sexual harassment claim was modeled on racial harassment claims. The first court to find hostile environment sexual harassment sex discrimination, *Bundy v. Jackson*,[141] cited *Rogers v. EEOC*,[142] which has been called "the seminal case regarding racially discriminatory work environment claims."[143] In drawing the parallel between so-called discriminatory environment cases and hostile environment sexual harassment, the court said:

> The relevance of these "discriminatory environment" cases to sexual harassment is beyond serious dispute. Racial or ethnic discrimination against a company's minority clients may reflect no intent to discriminate directly against the company's minority employees, but in poisoning the atmosphere it violates Title VII. Sexual stereotyping through

discriminatory dress requirements may be benign in intent, and may offend women only in a general, atmospheric manner, yet it violates Title VII. Racial slurs, though intentional and directed at individuals, may still be just verbal insults, yet they too may create Title VII liability. How then can sexual harassment, which injects the most demeaning sexual stereotypes into the general work environment and which always represents an intentional assault on an individual's innermost privacy, not be illegal?[144]

Rogers was also cited by the Supreme Court in its decision in *Meritor Savings Bank, FSB v. Vinson.*[145] And in *Henson,* the court states: "Sexual harassment which creates a hostile or offensive environment for members of one sex is every bit the arbitrary barrier to sexual equality at the workplace that racial harassment is to racial equality."[146]

According to some legal scholars, racial and sexual hostile environment claims have not been treated the same by the courts. Robert Gregory argues that since at least 1986, courts have accepted the view that racial and sexual hostile environment harassment should be governed by the same legal standard, but that, in fact, they are not.[147]

> The critical inquiry in cases of hostile environment harassment is whether the harassing behavior is, first, race- or sex-based and, second, "sufficiently severe or pervasive to alter the conditions of the victim's employment." In the race context, courts seem particularly receptive to claims that racially harassing behavior has affected the terms or conditions of an individual's employment, resolving any ambiguities in favor of the claimant and de-emphasizing the need for any specific number of instances of harassment. In the sex context, the judicial reaction seems less solicitous, with courts more often stressing the ambiguities in the conduct at issue and the need for repeated instances of harassing conduct.[148]

The differences in the ways that courts address these cases is interesting. Gregory provides evidence that

> [c]ourts, in particular, have insisted upon specific proof that the conduct stems from an anti-male or -female animus. Courts have also stressed that instances of sexual conduct "that prove equally offensive to male and female workers would not support a Title VII sexual harassment charge," a principle that appears to have no analog in the race context. Courts have suggested that even the most "gendered" conduct is not discriminatory if the harasser is motivated by a personal dislike, rather than a sexual animus. In contrast to race cases, where animus is typically inferred from the statement or conduct itself, courts in sex cases seem far more willing to probe the context of the statement or conduct and the underlying motivation of the individual engaging in the harassing behavior.[149]

This suggests that judges are considering the *causes* of apparently harassing behavior in deliberating on such cases. They perceive animus in race cases, but not so readily in sex cases. It seems that they see other possible causes. But what does the cause matter? Apparently, in race cases it is easier for judges to see that the abusive behavior is based on the *race* of the victim. If personal dislike is the cause of some kind of behavior, then the behavior may not be based on *sex*, but on *the person*.

This distinction recalls the natural/biological perspective on sexual harassment. Kingsley Browne claims that much of the gendered harassment of women by men is not based on the sex of the victim. Rather, the harasser is using the kinds of epithets he thinks will be most effective in intimidating or humiliating the woman, and those are often sexual and, when sexual, sex-specific.[150] If he were belittling a man, he might use other language, but it might also be sex-specific. According to Browne, the use of sex-specific expressions in the demeaning or annoying of a person does not imply that the person is being picked on because of their sex or gender: "Courts commonly, but incorrectly, conclude that vulgar sexually oriented epithets show that the hostility they embody is necessarily based upon sex. . . . The particular abusive words were no doubt chosen because she was a woman, but it is a different question whether she was selected for abuse in the first place because she was a woman."[151] Once this explanation is articulated, it is clear that it might also be used to explain racial harassment. People often resort to racial slurs and epithets when abusing a person because they know the sensitivities of the targeted individual. But whether or not the person is targeted because of their race is a different question.

This explanation of sexual or racial language or conduct, however convincing it may seem on the surface, omits something important. The speaker would probably not *think* of using racially or sexually explicit language to try to demean or annoy if he or she did not already consider race or sex to mark inferiority. Suppose that you know that I am a poor cook, and that I am sensitive about it. You might seek to hurt me by using language that prodded this sensitivity. However, you may not have any opinion about whether being a good cook makes one a person who is competent or who deserves respect. Racially and sexually specific expressions seem different. Nearly every woman knows that calling her a "dumb-ass woman" is an attempt to demean.[152] Such an expression is not chosen only because the speaker knows that many women are sensitive about being women. The epithet is chosen because the speaker believes women to be inferior and knows that, in many ways, the culture reinforces this belief. That is why racial and sexual *epithets* exist, ready to hand, as it were. Some who argue as Browne does would claim that the *personal* nature of the attack, which shows that it is not sex based, is evident because there are other women whom the harasser does not seek to demean. However, most of us, by now, recognize the inadequacy of the "some of my best friends are *x*" defense.

Many seek to distinguish racial from sexual harassment by remarking that, in cases of racial harassment, it is always clear that the behavior is harassing, whereas in cases of sexual harassment, this is not always obvious.

The "unwelcome" requirement is peculiar to sexual harassment. Harassment as a general matter is considered to be inherently unwelcome. Thus, potentially offensive conduct based on race or national origin is presumably offensive and unwelcome to whomever it is directed. Sexual advances are different, in that sexual advances, while potentially offensive, may reflect a friendly, romantic interest in the recipient and often are welcome, or at least not offensive.[153]

Sometimes this point is made by saying that in cases of racialized behavior, ill-will toward members of the victim's race is assumed, whereas in cases of sexualized behavior, such ill-will is not assumed.

It seems to me that this difference between sexual and racial harassment is overemphasized. Whether something counts as a racial epithet, or as evidence of racial prejudice, seems to depend just as much on context as does whether sexualized or gendered behavior is harassing. However, the legal understanding of sexual harassment does seem to diverge from the legal understanding of racial harassment at just this point. This is evident in the inclusion of the expression "unwelcome" in the EEOC definition of sexual harassment.

> *Unwelcome* sexual advances, requests for sexual favors, and other verbal or physical conduct of a sexual nature constitute sexual harassment when (1) submission to such conduct is made either explicitly or implicitly a term or condition of an individual's employment, (2) submission to or rejection of such conduct by an individual is used as the basis for employment decisions affecting such individual, or (3) such conduct has the purpose or effect of unreasonably interfering with an individual's work performance or creating an intimidating, hostile, or offensive working environment.[154] [My emphasis.]

Robert Gregory argues that the standards are more rigorous for hostile environment sexual harassment than for hostile environment racial harassment, even though the legal standards governing them are the same.[155] As a result, victims of sexual harassment are not given the same level of protection as are victims of racial harassment. His argument is based on two cases which seem to show that,

> [i]n the race context, courts seem particularly receptive to claims that racially harassing behavior has affected the terms or conditions of an individual's employment, resolving any ambiguities in favor of the claimant and de-emphasizing the need for any specific number of instances of harassment. In the sex context, the judicial reaction seems less solicitous, with courts more often stressing the ambiguities in the conduct at issue and the need for repeated instances of harassing conduct.[156]

Whether or not this is generally true, some judges seem to distinguish between racial and sexual harassment, particularly with regard to motive of the harasser.[157] Again, we see that sexual harassment is considered differently from other forms of harassment under Title VII.

If this difference between sexual harassment and racial harassment exists in the law, the question is whether it *should*. One way of sharpening the issue is to focus on the requirement that sexual harassment be "unwelcome" to constitute discrimination. This requirement is present in race cases, but, as Gregory points out, it is almost never at issue. However, this requirement is often at issue in sexual harassment cases.[158]

Michael Vhay and others take issue with this aspect of the understanding of sexual harassment, pointing out that "*Vinson, Henson* and the EEOC Guidelines do not explain why a victim of this form of discriminatory harassment, as opposed to racial, religious, or national origin harassment, must prove that the offensive activity was unwelcome."[159] Vhay's point is a legal one, concerning the requirement placed on the plaintiff to, in effect, rebut the defendant's defense in his or her prima facie case.[160] In most cases of alleged discrimination, the plaintiff presents her or his case initially by showing that they have been the recipient of the alleged behavior: "In the traditional disparate treatment claim of sex discrimination under Title VII, the complainant makes out a prima facie case by proving the basis (gender), the issue (a tangible job detriment), and the causal connection between the basis and the issue (but for the complainant's gender the complaint would not have suffered the job detriment)."[161] The defendant is then given the opportunity to "rebut elements of the prima facie case."[162] This may involve denying that the behavior in question ever took place, or showing that there was some "legitimate, nondiscriminatory reason" for the behavior in question.[163] The plaintiff may then seek to establish that the alleged nondiscriminatory reason for the behavior is a pretext for discrimination.

In cases of quid pro quo sexual harassment, the establishment of the prima facie case involves showing that a sexual advance was made and that it was unwelcome. Often, the defendant responds by trying to show that the sexual advance was not unwelcome. Since a showing of sex discrimination requires that the sexual advance be unwelcome, showing that it was in fact welcome would mean that sex discrimination did not take place. Vhay's point, then, is that by including the "unwelcomeness" requirement in the establishment of the prima facie case, the plaintiff is, in effect, being required to provide a rebuttal of a possible defense.[164]

The most obvious explanation for including "unwelcomeness" as an element is that the courts and the EEOC see sexual harassment as *sexual*, and they want to distinguish sexual harassment from consensual sexual behavior in the workplace. They seem to think that the *very same behaviors* could be illegal sexual harassment in one context, but not in another. Indeed, as Vhay shows, the EEOC says something very like this in its brief in *Meritor Savings Bank, FSB v. Vinson*.[165]

[S]exual harassment differs from other class-based harassment because some sexual expressions are normal in the workplace. The EEOC thus concluded that special rules are warranted so as to avoid intrusions into "purely personal, social relationships." The EEOC argued that courts must insist that plaintiffs demonstrate unwelcomeness in sexual harassment suits in order to "ensure that sexual harassment charges do not become a tool by which one party to a consensual sexual relationship may punish the other."[166]

Vhay sees this as revealing an antiquated and stereotypical view of women. It seems to be based on the fear that women will bring sexual harassment suits in revenge after a consensual relationship ends badly.[167] To prevent this misuse of Title VII, the plaintiff must show that the advances, or whatever the behavior in question is, were "unwelcome." The court says that this may be done by showing that the plaintiff did not incite or solicit the conduct, and that he or she found the conduct undesirable or offensive. Vhay argues that there is no justification for the inclusion of this element in sexual harassment cases, and he advocates treating sexual harassment cases like other discrimination cases, where "unwelcomeness" is assumed.[168] Vhay maintains that "the courts should not distinguish harassment from other forms of discrimination."[169] In the case of sexual harassment, this would mean shifting the burden of proof of *welcomeness* from the plaintiff to the defendant.

To drive the point home, Vhay cites *Jackson-Coley v. Corps of Engineers,*[170] a case in which the court required the victim to show that a sexual advance was unwelcome "in the sense that the employee deliberately and clearly makes her nonreceptiveness known to the alleged offender" in order to prove voluntariness. Vhay remarks, "[O]ne cannot imagine the same court requiring a black employee, for example, to state 'deliberately and clearly' his desire not to be insulted on account of his race."[171]

Of course, one can—but it should never happen. However, one can imagine a court requiring a black employee to prove that a particular sort of behavior or expression *is* an insult. At issue is whether every sexual advance is an "insult." If not, how is a person to determine beforehand whether a particular sexual advance will be regarded as an insult?

The question is, *should* sexual harassment be treated in just the same way as racial harassment—or, more broadly, should sex discrimination be treated identically to race discrimination. If there is a relevant difference between sexual advances and racial insults, then the answer may be no. And I think that, at this point in our social evolution, the answer is that there *is* a relevant difference between the two. Sexual advances are sometimes romantic overtures, even when they are from people with whom one works, and even when one is not interested in the advance. Racial insults are rarely anything else—certainly, they are never anything like romantic overtures.

Vhay argues that,

[a]s empirical studies have shown, all of the motivations behind sexual advances in the workplace contain discrimination. To purge the workplace of discriminatory barriers to equal opportunity, it should be presumed that a sexual advance, if it imposes such a barrier, is unlawful discrimination. . . . As with other discrimination actions, the defendant will always have the opportunity to assert a defense in order to defeat the presumption of unlawful conduct. Current law, however, begins

with the presumption that sexual advance is permissible until proven unwelcome. A presumption consistent with the general body of discrimination law is that a sexual advance is discrimination, unless the one making the advance can provide a justification.[172]

I do not know how this claim could be proved empirically. In any case, we must decide, as a society, whether this recommended shift reflects what women want in their workplaces and educational institutions. Otherwise, some standard for determining nondiscriminatory from discriminatory sexual behavior in the workplace will be necessary. If not the "welcomeness" criterion, then some other.

This problem is exacerbated by the differences between quid pro quo sexual harassment and hostile environment sexual harassment. One might argue that sexual advances from supervisors, or from other people who have authority over one in one's place of work, always threaten coercion. The economic power of the authority lessens the freedom of the person approached to consent. They may feel unable to say no. So, perhaps the assumption should be that advances from such persons are always prima facie wrong. Perhaps Vhay's suggested shift in presumption should be adopted for quid pro quo harassment by supervisors.

However, things get more complicated when one recalls that co-workers are also capable of sexual harassment, and that most sexual harassment seems to be carried out by co-workers. Without the "unwelcome" requirement, or something like it, romantic overtures in the workplace would seem to be prima facie illegal. And that seems wrong—especially since both men and women are finding romantic partners at work in increasing numbers. Vhay and others seem to ignore the fact that it is still the norm for men to initiate romantic or sexual encounters in heterosexual relationships, and that people see the workplace as a source of sexual partners. Perhaps they think this is wrong. But it is still the practice at this time.

Comparing sexual harassment to racial harassment highlights another feature of sexual harassment. Most of the emphasis in both the literature and court cases has been on *sexual* behavior. The EEOC definition emphasizes this. However, *gender* harassment is, in some ways, easier to see as a form of sex discrimination. The distinction is made clear by Lindemann and Kadue: "Sexual harassment reflecting gender-based animosity resembles harassment based on race or national origins. The hostile behavior arises when women enter male-dominated jobs or workplaces. . . . Behavior motivated by gender-based animosity usually takes one of two forms: (1) hostile conduct of a sexual nature (gender baiting), or (2) nonsexual hazing based on gender."[173] *Gender harassment* is "nonsexual hazing based on gender." Examples of gender harassment include the treatment of Sylvia DeAngelis. DeAngelis was the first woman sergeant in the El Paso Police Department. She filed a sex discrimination suit after being ridiculed in a work-related newsletter. Women in general were dismissed as incompetent as police, and DeAngelis was called a "dingy woman." The remarks were not sexual in nature, but they did question the competence of women to be police and, in particular, questioned DeAngelis's competence, as a woman.[174] In *Hall v. Gus Construction Co.*,[175] several women workers were harassed by their co-workers, who, among other things, urinated in the gas tank of a truck and failed to fix a truck that gave off fumes, and who called them "fucking flag girls."

> In Hall v. Gus Construction Co., the Eighth Circuit recognized that gender discrimination in the work environment is actionable regardless of whether it is sexually motivated. Hall involved a claim by three female employees of a construction company that their supervisors and co-workers subjected them to persistent discriminatory treatment. The pattern of abuse alleged by these employees included certain acts of gender-based harassment: references to one plaintiff as "Herpes" because of a skin condition; male crew members urinating in the gas tank of another plaintiff's car (characterized as a practical joke); and the company's failure to fix certain equipment while female employees were operating it.[176]

There was also "sexualized" behavior alleged in *Hall*, but this case is perceived to be important because, though the defendant wanted the "gender-based" harassment not to be considered, the court said it must be considered. The Eighth Circuit said, "Intimidation and hostility toward women because they are women can obviously result from conduct other than explicit sexual advances."[177] There have been other cases in which male co-workers sabotaged women's tools and refused to share work-related information.[178]

These so-called gender harassment cases seem more analogous to most racial harassment cases than to quid pro quo sexual harassment cases or hostile environment cases involving sexualized behavior. Ruth Colker has argued that courts seem to be more willing to find discrimination in harassment cases involving clearly sexualized behavior directed at women than in cases involving only gender-based behavior.[179] It is as if sexual harassment is usurping the category of sex discrimination, and heterosexual sexualized behavior becoming the only genuine form of sexual harassment. This emphasis has spilled over onto racial harassment cases. The only sexual harassment cases considered violations of Title VII involve sexual advances toward women by men. The only racial harassment cases considered violations of Title VII are those involving explicit racial epithets.

> [S]exual harassment doctrine has narrowed to include only the claims of a small subset of women who might face gender-based harassment at work. These women's claims constitute "sexualized" harassment because of the explicit references to sexuality or body parts . . . sexual harassment doctrine has . . . narrowed to include only heterosexualized claims . . . race discrimination doctrine has followed a trend parallel to the one that I observe for gender discrimination. Many courts are requiring minority plaintiffs to produce evidence of explicit racial epithets in order to recover.[180]

This trend, if supported, shows that it is important to consider all forms of harassment and all forms of discrimination together. Treatment of one sort bears on treatment of another, sometimes in ways that are not obvious without a comprehensive view. Such comparisons can show us inconsistencies in how the laws are being applied to racial and sexual harassment. This can lead to further consideration of what we think racial and sexual harassment are. This can then be used to decide future cases, to make future laws.

Religious Harassment   Racial, sexual, and national origin harassment have been discussed together, and, as we have seen, judicial decisions from one area seem to influence decisions in other areas. Few protested the suggestion by the EEOC that racial, national origin, and gender harassment be treated similarly. The remaining categories have been treated quite differently, though for different reasons. Age and disability discrimination became illegal under civil rights laws relatively recently. They were not included in the original Civil Rights Act of 1964. Therefore, people are just beginning to work out the legal and conceptual issues involved in discrimination based on age or disability. Religious discrimination seems to be conceptualized differently from any of the other kinds of discrimination.

The 1976 case *Compston v. Borden, Inc.*,[181] was the first to recognize religious harassment under Title VII. There have not been many religious harassment cases since.[182]

Religion is different from the other protected categories. The category of "religion" is, unlike the other protected categories (except some disabilities, and perhaps "sex"), not immutable.[183] In addition: "First, the other bases of discrimination are questions of status; religion is a set of beliefs. Second, the other bases of discrimination are relatively narrow in scope and more easily determined by observation, while religious affiliation is not readily apparent. Third, in the religious context, courts have held that a religious belief can be unique to the individual."[184] Perhaps the most significant difference between religious harassment and other forms of harassment is that in the case of religious harassment, there is a clear, acknowledged right on the side of the harasser that must be protected. "While an employee's interest in making sexual or racial comments may be questionable, many employees have a fundamental, societally recognized interest in commenting on religious matters. To those who believe that it is their duty to proselytize to others, an inflexible proscription against this activity may be an unbearable impairment to their religious practice."[185] Some of those who object to the extent of sexual harassment protection seem to be articulating something analogous to this for alleged sexual harassers. They perceive a right to sexual expression that should not be ignored in considering alleged sexual harassment. However, while religious expression is protected by the First Amendment explicitly, sexual expression is not.

Title VII requires employers to "accommodate an employee's religious observance, unless to do so would result in an undue burden or hardship on the employer's business."[186] Most early claims of religious harassment were by people whose supervisors or co-workers harassed them because of their religious beliefs.[187] More recently, people are claiming that the religious expressions of supervisors or co-workers is creating a hostile environment.[188] Thus, a conflict has developed between two possible demands issuing from the Title VII language on religious discrimination: religious practice and expression must be accommodated, and religious practice and expression must not create a hostile environment for others. "Legally, discrimination on the basis of religion is forbidden. Further, an employer is required to accommodate an employee's religious practice or observance. An employer is also required, however, to provide a working environment free from hostile or offensive harassment. Thus, a conflict may arise when one employee's religious practice is hostile or offensive to a co-worker."[189]

Because of these conflicting demands, criteria for the occurrence of religious hostile environment harassment should probably differ from those for, for example, sexual harassment. A balance must be struck between accommodating religious practices of employees and maintaining a nonabusive environment for employees. One suggestion is that, instead of the reasonable person or reasonable victim standard, the determination of whether religious harassment has taken place should be determined by whether the work environment is disrupted. This is because, "[u]pon actual evidence of a disruption of the work environment, the employer can argue that undue hardship prevents accommodation of a particular employee's religious habit."[190]

In spite of these differences between religion and other protected categories, the development of religious harassment law shows that court decisions have used cases involving other forms of harassment as models. For example, a significant case in religious harassment law, *Weiss v. United States*,[191] drew a distinction between quid pro quo and hostile environment religious harassment:

> the Weiss court noted that religious harassment can arise in either of two forms: "[Q]uid pro quo" harassment, in which a supervisor demands that an employee conform to a specified religious doctrine in order to secure job benefits, or "condition of work" harassment, in which the challenged conduct creates "an intimidating, offensive environment." This dichotomy was imported verbatim from the law of sexual harassment, and the symmetry between the "condition of work" doctrine of sexual harassment law and the doctrine of "religious intimidation," which had developed independently in the early religious harassment cases, demonstrates the growing sophistication and interdependency of harassment doctrine under Title VII.[192]

In its rulings on sexual harassment cases, the Supreme Court has affirmed that all forms of harassment should be treated similarly. This was stated explicitly in *Meritor* and again in *Harris*.[193] The proposed 1993 EEOC *Guidelines* simply articulated this.[194] However, people objected vehemently, claiming that the EEOC was trying to overstep its authority by, in effect, making law, and that the effect of following the *Guidelines* would be a chill on expression of religion in the workplace.[195] However, if, as has been argued, the *Guidelines* merely articulated the way in which religious harassment law has developed, then the first charge is not true. The second criticism suggests a way in which religious harassment may genuinely differ from other forms of harassment. Religious harassment seems to differ from racial or national origin harassment in that it appears to conflict with the First Amendment guarantee of freedom of religion.[196] Religion is specifically protected by the First Amendment, indicating that there is positive value in religious expression: "Religion is unique among the prohibited classifications found in Title VII and other civil rights statutes. Only religious speech, exercise, and expression have intrinsic, societally recognized and constitutionally enunciated value."[197] There is no directly comparable constitutionally guaranteed liberty in conflict with any of the other forms of harassment. A conflict between freedom of speech and certain kinds of sexual harassment has been discussed in legal literature. However, it can be argued that the conflict in sexual harassment cases is not a true conflict; whereas the conflict between religious harassment and freedom of religious expression is a true conflict.[198]

> This tension between the antidiscrimination mandate of Title VII and the free exercise principle of the First Amendment has been the Achilles heel of hostile work environment harassment doctrine ever since its inception. Whereas previous debate on this question has focused almost exclusively on sexually suggestive speech, a value which at best is outside the core of the First Amendment, the religious harassment debate exposed the fundamental (and arguably irreconcilable) tension between the antidiscrimination principle of Title VII and the free exercise guarantee of the First Amendment. In other words, whereas the tension between sexual harassment doctrine and the First Amendment may be rationalized as a "false conflict" due to the minimal constitutional value of sexually suggestive speech, a similar competition between the religious harassment doctrine of Title VII and the Free Exercise Clause creates a "true conflict" that cannot be elided by doctrinal formalisms. Restrictions on religious expression implicate the very core of the First Amendment, and thus raise much more significant concerns about the scope of Title VII harassment doctrine. These two competing principles are of "equal dignity" in modern constitutional thought, and the religious harassment debate exposes our struggle to reconcile them to each other.[199]

Another difference between Title VII protections of religion and other protected classes is that religious corporations and educational institutions which are affiliated with religions are exempt.[200] These two latter differences are not unrelated.

If the Title VII prohibition of religious harassment is considered to be in conflict with the First Amendment, then victims of religious harassment may not receive the same protection as victims of other sorts of harassment.

Another set of issues concerns the kind of language typical in harassing situations. Particularly in the case of hostile environment harassment, language plays a large role. Certain epithets are inherently offensive; others seem to depend for their offensiveness on context. One commentator distinguished religious harassment from sexual harassment in the following terms:

Religious expression is unique in that many religious statements are inherently offensive. Many religions, for example, preach that an individual must follow their doctrines to obtain salvation and get to heaven. A passive statement by a religious employee that a nonbeliever would go to hell has the effect of hostility toward a nonbeliever or believer of a different religion, regardless of the speaker's purpose.[201]

The author argues that simple expressions of religious belief can be disparaging of another's religious belief. However, it seems that religious expression is not unique in this respect. There are similar expressions of racial and sexual beliefs, for example, that are disparaging of a race of people, or of one sex.

Harassment on the Basis of Disability   Discrimination on the basis of disability is prohibited by the Americans with Disabilities Act of 1991(ADA).[202] The ADA "prohibits discriminatory employment practices against qualified individuals with disabilities, and requires employers to reasonably accommodate such individuals unless accommodation would constitute an undue hardship on the employer."[203] So far, the focus has been on providing reasonable accommodation for people with disabilities to remove barriers to employment, education, and housing. There has not yet been much attention paid disability *harassment*, though it was included in the proposed 1993 EEOC *Guidelines*: "(a) Harassment on the basis of race, color, religion, gender, national origin, age, or disability constitutes discrimination in the terms, conditions, and privileges of employment and, as such, violates title VII of the Civil Rights Act of 1964 . . . the Age Discrimination in Employment Act . . . the Americans with Disabilities Act . . . or the Rehabilitation Act of 1973. . . ." [204] Though these proposed *Guidelines* were eventually rescinded, commentators have argued that harassment on the basis of disability is prohibited by the ADA. [205]

Some have argued that harassment against individuals with disabilities has unique features which distinguish this kind of harassment from all other sorts. One feature is that, "[u]nlike other classes covered by anti-discrimination statutes, which are defined by a single trait, such as sex or race, individuals with disabilities are discriminated against based on the numerous and varied characteristics inherent in the hundreds of disabilities covered by the ADA."[206]

As of 1993, there had not been any cases claiming harassment on the basis of disability brought under ADA, although a number of disabled people have brought actions under the Rehabilitation Act of 1973.[207] However, these actions were not based on discrimination laws. They were based on common law theories such as constructive discharge and intentional infliction of emotional distress.[208]

The Rehabilitation Act's employment provisions have been utilized primarily to require that employers receiving government funds provide reasonable accommodation to disabled individuals. Because the focus of the Rehabilitation Act has been on reasonable accommodation . . . claims of harassment brought under the Rehabilitation Act were usually based on common law theories, and brought in conjunction with, or pendant to, a claim that an employer failed to reasonably accommodate.[209]

The ADA does contain provisions not present in Title VII. In particular, it requires an employer to reasonably accommodate employees, making it possible for them to do their work. However, a requirement of accommodation also attaches to Title VII protection from religious discrimination.[210]

In spite of the withdrawal of the proposed EEOC *Guidelines*, it seems that people can bring harassment charges under the ADEA. What kinds of similarities and differences will be found between this kind of harassment and sexual harassment remains to be seen.

Harassment on the Basis of Age   Discrimination based on age is prohibited by the Age Discrimination in Employment Act of 1988 (ADEA).[211] The ADEA applies to people over forty years old. The 1993 *Guidelines* included age in its list of categories against which hostile environment harassment was prohibited.

The category of age involves features which distinguish it from other sorts of protected categories. "The notable distinction between age and other bases for discrimination is that with advanced age one's physical and mental capabilities are invariably negatively affected."[212] This has led to the inclusion of a *bona fide occupational qualification* clause in the ADEA, similar to that applied to the category of sex under Title VII. "For the exception to apply, an age restriction must be 'reasonably necessary to the normal operation of the particular business.' Thus, if an employer can point to specific job requirements whereby advanced age would be a definite handicap to the safe administration of the employee's job, then the employer may dismiss the older employee."[213]

At this point, legal scholars are arguing that hostile environment theory *should* be applied to aging because of the analogies between the purposes of the ADEA and Title VII, and because of actual discrimination against people on the basis of age. These scholars draw analogies between age discrimination and other forms of discrimination:

In fact, the victims of age discrimination seem to have much in common with their Title VII counterparts. Research supports the concept that sexual harassment "sends a message of inferiority and objectification directed against individual women and women as a class." These messages undoubtedly affect a person's performance at work. It seems logical that victims of age discrimination would suffer similar effects.[214]

At the time of writing, no case alleging hostile environment harassment on the basis of age has shown age discrimination, although there have been cases which apply hostile environment discrimination theory to aging.[215]

It seems that the jury is still out with regard to hostile environment claims based on age. However, the similarities of the ADEA to Title VII suggest that such claims could be upheld. One commentator arguing in favor of such claims says:

The future of age discrimination and the hostile environment theory is unclear. With the withdrawal of the 1993 EEOC guidelines, there is little push for the expansion of the hostile environment to ADEA cases. Although the guidelines were not withdrawn because of the inclusion of age discrimination, there has been no published activity on pursuing similar guidelines without the controversial religious component.[216]

However, another commentator, reflecting on the impact of the EEOC's withdrawal of the 1993 EEOC *Guidelines*, suggests that remarks by EEOC chair Gilbert Casellas imply that the content of the proposed EEOC *Guidelines*, at least with regard to religious harassment, will be enforced whether or not they are enacted.[217]

7

CONCLUSION

M y aim in this book has been to provide the information necessary for careful, critical thinking about the concept of sexual harassment, and to guide the reader through some of the controversial issues that arise in consideration of the concept. The conclusion will be my assessment of the concept of sexual harassment based on this information.

As we have seen, the concept of sexual harassment was formed in the 1970s by feminists in order to create a remedy for a kind of treatment they believed constituted a barrier to equal opportunity for women. From the beginning, sexual harassment was conceptualized as a type of sex discrimination. The courts did not at first consider sexual harassment to be sex discrimination under Title VII. They focused on quid pro quo harassment, which they interpreted as romantic relationships gone wrong. In order to fit quid pro quo harassment into the category of sex discrimination, they had first to decide that conduct that was not an official policy of an employer could constitute discrimination under Title VII. They then had to find a way of reasoning that sexual harassment constituted behavior that was "because of sex" in the sense prohibited by Title VII. We have seen that at least three arguments were used to establish the link between sexual harassment and sex discrimination: the sexual desire argument, the stereotype argument, and the differential treatment argument. Court decisions suggest that either the motive behind the conduct, the nature of the conduct, or differential treatment may be sufficient, but no one element necessary, to establishing that treatment is "because of sex."

These three arguments have ties to the three perspectives described in chapter 1. The sexual desire argument has ties to the natural/biological perspective. Using the motivation of sexual desire to argue that the behavior in question would not have occurred "but for" the sex of the harassee assumes that sexual desire does indeed motivate some sexual harassment. The notion that sexual harassment is at its base amatory behavior, and thus either inevitable or justified, is still with us. Justice Kennedy expressed this in his dissent in *Davis v. Monroe County Board of Education* when he claimed that "a teenager's romantic overtures to a classmate (even when persistent and unwelcome) are an inescapable part of adolescence."[1] Adherents of the natural/biological perspective tend to worry that no clear line can be drawn between ordinary, permissible romantic conduct and sexual harassment. In some cases, this may be so. However, in the cases that reach federal courts, such as *Davis*, the description of the behavior in question as "a teenager's romantic overtures" is difficult to maintain. The harasser in *Davis* pleaded guilty to sexual battery. Teenage romantic overtures do not typically involve sexual battery—and if they do, then certainly calling such conduct a "romantic overture" does not justify it.

Both the sex stereotype argument and the differential treatment argument are consistent with the liberal perspective, and the sex stereotype argument is consistent with some socioculturalist perspectives. Both these arguments can be based on the principle of equality: equals should be treated equally, and unequals unequally, in proportion to their differences.

MacKinnon does not support what I am calling the sexual desire argument. However, her sociocultural perspective is partially responsible for the tendency of judges to think of sexual harassment as motivated by sexual desire.[2] In her view, sexual harassment is "the unwanted imposition of sexual requirements in the context of a relationship of unequal power."[3] But she finds the sexual desire argument inadequate because it appeals to the differences approach: the link between sexual harassment and sex discrimination is made via sexual desire, which establishes that the person is targeted *because of her sex*. This argument works for men as well as for women. But MacKinnon distinguishes between sexual advances made by men to women, and those made by men or women to men. There is no symmetry. MacKinnon does not endorse either the stereotype or the differential treatment argument, though sex stereotypes are forbidden on her dominance approach.[4] Her dominance approach utilizes three arguments for the claim that sexual harassment is sex discrimination.

> Women are sexually harassed by men because they are women, that is, because of the social meaning of female sexuality, here, in the employment context. Three kinds of arguments support and illustrate this position: first, the exchange of sex for survival has historically assured women's economic dependence and inferiority as well as sexual availability to men. Second, sexual harassment expresses the male sex-role pattern of coercive sexual initiation toward women, often in vicious and unwanted ways. Third, women's sexuality largely defines women as women in this society, so violations of it are abuses of women as women.[5]

Thus, in spite of MacKinnon's tremendous influence on the development of sexual harassment law, her particular arguments for the claim that sexual harassment is sex discrimination have not been adopted by many courts, though occasionally elements of a dominance view can be discerned.

In the introduction, I suggested that we might be able to reach some sort of agreement on what ought to be done about sexual harassment without agreeing on just what sexual harassment is. That is, we might be able to acknowledge that people have very different perspectives on gender, morality, and politics, and yet reach a kind of compromise on what to do about the behaviors some wish to designate as sexual harassment.

One of the reasons for approaching the issue in this way is that there is no way of determining which of the three perspectives—the natural/biological, the sociocultural, or the liberal—is "true" without begging the question against the others. There is no neutral position from which to judge them. Empirical data will not settle the issue, since such data are not free of value judgments. The best we can do, it seems to me, is to acknowledge that we live in a liberal state and seek to find an approach that is consistent with liberal political values. Such an approach will probably satisfy few completely but may satisfy most sufficiently.

There is agreement among adherents of the three perspectives on some points. Let us begin by surveying the various perspectives to find out where there is agreement.

Most people now agree that quid pro quo sexual harassment is wrong, though their explanations of that wrong differ. This is something that adherents of all three perspectives—natural/biological, liberal, and sociocultural—can agree on. It strikes most as unfair that someone should have to submit to an employer's sexual demands in order to retain a position, or to receive a promotion, or to escape retaliation. Many see this kind of behavior as an abuse of power on the part of the supervisor. Representatives of all three perspectives consider quid pro quo harassment to be extortion. However, those holding the natural/biological perspective do not believe it to be sex discrimination under Title VII or Title IX. They are joined in this belief by some liberals.[6] Other liberals, and socioculturalists, consider quid pro quo sexual harassment to be sex discrimination.

There is less agreement about hostile environment sexual harassment. According to the natural/biological perspective, most of what is classified as hostile environment sexual harassment is not wrong at all; or if it is wrong, it is not based on sex or gender. It is a natural result of the conflicts engendered by the differing psychologies of women and men. Browne admits that some hostile environment sexual harassment is based on gender animus and so constitutes sex discrimination.[7] However, he argues that other so-called hostile environment harassment involves hostility, but not hostility toward women (or men). Because this hostility is not based on sex, it is not sex discrimination. Furthermore, unwanted sexual advances should not be considered sex discrimination unless some job-related benefit is conditioned on their acceptance, or some burden threatened should they be refused.

Liberals are divided on what constitutes hostile environment sexual harassment, if anything. Liberal feminists such as Katie Roiphe and Camille Paglia have ridiculed conceptions of sexual harassment that render any sexual conduct in an educational or employment context immoral and unlawful. They point out that such conceptions feed into traditional perceptions of women as in need of protection from male sexuality. Roiphe contends that true abuses of power are indeed wrong and should be regulated. She includes quid pro quo sexual harassment among these.[8] But she objects to "hostile environment" conceptions of sexual harassment.[9] Paglia admits that there are serious instances of sexual harassment, and that these should be regulated.[10] However, like Roiphe, she objects to "hostile environment" sexual harassment claims.[11] Ellen Frankel Paul recognizes both quid pro quo and hostile environment sexual harassment, though she draws the boundaries of the latter more narrowly than some liberals might do. She holds that both forms of sexual harassment should be handled with a new tort of sexual harassment.[12] Mane Hajdin seems to agree with Browne to a large extent. He denies that "sexual harassment" is a meaningful concept but acknowledges that discriminatory conduct that is "motivated by hostility toward the presence of women in the workplace" constitutes sex discrimination, and that quid pro quo sexual harassment constitutes sex discrimination.[13]

Others who adhere to a liberal perspective are closer to socioculturalists. In a recent article, Vicki Schultz sets out a new paradigm for understanding hostile environment sexual harassment.[14] It is worth describing her argument briefly since I believe that her view represents a significant development in the concept of sexual harassment.

Schultz argues that the concept of sexual harassment, as it has developed in the law, is both too broad and too narrow. It is too broad in the sense that it seems to prohibit any expression of sexuality in the workplace. It is too narrow in its focus on sexual conduct, to the exclusion of other gender harassment. According to Schultz, the prevailing paradigm for the concept of sexual harassment is "the sexual desire-dominance paradigm." She finds its roots in both the biological/natural perspective and the sociocultural perspective. In her view, this paradigm is adequate for quid pro quo sexual harassment, but not for hostile environment sexual harassment.

Schultz argues that the sexual desire–dominance paradigm is too restrictive. The paradigm focuses attention on sexual advances, thereby obscuring the real reason that sexual harassment constitutes sex discrimination. According to Schultz, "[H]ostile work environment harassment is closely linked to job segregation by sex. Harassment serves a gender-guarding, competence-undermining function: By subverting women's capacity to perform favored lines of work, harassment polices the boundaries of the work and protects its idealized masculine image—as well as the identity of those who do it."[15]

Schultz argues for a "competence-centered" paradigm. According to her paradigm, hostile environment sexual harassment has the effect of undermining the perceived competence of women, and of some men, to do work that is traditionally masculine. It is discriminatory because it is used to keep women out of certain desirable jobs, or at least to define them as inferior in those jobs. Schultz's competence-centered paradigm is based on the premise that "a drive to maintain the most highly rewarded forms of work as domains of masculine competence underlies many, if not most, forms of sex-based harassment on the job. Harassment has the form and function of denigrating women's competence for the purpose of keeping them away from male-dominated jobs or incorporating them as inferior, less capable workers."[16] There are both material and psychological benefits for men from maintaining job segregation by gender. The material benefits allow men to head households and government. The psychological benefits concern the identities of men as masculine and not feminine. Schultz claims that men want to "define their work (and themselves) in masculine terms," and that this can be done only if women are unable to do the work or are not really women if they can do the work.[17] The image of masculinity that is crucial to the identities of many men is inextricably bound up with work.

Schultz's competence-centered paradigm focuses on one significant kind of harassment: harassment aimed at keeping women out of certain kinds of jobs, or at generally undermining their perceived competence as workers. This paradigm explains the kind of harassment that is motivated by gender animosity, rather than by sexual desire. The character of the harassment may be sexual, or gendered, or neither. As she argues, her account also provides a reasoned way of understanding same-sex harassment, and of distinguishing between innocuous sexual expression and sexual harassment. Like Franke, Schultz recognizes male-on-male sexual harassment as a form of "gender policing," although Schultz distinguishes her view from Franke's by pointing out that the gender policing concerns work competence.[18] If a man is perceived as insufficiently masculine to uphold the image of the work as man's work, then his competence will be questioned, or he may be punished.

I find Schultz's competence-centered paradigm an improvement over the sexual desire–dominance paradigm for hostile environment sexual harassment. As she argues, courts seem to have gravitated toward the sexual desire–dominance paradigm in an effort to distinguish discriminatory behavior from nondiscriminatory behavior. However, she provides excellent evidence that it does not. Schultz's competence-centered paradigm refocuses attention on the real issue: equal opportunity. It also provides a test for determining when sexual behavior is discriminatory, and when not. The test is whether the sexual conduct has the effect of undermining the woman's competence as a worker.

Schultz's paradigm seems to leave quid pro quo sexual harassment as it is, but to redescribe hostile environment sexual harassment in a way that would be acceptable to some proponents of the natural/biological perspective and to those liberals, such as Paglia and Roiphe, who find hostile environment sexual harassment problematic. Protection from sex is not the issue. Protection of one's right to equal treatment is the issue. Schultz says explicitly that "women should not be able to sue because they are offended by someone else's sexual conversation or gestures."[19]

Schultz's reconceptualization of sexual harassment has an effect common to liberal analyses of sexual harassment.[20] It tends to create a conceptual division between quid pro quo harassment and hostile environment harassment. The competence-centered paradigm does not do a good job of explaining quid pro quo harassment. It may be true that in some cases, the competence of the harassed person is compromised, but that does not seem to be a necessary feature of such cases. Thus, we seem to be left with the sexual desire–dominance paradigm for quid pro quo, and the new competence-centered paradigm for hostile environment. This conceptual division between quid pro quo and hostile environment sexual harassment is present in both natural/biological accounts and liberal accounts of sexual harassment. It means that those who wish to argue that both are species of sex discrimination must use different arguments for each kind of harassment. This tends to support the view that there really is no coherent concept of sexual harassment.

It seems that the only way to offer a coherent concept of sexual harassment is to adopt a gendered approach. Some versions of the liberal perspective are gendered approaches, as are all sociocultural views. MacKinnon conceives of quid pro quo and hostile environment sexual harassment as two poles of a continuum: "Note that the distinction is actually two poles of a continuum. A constructive discharge, in which a woman leaves the job because of a constant condition of sexual harassment, is an environmental situation that becomes quid pro quo."[21] She is able to explain both forms of sexual harassment using one explanation because she assumes men dominate women by means of sexuality and by means of work, and that the two reinforce one another. Without some acknowledgment that women's employment and educational opportunities have been differentially affected by sexual and gendered conduct at work and in school, the coherence of sexual harassment as a category falls apart.

It seems to me that in order to conceive of quid pro quo sexual harassment as *sex discrimination*, some acknowledgment of the difference that gender makes is necessary. One must acknowledge that the employment and educational opportunities of *women* in particular have been, and continue to be, detrimentally affected by quid pro quo harassment. One need not adopt the sociocultural perspective to take such a position. Ronald Dworkin articulated an analogous position with regard to race in his response to the Supreme Court's decision in *Bakke v. University of California Regents*.[22] In that case, the Supreme Court held that Allan Bakke, a white male, had been a victim of racial discrimination because he was denied admission to Davis medical school because of his race. Dworkin claims that the principle underlying legitimate claims of race discrimination is something like, "Every citizen has a constitutional right that he not suffer disadvantage, at least in competition for any public benefit, because the race or religion or sect or region or other natural or artificial group to which he belongs is the object of prejudice or contempt."[23] Dworkin argued that Bakke could not claim that he was kept out of Davis because his race is the object of prejudice or contempt.

An analogous principle with regard to gender would be: Every citizen has a constitutional right that she not suffer disadvantage, at least in competition for any public benefit, because the gender to which she belongs is the object of prejudice or contempt. The category of "sex" was included in Title VII because women had been objects of prejudice or contempt *because of their gender*, and the form this prejudice and contempt took had direct consequences for their employment opportunities.

Many Americans understand this and agree that women's employment and educational opportunities should not be hampered because of the prejudice or contempt some have for women. The next step in the argument is to conceptualize both quid pro quo and hostile environment sexual harassment in these terms.

Hostile environment sexual harassment that is due to gender animus is pretty universally acknowledged to be due to prejudice or contempt toward women, and so to be wrongful discrimination. Even some of those who object to classifying any other kind of behavior collected under the rubric "sexual harassment" as sex discrimination agree that such behavior is sex discrimination. As we saw, Browne and Hajdin both make an exception for this kind of harassment. Vicki Schultz's competence-centered paradigm takes this kind of case as central.

Quid pro quo harassment is more problematic. One can argue that quid pro quo sexual harassment is a form of coercion, and that coercion is wrong, as Hughes and May do.[24] One can also argue that it is a form of extortion, as Browne and Paul do. However, these conceptions do not justify treating quid pro quo harassment as a form of sex discrimination. What is needed is some reason for claiming that such conduct discriminates on the basis of sex.

As we have seen, the courts argued that the fact that a quid pro quo harasser is motivated by sexual desire shows that the conduct is because of sex. This only goes part way toward proving that the conduct constitutes sex discrimination. While it is true that a person discriminates between the sexes when he or she is motivated by heterosexual desire, this in itself is not wrongful discrimination. Hajdin makes the point well when he claims that

> simply pointing out that in almost all sexual harassment cases, the conduct at issue is deliberately directed at members of only one sex, is not sufficient to subsume sexual harassment under the general principle prohibiting discrimination on the basis of sex. That prohibition is against wrongful discrimination . . . while pointing out that the conduct is directed at only one sex merely shows that those who engage in it discriminate in the wide sense of the word. Therefore, if the treatment of sexual harassment as a violation of the principle prohibiting discrimination on the basis of sex is to be justified, it needs to be proven that the differentiation between the sexes that is characteristic of sexual harassment is wrongful.[25]

Hajdin argues that quid pro quo sexual harassment is wrongful discrimination because it conditions employment benefits or burdens on acceptance or rejection of sexual advances. However, it seems to me that this is not enough to show that quid pro quo sexual harassment constitutes sex discrimination in the full sense. That is, I am nearly convinced by Judge Stern's opinion in *Tomkins v. Public Service Electric & Gas:* "In this instance the supervisor was male and the employee was female. But no immutable principle of psychology compels this alignment of parties. The gender lines might as easily have been reversed, or even not crossed at all. While sexual desire animated the parties, or at least one of them, the gender of each is incidental to the claim of abuse."[26] What is needed is some premise showing that *gender* is not incidental. What is needed is a claim that quid pro quo sexual harassment affects women as a group differently from the way it affects men as a group. Unless it is possible to include quid pro quo harassment and hostile environment harassment under one analysis, we should admit that they are not as similar as all that and seek different accounts and different names for the conduct involved. This seems to be the liberal's dilemma.

There are several ways in which a unified analysis might be done. One way would be to invoke some version of the stereotype argument, which is what the courts have done. I agree with Hughes and May that men as a group are not affected in the same way by quid pro quo sexual harassment as women as a group. Recall that they claim that women as a group are harmed by the tolerance of quid pro quo harassment by employers because it perpetuates certain debilitating stereotypes about women: "When a company tolerates coercive behavior against one woman, it perpetuates the social convention that a woman's merits are to be measured in terms of her sexual attractiveness and compliance, not in terms of her skills or job performance. Women as a group are injured by the supervisor's conduct. . . ."[27] There is no similar group stereotype or convention regarding men as a group. This seems true, but I find Superson's description of the group harm suffered by women more perspicuous, though I do not agree with her definition of sexual harassment. Superson says that sexual harassment expresses and perpetuates the view that women are inferior because of their sex, and that this harms women. According to Superson, "The group harm has to do primarily with the fact that the behavior reflects and reinforces sexist attitudes that women are inferior to men and that they do and ought to occupy certain sex roles" and not others.[28]

I think it can be argued that quid pro quo sexual harassment expresses and perpetuates the view that women are inferior to men in the workplace and in educational environments. A supervisor who tries to coerce an employee into having sex with him in order to secure a promotion or retain her job does not value her competence as an employee. There is a view abroad that female sexual characteristics and competence in work and education are incompatible. This is expressed in such sayings as, "Don't you worry your pretty little head." Thus, when a woman's sexual attractiveness is emphasized, her competence as an employee is de-emphasized.

This account of why quid pro quo sexual harassment should constitute sex discrimination allows a unified account of quid pro quo sexual harassment and hostile environment sexual harassment using Schultz's competence-centered paradigm. Both kinds of sexual harassment express and perpetuate the view that women are inferior workers or academics.

As some have argued, conceiving of quid pro quo sexual harassment as sex discrimination does not capture all of the harm of such conduct. Quid pro quo sexual harassment is an abuse of power on the part of the harasser. Such conduct does represent a kind of theft from the employer when the harasser is not the owner of a business or institution. It is also an abuse of the power of a teacher over a student. None of this is explicitly acknowledged in treating quid pro quo sexual harassment as a form of sex discrimination. However, the fact that the conception of quid pro quo sexual harassment is not fully included in the category of sex discrimination is not a fatal objection to treating quid pro quo sexual harassment as a form of sex discrimination under Title VII and Title IX.

My analysis suggests that men are not victims of sex discrimination when they are the victims of quid pro quo sexual harassment. However, the courts have determined that they may be. I think men should have the protection of Title VII and Title IX for those cases in which they are the victims of quid pro quo sexual harassment and hostile environment sexual harassment. However, the reasons for this are different for different kinds of cases. Some of these reasons are very like those for regarding the harassment of women as sex discrimination. Others are not.

As we saw in chapter 5, some men are harassed by other men. In my view, a man who is a victim of quid pro quo sexual harassment should be able to claim that he is being discriminated against if only men and no women are victims of quid pro quo sexual harassment. That is, he should be able to claim discrimination based on the principle of differential treatment. Recall that this was one of the arguments used by the courts to link sexual harassment and sex discrimination, and that it is one of Hughes and May's ways of arguing that quid pro quo sexual harassment constitutes sex discrimination.[29] However, unless there is some indication that the victim is chosen because he is perceived not to be sufficiently masculine, such harassment does not express or perpetuate the stereotype that such men are inferior workers or academics.

Men who suffer hostile environment sexual harassment that is based on animosity toward men who are not considered sufficiently masculine do, it seems to me, suffer sex discrimination in a sense that is more analogous to that suffered by women. Such men are deemed inferior members of their sex not competent for work and education, and so they are discriminated against on the basis of their gender.

What about the problem of the bisexual harasser? According to the differences approach, differential treatment is required—for a treatment to be discriminatory, only members of one sex can be subject to the treatment in question in a given environment. It is the most important element from the point of view of Justice Ruth Ginsburg: "The critical issue, Title VII's text indicates, is whether members of one sex are exposed to disadvantageous terms or conditions of employment to which members of the other sex are not exposed."[30] If one follows Ginsburg, it would seem that victims of a bisexual harasser would not be able to claim sex discrimination. According to MacKinnon's dominance approach, only the women would seem to have a claim.

The problem here seems to be with the scope of the requirement of "differential treatment." The courts seem to hold that a claim of sex discrimination requires that in each case, women and men be treated differently. The sociocultural approach to the issue does not require that women and men be treated differently in each individual case. The larger social context is one in which women and men are treated differently. It would follow that neither women nor men would have a claim against a bisexual harasser on the differences approach, and that only women would have such a claim on the sociocultural approach. The question is which should prevail.

To be consistent, I must go with the socioculturalists. In the case of a bisexual harasser, the woman has a claim of sex discrimination for the reasons just stated. The man may also have a claim if there is evidence that he was chosen because he is perceived to be an inferior member of the male sex. Otherwise, he does not have a claim. What this means is that differential treatment is a sufficient but not a necessary condition for a claim of sex discrimination on my view. In taking this line, I am in substantial agreement with Schultz and with Franke. Both discuss the tendency of male-on-male harassment to express and perpetuate the view that certain men are inferior because they are not sufficiently masculine.

I have offered an analysis of sexual harassment that takes into account both quid pro quo sexual harassment and harassment designed to keep women (and some men) out of certain fields or job classifications. I have said very little about other sorts of behavior often classified as sexual harassment.

As Schultz points out, the centrality of the sexual desire–dominance paradigm has led some to think that all sexual conduct or expression in the workplace (or in academe) should be illegal. The EEOC characterization of sexual harassment as "unwelcome sexual advances, requests for sexual favors, and other verbal or physical conduct of a sexual nature" suggests that there is no safe sexual expression or conduct. This is both unrealistic and undesirable. On Schultz's model, the whole context of the workplace should be taken into account when considering whether sexual conduct or expression is an indication of sex discrimination.

> To determine whether the conduct is based on sex within the meaning of Title VII, they should inquire . . . into whether it embodies gender-based expectations for the workers or work involved. . . . As part of this causation inquiry, the larger structural context of the workplace will be very relevant . . . courts should examine the record for structural indicia of gender inequality at work. For example: Was there a history of discrimination or exclusion of women from the relevant occupation or field, the workplace, or the job title?[31]

Schultz's broadening of the context for determining the presence of hostile work environment sexual harassment should enable us to distinguish between discriminatory sexual conduct and nondiscriminatory sexual conduct.[32]

There is one further type of conduct that has been classified as hostile environment sexual harassment that I have not yet addressed. This is the unwanted sexual advance that is not quid pro quo. I find this a difficult area to classify. There is no doubt that women's conditions of work are negatively affected by the persistent attentions of men. However, my analysis of sexually harassing conduct suggests that not all such cases qualify as sex discrimination. If the advances are part of a larger campaign to call into question the harassed woman's competence, then the woman is a victim of sex discrimination. If the advances are made by a supervisor, or someone the woman reasonably believes to have power over her employment or education, and she has reason to think that there is a threat of retaliation for noncompliance, then the woman is a victim of sex discrimination for the same reasons that a victim of quid pro quo harassment is. If the advances are from a co-worker with no supervisory power over her, but they are so bizarre that they affect the woman's ability to carry out her work, then I believe that she has a claim of sex discrimination. This is on the grounds of differential treatment.

Thus, most quid pro quo sexual harassment and some, but not all, of what people have considered hostile environment sexual harassment constitute sex discrimination. The determining factor is whether the conduct expresses and perpetuates the view that women are inferior employees or academics.

After thinking through the issues surrounding the nature and treatment of sexual harassment, I conclude that some sexually harassing behavior should continue to be considered a form of sex discrimination and so prohibited under Title VII. The focus on *sex* rather than on *gender* has led courts and much of the public to think of sexual harassment as a subset of sex discrimination—a form of discriminatory behavior that involves sexual overtures, or explicit sexual language or gestures. But the history of judicial decisions and the theoretical work of legal scholars convinces me that it is better to think of sexual harassment and sex discrimination as intersecting sets. Not all *sexual* harassment is sex discrimination, and not all sex discrimination is sexual harassment.

What I have said so far in this discussion deals primarily with the law. But, as I emphasized at the beginning of this work, sexual harassment is not only a legal concept. It is a moral concept, as well. In this wider realm, I find myself in partial agreement with the critics of the concept of sexual harassment. The concept of sexual harassment seems to include within its borders disparate kinds of behavior that are wrong for different reasons. Some of them are abuses of power. Some are invasions of privacy. However, as long as they result in the imposition of disadvantageous terms and conditions in employment or education because of sex, they should continue to be prohibited by Title VII and Title IX. It may be that hostile environment sexual harassment will come to be known simply as "gender harassment," so that its association with sexual harassment will become a thing of the past. In my view, this would be a good thing. To continue to categorize both quid pro quo and hostile environment sexual harassment as *sexual* harassment perpetuates two errors in thinking: (1) thinking that harassment that is sex discrimination is *sexual*, and (2) thinking that all *sexual* expression and conduct is harassment.

NOTES

Chapter 1

1. Lin Farley, *Sexual Shakedown: The Sexual Harassment of Women on the Job* (New York: McGraw-Hill, 1978), xi.

2. *Williams v. Saxbe*, 413 F. Supp. 654 (D.D.C. 1976), *rev'd on other grounds sub nom. Williams v. Bell*, 587 F.2d 1240 (D.C. Cir. 1978).

3. Amy Joyce, "Companies Insuring Selves against Discrimination Suits," *Washington Post*, May 17, 1998, Financial section.

4. See "No Bliss from Boy's Kiss," *Washington Post*, September 25, 1996. Apparently, the Department of Education decided that, in this case anyway, the six-year-old did not sexually harass his classmate: "In one incident a school reportedly punished a six-year-old boy, under its sexual harassment policy, for kissing a female classmate on the cheek. These incidents provide a good example of how the Guidance can assist schools in formulating appropriate responses to conduct of this type. The factors in the Guidance confirm that a kiss on the cheek by a first grader does not constitute sexual harassment" (Department of Education, Office for Civil Rights, "Sexual Harassment Guidance: Harassment of Students by School Employees, Other Students, or Third Parties," *Federal Register* 62, no. 49 [March 13, 1997]: 12035).

5. A great deal of attention has been paid this issue. See Peter DeChiara, "The Need for Universities to Have Rules on Consensual Sexual Relationships between Faculty Members and Students," *Columbia Journal of Law and Social Policy* 21 (1988): 137–162; Billie Wright Dziech and Linda Weiner, *The Lecherous Professor: Sexual Harassment on Campus* (Boston: Beacon Press, 1984); Thomas P. Hustoles, "Consensual Relations Issues in Higher Education," in *Sexual Harassment on Campus: A Legal Compendium*, ed. E. K. Cole (Washington, D.C.: National Association of College and University Attorneys, 1990), 251–255; Elisabeth A. Keller, "Consensual Amorous Relationships between Faculty and Students: Policy Implications and the Constitutional Right to Privacy," in *Sexual Harassment on Campus: A Legal Compendium*, ed. Joan Van Tol (Washington, D.C.: National Association of College and University Attorneys, 1987), 80–88; Sherry Young, "Getting to Yes: The Case against Banning Consensual Relationships in Higher Education," *American University*

Journal of Gender & Law 4 (Spring 1996): 269–302; Martha Chamallas, "Consent, Equality, and the Legal Control of Sexual Conduct," *Southern California Law Review* 61 (1988): 777–861; Sue Rosenberg Zalk, Judith Dederich, and Michele A. Paludi, "Women Students' Assessment of Consensual Relationships with Their Professors: Ivory Power Reconsidered," in *Sexual Harassment on Campus: A Legal Compendium*, ed. E. K. Cole (Washington, D.C.: National Association of College and University Attorneys, 1990), 103–133; Barry M. Dank, "Campus Romances and Consenting Adults," *Chronicle of Higher Education* 29 (June 1994): B4; and Margaret A. Crouch, "Campus Consensual Relationship Policies," in *Globalism and the Obsolescence of the State*, ed. Yeager Hudson (Lewiston, New York: Edwin Mellen Press, 1999), 317–343.

6. Philip Shenon, "Command Decision: Army Blames Its Leadership for Sex Harassment," *Ann Arbor News*, September 12, 1997.

7. See chapters 3 and 6.

8. See Catharine A. MacKinnon, *Sexual Harassment of Working Women: A Case of Sex Discrimination* (New Haven: Yale University Press, 1979), 250, note 13.

9. Philosophers sometimes refer to terms such as "carrot" and "canyon" as "natural kind terms." "Natural kind terms constitute a class of general terms and include both mass terms, like 'gold' and 'water', and certain sortal terms, like 'tiger' and 'apple.' Loosely, they may be said to denote types of naturally occurring stuffs and things" (*The Oxford Companion to Philosophy*, ed. Ted Honderich [New York: Oxford University Press, 1995], 446). I am not claiming that other moral-legal terms may not also begin as "terms of art." However, the origins of such terms are often in the distant past, and we do not remember the controversies surrounding them. It is interesting to read John Locke on the issue of moral concepts. Locke claims that moral concepts are "mixed modes," which are concepts created by human beings to fit the kinds of situations of interest to them. For example, we have a term for the killing of a human being by another human being, but not for the killing of a sheep by a human being; a term for the killing of a family member, but not of a neighbor. "['T]is the Mind, that combines several scattered independent *Ideas*, into one complex one; and by the common name it gives them, makes them the Essence of a certain Species, without regulating it self by any connexion they have in Nature. For what greater connexion in Nature, has the *Idea* of a Man, than the *Idea* of a Sheep with Killing, that this is made a particular Species of Action, signified by the word *Murder*, and the other not? Or what Union is there in Nature, between the *Idea* of the Relation of a Father, with Killing, than that of a Son, or Neighbour; that those are combined into one complex *Idea*, and thereby are made the Essence of the distinct Species *Parricide*, whilst the other make no distinct Species at all?" (John Locke, *An Essay Concerning Human Understanding* [Oxford: Clarendon Press, 1975], 430–431, book 3, ch. 5, sec. 6).

10. This perspective is described by Kenneth Clatterbaugh as the "moral conservative" view in his *Contemporary Perspectives on Masculinity: Men, Women, and Politics in Modern Society* (Boulder, Colorado: Westview Press, 1990), 15–36.

11. Katherine M. Franke, "The Central Mistake of Sex Discrimination Law: The Disaggregation of Sex from Gender," *University of Pennsylvania Law Review* 144 (1995): 8. See also Katherine M. Franke, "What's Wrong with Sexual Harassment?" *Stanford Law Review* 49, no. 4 (1997): 691–772.

12. Franke, "Central Mistake," 58–70. "Contemporary sumptuary laws have been used to enforce rigid gender norms, and these laws represent a legal attempt to minimize the possibility of confusion or fraud occasioned by misreading gender

when the sexually anomalous person misbehaves by performing his or her gender role ambiguously or incorrectly. By establishing and enforcing appropriate sartorial norms, these laws are designed to ensure social and sexual legibility within a language of difference that regards sex and gender as synonymous. Those people who present themselves in a way that conflicts with, or at a minimum draws into question, the epiphenomenal relationship between sex and gender are either punished for trying to get away with something or pathologized as freaks" (Franke, "Central Mistake," 61).

13. Ibid., 58.

14. See Richard A. Epstein, *Forbidden Grounds: The Case against Employment Discrimination Laws* (Cambridge: Harvard University Press, 1992).

15. The concept of "family resemblance" is attributable to Ludwig Wittgenstein, *Philosophical Investigations*, 3rd ed., trans. G. E. M. Anscombe (New York: Macmillan, 1968), 32, sec. 67.

16. Linda LeMoncheck and Mane Hajdin, *Sexual Harassment: A Debate* (Lanham, Maryland: Rowman & Littlefield, 1997), 170.

17. Yla Eason, "When the Boss Wants Sex," in *Feminist Frameworks: Alternative Accounts of the Relations between Women and Men*, ed. Alison M. Jaggar and Paula S. Rothenberg (New York: McGraw-Hill, 1993), 44–49.

18. Robert Chrisman and Robert L. Allen, eds., *Court of Appeal: The Black Community Speaks Out on the Racial and Sexual Politics of Thomas v. Hill* (New York: Ballantine Books, 1992); Anita Faye Hill and Emma Coleman Jordan, eds., *Race, Gender, and Power in America: The Legacy of the Hill-Thomas Hearings* (New York: Oxford University Press, 1995); Toni Morrison, ed., *Race-ing Justice, En-gendering Power: Essays on Anita Hill, Clarence Thomas, and the Construction of Social Reality* (New York: Pantheon Books, 1992).

19. See Jane Gallop, "The Lecherous Professor," *Differences: A Journal of Feminist Cultural Studies* 7 (1995): 8.

20. Many of those who write on sexual harassment do so as though the harasser was always male and the harassed always female. Acknowledgment that men are also harassed often occurs in a footnote, along with the claim that most often it is women who are harassed. See, for example, Stefanie H. Roth, "Sex Discrimination 101: Developing a Title IX Analysis for Sexual Harassment in Education," *Journal of Law and Education* 23, no. 4 (1994): 460, note 10: "Due to the statistical disparity between male and female victims of sexual harassment, this paper assumes, unless otherwise indicated, that the victims of sexual harassment are female and that the harassers are male." For exploration of the issue of men who are harassed by women, see Aimee L. Widor, "Fact or Fiction? Role-Reversal Sexual Harassment in the Modern Workplace," *University of Pittsburgh Law Review* 58 (1996): 225–254.

21. See, for example, Alan Vaux, "Paradigmatic Assumptions in Sexual Harassment Research: Being Guided without Being Misled," *Journal of Vocational Behavior* 42 (1993): 116–135. Vaux claims that more men are the victims of sexual harassing behavior than most empirical studies show. His claim is based on a survey according to which "the rates of harassment experiences reported by men . . . were far higher than conventional wisdom led us to expect, often similar to the rates for women" (Vaux, "Paradigmatic Assumptions," 119). Vaux also says that "the . . . survey findings suggested that most perpetrators were male, regardless of the target of harassment" (Vaux, "Paradigmatic Assumptions," 122).

22. Vicki Schultz, "Sex Is the Least of It: Let's Focus Harassment Law on Work, Not Sex," *Nation*, May 25, 1998, 14.

23. This is a theme in some feminist epistemology. See Sandra Harding, *Whose Science? Whose Knowledge? Thinking from Women's Lives* (Ithaca, New York: Cornell University Press, 1991), and Marilyn Frye, "The Possibility of Feminist Theory," in *Feminist Frameworks: Alternative Accounts of the Relations between Women and Men*, ed. Alison M. Jaggar and Paula S. Rothenberg, 3rd ed. (New York: McGraw-Hill, 1993), 103–112. Linda LeMoncheck argues for the necessity of "world" traveling, a concept she borrows from Maria Lugones. "World" traveling is the "attempt to understand another's social and psychological location" (LeMoncheck and Hajdin, *Sexual Harassment*, 60). See also Maria Lugones, "Playfulness, 'World'-Traveling, and Loving Perception," *Hypatia* 2, no. 2 (1987): 3–19.

24. *Civil Rights Act of 1964*, U.S. *Code*, vol. 42, secs. 2000e-2, 2000e-16 (1982 and Supp. 1987).

25. See F. M. Christensen, "'Sexual Harassment' Must Be Eliminated," *Public Affairs Quarterly* 8, no. 1 (January 1994): 1–17, and LeMoncheck and Hajdin, *Sexual Harassment*. Christensen argues that the concept sexual harassment is illegitimate, while Hajdin argues that it is not a morally significant concept (LeMoncheck and Hajdin, *Sexual Harassment*, 100).

26. According to Rosemarie Tong, "A private harm (tort) is so classified because it hurts an assignable individual(s), where 'hurt' is understood to mean either physical pain or mental distress of a certain requisite intensity caused either by personal or by property damage. Although this hurt may be intentional, it is often caused by recklessness or negligence" (Rosemarie Tong, *Women, Sex, and the Law* [Totowa, New Jersey: Rowman & Littlefield, 1984], 129).

27. See Phyllis Schlafly, "Feminist Assault on Reasonableness," *Phyllis Schlafly Report* 30, no. 5 (December 1996), and "Feminist Hypocrisy and Double Standards," *Phyllis Schlafly Report* 31, no. 10 (May 1998); Camille Paglia, introduction to *Vamps and Tramps* (New York: Vintage Books, 1994), ix-xxv.

28. Warren Farrell, *The Myth of Male Power: Why Men Are the Disposable Sex* (New York: Simon & Schuster, 1993); Edmund Wall, "The Definition of Sexual Harassment," in *Sexual Harassment: Confrontations and Decisions*, ed. Edmund Wall (Buffalo, New York: Prometheus Books, 1992), 69–85; see also judicial decisions for *Barnes v. Train*, 13 FEP (BNA) 123 (D.D.C. 1974) and *Corne v. Bausch & Lomb, Inc.*, 390 F. Supp. 161, 10 FEP Cases 289 (D.C. Ariz. 1975).

29. Kingsley R. Browne, "An Evolutionary Perspective on Sexual Harassment: Seeking Roots in Biology Rather Than Ideology," *Journal of Contemporary Legal Issues* 8 (1997): 5–77; David M. Buss, *The Evolution of Desire: Strategies of Human Mating* (New York: Basic Books, 1994).

30. This was the view advanced by early proponents of sexual harassment such as Lin Farley and Catharine A. MacKinnon. See Farley, *Sexual Shakedown*, and MacKinnon, *Sexual Harassment*. It is repeated by Schultz: "Sex harassment is a means for men to claim work as masculine turf" (Schultz, "Sex Is the Least of It," 12).

31. Camille Paglia, "No Law in the Arena: A Pagan Theory of Sexuality," in *Vamps and Tramps*, 19–94; Katie Roiphe, *The Morning After: Sex, Fear, and Feminism* (Boston: Little, Brown, 1993), 6, 104, 91; Naomi Wolf, *Fire with Fire: The New Female Power and How It Will Change the 21st Century* (New York: Random House, 1993).

32. See Widor, "Fact or Fiction," 225–254, and Rebecca A. Thacker and Stephen F. Gohmann, "Male/Female Differences in Perceptions and Effects of Hostile Environment Sexual Harassment: 'Reasonable Assumptions'?" *Public Personnel Management* 22, no. 3 (1993): 461.

33. For example, Buss seems to be in agreement with MacKinnon on some

issues: "Feminists' and evolutionists' conclusions converge in their implication that men's efforts to control female sexuality lie at the core of their efforts to control women. Our evolved sexual strategies account for why this occurs, and why control of women's sexuality is a central preoccupation of men. Over the course of human evolutionary history, men who failed to control women's sexuality—for example, by failing to attract a mate, failing to prevent cuckoldry, or failing to keep a mate—experienced lower reproductive success than men who succeeded in controlling women's sexuality. We come from a long and unbroken line of ancestral fathers who succeeded in obtaining mates, preventing their infidelity, and providing enough benefits to keep them from leaving. We also come from a long line of ancestral mothers who granted sexual access to men who provided beneficial resources" (Buss, *Evolution of Desire*, 213–214). In addition, some biologically based perspectives are compatible with the view that harassment is behavior between individuals rather than groups.

34. Anthologies on sexual harassment wanting to offer balanced perspectives include writings by people holding variations of these three views. See, for example, Karin L. Swisher, ed., *Sexual Harassment* (San Diego: Greenhaven Press, 1992), and Wall, *Sexual Harassment*. Wall includes an excerpt from Sandra S. Tangri, Martha R. Burt, and Leanor B. Johnson, "Sexual Harassment at Work: Three Explanatory Models," *Journal of Social Issues* 38, no. 4 (1982): 33–54.

35. MacKinnon, *Sexual Harassment*, 2, 83–92.

36. "We use the term 'model' for want of a better one; in many ways these are positions or preferences for interpreting sexually harassing behavior in particular ways, in the service of particular ends" (Tangri et al., "Explanatory Models," 34).

37. For a critique of Tangri, Burt, and Johnson's models, see Browne, "Evolutionary Perspective," 49–54.

38. See Anita M. Superson, "A Feminist Definition of Sexual Harassment," *Journal of Social Philosophy* 24, no. 1 (1993): 46–64.

39. See Superson, "Feminist Definition," Mackinnon, *Sexual Harassment*, 4–5, and John C. Hughes and Larry May, "Is Sexual Harassment Coercive?" in *Moral Rights in the Work Place*, ed. Gertrude Ezorsky (Albany: State University of New York Press, 1987), 65–68.

40. LeMoncheck and Hajdin identify the sociocultural perspective with a "gendered" approach to sexual harassment. See LeMoncheck and Hajdin, *Sexual Harassment*, ix.

41. "[S]exual harassment is a form of coercion, relying not only upon the harasser's power to create the target's dependence upon the harasser for continued workplace benefits, but also the ability to punish the target for noncompliance . . . such attempts at domination, relying as they do upon power, will necessarily affect more females than males, as males are more likely to hold positions of power in organizations, relative to females" (Thacker and Gohmann, "Male/Female Differences," 463). Thacker and Gohmann do argue that women perceive more behaviors to be sexual harassment than men, and that women are more negatively affected psychologically by harassment than men, but these facts are implicitly attributed to differences in male and female experience. Michael Crichton seems to express this view in his *Disclosure* (New York: Knopf, 1994).

42. Buss, *Evolution of Desire*, 3.

43. Ibid., 3.

44. Ibid., 5–6.

45. For example, "Why men marry poses a puzzle. Since all an ancestral man needed to do to reproduce was to impregnate a woman, casual sex without com-

mitment would have sufficed for him. For evolution to have produced men who desire marriage and who are willing to commit years of investment to a woman, there must have been powerful adaptive advantages, at least under some circumstances, to that state over seeking casual sex partners" (Buss, *Evolution of Desire*, 49). "At least some ancestral women must have practiced the behavior some of the time, because if all women historically had mated for life with a single man and had no premarital sex, the opportunities for casual sex with consenting women would have vanished" (Buss, *Evolution of Desire*, 73).

46. Ibid., 70.

47. Ibid., 88.

48. Ibid., 30.

49. Ibid., 12.

50. Buss says that sexual harassment "produces" conflict, but it seems that what he means to say is that sexual harassment is a form of conflict. See Buss, *Evolution of Desire*, 159. According to Browne, "Much of the conflict that is labeled 'sexual harassment' is traceable in part to the fact that evolution has resulted in conflicting interests between the sexes, which in turn have resulted in different sexual psychologies in men and women" (Browne, "Evolutionary Perspective," 8–9).

51. Ibid., 159.

52. Ibid.

53. Ibid., 161.

54. Browne, "Evolutionary Perspective," 23.

55. Ibid.

56. Ibid., 25–26.

57. Ibid., 26.

58. For a critical discussion of the relevant empirical data, see chapter 4.

59. See Browne, "Evolutionary Perspective," 26–28.

60. Ibid., 37–38.

61. Buss, *Evolution of Desire*, 215.

62. Ibid., 216.

63. Browne, "Evolutionary Perspective," 26, note 121.

64. Kingsley Browne, "Biology, Equality, and the Law: The Legal Significance of Biological Sex Differences," *Southwestern Law Journal* 38 (1984): 654.

65. See Philip Kitcher, *Vaulting Ambition: Sociobiology and the Quest for Human Nature* (Cambridge: MIT Press, 1985), 4–10. See also Buss: "Evolutionary psychology . . . has no political agenda" (Buss, *Evolution of Desire*, 18).

66. Steven Pinker, "Why They Kill Their Newborns," *New York Times Magazine*, November 2, 1997, 52. Pinker is summarizing the views of Martin Daly and Margo Wilson.

67. Ibid., 52.

68. "We can try to understand what would lead a mother to kill her newborn, remembering that to understand is not necessarily to forgive" (Pinker, "Why They Kill," 52).

69. Ibid., 54.

70. Browne, "Evolutionary Perspective," 38.

71. See E. O. Wilson, *On Human Nature* (Cambridge: Harvard University Press, 1978). Going "against nature" has certain costs. With regard to the question of sex equality, Wilson states that "the evidences of biological constraint alone cannot prescribe an ideal course of action. However, they can help us to define the options and to assess the price of each. The price is to be measured in the added energy required for education and reinforcement and in the attrition of indi-

vidual freedom and potential" (Wilson, *On Human Nature*, 134). This is related to what Wilson calls the "leash principle." According to this principle, while genetic natural selection does not determine human behavior, it keeps it on a leash. "The point of the leash principle is to assert both that culture can go against the promptings of the genes and that, if it does, it is eventually going to be pulled back" (Roger Trigg, *Understanding Social Science: A Philosophical Introduction to the Social Sciences* [Oxford: Basil Blackwell, 1985], 156).

72. Browne, "Biology, Equality," 656.

73. Ibid.

74. Ibid., 657.

75. Michael Root, *Philosophy of Social Science: The Methods, Ideals, and Politics of Social Inquiry* (Cambridge, Mass.: Blackwell, 1993), 92.

76. Ibid., 93.

77. Ibid., 94.

78. For MacKinnon's feminism, see her *Toward a Feminist Theory of the State* (Cambridge: Harvard University Press, 1989).

79. "Sex, in nature, is not a bipolarity; it is a continuum. In society it is made into a bipolarity. Once this is done, to require that one be the same as those who set the standard . . . simply means that sex equality is conceptually designed never to be achieved" (Catharine A. MacKinnon, "Difference and Dominance: On Sex Discrimination," in *Feminism Unmodified: Discourses on Life and Law* [Cambridge: Harvard University Press, 1987], 44).

80. Catharine A. MacKinnon, "Desire and Power," in *Feminism Unmodified: Discourses on Life and Law* (Cambridge: Harvard University Press, 1987), 50.

81. Catharine A. MacKinnon, "Sexual Harassment: Its First Decade in Court," in *Feminism Unmodified: Discourses on Life and Law* (Cambridge: Harvard University Press, 1987), 107.

82. "Since 1970, feminists have uncovered a vast amount of sexual abuse of women by men. Rape, battery, sexual harassment, sexual abuse of children, prostitution, and pornography, seen for the first time in their true scope and interconnectedness, form a distinctive pattern: the power of men over women in society" (Catharine A. MacKinnon, introduction to *Feminism Unmodified: Discourses on Life and Law* [Cambridge: Harvard University Press, 1987], 5).

83. The term "quid pro quo" for harassment in which a supervisor demands sexual favors for job retention or promotions or retaliates by depriving one of job-related benefits is attributed to MacKinnon. See Jill W. Henken, "Hostile Environment Claims of Sexual Harassment: The Continuing Expansion of Sexual Harassment Law," *Villanova Law Review* 34, no. 6 (1989): 1245, note 7, and *Henson v. City of Dundee*, 682 F.2d 897 (11th Cir. 1982), 908, note 18. "The quid pro quo claim (literally 'this for that') involves harassment in which a supervisory employee demands sexual favors in exchange for job benefits over which that supervisor has some control or influence. By conditioning some aspect of employment on submission to sexual demands, the supervisory employee imposes on females an additional burden as a prerequisite to employment which men need not suffer, and the employer may be sued for this action of its agent" (National Organization for Women, "NOW Legal Resource Kit: Overview of Federal Sexual Harassment Law," in *Sexual Harassment: Know Your Rights!* ed. Martin Eskenazi and David Gallen [New York: Carroll & Graf, 1992], 128–129).

84. See Epstein, *Forbidden Grounds*.

85. Drucilla Cornell, *The Imaginary Domain: Abortion, Pornography, and Sexual Harassment* (New York: Routledge, 1995); Ellen Frankel Paul, "Sexual Harass-

ment as Sex Discrimination: A Defective Paradigm," *Yale Law and Policy Review* 8, no. 2 (1990): 333; Ellen Frankel Paul, "Bared Buttocks and Federal Cases," *Society* 28, no. 4 (1991): 4–7; Barbara A. Gutek, *Sex and the Workplace: The Impact of Sexual Behavior and Harassment on Women, Men, and Organizations* (San Francisco: Jossey-Bass, 1985); and Crichton, *Disclosure.*

86. Cornell, *Imaginary Domain*, 4.

87. Ibid.

88. Ibid.

89. Ibid., 209.

90. Ibid., 193.

91. Ibid., 205.

92. Paul, "Bared Buttocks," 6.

93. Ibid.

94. Paul, "Defective Paradigm," 336.

95. Thomas A. Mappes and Jane S. Zembaty, eds., *Social Ethics: Morality and Social Policy*, 4th ed. (New York: McGraw-Hill, 1992), 290.

96. *U.S. Code*, vol. 41, sec. 2000e-2(a)(1), in *Sex Discrimination Handbook*, ed. Barbara S. Gamble (Washington, D.C.: Bureau of National Affairs, 1992), 227.

97. See Will Kymlicka, "Liberalism," in *The Oxford Companion to Philosophy*, ed. Ted Honderich (New York: Oxford University Press, 1995), 483–485.

98. See Rosemarie Tong, *Feminist Thought: A Comprehensive Introduction* (Boulder, Colorado: Westview Press, 1989), 12–13.

99. For proponents of liberal feminism, see Betty Friedan, *The Feminine Mystique* (New York: Dell, 1974), Janet Radcliffe Richards, *The Skeptical Feminist* (London: Routledge & Kegan Paul, 1980), and Nadine Strossen, *Defending Pornography* (New York: Anchor, 1996).

100. See Mike Leigh's *Career Girls* (1997), a recent film that explores the lack of understanding between the sexes. Two young women are portrayed as they move from their college days into their thirties. Neither is able to connect with a man in the way she desires. The men in the film are portrayed as self-centered and completely at sea about how to connect with women.

101. See, for example, Michel Foucault, *The History of Sexuality*, vol. 1: *An Introduction*, trans. Robert Hurley (New York: Vintage Books, 1978); Prudence Allen, *The Concept of Woman: The Aristotelian Revolution, 750 BC-AD 1250* (Grand Rapids, Michigan: Eerdmans, 1997); Sarah B. Pomeroy, *Goddesses, Whores, Wives, and Slaves: Women in Classical Antiquity* (New York: Shocken, 1975); David D. Gilmore, *Manhood in the Making: Cultural Concepts of Masculinity* (New Haven: Yale University Press, 1990), and Robert C. Solomon, "The Virtue of (Erotic) Love," in *The Philosophy of (Erotic) Love*, ed. Robert C. Solomon and Kathleen M. Higgins (Manhattanville: University Press of Kansas, 1991), 492–518.

102. See *Harris v. Forklift Systems, Inc.*, 114 S.Ct. 367 (1993). The concern over how to determine severity and pervasiveness gave rise to the reasonable woman standard in *Ellison v. Brady*, 924 F.2d 872 (9th Cir. 1991), discussed in chapters 3 and 6.

Chapter 2

1. The best sources for such material are Lin Farley, *Sexual Shakedown: The Sexual Harassment of Women on the Job* (New York: McGraw-Hill, 1978); Catharine A. MacKinnon, *Sexual Harassment of Working Women: A Case of Sex Discrimina-*

tion (New Haven: Yale University Press, 1979); Constance Backhouse and Leah Cohen, *Sexual Harassment on the Job* (Englewood Cliffs, New Jersey: Prentice-Hall, 1982); Mary Bularzik, "Sexual Harassment at the Workplace: Historical Notes," *Radical America* 12 (1978): 25–43; and Kerry Segrave, *The Sexual Harassment of Women in the Workplace, 1600–1993* (Jefferson, North Carolina: McFarland, 1994). Segrave cites good sources, but her interpretation is problematic. She never defines "sexual harassment," so that her claims regarding its existence are difficult to confirm. In addition, there are some factual errors. For example, she has Louisa May Alcott seeking employment in Dedham, England, in 1851 (Segrave, *Sexual Harassment*, 28).

2. See Mary H. Blewett, *We Will Rise in Our Might: Workingwomen's Voices from Nineteenth-Century New England* (Ithaca, New York: Cornell University Press, 1991).

3. See Segrave, *Sexual Harassment*, 25–27.

4. Ibid., 12–13.

5. Anna Clark, *Women's Silence, Men's Violence* (London: Pandora, 1987), 40–41. Cited in Segrave, *Sexual Harassment*, 25.

6. See, for example, stories related by Helen Campbell in *Prisoners of Poverty: Women Wage-Workers, Their Trades and Their Lives* (1887; reprint, New York: Garrett Press, 1970). "The foreman she hated made everything as difficult as possible. Though the bundle came ready from the cutting-room, he had managed more than once to slip out some essential piece, and thus lessened her week's wages, no price being paid where a garment was returned unfinished. He had often done this where girls had refused his advances, yet it was impossible to make complaint. The great house on Canal Street left these matters entirely with him, and regarded complaint as mere blackmailing" (Campbell, *Prisoners*, 97).

7. See, for example, Amy A. Bully and Margaret Whitley, *Women's Work* (London: Methuen, 1894). "But perhaps the question which touches women most closely is the nature of the supervision to which they are subjected. Unhappily this has sometimes been used for the purpose of 'driving' the workpeople—for instance, by exposing the names of those who had fallen below the standard of the labour driver in the shed—but immoral conduct has had to be submitted to. However, the Unions have taken a firm attitude in this latter respect, and indeed two strikes have recently taken place, one at Oldham and one at Nelson, with the result that in each case the obnoxious overlooker was removed. In the Nelson case the evidence was submitted to arbitrators, clergymen of the neighborhood, who, in giving their judgment, placed it on record that the offences of which the man had been judged guilty 'are not uncommon among men who have the oversight of the female operatives in other mills, and as ministers of religion we most earnestly appeal to the employers of labor practically to recognise their duty in this matter, and seriously consider how essential it is to the happiness and well-being of those under their charge, as well as to their credit, to make the moral conduct of their work-people the subject of nearer concern and of greater importance.' It is satisfactory to note that this award has created an improvement in the behavior of overseers generally, and has attracted the attention of employers" (Bully and Whitley, *Women's Work*, 99–100).

8. See Jacqueline Jones, *Labor of Love, Labor of Sorrow: Black Women and Work and the Family, from Slavery to the Present* (New York: Vintage Books, 1985), 20, 28, 37–38.

9. Backhouse and Cohen, *Sexual Harassment on the Job*, 53.

10. Jones, *Labor of Love*, 20, 38, and Segrave, *Sexual Harassment*, 16–20.

11. Judith K. Schafer, "Open and Notorious Concubinage," in *Black Women in American History: From Colonial Times through the Nineteenth Century*, vol. 4, ed. Darlene Hines (Brooklyn: Carlson, 1990), 1192–1194; cited in Segrave, *Sexual Harassment*, 17.

12. Segrave, *Sexual Harassment*, 20–22.

13. "More Slavery at the South," *The Independent* 72, no. 3295 (January 25, 1912): 197–200, in *Black Women in White America: A Documentary History*, ed. Gerda Lerner (New York: Pantheon Books, 1972), 155, quoted in Farley, *Sexual Shakedown*, 40.

14. Lerner, *Black Women*, 156.

15. Ibid., 157.

16. Lerner, *Black Women*, 165, quoted in Paula Giddings, *When and Where I Enter: The Impact of Black Women on Race and Sex in America* (New York: Bantam Books, 1984), 86–87.

17. Quotations from Dorothy Richardson, *The Long Day: The True Story of a New York Working Girl as Told by Herself* (New York, 1905), quoted in Robert W. Smuts, *Women and Work in America* (New York: Columbia University Press, 1959), 72. Also cited in Segrave, *Sexual Harassment*, 61–62.

18. Ordway Tead, *Instincts in Industry: A Study of Working-Class Psychology* (1918; reprint, New York: Arno & New York Times, 1969), 33–34. Cited in Segrave, *Sexual Harassment*, 66.

19. Tead, *Instincts in Industry*, 35. Cited in Segrave, *Sexual Harassment*, 140.

20. Maud Nathan, *The Story of an Epoch-Making Movement* (Garden City, New York: Doubleday, Page, 1926), 15–16. Cited in Segrave, *Sexual Harassment*, 125.

21. Nathan, *Epoch-Making Movement*, 7. Cited in Segrave, *Sexual Harassment*, 108.

22. Segrave discusses the experiences of women in Russia, Australia, India, Brazil, France, New Zealand, Saudi Arabia, Mexico, Japan, and other countries.

23. Friedrich Engels, *The Conditions of the Working Class in England* (Palo Alto: Stanford University Press, 1968), 167–168.

24. Backhouse and Cohen, *Sexual Harassment on the Job*, 61.

25. Carole Elizabeth Adams, *Women Clerks in Wilhelmine Germany* (New York: Cambridge University Press, 1988), 43, 59–60. Cited in Segrave, *Sexual Harassment*, 106.

26. Frances Maule, *She Strives to Conquer: Business Behavior, Opportunities, and Job Requirements for Women* (New York: Funk & Wagnalls, 1935), 155–157.

27. Ibid., 157.

28. Ibid., 158.

29. Philip S. Foner, *Women and the Labor Movement: From World War I to the Present* (New York: Free Press, 1980), 404. Cited in Segrave, *Sexual Harassment*, 66.

30. Warren Farrell, *The Myth of Male Power: Why Men Are the Disposable Sex* (New York: Simon & Schuster, 1993).

31. "We can regulate the work environment. We must have equal opportunity and sexual harassment guidelines, but you cannot legislate relationships . . . ." (Camille Paglia, "The Rape Debate, Continued," in *Sex, Art, and American Culture* [New York: Vintage, 1992], 68).

32. Camille Paglia, "The Strange Case of Clarence Thomas and Anita Hill," in Paglia, *Sex, Art, and American Culture*, 47.

33. Patricia J. Williams, "A Rare Case Study of Muleheadedness and Men," in *Race-ing Justice, En-gendering Power*, ed. Toni Morrison (New York: Pantheon

Books, 1992), 159–171. The first quotation is from Catharine A. MacKinnon, quoted in "Harassment: Men on Trial," *U.S. News and World Report*, October 12, 1991, 40; the second is from Camille Paglia, quoted in the same article, 40.

34. Elaine Lunsford Weeks et al., "The Transformation of Sexual Harassment from a Private Trouble into a Public Issue," *Sociological Inquiry* 56, no. 4 (1986): 432–433.

35. Vicki Schultz, "Sex Is the Least of It: Let's Focus Harassment Law on Work, Not Sex," *Nation*, May 25, 1998, 14–15.

36. Weeks et al. provide a sociological account of the series of events that helped make possible the recognition of sexual harassment as a public issue. See Weeks et al., "Transformation of Sexual Harassment," 432–455.

37. Farley, *Sexual Shakedown*, xi.

38. Ibid. Farley's description of how the notion of sexual harassment arose is remarkably similar to Marilyn Frye's description of how "patterns" of oppression are recognized through consciousness raising in "The Possibility of Feminist Theory," in *Feminist Frameworks: Alternative Theoretical Accounts of the Relations between Women and Men*, 3rd ed., ed. Alison M. Jaggar and Paula S. Rothenberg (New York: McGraw-Hill, 1993), 103–112.

39. Farley, *Sexual Shakedown*, xi.

40. The precise relationship between Farley and Working Women United is not clear. Farley does not mention either Working Women United or the Working Women United Institute in *Sexual Shakedown*. Farley claims that the Women's Section of the Human Affairs Program at Cornell University distributed the first sexual harassment survey, which elsewhere is attributed to Working Women United (see Weeks et al., "Transformation of Sexual Harassment"). Weeks et al. cite Peggy Crull as the source of their information (Week et al., "Transformation of Sexual Harassment," 35–36). Silverman claims: "The issue of sexual harassment was developed by the Working Women United Institute and by Lin Farley, Susan Meyer, Karen Sauvigne and Carmita Wood. These women and others helped found the institute, put on the first Speak-Out on Sexual Harassment, gathered the data discussed in this article, and first brought the issue to public attention" (Dierdre Silverman, "Sexual Harassment: Working Women's Dilemma," *Quest* 3 [1976–77]: 23).

The "Testimony of Working Women's Institute before U.S. Senate Labor and Human Resources Committee, April 21, 1981," seems to support Weeks et al.: "Working Women's Institute is a national resource/research/service center that deals exclusively with sexual harassment on the job. Indeed, in 1975 at the Institute's formation we coined the phrase 'sexual harassment' and gave a name to a formerly taboo dilemma faced by millions of working women. . . " (U.S. Congress, Senate Committee on Labor and Human Resources, *Sex Discrimination in the Workplace: Hearing before the Committee on Labor and Human Resources*, 97th Cong., 1st sess., 1981, 517).

MacKinnon credits "Working Women United Institute" with being the first to use the term "sexual harassment" as a *term of art*: "Working Women United Institute . . . seems to have been the first to use these words as anything approaching a term of art, at first in connection with the case of Carmita Wood in October, 1975. . . . The concept was also used and developed by the Alliance Against Sexual Coercion . . . for example, in their 'Position Paper #1' (September 1976) and appears in Carol Brodsky, *The Harassed Worker* (Lexington, Mass.: Heath, 1976), at 27–28" (MacKinnon, *Sexual Harassment*, 250, note 13).

41. Farley, *Sexual Shakedown*, 20. This seems to be the same survey that Silver-

man claims was distributed by Working Women United Institute in 1975 (Silverman, "Sexual Harassment," 17).

42. Farley, *Sexual Shakedown*, 20.

43. See *Meritor Savings Bank, FSB v. Vinson*, 477 U.S. 57 (1986), 68: "The gravamen of any sexual harassment claim is that the alleged sexual advances were 'unwelcome.'" Rather redundantly, one of the elements required to prove a claim of hostile environment sexual harassment set out in *Henson v. the City of Dundee*, 682 F.2d 897 (11th Cir. 1982), is: "The employee was subject to unwelcome sexual harassment" (*Henson v. the City of Dundee*, 903). This element of the definition has been challenged by Michael D. Vhay. He argues that "[c]urrent law . . . begins with the presumption that a sexual advance is permissible until proven unwelcome," which is not consistent with the "general body of discrimination law" (Michael D. Vhay, "The Harms of Asking: Towards a Comprehensive Treatment of Sexual Harassment," *University of Chicago Law Review* 55 [1988]: 356). The "unwelcome" requirement has also been challenged by A. C. Juliano, among others. See A. C. Juliano, "Did She Ask for It? The 'Unwelcome' Requirement in Sexual Harassment Cases," *Cornell Law Review* 77 (1992): 1558–1592.

44. The first sexual harassment cases to reach federal courts were *Miller v. Bank of America*, 418 F. Supp. 233, 234, 13 FEP Cases 439 (N.D. Cal. 1976), *Corne v. Bausch & Lomb*, 390 F. Supp. 161, 10 FEP Cases 289 (D.C. Ariz. 1975), *Barnes v. Train*, 13 FEP (BNA) 123 (D.D.C. 1974), *rev'd sub nom. Barnes v. Costle*, 561 F.2d 983 (D.C. Cir. 1977), *Tomkins v. Public Service Electric & Gas*, 422 F. Supp. 553 (D.C. N.J. 1976), and *Williams v. Saxbe*, 413 F. Supp. 654 (D.D.C. 1976). All were quid pro quo cases.

45. See *Harris v. Forklift Systems, Inc.*, 114 S.Ct. 367 (1993). The concern over how to determine offensiveness gave rise to the "reasonable woman" standard in *Ellison v. Brady*, 924 F.2d 872 (9th Cir. 1991). See chapter 3.

MacKinnon seems to hold that "hostile environment" sexual harassment (which she calls "sexual harassment as a condition of work") is not really different in kind from quid pro quo sexual harassment. Both require a woman to put up with some kind of unequal treatment as a condition of employment. "Note that the distinction is actually two poles of a continuum. A constructive discharge, in which a woman leaves the job because of a constant condition of sexual harassment, is an environmental situation that becomes quid pro quo" (Catharine A. MacKinnon, *Feminism Unmodified: Discourses on Life and Law* [Cambridge: Harvard University Press, 1987], 254, note 17).

46. See William Petrocelli and Barbara Kate Repa, *Sexual Harassment on the Job* (Berkeley, California: Nolo Press, 1992). "[A] sex-for-jobs situation is always considered severe without anything further" and "Cases involving intrusive types of touching or fondling are also usually considered severe, even if the offensive behavior occurs only once" (Petrocelli and Repa, *Sexual Harassment on the Job*, 2/19).

See also *Ellison v. Brady*, 924 F.2d 872 (9th Cir. 1991), p. 878: "the required showing of severity or seriousness of the harassing conduct varies inversely with the pervasiveness or frequency of the conduct"; and *King v. Board of Regents University of Wisconsin System*, 898 F.2d 533 (7th Cir. 1990). "'Although a single act can be enough, . . . generally, repeated incidents create a stronger claim depending on the number of incidents and the intensity of each incident'" (*King v. Board of Regents University of Wisconsin System*, 537).

47. See Vhay, "Harms of Asking," 349–360, for use of the expression "sexuality harassment." The first case to address this question directly was *McKinney v.*

Dole, 765 F.2d 1129 (D.C.Cir. 1985). The court decided that an act that was not sexual could count as sexual harassment.

48. "Sexual harassment, most broadly defined, refers to the unwanted imposition of sexual requirements in the context of a relationship of unequal power" (MacKinnon, *Sexual Harassment*, 1). See also Anita M. Superson, "A Feminist Definition of Sexual Harassment," *Journal of Social Philosophy* 24, no. 1 (1993): 46–64. "[A]ny behavior (verbal or physical) caused by a person, A, in the dominant class directed at another B, in the subjugated class, that expresses and perpetuates the attitude that B or members of B's sex is/are inferior because of their sex, thereby causing harm to either B and/or members of B's sex" (Superson, "Feminist Definition," 46); Larry May and John C. Hughes, "Is Sexual Harassment Coercive?" in *Sexual Harassment: Confrontations and Decisions*, ed. Edmund Wall (Buffalo, New York: Prometheus Books, 1992), 61–68. "The term sexual harassment refers to the intimidation of persons in subordinate positions by those holding power and authority over them in order to exact sexual favors that would ordinarily not have been granted" (May and Hughes, "Is Sexual Harassment Coercive," 61).

49. The notion that co-workers could harass as well as supervisors was contained in the EEOC *Guidelines* before any court had established this (Vhay "Harms of Asking," 336). Whether this is inconsistent with the definitions of MacKinnon, Superson, or May and Hughes is not clear (see chapter 5). They all seem to consider male co-workers to have some informal social power over the women they harass. However, the law does not require this understanding of the broad social relations between men and women. It is interesting to note that surveys of federal employees performed by the U.S. Merit Systems Protection Board in 1980, 1987, and 1994 found that most sexual harassment was by co-workers or persons with no supervisory authority over the victim. (U.S. Merit Systems Protection Board, *Sexual Harassment in the Federal Workplace: Is It a Problem?* [Washington, D.C.: U.S. Government Printing Office, 1981], 59–60; U.S. Merit Systems Protection Board, *Sexual Harassment in the Federal Government: An Update.* [Washington, D.C.: U.S. Government Printing Office, 1988], 3; U.S. Merit Systems Protection Board, *Sexual Harassment in the Federal Workplace: Trends, Progress, Continuing Challenges* [Washington, D.C.: U.S. Government Printing Office, 1995], 18).

50. Farley, *Sexual Shakedown*, 14–15.

51. Farley, *Sexual Shakedown*, xvii. She identifies three main effects of sexual harassment on women in the labor market: (1) maintenance of job segregation; (2) contribution to female unemployment; (3) women who are not "attractive" are economically penalized (Farley, *Sexual Shakedown*, 49).

52. Farley, *Sexual Shakedown*, 11. Recall that Ellen Frankel Paul, who represents the liberal perspective, also finds an analogy between at least some forms of sexual harassment and extortion. See chapter 1.

53. The name of Eleanor Holmes Norton should also be mentioned. Norton was the director of the New York City Human Rights Commission when Farley et al., brought their first complaint on behalf of Carmita Wood, and she was the head of the committee of the EEOC that developed the 1980 definition of sexual harassment for the EEOC *Guidelines*, declaring it to be an illegal form of sex discrimination.

54. MacKinnon, *Sexual Harassment*, 1–2.

55. Ibid., 32.

56. Ibid.

57. Catharine A. MacKinnon, "Sexual Harassment: Its First Decade in Court," in *Feminism Unmodified: Discourses on Life and Law* (Cambridge: Harvard University Press, 1987), 254, note 17.

58. MacKinnon, *Sexual Harassment*, 40.

59. Ellen Frankel Paul, "Bared Buttocks and Federal Cases," *Society* 28, no. 4 (1991): 6.

60. A brief survey of some of the most significant early cases shows that judges had trouble making sexual harassment fit Title VII sex discrimination legislation and case law. This problem has plagued the development of the concept in the law from the beginning, prompting Judge Robert Bork to comment on the artificiality of conceiving of sexual harassment as sex discrimination: "Perhaps some of the doctrinal difficulty in this area is due to the awkwardness of classifying sexual advances as 'discrimination.' Harassment is reprehensible, but Title VII was passed to outlaw discriminatory behavior and not simply behavior of which we strongly disapprove. The artificiality of the approach we have taken appears from the decisions in this circuit . . . . Had Congress been aiming at sexual harassment, it seems unlikely that a woman would be protected from unwelcome heterosexual or lesbian advances but left unprotected when a bisexual attacks. That bizarre result suggests that Congress was not thinking of individual harassment at all but of discrimination in conditions of employment because of gender" (*Vinson v. Taylor*, 753 F.2d 141, 36 FEP 1423 [D.C. Cir. 1985], Bork's Dissenting opinion on Appellees' suggestion for rehearing *en banc*, n. 7, p. 1332).

61. Richard A. Epstein, *Forbidden Grounds: The Case Against Employment Discrimination Laws* (Cambridge: Harvard University Press, 1992) and Janet Dine and Bob Watt, "Sexual Harassment: Moving Away from Discrimination," *Modern Law Review* 58 (1995): 343–363, recommend using existing tort laws, while Ellen Frankel Paul, "Bared Buttocks" and "Sexual Harassment as Sex Discrimination: A Defective Paradigm," *Yale Law and Policy Review* 8, no. 2 (1990): 333–365, speaks of creating a special sexual harassment tort.

62. Carrie N. Baker, "Sexual Extortion: Criminalizing Quid Pro Quo Sexual Harassment," *Law and Inequality Journal* 13 (1994): 213–251.

63. Backhouse and Cohen, *Sexual Harassment on the Job*, 126.

64. Epstein, *Forbidden Grounds*, 352–353.

65. MacKinnon, *Sexual Harassment*, 171.

66. Tong, *Women, Sex, and the Law*, 77.

67. See Farley, *Sexual Shakedown*, MacKinnon, *Sexual Harassment*, and Superson, "Feminist Definition."

Chapter 3

1. Barbara S. Gamble, ed., *Sex Discrimination Handbook* (Washington, D.C.: Bureau of National Affairs, 1992), 227.

2. See Deborah L Rhode, *Justice and Gender: Sex Discrimination and the Law* (Cambridge: Harvard University Press, 1989), 57, and Joan Hoff-Wilson, *Law, Gender, and Injustice: A Legal History of U.S. Women* (New York: New York University Press, 1991), 233–234.

3. Rhode, *Justice and Gender*, 58; Hoff-Wilson, *Law, Gender, and Injustice*: "Although the first EEOC director, Herman Edelsberg, sought to ignore the sex provision of Title VII, saying it was a 'fluke' and not the agency's first priority, well over one-third of all complaints processed during the agency's first year alleged sex discrimination" (Hoff-Wilson, *Law, Gender, and Injustice*, 235).

4. *Barnes v. Costle*, 561 F.2d 983 (D.C. Cir. 1977), 987.

5. Gamble, *Sex Discrimination Handbook*, 1.

6. Rhode, *Justice and Gender*, 58; Hoff-Wilson, *Law, Gender, and Injustice*, 235.

7. *Pittsburgh Press Co. v. Pittsburgh Commission on Human Relations*, 413 U.S. 376 (1973).

8. *Weeks v. Southern Bell*, 408 F.2d 228 (5th Cir. 1969).

9. *Laffey v. Northwest Airlines*, 366 F. Supp. 763 (D.D.C. 1974), aff'd in part and reversed in part, No. 74–1719 (D.C. Cir. Oct. 20, 1976).

10. *Rosenfeld v. Southern Pac. Co.*, 444 F.2d 1219 (9th Cir. 1971).

11. *Ridinger v. General Motors, Corp.*, 325 F. Supp. 1089 (D. Ohio 1971).

12. *Bartmess v. Drewrys U.S.A., Inc.*, 444 F.2d 1186 (7th Cir. 1971).

13. *Jurinko v. Edwin L. Wiegan Co.*, 331 F. Supp. 1184 (D.Pa.1971).

14. *Schattman v. Texas Employment Co.*, 330 F. Supp. 328 (D.Tex.1971).

15. *Sprogis v. United Airlines, Inc.*, 444 F.2d 1194 (7th Cir. 1971).

16. Hoff-Wilson, *Law, Gender, and Injustice*, 245.

17. *Vinson v. Taylor*, 753 F.2d 141, 36 FEP 1423 (D.C. Cir. 1985). Bork's Dissenting opinion on Appellees' suggestion for rehearing en banc, 1332, note 7.

18. *Barnes v. Train*, 13 FEP (BNA) 123 (D.D.C. 1974), rev'd sub nom. *Barnes v. Costle*, 561 F.2d 983 (D.C. Cir. 1977). According to MacKinnon, *Barnes v. Train* was the first case, but it was not reported until two years later. The first reported case was *Corne v. Bausch & Lomb*, Inc., 390 F. Supp. 161, 10 FEP Cases 289 (D.C. Ariz. 1975). See Catharine A. MacKinnon, *Sexual Harassment of Working Women: A Case of Sex Discrimination* (New Haven: Yale University Press, 1979), 60.

19. It should be noted that Barnes's original claim was based on race discrimination. Many have argued that race and sex discrimination often go hand-in-hand, and that to force their division into race discrimination *or* sex discrimination results in injustice. See Kimberle Crenshaw, "Demarginalizing the Intersection of Race and Sex: A Black Feminist Critique of Antidiscrimination Doctrine, Feminist Theory, and Antiracist Politics," *University of Chicago Legal Forum* 139 (1989): 139–167.

20. *Barnes v. Train*, 124.

21. Ibid.

22. *Corne v. Bausch and Lomb, Inc.*, Tomkins v. Public Service Electric & Gas, 422 F. Supp. 553 (D.C. N.J. 1976). *Corne v. Bausch & Lomb*, 390 F. Supp. 161, 10 FEP Cases 289

23. *Tomkins v. Public Service Electric & Gas*, 556.

24. MacKinnon, *Sexual Harassment*, 58.

25. *Tomkins v. Public Service Electric & Gas*, 556.

26. *Williams v. Saxbe*, 413 F. Supp. 654 (D.D.C. 1976), rev'd on other grounds sub nom. *Williams v. Bell*, 587 F.2d 1240 (D.C. Cir. 1978). Though, again, the term "sexual harassment" is never used.

27. *Williams v. Saxbe*, 655–656.

28. Ibid., 658.

29. Ibid.

30. Ibid.

31. *Barnes v. Costle*, 989.

32. Ibid., 990.

33. Ibid., 991.

34. *Sprogis v. United Air Lines, Inc.*, 444 F.2d 1194, (CA7 1971), 1198. Cited in *Price Waterhouse v. Hopkins*, 490 U.S. 228 (1989).

35. MacKinnon, *Sexual Harassment*, 179. MacKinnon states the argument as part of her critique of the argument.

36. A version of this argument can be constructed for hostile environment sexual harassment:

Sex Stereotype Argument—Hostile Environment

1. Title VII prohibits the use of sex stereotypes in determining an individual's terms and conditions of work.
2. Creating a work environment that is abusive to members of one gender by the use of sex stereotypes constitutes the use of sex stereotypes in determining an individual's terms and conditions of work.
3. So, creating a work environment that is abusive to members of one gender by the use of sex stereotypes is prohibited by Title VII.

37. MacKinnon, *Sexual Harassment*, 66. Cited from the Brief for Appellant in *Barnes v. Costle*.

38. MacKinnon describes the *Williams v. Saxbe* conception this way: "whether the requirement *was in fact* imposed upon one gender but not the other in the case at hand" (MacKinnon, *Sexual Harassment*, 58).

39. Michael D. Vhay, "The Harms of Asking: Towards a Comprehensive Treatment of Sexual Harassment," *University of Chicago Law Review* 55 (1988): 342. MacKinnon describes the interpretation of sex discrimination in *Barnes v. Costle* as: "whenever an employment requirement, such as engaging in sexual relations as the price of a job, is fixed upon one gender that *would not*, under the totality of the circumstances, be fixed upon the other, the condition is seen as based on sex" (MacKinnon, *Sexual Harassment*, 58). This reasoning is quite different from that of early feminist activists. See chapter 2.

40. Vhay, "Harms of Asking," 348. *Henson v. City of Dundee*, 682 F.2d 897 (11th Cir. 1982).

41. See MacKinnon, *Sexual Harassment*, 6; see also chapter 1.

42. *Barnes v. Costle*, 990.

43. See *Corne v. Bausch & Lomb, Inc.*, 163; *Bundy v. Jackson*, 641 F.2d 934 (D.C. Cir. 1981): "Only by a reductio ad absurdum could we imagine a case of harassment that is not sex discrimination—where a bisexual supervisor harasses men and women alike" (*Bundy v. Jackson*, 942, note 7); "there may be cases in which a supervisor makes sexual overtures to workers of both sexes or where the conduct complained of is equally offensive to male and female workers. . . . In such cases, the sexual harassment would not be based upon sex because men and women are accorded like treatment. Although the plaintiff might have a remedy under state law in such a situation, the plaintiff would have no remedy under Title VII" (*Henson v. City of Dundee*, 904).

44. MacKinnon, *Sexual Harassment*, 201.

45. Ibid., 203.

46. Ibid.

47. *Sprogis v. United Airlines, Inc.*, 444 F.2d 1194 (7th Cir. 1971).

48. MacKinnon, *Sexual Harassment*, 116.

49. Ibid., 174.

50. Ibid.

51. Ibid., 203.

52. See Anja Angelica Chan, *Women and Sexual Harassment: A Practical Guide to the Legal Protections of Title VII and the Hostile Environment Claim* (New York: Haworth Press, 1994), 9–10.

53. *Chiapuzio v. BLT Operating Corp.*, 826 F. Supp. 1334 (D. Wyo. 1993).

54. *Johnson v. Tower Air, Inc.*, 149 F.R.D. 461 (E.D.N.Y. 1993).

55. For further discussion, see Michael J. Zimmer et al., *Cases and Materials on Employment Discrimination*, 3rd ed. (New York: Little, Brown, 1994), 565–566.

56. *Corne v. Bausch & Lomb, Inc.*, 163.

57. *Barnes v. Costle*, 992–993.

58. See Vhay, "Harms of Asking," 342, note 64: "The debate since *Costle* has been largely over employer liability for an employee's prohibited conduct." See also Lloyd R. Cohen, "Sexual Harassment," *Society* 28, no. 4 (1991): 8–13. Cohen says of "vicarious liability": "normally it is only applied when the acts of an employee are intended to serve the business interests of the employer" (Cohen, "Sexual Harassment," 11).

59. *U.S. Code*, vol. 42, sec. 2000(e)(b).

60. MacKinnon, *Sexual Harassment*, 93.

61. *Corne v. Bausch & Lomb, Inc.*, 163. For a discussion of this point, see Ellen Frankel Paul, "Sexual Harassment as Sex Discrimination: A Defective Paradigm," *Yale Law and Policy Review* 8, no. 2 (1990): 339–340.

62. *Corne v. Bausch & Lomb, Inc.*, 163.

63. Cohen, "Sexual Harassment," 11.

64. Ibid., 12.

65. For a description of the case, see "Rough Traders of Wall Street," *Guardian Weekly*, May 3, 1998, 22.

66. *Corne v. Bausch & Lomb, Inc.*, 163.

67. *Miller v. Bank of America*, 418 F. Supp. 233, 234, 13 FEP Cases 439 (N.D. Cal. 1976).

68. Ibid., 234.

69. Ibid., 235.

70. *Miller v. Bank of America* was decided after *Williams v. Saxbe*, and it cites *Williams v. Saxbe*. However, the court found that, unlike *Williams v. Saxbe*, in which there were allegations of a practice of sexual advances by the supervisor, this was an isolated instance, and that the policy of the Bank of America was contrary to the behavior of the supervisor (*Miller v. Bank of America*, 235).

71. *Williams v. Saxbe*, 660.

72. Ibid., note 8.

73. *Corne v. Bausch & Lomb, Inc.*, 163–164.

74. *Tomkins v. Public Service Electric & Gas*, 557.

75. Ibid.

76. J. Hearn and W. Parkin, *'Sex' at 'Work': The Power and Paradox of Organisation and Sexuality* (New York: St. Martin's, 1987), 3–4.

77. *Barnes v. Costle*, 989–990, note 49.

78. Vhay, "Harms of Asking," 348–350.

79. See *Tomkins v. Public Service Electric & Gas*, 556–557, and *Miller v. Bank of America*, 235.

80. See *Hall v. Gus Constr. Co.*, 842 F.2d 1010 (8th Cir. 1988); *Andrews v. City of Philadelphia*, 895 F.2d 1469 (3d Cir. 1990); *Hicks v. Gates Rubber Co.*, 833 F.2d 1406 (10th Cir. 1987); *Bell v. Crackin Good Bakers, Inc.*, 777 F.2d 1497 (11th Cir. 1985); *McKinney v. Dole*, 765 F.2d 1129 (D.C. Cir. 1985); *Delgado v. Lehman*, 43 F.E.P. Cases 593 (E.D. Va. 1987). "Harassing conduct that follows a pattern of sex-based disparate treatment is also discriminatory even if not 'sexual' in nature. The most common mode of proof of discrimination is 'disparate treatment' proof, i.e. that a female is being treated differently than a similarly situated male. Accordingly, any harassing treatment, whether sexual in nature or not, could come within a Title

VII sexual harassment analysis" ("NOW Legal Resource Kit: Overview of Federal Sexual Harassment Law," in *Sexual Harassment: Know Your Rights!* ed. Martin Eskenazi and David Gallen [New York: Carroll & Graf, 1992], 134). The following definition appears in a 1992 government publication: "Sexual harassment in its broadest sense is the imposition of an unwanted condition on continued employment or on the receipt of an employment benefit because of the victim's gender. The acts underlying a sexual harassment claim generally are sexual in nature, although intimidation and hostility on the basis of gender that are severe enough to create a hostile working environment can be actionable under Title VII even though no explicit sexual advances occur" (Gamble, *Sex Discrimination Handbook*, 58).

81. 29 CFR Ch. XIV, sec. 1604.11.

82. *Bundy v. Jackson*, 641 F. 2d 934 (D.C. Cir. 1981).

83. Ibid., 940.

84. Ibid., 938.

85. *Bundy v. Jackson*, 943–944. The case to which the court refers in rendering its decision was a case involving race rather than sex. See *Rogers v. E.E.O.C.*, 454 F.2d 234 (5th Cir. 1971), *cert. denied*, 406 U.S. 957, 92 S.Ct. 2058, 32 L.Ed.2d 343 (1972). In *Bundy v. Jackson*, Judge Skelly quotes from *Rogers v. E.E.O.C.* "that 'terms, conditions, or privileges of employment' . . . is an expansive concept which sweeps within its protective ambit the practice of creating a work environment heavily charged with ethnic or racial discrimination. . . . One can readily envision working environments so heavily polluted with discrimination as to destroy completely the emotional and psychological stability of minority group workers. . ." (*Bundy v. Jackson*, 944; *Rogers v. E.E.O.C.*, 238). For more on the interaction between race discrimination law and sex discrimination law, see chapter 6.

86. *Bundy v. Jackson*, 943.

87. *Rogers v. E.E.O.C.*, 454 F.2d 234 (5th Cir. 1971), *cert. denied*, 406 U.S. 957, 92 S.Ct. 2058, 32 L.Ed.2d 343 (1972).

88. *Bundy v. Jackson*, 944.

89. *Bundy v. Jackson*, 944; *Rogers v. E.E.O.C.*, 238.

90. *Bundy v. Jackson*, 944; *Rogers v. E.E.O.C.*, 238.

91. *Bundy v. Jackson*, 945, note 10.

92. For the hearings on the proposed EEOC *Guidelines on Discrimination because of Sex*, see U.S. Congress, Senate Committee on Labor and Human Resources, *Sex Discrimination in the Workplace: Hearing before the Committee on Labor and Human Resources*, 97th Cong.,1st sess., 1981.

93. *Henson v. City of Dundee*, 682 F.2d 897 (11th Cir. 1982).

94. Ibid., 902.

95. Vhay, "Harms of Asking," 342–343.

96. *Henson v. City of Dundee*, 903–905.

97. For a discussion of the "unwelcomeness" requirement in sexual harassment cases, see chapter 6.

98. *Henson v. City of Dundee*, 910.

99. *Henson v. City of Dundee*, Judge Clark, concurring in part, dissenting in part, 913–914.

100. *Meritor Savings Bank, FSB v. Vinson*, U.S. 106 S.Ct. 2399, 2404, 40 FEP Cases 1822, 54 LW 4703 (1986).

101. *Vinson v. Taylor*, 23 FEP (BNA), (D.D.C. 1980), 42; cited in *Meritor Savings Bank, FSB v. Vinson*, 61.

102. *Meritor Savings Bank, FSB v. Vinson*, 64.

103. Ibid., 65.

104. Ibid.

105. Harassment based on race: *Firefighters Institute for Racial Equality v. St. Louis*, 549 F.2d 506, 514–515 (CA8), *cert. denied sub nom. Banta v. United States*, 434 U.S. 819 (1977), and *Gray v. Greyhound Lines, East*, 178 U.S.App.D.C. 91, 98, 545 F.2d 169, 176 (1976). Harassment based on religion: *Compston v. Borden, Inc.*, 424 F. Supp. 157 (SD Ohio 1976). Harassment based on national origin: *Carriddi v. Kansas City Chiefs Football Club*, 568 F.2d 87, 88 (CA8 1977).

106. *Meritor Savings Bank, FSB v. Vinson*, 68.

107. Ibid., 69.

108. Ibid., 72.

109. EEOC, *Policy Guidance on Sexual Harassment*, 1990, reprinted in Gamble, *Sex Discrimination Handbook*, 340–341.

110. 29 CFR 1604.11(c) (1980).

111. 29 CFR 1604.11(d) (1980).

112. *Burlington Industries, Inc. v. Ellerth* (97–569). Argued April 22, 1998—Decided June 26, 1998.

113. *Faragher v. City of Boca Raton* (97–282). Argued March 25, 1998—Decided June 26, 1998.

114. The defense must include two elements: "(a) that the employer exercised reasonable care to prevent and correct promptly any sexually harassing behavior, and (b) that the plaintiff employee unreasonably failed to take advantage of any preventive or corrective opportunities provided by the employer or to avoid harm otherwise." See *Burlington Industries, Inc. v. Ellerth*, No. 97–569.

115. *Meritor Savings Bank, FSB v. Vinson*, 67, citing *Henson v. City of Dundee*, 904.

116. See Saba Ashraf, "The Reasonableness of the 'Reasonable Woman' Standard: An Evaluation of Its Use in Hostile Environment Sexual Harassment Claims under Title VII of the Civil Rights Act," *Hofstra Law Review* 21 (1992): 486–487. See also Jill Henken, "Hostile Environment Claims of Sexual Harassment: The Continuing Expansion of Sexual Harassment Law," *Villanova Law Review* 34, no. 6 (1989): 1243–1264. "The court held that regardless of how offended the plaintiff was, it must be clear that the conduct would have interfered with the hypothetical reasonable person's ability to function effectively in the same or similar environment" (Henken, "Hostile Environment," 1255, note 60).

117. *Rabidue v. Osceola Refining Co.*, 805 F.2d 611 (6th Cir. 1986), *cert. denied*, 481 U.S. 1041 (1987).

118. *Rabidue v. Osceola Refining Co.*, 615.

119. Ibid., 620.

120. Ibid.

121. Ibid., 622.

122. Ibid., 626.

123. Ibid., 620–621.

124. Ibid., 621.

125. Ibid., 627.

126. *Ellison v. Brady*, 924 F.2d 872 (9th Cir. 1991).

127. Ibid., 873.

128. Cited in *Ellison v. Brady*, 876.

129. *Ellison v. Brady*, 878.

130. Ibid.

131. *Rabidue v. Osceola Refining Co.*, 627.

132. *Ellison v. Brady*, 879.

133. Ibid.

134. *Federal Register* 58, no. 189 (October 1, 1993): 51269.

135. Ibid.

136. *Harris v. Forklift Systems, Inc.*, 114 S.Ct. 367 (1993).

137. Ibid., 370.

138. Ibid., 371.

139. *Harris v. Forklift Systems, Inc.*, 114 S.Ct. 367 (1993), Justice Ginsburg, concurring, 372.

140. I thank Elizabeth Hackett for this point.

141. *Robinson v. Jacksonville Shipyards, Inc.*, 760 F. Supp. 1486 (M.D. Fla. 1991).

142. Ibid., 1523

143. See, for example, Jolynn Childers, "Is There a Place for a Reasonable Woman in the Law? A Discussion of Recent Developments in Hostile Environment Sexual Harassment," *Duke Law Journal* 42 (1993): 854–904. "A district court first acknowledged pornography as a form of harassment in Robinson v. Jacksonville Shipyards, 760 F. Supp. 1486, 1522 (M.D. Fla. 1991)" (Childers, "Reasonable Woman," 867, note 44).

144. Kathryn Abrams, "The Pursuit of Social and Political Equality: Complex Claimants and Reductive Moral Judgments: New Patterns in the Search for Equality," *University of Pittsburgh Law Review* 57 (1996): 337–362. "Lois Robinson, a welder at Jacksonville Shipyards, brought a sexual harassment charge based on the pervasive posting of pornography in her workplace, only to be met with a First Amendment defense. . . . Robinson won the First Amendment argument at the district court level . . . and this case of first impression was appealed to the Eleventh Circuit. . . . Before that court could render an opinion, however, the case was dismissed by stipulation of the parties, after the Jacksonville Shipyards closed" (Abrams, "Social and Political Equality," 340, note 18).

145. See Eugene Volokh, "Freedom of Speech and Workplace Harassment," *UCLA Law Review* 39 (1992): 1791–1872; Kingsley R. Browne, "Title VII as Censorship: Hostile-Environment Harassment and the First Amendment," *Ohio State Law Journal* 52 (1991): 481–550; Jules B. Gerard, "The First Amendment in a Hostile Environment: A Primer on Free Speech and Sexual Harassment," *Notre Dame Law Review* 68 (1993): 1003–1035; Suzanne Sangree, "Title VII Prohibitions against Hostile Environment Sexual Harassment and the First Amendment: No Collision in Sight," *Rutgers Law Review* 47(1995): 461–561; and Nadine Strossen, *Defending Pornography* (New York: Anchor, 1996).

146. Walter Christopher Arbery, "Individual Rights and the Powers of Government: Note: A Step Backward for Equality Principles: The 'Reasonable Woman' Standard in Title VII Hostile Work Environment Sexual Harassment Claims," *University of Georgia* 27 (1993): 504, note 9.

147. Robert S. Adler and Ellen R. Peirce, "The Legal, Ethical, and Social Implications of the 'Reasonable Woman' Standard in Sexual Harassment Cases," *Fordham Law Review* 61 (1993): 785, note 62.

148. See Paul N. Monnin, "Proving Welcomeness: The Admissibility of Evidence of Sexual History in Sexual Harassment Claims after the 1994 Amendments to Federal Rule of Evidence 412," *Vanderbilt Law Review* 48 (1995): 1155–1213; and Kenneth L. Pollack, "Current Issues in Sexual Harassment Law," *Vanderbilt Law*

Review 48 (1995): 1009–1018. "[T]he Federal Judicial Conference, fearing abuse of the unwelcomeness standard by sexual harassment defendants, extended Federal Rule of Evidence 412, the federal rape-shield rule, to civil cases. These recent statutory and rule changes make it more attractive for victims to bring sexual harassment claims by making available greater rewards and reducing the likelihood of further harassment during the litigation process" (Pollack, "Current Issues," 1011).

149. *Wright v. Methodist Youth Servs., Inc.*, 511 F. Supp. 307 (N.D. Ill. 1981).

150. See, for example, *Joyner v. AAA Cooper Transportation*, 597 F. Supp. 537 (M.D. Ala. 1983), aff'd without opinion, 749 F.2d 732 (11th Cir. 1984).

151. Kara Gross argues that sexual orientation is seen to be relevant to determining whether sexual harassment has occurred in same-sex cases, but not in different-sex cases. This seems to be true only because the court assumes that the harassers are heterosexual when the harasser is male and the harassed female. As the argument linking sexual harassment and sex discrimination reveals, sexual desire, and thus the sexual orientation of the harasser, is central to the argument. See Kara L. Gross, "Toward Gender Equality and Understanding: Recognizing that Same-Sex Sexual Harassment Is Sex Discrimination," *Brooklyn Law Review* 62 (1996): 1166–1215.

152. *Parrish v. Washington International Insurance Co.*, No. 89-C-4515, 1990 U.S. Dist. (N.D. Ill. Oct. 16, 1990).

153. Cited in Susan Perissinotto Woodhouse, "Same-Gender Sexual Harassment: Is It Sex Discrimination under Title VII?" *Santa Clara Law Review* 36 (1996): 1159.

154. Gross, "Toward Gender Equality," 1189. *McWilliams v. Fairfax County Board of Supervisors*, 72 F.3d 1191 (4th Cir.), cert. denied, 117 S.Ct. 72 (1996).

155. *Hopkins v. Baltimore Gas & Elec. Co.*, 871 F. Supp. 822 (D. Md. 1994), aff'd, 70 Fair Empl. Prac. Cas. (BNA) 184 (4th Cir. Mar. 5, 1996).

156. *Goluszek v. Smith*, 697 F. Supp. 1452 (N.D. Ill. 1988). Gross says that this case has been heavily criticized because it relied entirely on a law student's interpretation of Title VII for its argument. See Gross, "Toward Gender Equality," 1183–1184, note 97. Interestingly, the law student's interpretation was a version of MacKinnon's inequality approach.

157. For the details of the case, see Katherine M. Franke, "What's Wrong with Sexual Harassment?" *Stanford Law Review* 49, no. 4 (1997): 737–738.

158. *Goluszek v. Smith*, 1456.

159. Ibid.

160. *Vandeventer v. Wabash National Corp.*, 867 F. Supp. 790 (N.D. Ind. 1994). See Woodhouse, "Same-Gender," 1165.

161. *Vandeventer v. Wabash National Corp.*, 796.

162. *Garcia v. Elf Atochem North America*, 28 F.3d 446 (5th Cir. 1994).

163. Ibid., 451.

164. *Hopkins v. Baltimore Gas & Elec. Co.*, 871 F. Supp. 822 (D. Md. 1994), aff'd, 70 Fair Empl. Prac. Cas. (BNA) 184 (4th Cir. Mar. 5, 1996).

165. Cited in Franke, "What's Wrong," 754: "*Hopkins v. Baltimore Gas & Elec. Co.*, 871 F. Supp. 822, 833 (D. Md. 1994) (quoting Ellen Frankel Paul, Sexual Harassment as Sex Discrimination: A Defective Paradigm, 8 Yale L. & Pol. Rev. 333, 352 (1990)), aff'd, 77 F.3d 745 (4th Cir.), cert. denied, 117 S.Ct. 70 (1996)."

166. *Quick v. Donaldson Co.*, 90 F.3d 1372 (8th Cir. 1996). See Gross, "Toward Gender Equality": "The Eighth Circuit, in Quick v. Donaldson Co., is the only circuit thus far to hold that same-sex sexual harassment of a non-erotic nature may state a cause of action under Title VII. Quick, a male employee, brought a hostile

work environment suit alleging that his male coworkers subjected him to 'bagging,' physical assault and verbal harassment, including falsely labeling and taunting Quick about being homosexual. In fact, the record states that both Quick and his coworkers were heterosexual" (Gross, "Toward Gender Equality," 1192).

167. *Doe v. City of Belleville*, 119 F. 3d 563 (7th Cir. 1997).

168. A second case in the same district, *Johnson v. Hondo, Inc.* (7th Cir. 1997), cited *Doe* in support of its claim that same-sex sexual harassment is prohibited by Title VII.

169. *Doe v. City of Belleville*, 578.

170. *Price Waterhouse v. Hopkins*, 490 U.S. 228, 109 S.Ct. 1775 (1989).

171. Others also understand *Price Waterhouse* in this way. See Vicki Schultz, "Reconceptualizing Sexual Harassment," *Yale Law Journal* 107 (1998): 1691.

172. *Doe v. City of Belleville*, 580.

173. *Quick v. Donaldson Co.*, 90 F.3d 1372 (8th Cir. 1996). See Gross, "Towards Gender Equality," 1192–1193, for discussion.

174. See Gross, "Towards Gender Equality," 1193–1194.

175. *Harris v. Forklift Systems, Inc.*, 510 U.S. 17 (1993), 25, Ginsburg concurring.

176. MacKinnon, *Sexual Harassment*, 6.

177. *Oncale v. Sundowner Offshore Services, Inc., U.S. Supreme Court*, No. 96–568, March 4, 1998.

178. *Giddens v. Shell Oil Co.*, No. 92–8533 (5th Cir. Dec. 6, 1993) (unpublished).

179. *Giddens v. Shell Oil Co.*, No. 92–8533 (5th Cir. Dec. 6, 1993) (unpublished). Cited in *Garcia v. Elf Atochem North America*, 28 F.3d 446 (5th Cir. 1994).

180. *Oncale v. Sundowner Offshore Services, Inc.*, No. 96–568.

181. *Castaneda v. Partida*, 430 U.S. 482 (1977), 499.

182. *Oncale v. Sundowner Offshore Services, Inc.*, No. 96–568.

183. *Harris v. Forklift Systems, Inc.*, 25.

184. James B. Stewart, "Coming Out at Chrysler," *New Yorker*, July 21, 1997, 42.

185. *Oncale v. Sundowner Offshore Services, Inc., U.S. Supreme Court*, No. 96–568, March 4, 1998.

186. *Oncale v. Sundowner Offshore Services, Inc.* The case cited was *Johnson v. Transportation Agency, Santa Clara Cty.*, 480 U.S. 616 (1987).

187. *Oncale v. Sundowner Offshore Services, Inc.*

188. Franke, "What's Wrong," 758.

189. Katherine M. Franke, "The Central Mistake of Sex Discrimination Law: The Disaggregation of Sex from Gender," *University of Pennsylvania Law Review* 144 (1995): 96.

190. There is a large literature on sexual harassment in academe. Much of it has been confined to harassment in colleges and universities, though more recently, sexual harassment in elementary and secondary institutions has received attention. See Walter B. Connolly, Jr., and Alison B. Marshall, "Sexual Harassment of University or College Students by Faculty Members," *Journal of College and University Law* 15, no. 4 (1989): 381–403; Frances L. Hoffman, "Sexual Harassment in Academia: Feminist Theory and Institutional Practice," *Harvard Educational Review* 56, no. 2 (1986): 105–121; E. K. Cole, ed., *Sexual Harassment on Campus: A Legal Compendium* (Washington, D.C.: National Association of College and University Attorneys, 1990); Nancy Tuana, "Sexual Harassment in Academe: Issues of Power and Coercion," in *Sexual Harassment: Confrontations and Decisions*, ed. Edmund Wall (Buffalo, New York: Prometheus Books, 1992), 49–60.

191. *U. S. Code*, vol. 20, sec. 1681 (1982).

192. Barbara Watts, "Legal Issues," in *Sexual Harassment on College Campuses: Abusing the Ivory Power*, ed. Michele A. Paludi (Albany: State University of New York Press, 1996), 16.

193. See Rhode, *Justice and Gender*, 288–304.

194. *Alexander v. Yale University*, 631 F.2d 178 (2nd Cir. 1980), aff'g 459 F. Supp. 1 (D. Conn. 1977).

195. See Watts, "Legal Issues," 16. But see Elisa Kircher Cole, "Recent Developments in Sexual Harassment," *Journal of College and University Law* 13, no. 3 (1986): 267–284. "However, some courts have limited its expansion into employment matters, applying it only when the plaintiff has no recourse to a remedial statute such as Title VII" (Cole, "Recent Developments," 280). Further limitations followed *Grove City College v. Bell*, which "limited Title IX's enforceability to those programs or activities which receive direct federal assistance" (Cole, "Recent Developments," 180). But, since these limitations were removed by the action of Congress in 1988, nothing further shall be said about them here. "In March 1988, Congress overrode Reagan's veto, thus voiding the Supreme Court decision in *Grove City* and restoring Title IX to its previous potential. . ." (Hoff-Wilson, *Law, Gender, and Injustice*, 257).

196. *Alexander v. Yale University*, 631 F.2d 178 (2nd Cir. 1980), aff'g 459 F. Supp. 1 (D. Conn. 1977).

197. Watts, "Legal Issues," 18.

198. Cited in the appeal, *Alexander v. Yale University*, 182.

199. Carrie N. Baker, "Proposed Title IX Guidelines on Sex Based Harassment of Students," *Emory Law Journal* 43 (1994): 272.

200. Watts, "Legal Issues," 18.

201. *Moire v. Temple University School of Medicine*, 613 F. Supp. 1360 (E.D. Pa. 1985), aff'd, 800 F.2d 1136 (3d Circ. 1986).

202. Ibid., 1365.

203. Ibid., 1367, note 2.

204. See *Levitt v. University of Texas at El Paso*, 759 F.2d 1224 (5th Cir. 1985), *cert. denied*, 106 S.Ct. 599 (1986), and *Cockburn v. Santa Monica Community College District*, 161 Cal. Appl. 3d. 734 (Cal. Rptr. 589 (Ct. App. 2d Dist. 1984). Both cases involved professors who were terminated for engaging in sexual harassment of students. In both cases, the decision went against the professor.

205. "Sexual harassment consists of the sexualization of an instrumental relationship through the introduction or imposition of sexist or sexual remarks, requests or requirements, in the context of a formal power differential. Harassment can also occur where no such formal differential exists, if the behavior is unwanted by or offensive to the woman. Instances of harassment can be classified into the following general categories: gender harassment, seductive behavior, solicitation of sexual activity by promise of reward or threat of punishment, and sexual imposition or assault" (Louise F. Fitzgerald, "Sexual Harassment: The Definition and Measurement of a Construct," in *Sexual Harassment on College Campuses: Abusing the Ivory Power*, ed. Michele A. Paludi [Albany: State University of New York, 1996], 41).

206. Fitzgerald, "Sexual Harassment," 41.

207. Ibid., 41–42.

208. Billie Wright Dziech and Linda Weiner, *The Lecherous Professor: Sexual Harassment on Campus* (Boston: Beacon Press, 1984), 75.

209. Ibid., 74.

210. See *Korf v. Ball State University*, 726 F.2d 1222 (7th Cir. 1984), and *Naragon*

v. Wharton, 737 F.2d 1403 (5th Cir. 1984). See M. Cynara Stites, "What's Wrong with Faculty-Student Consensual Sexual Relationships?" in *Sexual Harassment on College Campuses: Abusing the Ivory Power*, ed. Michele A. Paludi (Albany: State University of New York Press, 1996), 118–119, and Elisabeth A. Keller, "Consensual Amorous Relationships between Faculty and Students: Policy Implications and the Constitutional Right to Privacy," in *Sexual Harassment on Campus: A Legal Compendium*, ed. Joan Van Tol (Washington, D.C.: National Association of College and University Attorneys, 1987), 80–88.

211. *Naragon v. Wharton*, 737 F.2d 1403 (5th Cir. 1984).

212. Ibid.,1404–1405.

213. *Korf v. Ball State University*, 726 F.2d 1222 (7th Cir. 1984).

214. Ibid.,1224.

215. Ibid. Cited from the committee findings.

216. Ibid.

217. Ibid.

218. Ibid.

219. Ibid.

220. *Meritor Savings Bank, FSB v. Vinson*, U.S. 106 S.Ct. 2399, 2404, 40 FEP Cases 1822, 54 LW 4703 (1986).

221. For a newspaper article explicitly making this connection, see Laura Mansnerus, "Colleges Break Up Dangerous Liaisons," *New York Times*, April 7, 1991: "Francis S. Smith, Howard's general counsel, said the school's policy was suggested by a 1986 Supreme Court decision, Meritor Savings Bank v. Vinson, which established that under Federal employment discrimination law, the fact that a sexual relationship between employee and supervisor seemed to be voluntary is not necessarily a defense to harassment."

222. See Mary Jo Small and Julia Mears, "To Draft a More Perfect Policy: The Development of the University of Iowa's Sexual Harassment Policy," in *Sexual Harassment on Campus: A Legal Compendium*, ed. Joan Van Tol (Washington, D.C.: National Association of College and University Attorneys, 1988), 138.

223. Peter DeChiara, "The Need for Universities to Have Rules on Consensual Sexual Relationships between Faculty Members and Students," *Columbia Journal Law and Social Policy* 21 (1988): 137–162; Thomas P. Hustoles, "Consensual Relations Issues in Higher Education," in *Sexual Harassment on Campus: A Legal Compendium*, ed. E. K. Cole (Washington, D.C.: National Association of College and University Attorneys, 1990), 251–255. See also, Patricia L. Winks, "Legal Implications of Sexual Contact between Teacher and Student," *Journal of Law and Education* 11, no. 4 (1982): 437–477, and Phyllis Coleman, "Sex in Power Dependency Relationships: Taking Unfair Advantage of the 'Fair' Sex," *Albany Law Review* 53 (1988): 95–141.

224. Employees of the Minnesota State University System are warned: "A university employee who enters into a sexual relationship with a student or a subordinate where a professional power relationship exists is warned that, if a charge of sexual harassment is subsequently made, the student or subordinate may assert that the relationship was not one of mutual or voluntary consent" (Minnesota State Colleges and Universities, "Policy Statement on Sexual/Gender Harassment, Sexual Violence, and Racial and Disability Harassment," in *Carry Forward Policies—State Universities* [St. Paul: Minnesota State Colleges and Universities, 1992]).

Hope College maintains that "the initiation of or consent to a romantic or sexual relationship between an employee of Hope College and any current Hope College student for whom the employee has a direct professional responsibility is unacceptable. . . . If a complaint by the involved student is filed, it is defined as a complaint of sexual harassment" (Hope College, "Policy Statement on Sexual Harassment and Grievance Procedure," in *Hope College Faculty Handbook* [Holland, Michigan: Hope College, 1995]).

The University of Wisconsin system policy says that "where power differentials exists, even in a seemingly consensual relationship, there are limited after-the-fact defenses against charges of sexual harassment" (University of Wisconsin System, "Consensual Relationship Policy," *System Policies and Procedures* [1991]).

225. *Franklin v. Gwinnett County Public Schools*, 112 S.Ct. 1028 (1992).

226. Watts, "Legal Issues," 19.

227. Baker, "Proposed Title IX Guidelines," and Stephanie H. Roth, "Sex Discrimination 101: Developing a Title IX Analysis for Sexual Harassment in Education," *Journal of Law & Education* 23 (1994): 459–521.

228. Baker, "Proposed Title IX Guidelines," 295. See also Roth, "Sex Discrimination 101": "A Title IX analysis of sexual harassment should either abandon the unwelcomeness requirement or deem sexual advances or attentions by a teacher or other school official at any educational institution to be presumptively unwelcome" (Roth, "Sex Discrimination 101," 506).

229. Roth, "Sex Discrimination 101," 507.

230. Ibid. See also Baker, "Proposed Title IX Guidelines": "Even with regard to adult students, some have questioned whether they can 'consent' to sexual advances of a teacher. However, assuming consensual relationships may occur between adult students and their teachers, the asymmetry of power threatens the fundamental purpose of the relationship—the student's education. . . . Therefore, Title IX guidelines should not put the burden of proving unwelcomeness upon the plaintiff. Instead, they should allow a defense of welcomeness to a charge of quid pro quo sexual harassment when the student is not a minor" (Baker, "Proposed Title IX Guidelines," 296–297).

231. Roth, "Sex Discrimination 101," 508.

232. Some reports of sexual advances to graduate students, and the consequences to their educations of either accepting or rejecting them, are appalling. See R. D. Glaser and J. Thorpe, "Unethical Intimacy: A Survey of Contact and Advances between Psychology Educators and Female Graduate Students," *American Psychologist* 41 (1986): 43–51; K. Pope, H. Levenson, and L. Schover, "Sexual Intimacy in Psychology Training: Results and Implications of a National Survey," *American Psychologist* 34, no. 3 (1979): 682–689; M. Bond, "Division 27 Sexual Harassment Survey: Definition, Impact, Environmental Context," *Community Psychologist* 21 (1988): 7–10; W. Robinson and P. Reid, "Sexual Intimacies in Psychology Revisited," *Professional Psychology: Research and Practice* 16, no. 4 (1985): 512–520. See also Robin West, *Narrative, Authority, and Law* (Ann Arbor: University of Michigan Press, 1993).

233. See Jane Gallop, "The Lecherous Professor," *Differences: A Journal of Feminist Cultural Studies* 7 (1995): 1–14, and Jane Gallop, *Feminist Accused of Sexual Harassment* (Durham: Duke University Press, 1997).

234. Gallop, *Feminist Accused*, 28.

235. Ibid., 38.

236. See Margaret A. Crouch, "Campus Consensual Relationship Policies," in *Globalism and the Obsolescence of the State*, ed. Yeager Hudson (Lewiston, New York: Edwin Mellen Press, 1999), 317–343.

237. Gallop, *Feminist Accused*, 38–39.

238. Department of Education, Office for Civil Rights, "Sexual Harassment Guidance: Harassment of Students by School Employees, Other Students, or Third Parties," *Federal Register* 62, no. 49 (March 13, 1997): 12033–12051. The assistant secretary for civil rights issued a final document entitled "Sexual Harassment Guidance." Its purpose: "Sexual harassment of students is prohibited by Title IX of the Education Amendments of 1972 under the circumstances described in the Guidance. The Guidance provides educational institutions with information regarding the standards that are used by the Office for Civil Rights (OCR), and that institutions should use, to investigate and resolve allegations of sexual harassment of students engaged in by school employees, other students (peers), or third parties" (Department of Education, "Sexual Harassment Guidance," 12034).

239. Department of Education, "Sexual Harassment Guidance," 12038.

240. Ibid.

241. Ibid.,12040.

242. Ibid.

243. Ibid.,12041.

244. The Department of Education cites *Harris*'s use of both a "subjective" and an "objective" perspective. The subjective criterion is met if the victim perceives the conduct in question to be sufficiently severe, persistent, and pervasive to interfere with her or his education. The objective criterion is not as clear: "The Supreme Court used a 'reasonable person' standard in Harris, 114 S.Ct. at 370–71 to determine whether sexual conduct constituted harassment. This standard has been applied under Title VII to take into account the sex of the subject of the harassment, see, e.g., *Ellison*, 924 F.2d at 878–79 (applying a 'reasonable woman' standard to sexual harassment), and has been adapted to sexual harassment in education, *Davis*, 74 F.3d at 1126 (relying on Harris to adopt an objective, reasonable person standard), vacated, reh'g granted; *Patricia H. v. Berkeley Unified School Dist.*, 830 F. Supp. 1288, 1296 (N.D. Cal. 1993) (adopting a 'reasonable victim' standard and referring to OCR's use of it); *Racial Harassment Guidance*, 59 FR 11452 (the standard must take into account the characteristics and circumstances of victims on a case-by-case basis, particularly the victim's race and age)" (Department of Education, "Sexual Harassment Guidance," 12041, note 44).

245. Department of Education, "Sexual Harassment Guidance," 12045.

246. *Silva v. University of New Hampshire*, 883 F. Supp. 293 (D.N.H. 1994).

247. See Timothy E. Di Domenico, "Silva v. University of New Hampshire: The Precarious Balance between Student Hostile Environment Claims and Academic Freedom," *St. John's Law Review* 69 (1995): 609–632.

248. *Silva v. University of New Hampshire*, 299. Cited in Di Domenico, "Silva," 614, note 20.

249. *Silva v. University of New Hampshire*, 299.

250. Ibid. This explanation, cited in the court's decision, is taken from a letter to Dr. Brian A. Giles, director of the Thompson School and one of the defendants in the case.

251. *Silva v. University of New Hampshire*, 310, 305, 302. Cited in Di Domenico, "Silva," 614.

252. *Silva v. University of New Hampshire*, 307. Cited in Di Domenico, "Silva," 615, note 23.

253. *Silva v. University of New Hampshire*, 311.

254. See Di Domenico, "Silva": "It is submitted that the Silva court erred in

holding that Silva's speech was related to matters of public concern and constitutionally protected under the First and Fourteenth Amendments" (Di Domenico, "Silva," 619).

255. *Silva v. University of New Hampshire*, 313.

256. Ibid.,314.

257. *Cohen v. San Bernardino Valley College*, 9th Cir., No. 95–55936, filed August 19, 1996.

258. Department of Education, "Sexual Harassment Guidance," 12046.

259. *Gebsere et al. v. Lago Vista Indep. School Dist.* (96–1866). Argued March 25, 1998–Decided June 22, 1998.

260. Majority opinion, *Gebsere et al. v. Lago Vista Indep. School Dist.*

261. Dissenting opinion, *Gebsere et al. v. Lago Vista Indep. School Dist.*

262. Ibid.

263. See Margaret Mead, "A Proposal: We Need Taboos on Sex at Work," *Redbook*, April 1978, 31.

264. See Monica L. Sherer, "No Longer Just Child's Play: School Liability under Title IX for Peer Sexual Harassment," *University of Pennsylvania Law Review* 141 (1993): 2119–2158.

265. See Christina Hoff Sommers, *Who Stole Feminism? How Women Have Betrayed Women* (New York: Simon & Schuster, 1994), 46.

266. See Cynthia Gorney, "Teaching Johnny the Appropriate Way to Flirt," *New York Times Magazine*, June 13, 1999, 42–47, 67, 73, 80, 82–83.

267. *Doe v. Petaluma City School Dist.*, 830 F. Supp. 1560 (N.D. Cal. 1993) rev'd in part on other grounds, 54 F.3d 1447 (9th Cir. 1995). See also *Burrow v. Postville Community School District*, 929 F. Supp. 1193, 1205 (N.D. Iowa 1996), and *Davis v. Monroe County Bd. Of Education*, 74 F.3d 1186, 1193 (11th Cir. 1996), vacated, reh'g granted, 91 F.3d 1418 (11th Cir. 1996).

268. "[T]he court set the standard for peer-based sexual harassment at intentional discrimination on the basis of sex. The Petaluma court reasoned that unless the school actually meant to discriminate, discriminatory intent cannot be found. . . . because Doe did not allege evidence of intentional discrimination on the basis of sex in her initial suit, the court dismissed the claim without prejudice" (Sylvia Hermann Bukoffsky, "School District Liability for Student-Inflicted Sexual Harassment: School Administrators Learn a Lesson under Title IX," *Wayne Law Review* 42 [1995]: 183–184).

269. See Bukoffsky, "School District Liability," 184–186.

270. Department of Education, "Sexual Harassment Guidance," 12036. *Rowinsky v. Bryan Independent School District*, 80 F.3d 1006 (5th Cir. 1996), cert. denied, 117 S.Ct. 165 (1996).

271. Department of Education, "Sexual Harassment Guidance," 12039–12040.

272. *Davis v. Monroe County Board of Education* (97–843). Argued January 12, 1999—Decided May 24, 1999.

273. Ibid.

274. *Davis v. Monroe County Board of Education*, 97–843, Justice Kennedy dissenting.

275. Ibid.

276. International Labour Organization, *Conditions of Work Digest* 11, no. 1 (1992).

277. ILO, *Conditions of Work*, 51.

278. Jane Aeberhard-Hodges, "Sexual Harassment in Employment: Recent Judicial and Arbitral Trends," *International Labour Review* 125, no. 5 (1996): 499.

279. The following are EC Member States: Belgium, Denmark, Germany, Greece, France, Ireland, Italy, Luxembourg, the Netherlands, Portugal, Spain, and the United Kingdom.

280. ILO, *Conditions of Work Digest*, 23.

281. Ibid.

282. Ibid., 26–28.

283. Ibid., 24.

284. Ibid., 29.

285. Ibid., 24.

286. Ibid., 32–39.

287. Ibid., 32.

288. Ibid., 40

289. Victoria A. Carter, "Working on Dignity: EC Initiatives on Sexual Harassment in the Workplace," *Journal of International Law and Business* 12 (1992): 440.

290. Carter, "Working on Dignity," 442–423: "The Recommendation and Code of Practice are influential but not legally binding measures. The European Court of Justice has held, in the context of social policy, that national courts should consider Commission recommendations when adjudicating complaints. In the few Member States that offer victims of sexual harassment legal redress, the Recommendation may influence judicial interpretations of law. What are needed, however, are national laws prohibiting sexual harassment under which victims can seek legal redress. A Commission recommendation cannot provide this." However, see Joseph M. Kelly and Bob Watt, "Damages in Sex Harassment Cases: A Comparative Study of American, Canadian, and British Law," *New York Law School Journal of International and Comparative Law* 16 (1996):

the legal status of the Recommendations of the Commission is at best unclear, and they may not grant enforceable rights under European Community law. The most authoritative view of the status of the Recommendations comes from the European Court of Justice's decision in Grimaldi v. Fonds des maladies professionelles. While the Grimaldi court held that the Recommendations cannot create rights on which individuals may rely before a national court, the Recommendations are not legally impotent. The court decided that domestic courts are bound to consider the Recommendations when they clarify the interpretation of national provisions adopted to implement them or when they are designed to supplement binding European Community measures. This means that the protected right is based in domestic law and the Community Recommendation is to be regarded simply as an interpretive tool.

Arguably, the Recommendation regarding sexual harassment creates a right under European Community law upon which plaintiffs may rely. If a court were to find that a right guaranteed by European Community law is infringed when a person is sexually harassed, the rules recently expounded by the Court of Justice of the European Community in Marshall v. Southampton and South West Hampshire Health Authority (No. 2) would be brought into effect. In Marshall (No. 2), the court held that national laws, such as the relevant provisions of the Sex Discrimination Act of 1975, which restrict remedies for the infringement of rights guaranteed under the Treaty of Rome, are unlawful as a matter of European Community law. The court further held that the remedy granted must compensate the plaintiff for the entire loss suffered. Marshall (No. 2) concerned inequalities in retirement age as enforced by a Health Authority (which is viewed as an institution controlled by the state). In the first Marshall case, the court found that such inequitable enforcement was a clear infringement of European Community law. (Kelly and Watt, "Damages in Sex Harassment Cases," 123–125)

291. Convention on the Elimination of all Forms of Discrimination against Women, U.N. G.A. Res. 280(XXXIV 1979), 19 I.L.M. 33 (1980). See Beverley H. Earle and Gerald A. Madek, "An International Perspective on Sexual Harassment Law," *Law and Inequality* 12 (1993): 72. The convention has been ratified by over one hundred nations, though many had religious objections. Secretary of State Madeleine Albright has called for ratification of the convention by the United States. See Thomas W. Lippman, "State Dept. Seeks Gains for Women," *Washington Post*, March 25, 1997, sec. A01.

292. Objections to ratification of the U.N. Convention on the Elimination of All Forms of Discrimination against Women are also based on general opposition to the United Nations. See, for example, Phyllis Schlafly, "President Clinton Is Embarrassed," www.eagleforum.org/column/dec96/96-12-26.html.

293. ILO, *Conditions of Work Digest*, 24.

294. Ibid., 41: "Paragraph 139. The working conditions of women should be improved.... Appropriate measures should be taken to prevent sexual harassment on the job and sexual exploitation in specific jobs." See United Nations, *The Nairobi Forward-Looking Strategies for the Advancement of Women*, document adopted by the World Conference to Review and Appraise the Achievements of the United Nations Decade for Women: Equality, Development and Peace, Nairobi, Kenya, July 15–26, 1985.

295. ILO, *Conditions of Work Digest*, 41–42.

296. Ibid., 42–43.

297. Ibid., 44.

298. Ibid.

299. Ibid., 44–45.

300. Ibid., 45.

301. Anita Bernstein. "Law, Culture, and Harassment," *University of Pennsylvania Law Review* 142 (1994): 1227–1331. In general, I agree with Bernstein that approaches to sexual harassment in the United States are more concerned than European approaches with fault and personal injury. However, the "Puritanism" to which she calls attention is not unique to the United States.

302. This is discussed in the context of law by Bernstein. She argues that the approach taken by the United States is concerned with placing blame on an individual for a wrong done to another individual. The European approach emphasizes work conditions and the rights of people to be treated with dignity. "While Americans see the problem of sexual harassment as either wrongful private conduct between two people or as sex discrimination, Europeans have shaped it as a problem of workers, and sited the problem in the workplace. In the United States, sexual harassment is a legal wrong; in Europe, . . . sexual harassment is atmosphere, conditions, an obstruction, or trouble, with very little blame from the law" (Bernstein, "Law, Culture, and Harassment," 1233).

303. For a summary of legislative actions since 1990, see Aeberhard-Hodges, "Sexual Harassment in Employment," 501–503. Legislative Acts prohibiting sexual harassment have been passed in Costa Rica and the Philippines. New Zealand has amended the Human Rights Act of 1993 to cover sexual harassment. Austria has amended the Equality of Treatment Act of 1979 to include sexual harassment, and has an act that equates sexual harassment with sex discrimination, which was already prohibited, in the federal public service. Finland has amended

its Equality Act of 1986. Germany's Second Act on Equality for Men and Women of June 24, 1994, includes the Employee Protection Act, which protects the dignity of women and men by prohibiting sexual harassment. Ireland's Employment Equality Bill No. 38 of 1996 bans sexual harassment. Switzerland's Federal Act on Equality between Women and Men of 1995 designates sexual harassment as sex discrimination. In Argentina, a presidential decree penalizes sexual harassment in public service, but there is no penalty for sexual harassment in the private sector. See also "UN Committee on Elimination of Discrimination against Women Concludes Seventeenth Session at HQ," *M2 Presswire*, July 29, 1997.

304. The Canadian Human Rights Act is not as broad as Title VII. See Joseph M. Pelliciotti, "Workplace Sexual Harassment Law in Canada and the United States: A Comparative Study of the Doctrinal Development concerning the Nature of Actionable Sexual Harassment," *Pace International Law Review* 8 (1996): 339–397. "Canadian federal law reaches only those within the jurisdiction of the federal government. Unlike discrimination laws in the United States, such as Title VII of the Civil Rights Act of 1964 which serves as a powerful vehicle for broad, national regulation by Congress via the constitutional authority of the commerce clause, federal legislation in Canada has a significantly more limited span. Essentially, federal human rights legislation in Canada reaches federal governmental entities, key private, inter-provincial operations in communications and transportation, federally-chartered banks, and some mining operations. The Canadian provincial and territorial laws reach those unprotected by the federal legislation within their respective jurisdictions" (Pelliciotti, "Workplace Sexual Harassment Law in Canada," 348–349).

305. ILO, *Conditions of Work Digest*, 82. Provinces or territories that mention sexual harassment in their codes or acts include Manitoba, Newfoundland, Nova Scotia, Ontario, Quebec, New Brunswick, Alberta, and Yukon Territory. For a more detailed explanation of the Canadian constitutional and legal structure, see Pelliciotti, "Workplace Sexual Harassment Law in Canada," 340–350.

306. ILO, *Conditions of Work Digest*, 84. See also Kelly and Watt, "Damages in Sex Harassment Cases," 107–108.

307. *C. Bell v. The Flaming Steer Steak House Tavern Inc.*, 1 *Canadian Human Rights Report* (C.H.R.R.) D/155 (Ont. 1980). ILO, *Conditions of Work Digest*, 82. See also Pelliciotti, "Workplace Sexual Harassment Law in Canada," 358: "The line of Canadian cases equating sexual harassment with illegal sex discrimination, which began with Bell in 1980, continued uninterrupted until the Manitoba Court of Appeal departed from that precedent in 1986, in Janzen v. Platy Enterprises Ltd. The Manitoba court's decision set the stage for the appeal to the Canadian Supreme Court, and the Canadian high court's landmark 1989 Janzen decision."

308. *Janzen v. Platy Enterprises, Ltd.*, 59 D.L.R. 4th 352, 10 C.H.R.R. D/6205 (Can. 1989).

309. "While the distinction may have been important to illustrate forcefully the range of behaviour that constitutes harassment at a time before sexual harassment was widely viewed as actionable . . . there is no longer any need to characterize harassment as one of these forms. The main point in allegations of sexual harassment is that unwelcome sexual conduct has invaded the workplace, irrespective of whether the consequences of the harassment included a denial of concrete employment rewards for refusing to participate in sexual activity" (*Janzen v. Platy Enterprises, Ltd.*, D/6226).

310. *Janzen v. Platy Enterprises, Ltd.*, D/6227.

311. Ibid.

312. See Kelly and Watt, "Damages in Sex Harassment Cases," 111.

313. Pellicciotti, "Workplace Sexual Harassment Law in Canada," 357.

314. *Rabidue v. Osceola Refining Co.*, 805 F.2d 611, 620 (6th Cir. 1986), *cert. denied*, 481 U.S. 1041 (1987).

315. Arjun P. Aggarwal, *Sexual Harassment in the Workplace*, 2nd ed. (Toronto: Butterworths, 1992), 95–96.

316. See "U.K.: Why Business Is in Two Minds over Europe,"" Aberdeen Press and Journal, 14 May 14, 1997.

317. Nicolle R. Lipper, "Sexual Harassment in the Workplace: A Comparative Study of Great Britain and the United States," *Comparative Labor Law Journal* 13 (1992): 294.

318. *Sex Discrimination Act*, 1975, ch. 7, 63 (Eng.). See Kelly and Watt, "Damages in Sex Harassment Cases," 120.

319. *Porcelli v. Strathclyde Regional Council*, (1986) 15 *Industrial Relations Law Reports* (I.R.L.R.) 134 (Ct. Spec. Sess.) (Eng.).

320. Kelly and Watt, "Damages in Sex Harassment Cases," 120–121.

321. Lipper, "Comparative Study," 318–319.

322. Tanya Martinez Shively, "Sexual Harassment in the European Union: King Rex Meets Potiphar's Wife," *Louisiana Law Review* 55 (1995): 1137.

323. Bernstein, "Law, Culture, and Harassment," 1279.

324. Aeberhard-Hodges, "Sexual Harassment in Employment," 503.

325. See Michael Rubenstein, "Dealing with Sexual Harassment at Work: The Experience of Industrialized Countries," in ILO, *Conditions of Work Digest*, 14: "There are, however, two fundamental problems with restricting a prohibition on sexual harassment to harassment which takes the form of sexual blackmail by the employer . . . it excludes conduct between colleagues. This is the conscious approach in France, where the stated aim is to legislate without making 'flirting' into an offence."

326. See ILO, *Conditions of Work Digest*, 97.

327. "France: Law against Sexual Harassment," *International Labour Review* 132, no. 1 (1993): 5.

328. Earle and Madek, "An International Perspective," 80. *Code Penal art.* 222–23 *Tire II* (Fr.), trans. Beverley Earle.

329. Earle and Madek, "An International Perspective," 81. *Code du travail art.* L. 122–46, trans. Beverley Earle.

330. ILO, *Conditions of Work Digest*, 98.

331. See Ellen Frankel Paul, "Sexual Harassment as Sex Discrimination: A Defective Paradigm," *Yale Law and Policy Review* 8, no. 2 (1990): 333–365; Ellen Frankel Paul, "Bared Buttocks and Federal Cases," *Society* 28, no. 4 (1991): 4–7. However, see Carrie N. Baker, "Sexual Extortion: Criminalizing Quid Pro Quo Sexual Harassment," *Law and Inequality Journal* 13 (1994): 213–251.

332. ILO, *Conditions of Work Digest*, 143.

333. Workers Charter, 5272 Act 3/1989 of 3 March 1989—s.4(2)(e). Cited in Michael Rubenstein and Ineke M. de Vries, *How to Combat Sexual Harassment at Work: A Guide to Implementing the European Commission Code of Practice* (Luxembourg: Commission of the European Communities, Office for Official Publication of the European Communities, 1993), 29.

334. Salvador del Rey Guanter, "Employee Privacy in Spanish Labor Relations," *Comparative Labor Law Journal* 17 (1995): 128.

335. Drucilla Cornell, *The Imaginary Domain: Abortion, Pornography, and Sexual Harassment* (New York: Routledge, 1995). See chapter 5.

336. del Rey Guanter, "Employee Privacy," 128.

337. See "Spain Revises 147-year-old Penal Code," *Reuters North American Wire*, November 8, 1995, and David White, "Spain Overhauls Penal Code," *Financial Times* (London), November 9, 1995, p. 3.

338. Aeberhard-Hodges, "Sexual Harassment in Employment," 517. "In Spain, [sexual harassment] is perceived more as a violation of the right to health and safety at work under the Worker's Statute, 1980, and of the General Ordinance Safety and Health at Work, 1971" (Aeberhard-Hodges, "Sexual Harassment in Employment," 503).

339. *Employment Contracts Act of 1991*, Section 29(1). Cited in ILO, *Conditions of Work Digest*, 131.

340. Hiroko Hayashi, "Women's Rights as International Human Rights: Sexual Harassment in the Workplace and Equal Employment Legislation," *St. John's Law Review* 69 (1995): 56.

341. Decision of the Fukuoka District Court, Decision No. 1992/1872. Cited in Tariq Mundiya, "Book Review: Conditions of Work Digest: Combating Sexual Harassment at Work," *Comparative Labor Law Journal* 15 (1993): 124–125. See also ILO, *Conditions of Work Digest*, 117.

342. Hayashi, "Women's Rights," 50.

343. Ibid., 50–51.

344. Ibid., 57–58. However, Leon Wolff argues that academics and the courts are finding ways to argue that sexual harassment is sex discrimination under existing Japanese law. See Leon Wolff, "Eastern Twists on Western Concepts: Equality Jurisprudence and Sexual Harassment in Japan," *Pacific Rim Law & Policy Journal* 5 (1996): 509–535.

345. "Japan Adopts Action Plan on Sexual Discrimination," *Reuters North American Wire*, December 13, 1996.

346. "Women's Groups, Unions Press for Sexual Harassment Ban," *Japan Weekly Monitor*, August 26, 1996.

347. "Japan Adopts Action Plan."

348. "Over 90% of Firms Lack Steps on Sexual Harassment," *Japan Economic Newswire*, December 12, 1996. The survey was conducted by the Management and Coordinating Agency during April and June of 1996. See also "Japan Firms Have No Sex Harassment Countermeasures," *Reuters World Service*, December 12, 1996.

349. Yomiuri Shimbun, "Beefing Up Sexual Harassment Policies," *Daily Yomiuri*, May 8, 1996.

350. "Women's Groups, Unions."

351. Shimbun, "Beefing Up Sexual Harassment Policies."

352. Kirstin Downey Grimsely, "Mitsubishi Settles for $34 Million," *Washington Post*, June 12, 1998.

353. See MacKinnon, *Sexual Harassment*, 166, and 283–284, note 70.

354. Public forms of harassment such as subway groping are receiving attention from scholars and governments alike. In India, laws have been passed prohibiting a phenomenon known as "Eve-teasing." Eve-teasing occurs in public places such as bus stops, trains and buses, the street, cinemas, and shopping areas. Men direct indecent remarks, songs, and gestures toward women, grope them, tug on their braids, jostle against women, and spit on women. This behavior is categorized as "indecent behavior" under the Indian Penal Code, which construes such behavior as an insult to a woman's modesty. See Padma Anagol-McGinn, "Sexual Harassment in India: A Case Study of Eve-teasing in Historical Perspective," in *Rethinking Sexual Harassment*, ed. Clare Brant and Yun Lee Too

(London: Pluto Press, 1994), 220–234. See also Cynthia Grant Bowman, "Street Harassment and the Informal Ghettoization of Women," *Harvard Law Review* 106, no. 3 (1993): 517–580.

355. Lance Compa and Tashia Hinchliffe-Darricarrere, "Doing Business in China and Latin America: Developments in Comparative and International Labor Law: Enforcing International Labor Rights through Corporate Codes of Conduct," *Columbia Journal of Transnational Law* 33 (1995): 672–673.

Chapter 4

1. "The problem of sexual harassment in the workplace apparently is widespread. . . . See also U.S. Merit Systems Protection Board, *Sexual Harassment in the Federal Workplace: Is It a Problem?* (1981): . . . (*Henson v. City of Dundee*, 682 F.2d 897 [11th Cir. 1982], note 5, p. 902); "Over 40 percent of female employees reported incidents of sexual harassment in 1987, roughly the same number as in 1980. United States Merit Systems Protection Board, *Sexual Harassment in the Federal Government: An Update* 11 (1988)" (*Ellison v. Brady*, 924 F.2d 872 [9th Cir. 1991], note 15, p. 880). See also U.S. Congress, Senate Committee on Labor and Human Resources, *Sex Discrimination in the Workplace: Hearing before the Committee on Labor and Human Resources*, 97th Cong.,1st sess., 1981, 336–342.

2. See, for example, Michele A. Paludi, ed., *Sexual Harassment on College Campuses: Abusing the Ivory Power* (Albany: State University of New York, 1996), 5–6; Robert O. Riggs, Patricia H. Murrell, and JoAnne C. Cutting, *Sexual Harassment in Higher Education: From Conflict to Community* (Washington, D.C.: ASHE-ERIC Higher Education Report 93–2, 1993), 17–23; Anja Angelica Chan, *Women and Sexual Harassment: A Practical Guide to the Legal Protections of Title VII and the Hostile Environment Claim* (New York: Haworth Press, 1994), 3; Anita M. Superson, "A Feminist Definition of Sexual Harassment," *Journal of Social Philosophy* 24, no. 1 (1993): 46, note 2; Monica L. Sherer, "No Longer Just Child's Play: School Liability under Title IX for Peer Sexual Harassment," *University of Pennsylvania Law Review* 141 (1993): 2120, note 7; Jehan A. Abdel-Gawad, "Kiddie Sex Harassment: How Title IX Could Level the Playing Field without Leveling the Playground," *Arizona Law Review* 39 (1997): 727, notes 4 and 5; Stefanie H. Roth, "Sex Discrimination 101: Developing a Title IX Analysis for Sexual Harassment in Education," *Journal of Law and Education* 23, no. 4 (1994): 459–465; and Michael Rubenstein, *The Dignity of Women at Work: A Report on the Problem of Sexual Harassment in the Member States of the European Communities* (Luxembourg: Commission of the European Communities, Office for Official Publications of the European Communities, 1988), 15–18.

3. See *Robinson v. Jacksonville Shipyards, Inc.*, 760 F. Supp. 1486 (M.D. Fla. 1991), 1507.

4. See Rubenstein, *The Dignity of Women at Work*, 15.

5. Mark L. Lengnick-Hall, "Sexual Harassment Research: A Methodological Critique," *Personnel Psychology* 48, no. 4 (1995): 290.

6. The 1976 *Redbook* survey (Claire Safran, "What Men Do to Women on the Job: A Shocking Look at Sexual Harassment," *Redbook*, November 1976, 149, 217–224), discussed later in the chapter, continued to be cited into the 1990s to show high levels of sexual harassment. However, this study is methodologically flawed and is now over twenty years old. In my view, very little can be inferred from this study about the prevalence of sexual harassment in 1976, and nothing can be inferred about current levels of sexual harassment. For recent citations

of this survey, see Chan, *Women and Sexual Harassment*, 3; Superson, "Feminist Definition," 1, note 2; Rosemarie Skaine, *Power and Gender: Issues in Sexual Dominance and Harassment* (Jefferson, North Carolina: McFarland & Company, 1996), 153; Vaughana Macy Feary, "Sexual Harassment: Why the Corporate World Still Doesn't 'Get It,'" *Journal of Business Ethics* 13 (1994): 649; and Barry S. Roberts and Richard A. Mann, "Sexual Harassment in the Workplace: A Primer," *Akron Law Review* 29 (1996): 270–271. Nicolle Lipper acknowledges that the study is flawed but cites it anyway, because everyone else has: "Although the 1976 Redbook magazine survey was a voluntary study with results that may not have been empirically reliable, the poll was treated seriously and has been referred to in many works as an early step towards recognizing the magnitude and gravity of the problem of sexual harassment in the American workplace" (Nicolle R. Lipper, "Sexual Harassment in the Workplace: A Comparative Study of Great Britain and the United States," *Comparative Labor Law Journal* 13 [1992]: 297, note 14).

7. Keith E. Stanovich, *How to Think Straight about Psychology*, 5th ed. (New York: Longman, 1998), 40.

8. Ibid., 40–41.

9. Richard M. Hessler, *Social Research Methods* (St. Paul, Minn.: West, 1992), 20. See also Trudy Govier, *A Practical Study of Argument*, 2nd ed. (Belmont, California: Wadsworth, 1988), 266–269.

10. See Edmund Wall, ed., introduction to *Sexual Harassment: Confrontations and Decisions* (Buffalo, New York: Prometheus Books, 1992), 11–13, and Louise F. Fitzgerald et al., "The Incidence and Dimensions of Sexual Harassment in Academia and the Workplace," *Journal of Vocational Behavior* 32 (1988): 152–175.

11. Claire Safran, "How Do You Handle Sex on the Job?" *Redbook*, January 1976, 75.

12. Lengnick-Hall, "Sexual Harassment Research," 295.

13. Richard D. Arvey and Marcie A. Cavanaugh, "Using Surveys to Assess the Prevalence of Sexual Harassment: Some Methodological Problems," *Journal of Social Issues* 51, no. 1 (1995): 39–53.

14. Ibid., 42.

15. Safran, "What Men Do to Women," 149, 217–224.

16. U.S. Merit Systems Protection Board, *Sexual Harassment in the Federal Workplace: Trends, Progress, Continuing Challenges* (Washington, D.C.: U.S. Government Printing Office, 1995).

17. Barbara Gutek, *Sex and the Workplace: The Impact of Sexual Behavior and Harassment on Women, Men, and Organizations* (San Francisco: Jossey-Bass, 1985), 49.

18. Billie Wright Dziech and Linda Weiner, *The Lecherous Professor* (Boston: Beacon Press, 1984).

19. Ibid., 15. Dziech and Weiner make this claim in spite of the fact that one of the studies they cite, from the University of Arizona, reports that only 13 percent of the students experienced sexual harassment.

20. Arvey and Cavanaugh, "Using Surveys," 45.

21. Lengnick-Hall, "Sexual Harassment Research," 297. Reference omitted.

22. Arvey and Cavanaugh, "Using Surveys," 44.

23. Ibid.

24. Lengnick-Hall, "Sexual Harassment Research," 295. References omitted.

25. Julia T. Wood, "Saying It Makes It So: The Discursive Construction of Sexual Harassment," in *Conceptualizing Sexual Harassment as Discursive Practice*, ed. Shereen G. Bingham (Westport, Connecticut: Praeger, 1994), citing L. Brooks

and A. Perot, "Reporting Sexual Harassment: Exploring a Predictive Model," *Psychology of Women Quarterly* 15 (1991): 31–47.

26. A similar point is made in Arvey and Cavanaugh, "Using Surveys," 43.

27. Louise F. Fitzgerald et al., "Academic Harassment: Sex and Denial in Scholarly Garb," *Psychology of Women Quarterly* 12 (1988): 332.

28. Ibid., 338.

29. Ibid.

30. In addition to the works listed earlier, all of the following cite the *Redbook* study as evidence of the magnitude of the problem of sexual harassment for women: Rosemarie Tong, *Women, Sex, and the Law* (Totowa, New Jersey: Rowman & Littlefield, 1984), 66; Catharine A. MacKinnon, *Sexual Harassment of Working Women: A Case of Sex Discrimination* (New Haven: Yale University Press, 1979), 26; and Constance Backhouse and Leah Cohen, *Sexual Harassment on the Job* (Englewood Cliffs, New Jersey: Prentice-Hall, 1982), 34.

31. Safran, "What Men Do to Women,"149.

32. Ibid., 217. Elsewhere, the number is given as 88 percent.

33. Safran, "How Do You Handle Sex," 75.

34. Safran acknowledges that "the women in our survey are what statisticians like to call a 'self-selected group'—meaning women who felt strongly about this problem, probably because they had experienced it, were likelier to fill out our questionnaire than women who had escaped it" (Safran, "What Men Do to Women," 218), but, since their figure is comparable to that found by the Women Worker's United survey, described in chapter 2 (70 percent of those surveyed had experienced sexual harassment), they are satisfied with their results.

35. Safran, "How Do You Handle Sex," 76.

36. See Michael D. Vhay, "The Harms of Asking: Towards a Comprehensive Treatment of Sexual Harassment," *University of Chicago Law Review* 55 (1988): 349–360, for use of this expression.

37. Frank J. Till, *Sexual Harassment: A Report on the Sexual Harassment of Students*, (Washington, D.C.: U.S. Department of Education, 1980), 7; cited in Nancy Tuana, "Sexual Harassment in Academe: Issues of Power and Coercion," in *Sexual Harassment: Confrontations and Decisions*, ed. Edmund Wall (Buffalo, New York: Prometheus Books, 1992), 49–60; Louise F. Fitzgerald et al., "Incidence and Dimensions of Sexual Harassment," 157, and Michele A. Paludi and Richard Barickman, *Academic and Workplace Sexual Harassment: A Resource Manual* (Albany: State University of New York, 1991), 6.

38. Till, *Sexual Harassment of Students*, part 1, 6.

39. Ibid., 7.

40. Fitzgerald et al., "Incidence and Dimensions of Sexual Harassment," 152–175.

41. Till, *Sexual Harassment of Students*, part 1, 8.

42. Ibid.

43. "Estimates of frequency are beyond the scope of this report" (Till, *Sexual Harassment of Students*, part 1, 39).

44. Ibid., 18.

45. Reported in U.S. Merit Systems Protection Board, *Sexual Harassment in the Federal Workplace: Is It a Problem* (Washington, D.C.: U.S. Government Printing Office, 1981) and U.S. Merit Systems Protection board, *Sexual Harassment in the Federal Government: An Update* (Washington, D.C.: U.S. Government Printing Office, 1988). All of the following cite the Merit studies: Wall, *Confrontations and Decisions*, 12; Paludi and Barickman, *Academic and Workplace Sexual Harassment*,

11; Deborah L. Rhode, *Justice and Gender: Sex Discrimination and the Law* (Cambridge: Harvard University Press, 1989), 232; Ellen Frankel Paul, "Bared Buttocks and Federal Cases," *Society* 28, no. 4 (1991): 5; Fitzgerald et al., "Incidence and Dimensions of Sexual Harassment," 153; International Labour Organization, "Combating Sexual Harassment at Work," *Conditions of Work Digest* 11, no. 1 (1992): 288; and Arjun P. Aggarwal, *Sexual Harassment in the Workplace*, 2nd ed. (Toronto: Butterworths, 1992), 3.

46. U.S. Merit Systems Protection Board, *Sexual Harassment . . . Is It a Problem*, 19.

47. Ibid., 2.

48. Ibid., from the survey questionnaire, appendix C, 8.

49. Ibid., 21.

50. Ibid., 2.

51. Ibid., 26.

52. Ibid., 28.

53. Ibid., 36.

54. U.S. Merit Systems Protection Board, *Sexual Harassment . . . An Update*, 1. The sample does not seem to have been as carefully designed in the 1987 survey. The 13,000 were "full-time permanent Federal employees during March 1987" (U.S. Merit Systems Protection Board, *Sexual Harassment . . . An Update*, 9).

55. Ibid., 2.

56. Ibid.

57. Ibid.

58. Ibid., 13.

59. Ibid., 12.

60. Ibid., 13.

61. Ibid., 13–14.

62. U.S. Merit Systems Protection Board, *Sexual Harassment in the Federal Workplace: Trends, Progress, Continuing Challenges* (Washington, D.C.: U.S. Government Printing Office, 1995).

63. Ibid., 13.

64. Ibid., 7.

65. "Harassers of women usually (in 65% of all incidents) are coworkers or 'others' Federal employees having no supervisory authority over the victim. In a sizeable number of the incidents (37%), however, the women were harassed by their immediate supervisor or a higher level supervisor. Subordinates were harassers in only 4% of the incidents. . . ." (U.S. Merit Systems Protection Board, *Sexual Harassment . . . Is It a Problem*, 59); "Most harassers are coworkers, but many women are harassed by supervisors" (U.S. Merit Systems Protection Board, *Sexual Harassment . . . Is It a Problem*, 57); "About 79 percent of male victims and 77 percent of female victims were subjected to unwanted behaviors by people they identified as coworkers or other employees without supervisory authority over them. Some 14 percent of male and 28 percent of female victims were sexually harassed by persons in their supervisory chains" (U.S. Merit Protection Board, *Sexual Harassment . . . Trends*, 18).

66. Ibid., 23.

67. Gutek, *Sex and the Workplace*.

68. Louise F. Fitzgerald and Matthew Hesson-McInnis, "The Dimensions of Sexual Harassment: A Structural Analysis," *Journal of Vocational Behavior* 35 (1989): 309–310; Louise F. Fitzgerald, "Sexual Harassment: The Definition and Measurement of a Construct," in *Sexual Harassment on College Campuses: Abusing*

the Ivory Power, ed. Michele A. Paludi (Albany: State University of New York Press, 1996), 25–47; and Fitzgerald et al., "Incidence and Dimensions of Sexual Harassment," 152–175.

69. Gutek, *Sex and the Workplace*, 74.

70. Ibid., 20–21, appendix B.

71. Ibid., 43.

72. Ibid., 43, table 1.

73. Ibid., 45.

74. Ibid.

75. Ibid., 49.

76. Ibid., 158.

77. Fitzgerald et al., "Incidence and Dimensions of Sexual Harassment," 157.

78. Fitzgerald, "Sexual Harassment," 36–37.

79. Ibid., 37.

80. Paludi and Barickman, *Academic and Workplace Sexual Harassment*, 6.

81. Ibid., 17, table 1.8.

82. Ibid.

83. Ibid.

84. Quoted in Paludi and Barickman, *Academic and Workplace Sexual Harassment*, 7. From Fitzgerald, "Sexual Harassment."

85. American Association of University Women, *Hostile Hallways: The AAUW Survey on Sexual Harassment in American Schools* (Washington, D.C.: American Association of University Women, 1993).

86. Ibid., 5.

87. Ibid., 6.

88. Ibid., 5.

89. Ibid., 7.

90. Ibid., 20.

91. Ibid., 6.

92. Ibid., 25.

93. Christina Hoff Sommers, *Who Stole Feminism? How Women Have Betrayed Women* (New York: Simon & Schuster, 1994), 184.

94. Ibid., 185.

95. See Sommers, *Who Stole Feminism*, 293, note 84. She cites figures from the 1992 *Digest of Educational Statistics*, p. 142: "10.6 percent of male and 7.1 percent of female eighth-graders cut classes 'at least sometimes'; and 89.4 percent of boys and 92.9 percent of girls say they do it 'never or almost never.'" It should be pointed out that this statistic appears to be based on what students *say*, not what they actually do. So, perhaps more girls than boys actually cut classes.

96. "Sample size and differences in questions asked make the figures given above unreliable as an indication of any differences between countries in terms of the magnitude of the problem. There is reason to believe that, on the whole, the higher the consciousness of sexual harassment as a concept, the more women will report having experienced the problem. . . ." (Rubenstein, *The Dignity of Women at Work* , 18, note 19).

97. Victoria A. Carter, "Working on Dignity: EC Initiatives on Sexual Harassment in the Workplace," *Journal of International Law & Business* 12 (1992): 433, note 8.

98. International Labour Organization, "Combating Sexual Harassment," *Conditions of Work Digest* 11, no. 1 (1992).

99. "The results of such surveys of course depend very much on the definition

of sexual harassment that was used . . . and the time span covered. The size and characteristics of the sample population also affect the findings" (ILO, "Combating Sexual Harassment," 285).

100. Rubenstein, *The Dignity of Women at Work*, 16, and ILO, "Combating Sexual Harassment," 287. The study was commissioned by the Secretaría de la Mujer (Women's Section) of the Unión General de Trabajadores (UGT) (General Union of Workers).

101. ILO, "Combating Sexual Harassment," 287.

102. Ibid.

103. Ibid., 288. The study was sponsored by the Jämställdhetsombudsmannen (Equal Opportunity Ombudsman).

104. Ibid., 286.

105. Ibid., 288.

106. Ibid.

107. *Unwanted Sexual Attention and Sexual Harassment: Results of a Survey of Canadians* (Ottawa: Canadian Human Rights Commission, 1983). Cited in Aggarwal, *Sexual Harassment in the Workplace*, 5.

108. "Women's Groups, Unions Press for Sexual Harassment Ban," *Japan Weekly Monitor*, August 25, 1996.

109. "Female Kyoto University Graduates Report Sexual Harassment," *Japan Weekly Monitor*, November 18, 1996.

110. Lengnick-Hall, "Sexual Harassment Research," 294.

111. Alan Vaux, "Paradigmatic Assumptions in Sexual Harassment Research: Being Guided without Being Misled," *Journal of Vocational Behavior* 42 (1993): 119.

112. Ibid., 120.

113. Fitzgerald et al., "Incidence and Dimensions of Sexual Harassment." He also cites D. B. Mazer and E. F. Percival, "Students' Experience of Sexual Harassment at a Small University," *Sex Roles* 20 (1989): 1–22.

114. Vaux, "Paradigmatic Assumptions," 124. M. E. Reilly, B. Lott, and S. M. Gallogy, "Sexual Harassment of University Students," *Sex Roles* 15 (1986): 333–358.

115. Vaux, "Paradigmatic Assumptions," 122.

116. See Robert D. Glaser and Joseph S. Thorpe, "Unethical Intimacy: A Survey of Sexual Contact and Advances between Psychology Educators and Female Graduate Students," *American Psychologist* 41, no. 1 (1986): 43–51.

117. Michael Rubenstein, "Dealing with Sexual Harassment at Work: The Experience of Industrialized Countries," *Conditions of Work Digest* 11, no. 1 (1992): 8.

118. U.S. Merit Systems Protection Board, *Sexual Harassment . . . Trends*; David E. Terpstra and Susan E. Cook, "Complaint Characteristics and Reported Behaviors and Consequences Associated with Formal Sexual Harassment Charges, *Personnel Psychology* 38 (1985): 564; Rubenstein, "Dealing with Sexual Harassment at Work," 8. "Marital status is strongly related to sexual harassment. Working women who are married or widowed are less likely to be harassed than working women who are divorced, separated, or never married" (Gutek, *Sex and the Workplace*, 55).

119. "Female victims tend to be younger than the general female working population" (Gutek, *Sex and the Workplace*, 55); Terpstra and Cook, "Complaint Characteristics," 563, and Rubenstein, "Dealing with Sexual Harassment at Work," 8. U.S. Merit Systems Protection Board, *Sexual Harassment . . . An Update*, 20: "between the ages of 20 and 44."

120. Judy T. Ellis, "Sexual Harassment and Race: A Legal Analysis of Discrimination," *Journal of Legislation* 8, no. 1 (1981): 39.

121. "The survey suggests that minority women are not particularly more vulnerable to sexual harassment than Caucasian women. In fact, Caucasian women report somewhat higher rates of sexual harassment and are more likely to quit a job because of sexual harassment. A variety of factors may contribute to these findings: minority women may report fewer of their experiences and Caucasian women may represent the cultural standard of attractiveness" (Gutek, *Sex and the Workplace*, 56).

122. Rubenstein, "Dealing with Sexual Harassment at Work," 8.

123. Gutek reports, "Women of all occupations are about equally likely to be sexually harassed, although women managers are slightly more likely than other women to be harassed" (Gutek, *Sex and the Workplace*, 56).

124. U.S. Merit Systems Protection Board, *Sexual Harassment . . . Trends*, 17; Terpstra and Cook, "Complaint Characteristics," 564; Gutek found that "[w]omen who are well-educated are generally as likely to be sexually harassed as women who are less well educated. If anything, victims of harassment are even more likely to have advanced education" (Gutek, *Sex and the Workplace*, 55).

125. U.S. Merit Systems Protection Board, *Sexual Harassment . . . An Update*, 20.

126. Ibid.

127. Skaine, *Power and Gender*, 180, note 13.

128. U.S. Merit Systems Protection Board, *Sexual Harassment . . . Trends*, 17.

129. Gutek, *Sex and the Workplace*, 57.

130. U.S. Merit Systems Protection Board, *Sexual Harassment . . . An Update*, 20; Gutek, *Sex and the Workplace*, 57.

131. U.S. Merit Systems Protection Board, *Sexual Harassment . . . An Update*, 20. Gutek reports, "In general, men in different categories did not report instances of sexual harassment more often, except for men in managerial positions" (Gutek, *Sex and the Workplace*, 57–58).

132. U.S. Merit Systems Protection Board, *Sexual Harassment . . . Is It a Problem*, 6.

133. MacKinnon, *Sexual Harassment*, 28.

134. See Darlene C. DeFour, "The Interface of Racism and Sexism on College Campuses," in *Sexual Harassment on College Campuses: Abusing the Ivory Power*, ed. Michele A. Paludi (Albany: State University of New York Press, 1996), 49. In 1981, Ellis said that "[s]tatistics on the sexual harassment of black women are scarce" (Ellis, "Sexual Harassment and Race," 40). It seems this is still true.

135. See Ellis, "Sexual Harassment and Race," 39.

136. See Kathryn Abrams, "Title VII and the Complex Female Subject," *Michigan Law Review* 92 (1994): 2501.

137. See Ellis, "Sexual Harassment and Race"; Virginia W. Wei, "Asian Women and Employment Discrimination: Using Intersectionality Theory to Address Title VII Claims Based on Combined Factors of Race, Gender, and National Origin," *Boston College Law Review* 37 (1996): 771–812; and Judith A. Winston, "Mirror, Mirror on the Wall: Title VII, Section 1981, and the Intersection of Race and Gender in the Civil Rights Act of 1990," *California Law Review* 79 (1991): 775–805.

138. Paula M. Popovich et al., "Perceptions of Sexual Harassment as a Function of Sex of Rater and Incident Form and Consequence," *Sex Roles* 27, nos. 11/12 (1992): 610. In support of their claim, the authors cite B. A. Gutek, B. Morasch, and A. G. Cohen, "Interpreting Social-Sexual Behavior in a Work Setting," *Journal of Vocational Behavior* 22 (1983): 30–48; S. C. Padgitt and J. S. Padgitt, "Cognitive

Structure of Sexual Harassment: Implications of University Policy," *Journal of College Student Personnel* (January 1986): 34–39; and P. M. Popovich et al., "Assessing the Incidence and Perceptions of Sexual Harassment Behaviors among American Undergraduates," *Journal of Psychology* 120 (1986): 387–396.

139. Riggs et al., *Sexual Harassment in Higher Education*, 22–23.

140. Mary A. Gowan and Raymond A. Zimmerman, "Impact of Ethnicity, Gender, and Previous Experience on Juror Judgments in Sexual Harassment Cases," *Journal of Applied Social Psychology* 26, no. 7 (1996): 598–599.

141. Ibid., 599.

142. Carol L. Baird et al., "Gender Influence on Perceptions of Hostile Environment Sexual Harassment," *Psychological Reports* 77 (1995): 79.

143. A similar point is made in Arvey and Cavanaugh, "Using Surveys," 42.

144. Gowan and Zimmerman, "Impact of Ethnicity," 608.

145. Ibid., 611.

146. Gowan and Zimmerman, "Impact of Ethnicity," 613, agreeing with Jasmine Tata, "The Structure and Phenomenon of Sexual Harassment: Impact of Category of Sexually Harassing Behavior, Gender, and Hierarchical Level," *Journal of Applied Social Psychology* 23 (1993): 199–211.

147. Gowan and Zimmerman, "Impact of Ethnicity," 604.

148. Ibid., 610.

149. Ibid., 611.

150. Ibid., 612–613.

151. Popovich et al., "Perceptions of Sexual Harassment," 609–625.

152. Ibid., 613.

153. Ibid., 614.

154. Ibid., 615.

155. Ibid., 617–618.

156. Ibid., 618–619.

157. Ibid., 622.

158. A similar point is made in Barbara A. Gutek and Maureen O'Connor, "The Empirical Basis for the Reasonable Woman Standard," *Journal of Social Issues* 51, no. 1 (1995): 157.

159. U.S. Merit Systems Protection Board, *Sexual Harassment . . . An Update*, 2. U.S. Merit Systems Protection Board, *Sexual harassment . . . Trends*, 7.

160. Gutek and O'Connor, "Empirical Basis," 151.

161. Ibid.

162. Ibid., 154–155.

163. Ibid., 155.

164. Ibid.

165. Ibid., 155–156.

166. Ibid., 156.

167. Ibid.

168. Ibid., 156–157.

169. Ibid., 157.

170. Ibid., 158.

171. Ibid.

172. Ibid., 160–161.

173. Sandra S. Tangri, Martha R. Burt, and Leanor B. Johnson, "Sexual Harassment at Work: Three Explanatory Models," *Journal of Social Issues* 38, no. 4 (1982): 33–54.

174. U.S. Merit Systems Protection Board, *Sexual Harassment . . . Is It a Problem.*

175. Kingsley Browne criticizes Tangri et al.'s characterization of the natural/biological model. See Kingsley R. Browne, "An Evolutionary Perspective on Sexual Harassment: Seeking Roots in Biology Rather than Ideology," *Journal of Contemporary Legal Issues* 8 (1997): 49–54.

176. Tangri, Burt, and Johnson, "Explanatory Models," 35.

177. Ibid., 36.

178. Ibid., 35–36.

179. Ibid., 35.

180. Ibid., 99.

181. Ibid.

182. David M. Buss, *The Evolution of Desire: Strategies of Human Mating* (New York: Basic Books, 1994), 159.

183. Ibid.

184. Ibid., 160–161.

185. Tangri, Burt, and Johnson, "Explanatory Models," 38–39.

186. Browne, "Evolutionary Perspective," 31.

187. Ibid., 40.

188. Ibid.

189. Ibid. Browne seems to think that empirical research can settle the question, however, for he recommends that "More empirical research could usefully be employed to discern whether the standard does in fact make a difference" (Browne, "Evolutionary Perspective," 41).

190. "Other things being equal, the more phenomena an explanation explains, the better" (Brooke Noel Moore and Richard Parker, *Critical Thinking*, 4th ed. [Mountain View, California: Mayfield, 1995], 204). This criterion could be applied to the wider perspectives under discussion, but I am interested here only in the scope of their explanations of sexual harassment.

191. Browne may ultimately deny that there is any such thing as "sexual harassment." He seems to want to explain the different behaviors commonly collected under that term in different ways. None of them is explained as discriminatory toward women. His language suggests this. For example, he says, "The behaviors described above have in common that they harm, or at least are thought to harm, either individual women or women as a class" (Browne, "Evolutionary Perspective," 7).

192. For more about race and sexual harassment, see chapters 2 and 6. The natural/biological perspective says almost nothing about race and sexual harassment. MacKinnon discusses race and sexuality in several of her works, including her *Sexual Harassment* and *Only Words* (Cambridge: Harvard University Press, 1993). However, her analogies between racial harassment and sexual harassment are problematic. Varieties of harassment are discussed in more detail in chapter 6. For an interesting argument that heterosexism is at the center of most conceptions of sexual harassment, see Jane Gallop, "The Lecherous Professor," *Differences: A Journal of Feminist Cultural Studies* 7 (1995): 1–14. Gallop argues that there is a heterosexist assumption underlying a mistake that is made in most views of sexual harassment. The assumption is "that sexuality and relations between the sexes are synonymous. The presumption that any relation to the opposite sex is sexual necessarily follows from that assumption" (Gallop, "Lecherous Professor," 10). "The mistake is to understand the 'sexual' in sexual harassment as referring to sex rather than to sexism. Whereas the harasser's heterosexism

leads him to discriminate by being sexual, the antiharasser's heterosexism leads her to assume that all sexuality is discriminatory" (Gallop, "Lecherous Professor," 11). But this is wrong.

193. Jennifer Trusted, *Inquiry and Understanding: An Introduction to Explanation in the Physical and Human Sciences* (London: MacMillan Education, 1987), 240.

194. Many philosophers who investigate the methodologies of the physical and social sciences have reached the conclusion that empirical data alone is never sufficient for rational choice between theories. This is because facts and values are not clearly distinguishable, and different approaches are not value neutral. Values always enter into our science. See Hilary Putnam, *Reason, Truth, and History* (New York: Cambridge University Press, 1981), Michael Root, *Philosophy of Social Science: The Methods, Ideals, and Politics of Social Inquiry* (Cambridge, Massachusetts: Blackwell, 1993), Sandra Harding, *The Science Question in Feminism* (Ithaca, New York: Cornell University Press, 1986). This being the case, some recommend that we use values in determining which of several theories is better.

195. Trusted, *Inquiry and Understanding*, 5–6.

Chapter 5

1. The epigraph that introduces this chapter is adapted from Jeffrie Murphy and Jules Coleman, *The Philosophy of Law: An Introduction to Jurisprudence* (Totowa, New Jersey: Rowman & Allanheld, Publishers, 1984), 3. The original wording is: "The philosophical analysis of a concept, while by no means indifferent to ordinary usage . . . is concerned to give a *rational account* of such usage. It is concerned, for example, to answer the question: What is there about all cases of negligence that makes us group them under one concept and thus use the same word?"

2. MacKinnon argues that sexual harassment is "not a moral issue." This is actually the title of an essay on pornography, but she holds the same view with regard to sexual harassment. See MacKinnon, "Not a Moral Issue," in *Feminism Unmodified: Discourses on Life and Law* (Cambridge: Harvard University Press, 1987), 146–162. For her application of this view to sexual harassment, see *Sexual Harassment of Working Women* (New Haven: Yale University Press, 1979), 173. Part of this denial of morality can be explained by her Marxist perspective. But Carol Smart (*Law, Crime and Sexuality: Essays in Feminism* [London: Sage Publications, 1995]) explains it as a strategy. If feminists focus on power relations, liberals cannot say that sexual harassment is merely a matter of the private sphere, and so not appropriately a matter for discrimination law. By denying that sexual harassment is first and foremost a matter of sexual morality, MacKinnon seeks to shift attention from issues of sexual "moralism" and protection of female virtue to protection of women's equality of opportunity. See MacKinnon, *Sexual Harassment*, 172–173.

3. Other political perspectives do not require specific harm to legitimate laws, and sometimes the liberal perspective does not either. However, much of the concern to pin down the specific harm of sexual harassment can best be understood in the context of liberal political philosophy, since many of those concerned about it seek to justify the regulation of sexual harassment—or not—in our liberal state. MacKinnon wants to present an alternative rationale for laws prohibiting sexual harassment. She claims that sexual harassment ought to be illegal because it prevents women from obtaining social equality. Her focus is not on the individual

woman, but on women as a group. Liberal theory tends to interpret sexual harassment as an individual harm to individuals, who may be members of a particular group.

4. For criteria for evaluating definitions, see Trudy Govier, *A Practical Study of Argument*, 2nd ed. (Belmont, California: Wadsworth, 1988). "If you can find a case where people would typically not use the word defined, even though the definition would allow it, the definition is too broad. If you can find a case where people would typically use the word although the definition would not allow it, the definition is too narrow" (Govier, *Practical Study of Argument*, 40). Of course, if the term in question is one the meaning of which is not settled, these criteria for narrowness and broadness are problematic. See comments on Mane Hajdin's discussion of sexual harassment that follow.

5. MacKinnon, *Sexual Harassment*, 1.

6. Ibid., 1–2.

7. Ibid., 216.

8. Ibid., 31.

9. Ibid., 4–5.

10. Drucilla Cornell, *The Imaginary Domain: Abortion, Pornography, and Sexual Harassment* (New York: Routledge, 1995), 174–175.

11. MacKinnon is not as clear about this as she might be. She uses an analogy with race: "It has never been thought that simply because people are black, their situation is so noncomparable with that of whites that it is impossible to tell whether blacks are compatively [*sic*] disadvantaged. Yet it is widely recognized that the content of the social meaning of being black is very different from that of being white, such that black and white skin color cannot be treated as if they are the same. As with skin privilege, so also sex privilege. Both genders possess sexuality. Women and men can, then, be compared with regard to the underlying variable: sexuality in the context of employment. Both sexes can be sexually harassed. When women's sexuality is treated differently from men's sexuality, similarly situated women and men will have been differently treated, to women's comparative disadvantage, and that is sex discrimination" (MacKinnon, *Sexual Harassment*, 215–216).

12. Ellen Frankel Paul, "Sexual Harassment as Sex Discrimination: A Defective Paradigm," *Yale Law and Policy Review* 8, no. 2 (1990): 335. See also Cornell, *Imaginary Domain*, 26: "The primary reliance on practical reason in the elaboration and defense of an egalitarian vision for all forms of sexuate being through a minimum of conditions of individuation does not deny that feminism needs a theoretical account of the abjection, the simultaneous repudiation and making-other, of the feminine. But the argument here is that this account should not be directly incorporated into any ideal of equality. Politically, this reliance on practical reason allows us to create legal alliances with those who are not feminist and who would reject any comprehensive and general feminist analysis. Rawls' conception of an overlapping consensus stems from the possibility of an agreement about fundamental political values within and alongside the public culture's understanding that there will always be considerable disagreement on the theoretical bases about those shared political values. In other words, citizens who are not feminists could still endorse feminist positions in the public sphere without justifying them on any special basis of a feminist position" (Cornell, *Imaginary Domain*, 26).

13. "Never is it asked whether, under conditions of male supremacy, the notion of consent has any real meaning for women. . . . Consent is not scrutinized to see

whether it is a structural fiction to legitimize the real coercion built into the normal social definitions of heterosexual intercourse" (MacKinnon, *Sexual Harassment*, 298, note 8).

14. See, for example, bell hooks, *Feminist Theory: From Margin to Center* (Boston: South End Press, 1984); Angela Davis, *Women, Race, and Class* (New York: Random House, 1982); Audre Lorde, *Sister Outsider* (Trumansburg, New York: Crossing Press, 1984); and Angela P. Harris, "Race and Essentialism in Feminist Legal Theory," *Stanford Law Review* 42 (1990): 581–616. For a critique of gender essentialism, see Elizabeth V. Spelman, *Inessential Woman: Problems of Exclusion in Feminist Thought* (Boston: Beacon Press, 1988).

15. See Thomas E. Wartenberg, *The Forms of Power: From Domination to Transformation* (Philadelphia: Temple University Press, 1990). Wartenberg describes what he calls a "transformative use of power" as "one in which an agent uses her power over another agent in order to help that other attain certain skills or abilities" (Wartenberg, *Forms of Power*, 7).

16. See Katherine M. Franke, "The Central Mistake of Sex Discrimination Law: The Disaggregation of Sex from Gender," *University of Pennsylvania Law Review* 144 (1995): 1–99; Katherine M. Franke, "What's Wrong with Sexual Harassment?" *Stanford Law Review* 49, no. 4 (1997): 691–772; Cornell, *Imaginary Domain*. See also Kathryn Abrams, "Title VII and the Complex Female Subject," *Michigan Law Review* 92 (1994): 2479–2540.

17. Catharine A. MacKinnon, "Sexual Harassment: Its First Decade in Court," in *Feminism Unmodified: Discourses on Life and Law* (Cambridge: Harvard University Press, 1987), 103.

18. James B. Stewart, "Coming Out at Chrysler," *New Yorker*, July 21, 1997, 38–49. Woods was hit, jeered at, and threatened and had degrading epithets directed at him written in his work area. His work evaluations suffered, he lost the support of his union, and he had to be transferred because of threats to his safety.

19. Anita M. Superson, "A Feminist Definition of Sexual Harassment," *Journal of Social Philosophy* 24, no. 1 (1993): 46–64.

20. Ibid., 46.

21. Ibid.

22. Ibid., 51. Quoted from Mari Matsuda, "Public Response to Racist Speech: Considering the Victim's Story," *Michigan Law Review* 87, no. 8 (1989): 2348.

23. Superson, "Feminist Definition," 51.

24. Ibid., 52.

25. Ibid.

26. Ibid., 53.

27. Ibid.

28. Ibid.

29. Ibid., 55.

30. Ibid., 55–56.

31. Ibid., 58.

32. Ibid., 60.

33. Ibid.

34. Ibid., 61.

35. Ibid.

36. Ibid., 62.

37. Kingsley R. Browne, "An Evolutionary Perspective on Sexual Harassment: Seeking Roots in Biology Rather Than Ideology," *Journal of Contemporary Legal Issues* 8 (1997): 72.

38. Superson, "Feminist Definition," 51–52.

39. Ibid., 54.

40. Ibid., 50.

41. Larry May and John C. Hughes, "Is Sexual Harassment Coercive?" in *Sexual Harassment: Confrontations and Decisions*, ed. Edmund Wall (Buffalo, New York: Prometheus Books, 1992), 61–68. See also John C. Hughes and Larry May, "Sexual Harassment," *Social Theory and Practice* 6 (1980): 249–280, and John C. Hughes and Larry May, "Is Sexual Harassment Coercive?" in *Moral Rights in the Workplace*, ed. Gertrude Ezorsky (Albany: State University of New York Press, 1987), 115–122.

42. Hughes and May, "Is Sexual Harassment Coercive," 61.

43. I consider their definition to be consistent with Farley's version, according to which sexual harassment is "extortion":

The end result of male sexual harassment of women on the job is the extortion of female subservience at work. As a consequence, the broad range of male aggression brought to bear against working women—which includes, but is not limited to, forced sex either by rape or in exchange for work—cannot be seen as anything more (or less) than the means by which this extortion is effected.

Work is the key element in understanding sexual harassment, because this is the prize men are controlling through their extortion. . . . The consequences of such extortion—being denied work or being forced out of work or being intimidated on the job as a result of male sexual aggression—are at the heart of the problem of sexual harassment. (Lin Farley, *Sexual Shakedown: The Sexual Harassment of Women on the Job* [New York: McGraw-Hill, 1978], 11)

44. May and Hughes, "Is Sexual Harassment Coercive," 61.

45. Ibid., 62.

46. Ibid., 63.

47. Ibid., 66.

48. Ibid., 67.

49. Ibid., 64.

50. Ibid., 65.

51. Hughes and May, "Sexual Harassment," 263.

52. Ibid., 267–268.

53. Ibid., 268.

54. Ibid., 267–268.

55. See Wall's criticism on this ground later in the text.

56. See Barbara Lindemann and David D. Kadue, *Sexual Harassment in Employment Law* (Washington, D.C.: Bureau of National Affairs, 1992), 86–87: "In the typical sexual favoritism case, a supervisor favors subordinates who satisfy the sexual demands of supervisors, thereby creating an implicit quid pro quo. In this situation, even though sexual activity may not be directly required of the complainant, the complainant is nonetheless disadvantaged" (Lindemann and Kadue, *Sexual Harassment in Employment Law*, 86–87). One such case was *Broderick v. Ruder*, 685 F. Supp. 1269, 46 FEP Cases 1272 (D.D.C. 1988). "*Broderick* stands for the proposition that the complainant need not be the direct victim of the harassing conduct in a sexually charged workplace to maintain an action under Title VII. The *Broderick* claimant suffered harassment because she was denied opportunities available to those who participated in the sexual politics of the office and because the atmosphere of sexual politics based on explicit sexual favoritism created a hostile, offensive, and intimidating environment" (Lindemann and Kadue, *Sexual Harassment in Employment Law*, 93).

57. Paul, "Defective Paradigm," 333; Ellen Frankel Paul, "Bared Buttocks and Federal Cases," *Society* 28, no. 4 (1991): 4–7; Farley, *Sexual Shakedown*.

58. Edmund Wall, "The Definition of Sexual Harassment," in *Sexual Harassment: Confrontations and Decisions* (Buffalo, New York: Prometheus Books, 1992), 69.

59. Ibid.

60. Ibid., 73.

61. Ibid., 74.

62. Ibid.

63. Ibid.

64. Ibid.

65. Ibid.

66. Ibid., 75.

67. Ibid., 76.

68. Catharine A. MacKinnon, *Only Words* (Cambridge: Harvard University Press, 1993). This view was satirized in Carlin Romano's famous article in *The Nation*. See Carlin Romano, review of *Only Words*, by Catharine A. MacKinnon, *Nation*, November 15, 1993, 563–570.

69. MacKinnon, *Only Words*, 33.

70. An example of what I have in mind here is the discomfort some feel in a classroom setting when the discussion turns to sex. Certain expressions may trigger sexual arousal, despite what the hearer wishes. People may blush, become agitated, defensive, embarrassed. A famous case in California involved a male student who objected to material on female masturbation presented in a psychology class. The language used by the student in describing his experience comes very close to exemplifying MacKinnon's description. See *20/20*: "The Speech Police: Is Sexual Speech Sexual Harassment?" (ABC television broadcast, May 12, 1995), available in LEXIS, News Library, Script File. Craig Rogers, the student in the case, stated: "I had no power. I had no control. I was being aroused and didn't want it. I felt like I was being held down." See also George Will, "Sex in Sacramento," *Newsweek*, April 3, 1995, 76.

71. Wall, "Definition of Sexual Harassment," 69.

72. Kathleen M. Franke makes a similar point in a critique of the "but for" analysis in sex discrimination law ("What's Wrong," 746). I was reminded of this point by a newspaper report of the result of a sexual assault case. The defendant said that "the woman did not tell him that she did not want to have sex," and that "he was confused by her actions when he tried to touch her again." His attorney claimed that she "did not make her intentions clear . . . about not wanting to have sex" (*Ann Arbor News*, September 28, 1997, sec. C, 4).

73. Linda LeMoncheck and Mane Hajdin, *Sexual Harassment: A Debate* (Lanham, Maryland: Rowman & Littlefield, 1997), 142.

74. Ibid., 143.

75. Wall, "Definition of Sexual Harassment," 74.

76. Ibid., 76.

77. Ibid., 77. I have made a similar point earlier here.

78. Cornell, *Imaginary Domain*, 4.

79. Ibid.

80. Ibid., 5–6.

81. Ibid., 170–171.

82. *Meritor Savings Bank, FSB v. Vinson*, U.S. 106 S.Ct. 2399, 2404, 40 FEP Cases 1822, 54 LW 4703 (1986), 69.

83. Cornell, *Imaginary Domain*, 172.

84. Ibid., 170.

85. Ibid.

86. Ibid., 190–191, 193.

87. Ibid., 195.

88. Ibid.

89. Ibid., 193.

90. Ibid., 201.

91. This is her variation on "John Rawls' argument that self-respect should be guaranteed to each one of us in a just society as a primary good" (Cornell, *Imaginary Domain*, 171).

92. Ibid., 172.

93. Ibid.

94. Cornell also argues that it avoids the incorporation of a "fault-based tort scheme" into discrimination law (*Imaginary Domain*, 171). For more on tort law and sexual harassment, see chapter 6.

95. Ibid., 173.

96. Ibid., 193.

97. Ibid., 205.

98. Ibid., 169.

99. Nancy "Ann" Davis, "Sexual Harassment in the University," in *Morality, Responsibility, and the University: Studies in Academic Ethics*, ed. Steven M. Cahn (Philadelphia: Temple University Press, 1990), 154.

100. Ibid., 156.

101. Ibid., 154.

102. F. M. Christensen argues that "sexual harassment" is not a legitimate concept in "'Sexual Harassment' Must Be Eliminated," *Public Affairs Quarterly* 8, no. 1 (January 1994): 1–17. LeMoncheck and Hajdin, *Sexual Harassment*. Hajdin argues that it is not a "morally significant concept" (LeMoncheck and Hajdin, *Sexual Harassment*, 100).

103. Christensen, "'Sexual Harassment' Must Be Eliminated," 1.

104. LeMoncheck and Hajdin, *Sexual Harassment*, 100.

105. See Browne, "Evolutionary Perspective," 6–7. He lists behaviors taken from legal cases. They include "forcible rape; extorting sex for job benefits; sexual touching; granting preferential treatment to a woman who is engaged in a consensual relationship with her supervisor; the existence of pervasive consensual sexual conduct in the office; sexual jokes, sexually suggestive pictures or cartoons, sexist comments, sexual propositions, and vulgar language; obscene language and gestures on a picket line; romantic overtures; 'well-intended compliments'; failure to squelch false rumors that an employee was having an affair with her supervisor; violent attacks on a former lover; attempts to maintain a soured relationship; and harassing actions of a non-sexual form."

106. A similar point is made by Hajdin, *Sexual Harassment*, 154–157.

107. Christensen, "'Sexual Harassment' Must Be Eliminated," 1.

108. Ibid., 2.

109. Ibid., 3.

110. Ibid., 4.

111. Ibid.

112. Ibid., 5.

113. Davis, "Sexual Harassment in the University," 156. Davis goes on to argue

that the case of "homicide" is not like that of "sexual harassment" because, while the former is a neutral term, the latter is not. So, she would not agree with my use of her example.

114. The vehemence of the response to Silva is an example of this. See Timothy E. Di Domenico, "Silva v. University of New Hampshire: The Precarious Balance between Student Hostile Environment Claims and Academic Freedom," *St. John's Law Review* 69 (1995): 609–632.

115. Maria L. Ontiveros, "Fictionalizing Harassment—Disclosing the Truth," *Michigan Law Review* 93 (1995): 1381–1382.

116. Smart, *Law, Crime, and Sexuality*, 94.

117. Christensen, "'Sexual Harassment' Must Be Eliminated," 2.

118. LeMoncheck and Hajdin, *Sexual Harassment*, 127.

119. Ibid., 166.

120. Christensen, "'Sexual Harassment' Must Be Eliminated," 9.

121. Ibid.

122. Ibid.

123. See chapter 6 for a discussion of these arguments.

124. However, interestingly, at the end of his discussion, Christensen suddenly brings in the gender reality, to argue that sexual harassment law discriminates against men.

Chapter 6

1. Rosemarie Tong, *Women, Sex, and the Law* (Totowa, New Jersey: Rowman & Littlefield, 1984), 13–14.

2. Carol Smart, *Law, Crime, and Sexuality: Essays in Feminism* (London: Sage Publications, 1995), 124–125.

3. "[I]t may be too soon to know whether the law against sexual harassment will be taken away from us or turn to nothing or turn ugly in our hands. The fact is, this law is working surprisingly well for women by any standards, particularly when compared with the rest of sex discrimination law. If the question is whether a law designed from women's standpoint and administered through this legal system can do anything for women—which always seems to me to be a good question—this experience so far gives a qualified and limited yes" (Catharine MacKinnon, "Sexual Harassment: Its First Decade in Court," in *Feminism Unmodified: Discourses on Life and Law* [Cambridge: Harvard University Press, 1987], 105).

4. For those favoring tort law, see Richard A. Epstein, *Forbidden Grounds: The Case against Employment Discrimination Laws* (Cambridge: Harvard University Press, 1992), 350–366; Janet Dine and Bob Watt, "Sexual Harassment: Moving Away from Discrimination," *Modern Law Review* 58 (1995): 343–363; and Ellen Frankel Paul, "Bared Buttocks and Federal Cases," *Society* 28, no. 4 (1991): 4–7, and "Sexual Harassment as Sex Discrimination: A Defective Paradigm," *Yale Law and Policy Review* 8 (1990): 333–365. Drucilla Cornell favors discrimination law. See her *The Imaginary Domain: Abortion, Pornography, and Sexual Harassment* (New York: Routledge, 1995).

5. Mark McLaughlin Hager, "Harassment as a Tort: Why Title VII Hostile Environment Liability Should Be Curtailed," *Connecticut Law Review* 30, no. 2 (1998): 375–439.

6. Epstein (*Forbidden Grounds*) and Dine and Watt ("Sexual Harassment") recommend using existing tort laws, while Paul ("Bared Buttocks" and "Defective Paradigm") speaks of creating a special sexual harassment tort.

7. Carrie N. Baker, "Sexual Extortion: Criminalizing Quid Pro Quo Sexual Harassment," *Law and Inequality Journal* 13 (1994): 213–251.

8. Constance Backhouse and Leah Cohen, *Sexual Harassment on the Job* (Englewood Cliffs, New Jersey: Prentice-Hall, 1982), 126.

9. Epstein, *Forbidden Grounds*, 352–353.

10. "In tort perspective, the injury of sexual harassment would be seen as an injury to the individual person, to personal sexual integrity, with damages extending to the job" (Catharine A. MacKinnon, *Sexual Harassment of Working Women: A Case of Sex Discrimination* [New Haven: Yale University Press, 1979], 171).

11. Tong, *Women, Sex, and the Law*, 77.

12. See Lin Farley, *Sexual Shakedown: The Sexual Harassment of Women on the Job* (New York: McGraw-Hill, 1978), MacKinnon, *Sexual Harassment*, and Anita M. Superson, "A Feminist Definition of Sexual Harassment," *Journal of Social Philosophy* 24, no. 1 (1993): 46–64.

13. Michael D. Vhay, "The Harms of Asking: Towards a Comprehensive Treatment of Sexual Harassment," *University of Chicago Law Review* 55 (1988): 355–362.

14. MacKinnon, *Sexual Harassment*, 171. "The essential purpose of tort law . . . is to compensate individuals one at a time for mischief which befalls them as a consequence of the one-time ineptitude or nastiness of other individuals. . . . Sexual harassment as understood in this book is not merely a parade of interconnected consequences with the potential for discrete repetition by other individuals, so that precedent will suffice. Rather, it is a group-defined injury which occurs to many different individuals regardless of unique qualities or circumstances, in ways that connect with other deprivations of the same individuals, among all of whom a single characteristic—female sex—is shared. Such an injury is *in essence* a group injury. . . . Tort law compensates individuals for injuries while spreading their costs and perhaps setting examples for foresightful perpetrators; the purpose of discrimination law is to change the society so that this kind of injury need not and does not recur. Tort law considers individual and compensable something which is fundamentally social and should be eliminated" (MacKinnon, *Sexual Harassment*, 172).

15. "If the harasser engaged in touching without consent, he committed a battery. [See Restatement (Second) of Torts Sec. 18 (1965), imposing liability for intentional offensive contact with another person.] If the touching was only threatened but not consummated, he committed an assault. [See Restatement (Second) of Torts Sec. 21 (1965), subjecting a defendant to liability if 'he acts intending to cause a harmful or offensive contact with the person of the other.'] If the threat was for future physical harm, he committed the tort of intentional infliction of emotional distress. [See Restatement (Second) of Torts Sec. 46 (1965), governing 'outrageous conduct causing severe emotional distress.'] If the challenged conduct involved shadowing or following a person, he committed the tort of invasion of privacy. . . . [See Restatement (Second) of Torts Sec. 652B (1965), governing intrusion upon seclusion]" (Epstein, *Forbidden Grounds*, 353).

16. Ibid., 505.

17. Ibid., 351–352.

18. Ibid., 357.

19. Paul, "Defective Paradigm," and Vhay, "Harms of Asking." Paul recommends a sexual harassment tort *instead* of use of antidiscrimination law. Vhay recommends a sexual harassment tort ("advances in inappropriate contexts") *in*

addition to existing torts and antidiscrimination law (Vhay, "Harms of Asking," 356–360).

20. Paul, "Bared Buttocks," 6. Paul calls for the "de-ideologizing" of the sexual harassment issue. However, she seems to ignore the clearly ideological basis of her own view. She claims that quid pro quo sexual harassment is "analogous to extortion" and that "The harasser extorts property (i.e., the use of the woman's body) through the leverage of fear for her job." Surely, conceiving of quid pro quo sexual harassment as first and foremost a property crime is as ideological as conceiving of it as sex discrimination. Furthermore, conceiving of sexual harassment as a property crime does nothing to explain why it is primarily directed at women. That Paul does conceive of sexual harassment as a crime against property is confirmed by her concern for the employer. The harasser is stealing from his or her employer by taking benefits of the job and using them for his or her personal benefit, rather than for the employer's benefit. Paul should admit that she is substituting one ideology for another and argue for her perspective on the grounds that her ideology is preferable.

21. See chapter 3, p. 63.

22. Paul, "Bared Buttocks," 6. Paul also argues that it was not the intention of Title VII legislation to prohibit sexual harassment. See Paul, "Defective Paradigm," 345–346.

23. "The debate since *Costle* has been largely over employer liability for an employee's prohibited conduct" (Vhay, "Harms of Asking," 342, note 64). See also Lloyd R. Cohen, "Sexual Harassment and the Law," *Society* 28, no. 4 (1991): 8–13. Cohen says of "vicarious liability": "normally it is only applied when the acts of an employee are intended to serve the business interests of the employer" (Cohen, "Sexual Harassment," 11).

24. "[O]ne wonders why the market has not already substantially eliminate it. Precisely because sexual harassment imposes costs on employers that will ultimately be shifted to the harasser, it is hard to see how true large-scale sexual harassment in the workplace can survive a market test.

"In support of this proposition, the results of a sifting of the records of sexual harassment cases indicate that a grossly disproportionate number of sexual harassment suits come from public sector employment. Since government employers do not face the market constraints of private employers and have less discretion in dismissing employees, they have less incentive and ability to discipline sexual harassment" (Cohen, "Sexual Harassment," 12–13). Cohen's explanation for why the market has not eliminated sexual harassment seems to be that it has, except where the market is not allowed to operate freely. MacKinnon, of course, would offer a different explanation.

25. Paul, "Bared Buttocks," 6.

26. Paul, "Defective Paradigm," 335.

27. Ibid., 349.

28. Ibid., 350.

29. Ibid., 352.

30. Ibid., 360.

31. Ibid., 361.

32. Cited in Paul, "Defective Paradigm," 361. From *Restatement (Second) of Torts* 46 (1965), comment a.

33. Cited in Paul, "Defective Paradigm," 361. From *Restatement (Second) of Torts* 46 (1965), comment j.34. Cited in Paul, "Defective Paradigm," 361. From *Restatement (Second) of Torts* 46 (1965), comment a.

35. Paul, "Defective Paradigm," 362.

36. Vhay, "Harms of Asking," 358–359.

37. "Common law causes of action such as constructive discharge impose a greater burden on the complainant than does hostile work environment" (Frank Ravitch, "Beyond Reasonable Accommodation: The Availability and Structure of a Cause of Action for Workplace Harassment under the Americans with Disabilities Act," *Cardozo Law Review* 15 (1994): 1494, note 91).

38. William Petrocelli and Barbara Kate Repa, *Sexual Harassment on the Job* (Berkeley, California: Nolo Press, 1992), 5/7.

39. Anita Bernstein, "Law, Culture, and Harassment," *University of Pennsylvania Law Review* 142 (1994): 1227–1331.

40. Ibid., 1233.

41. Ibid.

42. Ibid., 1239.

43. Ibid., 1244–1245.

44. Ibid. Other commentators on the European scene agree with Bernstein that Europeans put less emphasis on sex discrimination in their treatment of sexual harassment. However, they see in both the United States and in Europe a trend toward conceptualizing sexual harassment as a misuse of sexuality. See Dine and Watt, "Sexual Harassment," 347.

45. Bernstein, "Law, Culture, and Harassment," 1259.

46. Ibid., 1281.

47. Ibid., 1285.

48. Ibid., 1289.

49. "The reasonableness standard that has been adopted by the courts is a tort reasonableness standard which appeals to the reasonable man as the basis for what it is reasonable for people to expect in our society and, from that perspective, what constitutes harm. The reasonableness test purports to give objectivity to the perspective that is allowed to determine the conduct as harassment" (Cornell, *Imaginary Domain*, 176).

50. See Aimee L. Widor, "Comment: Fact or Fiction? Role-Reversal Sexual Harassment in the Modern Workplace," *University of Pittsburgh Law Review* 58 (1996): 248–249. See also Robert S. Adler and Ellen R. Peirce, "The Legal, Ethical, and Social Implications of the 'Reasonable Woman' Standard in Sexual Harassment Cases," *Fordham Law Review* 61 (1993): 773–774: "In a 1986 decision, the Supreme Court directed lower courts to assess, in examining allegedly harassing conduct, whether the conduct was both unwelcome and so severe or pervasive that it altered the plaintiff's working environment. This directive, however, leaves open the question of whose perspective—that of the particular victim, a reasonable person undifferentiated by sex, or a reasonable woman—the fact finder should use to assess the seriousness of the offense" (Adler and Peirce, "Legal, Ethical, and Social Implications," 773–774).

51. *Meritor Savings Bank, FSB v. Vinson*, U.S. 106 S.Ct., 67. See also *Henson v. City of Dundee*, 682 F.2d 897 (11th Cir. 1982), 904.

52. See Saba Ashraf, "The Reasonableness of the 'Reasonable Woman' Standard: An Evaluation of Its Use in Hostile Environment Sexual Harassment Claims under Title VII of the Civil Rights Act," *Hofstra Law Review* 21 (1992): 486–487.

53. "Conduct that is not severe or pervasive enough to create an objectively hostile or abusive work environment—an environment that a reasonable person would find hostile or abusive—is beyond Title VII's purview. Likewise, if the victim does not subjectively perceive the environment to be abusive, the conduct has not

actually altered the conditions of the victim's employment, and there is no Title VII violation" (*Harris v. Forklift Systems, Inc.*, 114 S.Ct. 367 [1993], 370).

54. *Rabidue v. Osceola Refining Co.*, 805 F.2d 611, 620 (6th Cir. 1986), 620–622.

55. Ibid., 626.

56. Adler and Peirce, "Legal, Ethical, and Social Implications," 774, note 3.

57. Ibid., 799.

58. Note, "Sexual Harassment Claims of Abusive Work Environment under Title VII," *Harvard Law Review* 97 (1984): 1449–1467.

59. *Rabidue v. Osceola Refining Co.*, 805 F.2d 611, 620 (6th Cir. 1986), *cert. denied*, 481 U.S. 1041 (1987), citation of Note, 626.

60. Liesa L. Bernardin, "Does the Reasonable Woman Exist and Does She Have Any Place in Hostile Environment Sexual Harassment Claims under Title VII after Harris?" *Florida Law Review* 46 (1994): 301.

61. Ibid.

62. See Ravitch, "Beyond Reasonable Accommodation," 1479, note 21; Russell S. Post, "The Serpentine Wall and the Serpent's Tongue: Rethinking the Religious Harassment Debate," *Virginia Law Review* 83 (1997): 193, note 71.

63. Ravitch, "Beyond Reasonable Accommodation," 1483, note 37.

64. Adler and Peirce, "Legal, Ethical, and Social Implications," 775, note 11.

65. Ibid., 807.

66. Ibid., 807–808.

67. This is the argument presented by Deborah S. Brenneman, "From a Woman's Point of View: The Use of the Reasonable Woman Standard in Sexual Harassment Cases," *University of Cincinnati* 60 (1992): 1285–1289.

68. *Caleshu v. Merrill Lynch, Pierce, Fenner & Smith*, 737 F. Supp. 1070 (E.D. Mo. 1990); *Ebert v. Lamar Truck Plaza*, 715 F. Supp. 1496, 1499 (D. Colo. 1987), aff'd, 878 F.2d 338 (10th Cir. 1989).

69. Kingsley R. Browne, "An Evolutionary Perspective on Sexual Harassment: Seeking Roots in Biology Rather Than Ideology," *Journal of Contemporary Legal Issues* 8 (1997): 31.

70. Kathryn Abrams, "The Reasonable Woman: Sense and Sensibility in Sexual Harassment Law," *Dissent*, Winter 1995, 51. Abrams refers to the amicus brief filed by Catharine MacKinnon and the Women's Legal Defense and Education Fund, which argued that *any* reasonableness standard would "reinforce stereotypes and distract the courts from the primary issue—the conduct of the defendant" (Abrams, "Reasonable Woman," 51).

71. Debra A. DeBruin, "Identifying Sexual Harassment: The Reasonable Woman Standard," in *Violence against Women: Philosophical Perspectives*, ed. Stanley French, Laura Purdy, and Wanda Teays (Ithaca, New York: Cornell University Press, 1998), 107–122.

72. It is interesting to compare DeBruin's interpretation of the *Ellison* case with Browne's. Though they both support the reasonable woman standard, their political perspectives are very different, leading to conflicting readings of particular cases. DeBruin sees Ellison as justifiably frightened by Gray's behavior; Browne sees the situation as one of miscommunication, unfairly blamed on the man involved. One could say that this is evidence that reasonable women and reasonable men perceive such events differently. However, that would ignore the political commitments of both interpreters.

73. DeBruin, "Identifying Sexual Harassment," 122.

74. This thought is also found in Martha Chamallas, "Feminist Constructions of Objectivity: Multiple Perspectives in Sexual and Racial Harassment Litigation,"

Texas Journal of Women and Legislation 1 (1992). "[T]he hypothetical reasonable woman will not be the average woman who has found a way to cope with, but not to challenge, sexually harassing conduct. . ." (Chamallas, "Feminist Constructions of Objectivity, 135).

75. DeBruin, "Identifying Sexual Harassment," 120–121.

76. Ibid., 121.

77. Abrams, "Reasonable Woman," 52.

78. Ibid., 52–53.

79. Katherine M. Franke, "What's Wrong with Sexual Harassment?" *Stanford Law Review* 49, no. 4 (1997): 752. Ultimately, Franke does not think Abrams's standard goes far enough.

80. Cited in DeBruin, "Identifying Sexual Harassment," 7–8, from *Radke v. Everett*, 501 N.W. 2d 155 (Mich. 1993), 167.

81. Adler and Peirce, "Legal, Ethical, and Social Implications," 772.

82. Ibid., 802.

83. See Nancy "Ann" Davis, "Sexual Harassment in the University," in *Morality, Responsibility, and the University: Studies in Academic Ethics*, ed. Steven M. Cahn (Philadelphia: Temple University Press, 1990), 155–156; Browne, "Evolutionary Perspective," 33–39; Edmund Wall, "The Definition of Sexual Harassment," in *Sexual Harassment: Confrontations and Decisions*, ed. Edmund Wall (Buffalo, New York: Prometheus Books, 1992), 75–76.

84. Wall, "Definition of Sexual Harassment," 75.

85. Ibid., 75.

86. Browne, "Evolutionary Perspective," 37.

87. Ibid., 38–39.

88. Adler and Pierce, "Legal, Ethical, and Social Implications," 822–823. See also Robert Unikel, "'Reasonable' Doubts: A Critique of the Reasonable Woman Standard in American Jurisprudence," *Northwestern University Law Review* 87 (1992). "[T]he judicial policies underlying the development of the reasonable woman standard dictate the creation of a multitude of highly specific reasonableness standards incorporating the norms and ideals of particular groups into the decisionmaking process. Even if these standards were established only for those groups that could be legitimately classified as 'suspect' or 'quasi-suspect,' the required number would be dizzying. . . . Furthermore, because each person is inevitably a member of more than one group (for example, the 'Caucasian' and 'female'), in order for reasonableness standards adequately to reflect the entire spectrum of group norms relevant to any situation, those standards must be drawn to include all of a person's significant group associations. For example, a 'reasonable black woman' standard, a 'reasonable Asian, gay man' standard, or a 'reasonable Russian, Jewish woman' standard may be required in certain circumstances, depending on the particular group affiliations of the person or persons involved. Consequently, a potentially infinite number of specifically designed reasonableness standards is required in order adequately to incorporate each individual's relevant group connections" (Unikel, "'Reasonable' Doubts," 354–355).

89. *Harris v. International Paper Co.*, 765 F. Supp. 1509 (D. Me. 1991).

90. Adler and Pierce, "Legal, Ethical, and Social Implications," 823.

91. *Harris v. International Paper Co.*, 1515–1516.

92. *Murray v. City of Austin*, 947 F.2d 147 (5th Cir. 1991), cert. denied, 112 S.Ct. 3028 (1992). See Adler and Pierce, "Legal, Ethical, and Social Implications," 823.

93. *Stingley v. Arizona*, 796 F. Supp. 424 (D. Ariz. 1992).

94. Ibid., 428.

95. See Ashraf, "Reasonableness of the 'Reasonable Woman' Standard," 496–497.

96. Adler and Pierce, "Legal, Ethical, and Social Implications," 823–824.

97. Ravitch, "Beyond Reasonable Accommodation," 1505–1506.

98. Linda LeMoncheck argues that courts should engage in 'world'-traveling—attempt to understand other's social and psychological locations—in Linda LeMoncheck and Mane Hajdin, *Sexual Harassment: A Debate* (Lanham, Maryland: Rowman & Littlefield, 1997), 60–61.

99. See Abrams, "Reasonable Woman," 48–54.

100. See Widor, "Fact or Fiction," 248.

101. Franke, "What's Wrong," 752.

102. L. Camille Hebert, "Sexual Harassment Is Gender Harassment," *Kansas Law Review* 43 (1995): 587–588.

103. "Despite the uproar following the Clarence Thomas hearings, sexual harrassment [sic] in the workplace is not common, and the vast majority of Americans are satisfied with the way their employers are treating the problems. . . . Moreover, the survey finds no great difference between men and women in their perceptions of the relative severity of the problem and on the definitions of what constitutes sexual harassment" ("Most Americans Say Sexual Harassment At Work Not A Problem," *Roper Reports*, No. 92–1 [1992]). The poll was based on interviews with 1,026 employed men and women. Cited in Adler and Pierce, "Legal, Ethical, and Social Implications," 806. I do not know what the questions asked in the poll were.

104. Chamallas, "Feminist Constructions of Objectivity," 135.

105. For a discussion of cases in which women allegedly harassed men see Widor, "Fact or Fiction." Such cases include *Harvey v. Blake*, 913 F.2d 226, 227 (5th Cir. 1990) and *Huebschen v. Wisconsin Dep't of Health & Social Servs.*, 716 F.2d 1167, 32 FEP Cases 1582, 1582–3 (7th Cir. 1983). Cases in which men allegedly harassed men include *Prescott v. Independent Life & Accs. Ins. Co.*, 878 F. Supp. 1545 (M.D. Ala. 1995), *EEOC v. Walden Books Co.*, 885 F. Supp. 1100 (M.D. Tenn. 1995), and *Wright v. Methodist Youth Services, Inc.*, 511 F. Supp. 307 (N.D. Ill. 1981). Cases in which women allegedly harassed women include *Barlow v. Northwestern Memorial Hosp.*, 30 FEP Cases 223 (N.D. Ill. 1980).

106. Widor, "Fact or Fiction, " 225, note 3.

107. Ibid., 233. One case in which a man successfully sued for quid pro quo sexual harassment was *Gardinella v. General Electric Co.*, 833 F. Supp. 617 (W.D. Ky. 1993).

108. Widor mentions a case in which a man received $1 million for emotional distress, economic losses, and punitive damages (Widor, "Fact or Fiction," 241–242). Other cases include the Jenny Craig, Inc., case, a case against a city councilwoman in St. Paul that was settled out of court, and a case brought by the EEOC on behalf of a male employee against Domino's Pizza.

109. A similar point is made in Frank, "What's Wrong," 691–772.

110. Portions of this section are taken from Margaret A. Crouch, "The Coherence of Sexual Harassment Law: The Problem of Same-Sex Harassment," presented at the Michigan Academy of Sciences and Letters, March 1999.

111. Kara L. Gross, "Toward Gender Equality and Understanding: Recognizing That Same-Sex Sexual Harassment Is Sex Discrimination," *Brooklyn Law Review* 62 (1996): 1166.

112. I am inferring this from her discussion of "exactly the same behavior" by a

male toward a male as occurred in *Meritor*. See Gross, "Toward Gender Equality," 1197.

113. According to MacKinnon, this is a point at which the differences approach and the dominance approach diverge. According to the differences approach, different treatment of women and men is justified if it is based on a factual difference between them. The dominance approach does not regard *any* differential treatment based on sex as justified. Thus, Gross would seem to represent a hybrid of the two approaches. For more on the dominance approach, see the text that follows.

114. Gross, "Toward Gender Equality," 1166.

115. See *Oncale v. Sundowner Offshore Services, Inc., U.S. Supreme Court*, No. 96–568, March 4, 1998.

116. MacKinnon, *Sexual Harassment*, 1.

117. Ibid., 216.

118. Ibid., 4–5.

119. See chapter 5, note 11.

120. Susan Perissinotto Woodhouse, "Same-Gender Sexual Harassment: Is It Sex Discrimination under Title VII?" *Santa Clara Law Review* 36 (1996): 1168.

121. "It is argued that same-gender sexual harassment does not have the same effects, nor does it further the goals of Title VII to empower the powerless and eliminate discrimination based on sex" (Woodhouse, "Same-Gender," 1150).

122. Chamallas, "Feminist Constructions of Objectivity," 130.

123. Franke, "What's Wrong," 772.

124. Ibid., 758.

125. Katherine M. Franke, "The Central Mistake of Sex Discrimination Law: The Disaggregation of Sex from Gender," *University of Pennsylvania* 144 (1995): 96. Franke does not say what kind of right this is—moral or legal.

126. *Doe v. City of Belleville*, 119 F. 3d 563 (7th Cir. 1997).

127. See Gross, "Toward Gender Equality," 1205, and Woodhouse, "Same-Gender," 1147, note 3.

128. *Goluszek v. Smith*. 697 F. Supp. 1452 (N.D. Ill. 1988). *Vandeventer v. Wabash National Corp.* speaks of the "dominant gender."

129. *Oncale v. Sundowner Offshore Services, Inc.*

130. Ibid.

131. The original Civil Rights Act of 1964 included the categories of race, sex, religion, and national origin. Age is protected by the Age Discrimination in Employment Act of 1988 and disability by the Americans with Disabilities Act of 1991. See Julie Vigil, "Expanding the Hostile Environment Theory to Cover Age Discrimination: How Far Is Too Far?" *Pepperdine Law Review* 23 (1996): 565–606, and Ravitch, "Beyond Reasonable Accommodation."

132. Hostile-environment theory was approved for Title IX cases in *Doe v. Petaluma City School Dist.*, 830 F. Supp. 1560, 1563 (N.D. Cal. 1993).

133. See Vhay, "Harms of Asking," 336.

134. Ibid., 337.

135. One need simply do a search of law review articles on LEXIS to see this.

136. "Proposed Rules," *Federal Register* 58, no. 189 (October 1, 1993): 51266.

137. See Post, "Serpentine Wall."

138. See Virginia I. Postrel, "Persecution Complex," *Reason*, August 26/September 1994, 6.

139. See MacKinnon, *Sexual Harassment*, 237. In her book, MacKinnon is ex-

plicitly concerned with comparing sex discrimination and racial discrimination (see MacKinnon, *Sexual Harassment*, 14, for example). It is from this and from examples she uses that I infer that the concept of sexual harassment as sex discrimination is developed at least in part on analogy with racial harassment.

140. "Part of the courts' and commentators' difficulties in constructing an adequate analytic framework for sex-based discrimination has stemmed from a reliance on prior race-based paradigms that cannot capture the complexities of gender" (Deborah L. Rhode, *Justice and Gender: Sex Discrimination and the Law* [Cambridge: Harvard University Press, 1989], 89–90).

141. *Bundy v. Jackson*, 641 F.2d 934 (D.C. Cir.1981).

142. *Rogers v. E.E.O.C.*, 454 F.2d 234 (5th Cir. 1971), *cert. denied*, 406 U.S. 957, 92 S.Ct. 2058, 32 L.Ed.2d 343 (1972). This is considered to be a racial harassment case, but it is not clear to me why it is not a national origin harassment case. Most commentators do not treat racial and national origin sexual harassment separately, so I shall simply use "racial harassment" as proxy for race and national-origin harassment. I do this reluctantly, since an investigation into the ways in which racial and national origin harassment differ is needed.

143. Jill W. Henken, "Hostile Environment Claims of Sexual Harassment: The Continuing Expansion of Sexual Harassment Law," *Villanova Law Review* 34 (1989): 1248, note 21.

144. *Bundy v. Jackson*, 641 F.2d 934 (D.C. Cir. 1981), 945.

145. *Meritor Savings Bank, FSB v. Vinson*, U.S. 106 S.Ct. (1986), 65–66.

146. *Henson v. City of Dundee*, 682 F.2d 897 (11th Cir. 1982), 902. Cited in Vhay, "Harms of Asking," 349.

147. "What is clear from this review of the development of harassing environment law is that sexual harassment was seldom treated as the equivalent of harassment on the basis of religion, race, or national origin. Animus, unwelcomeness, and resultant harm were commonly assumed in religion, race, or national origin categories, even when the comments were dismissed by defendants as bantering or 'just joking.' Courts were reluctant to view gender-based comments in the same light. . ." (Terry Morehead Dworkin and Ellen R. Peirce, "Is Religious Harassment 'More Equal'?" *Seton Hall Law Review* 26 [1995]: 61–62).

148. Robert J. Gregory, "You Can Call Me a 'Bitch' Just Don't Use the 'N-Word': Some Thoughts on *Galloway v. General Motors Service Parts Operations* and *Rodgers v. Western-Southern Life Insurance Co.*," *DePaul Law Review* 46 (1997): 741–742. I am not convinced that Gregory is right about this. Many of the cases he cites suggest that there is simply a great deal of variation in the way judges perceive hostile environment cases involving sex. Perhaps this is enough—there is not so much variation when the case involves race.

149. Ibid., 746–747. Citations omitted.

150. "People sensitive to sexually oriented attacks—women and particularly sensitive men—are likely to be attacked in that way" (Browne, "Evolutionary Perspective," 72).

151. Ibid., 68–69.

152. See Ruth Colker, "Whores, Fags, Dumb-Ass Women, Surly Blacks, and Competent Heterosexual White Men: The Sexual and Racial Morality Underlying Anti-Discrimination Doctrine," *Yale Journal of Law and Feminism* 7 (1995): 208. This expression was used to refer to Teresa Harris in *Harris v. Forklift Systems, Inc.*, 114 S.Ct. 367 (1993).

153. Barbara Lindemann and David D. Kadue, *Sexual Harassment in Employ-*

ment Law (Washington, D.C.: Bureau of National Affairs, 1992), 135. See also Ronna Greff Schneider, "Sexual Harassment and Higher Education," *Texas Law Review* 65 (1987): 533: "Sexual harassment is difficult to identify. Unlike racial, ethnic, or religious harassment, which are intrinsically offensive and presumptively unwelcome, sexual advances are ambiguous" (Schneider, "Sexual Harassment and Higher Education," 533).

154. 29 CFR Ch. XIV, Sec. 1604.11.

155. Gregory, "You Can Call Me a 'Bitch,'" 741.

156. Ibid.

157. Ibid., 765.

158. Ibid., 766–767.

159. Vhay, "Harms of Asking," 344. See also Susan Estrich, "Sex at Work," *Stanford Law Review* 43 (1991): 826–833. Estrich claims that the "unwelcomeness" requirement "has served as a vehicle to import some of the most pernicious doctrines of rape law into Title VII cases" ("Sex at Work," 826).

160. Vhay, "Harms of Asking," 344.

161. Lindemann and Kadue, *Sexual Harassment in Employment Law*, 131.

162. Ibid., 153.

163. Ibid.

164. "[M]ost areas of the law do not require a victim to anticipate her antagonist's defenses in her prima facie case, and Title VII is no exception" (Vhay, "Harms of Asking," 344).

165. *Meritor Savings Bank, FSB v. Vinson*, U.S. 106 S.Ct. 2399 (1986).

166. Vhay, "Harms of Asking," 344. The brief from which he quotes is "Brief for the United States and the Equal Employment Opportunity Commission as Amici Curiae, *Meritor Savings Bank v. Vinson*," No. 84–1979 (Dec. 11, 1985).

167. This same worry appeared in earlier cases: "An invitation to dinner could become an invitation to a federal lawsuit if a once harmonious relationship turned sour at some later time" (*Tomkins v. Public Service Electric & Gas*, 422 F. Supp. 553 [D.C. N.J. 1976], 557).

168. Vhay, "Harms of Asking," 356, note 113.

169. Ibid., 355.

170. *Jackson-Coley v. Corps of Engineers*, 43 F.E.P. Cases 617, 620 (E.D.Mich. 1987).

171. Vhay, "Harms of Asking," 356, Note 113.

172. Ibid., 356.

173. Lindemann and Kadue, *Sexual Harassment in Employment Law*, 75.

174. *DeAngelis v. El Paso Municipal Police Officers Association*, 51 F.3d 591 (5th Cir. 1995).

175. *Hall v. Gus Construction Co.*, 842 F.2d 1010 (8th Cir. 1988).

176. Joshua F. Thorpe, "Gender-Based Harassment and the Hostile Work Environment," *Duke Law Journal* (1990): 1392.

177. *Hall v. Gus Construction Co.*, 1014.

178. See Suzanne Sangree, "Title VII Prohibitions against Hostile Environment Sexual Harassment and the First Amendment: No Collision in Sight," *Rutgers Law Review* 47 (1995): 494–495.

179. Colker, "Whores, Fags, Dumb-Ass Women."

180. Ibid., 199–200.

181. *Compston v. Borden, Inc.*, 424 F. Supp. 157, 160–61 (S.D. Ohio 1976).

182. *Smallzman v. Sea Breeze*, 60 Fair Empl. Prac. Cas. (BNA) 1031 (D. Md. Jan,

7, 1993); *Weiss v. United States*, 595 F. Supp. 1050 (E.D. Va. 1984); *Obradovich v. Federal Reserve Bank*, 569 F. Supp. 785 (S.D.N.Y. 1983) (from Dworkin and Peirce, "Is Religious Harassment 'More Equal'?" 49, note 28).

183. "Of all the protected categories under Title VII, religion is the only one that is not an immutable characteristic" (Julia Spoor, "Go Tell It on the Mountain, but Keep It out of the Office: Religious Harassment in the Workplace," *Valparaiso University Law Review* 31 [1997]: 1005, note 195).

184. Betty L. Dunkum, "Where to Draw the Line: Handling Religious Harassment Issues in the Wake of the Failed EEOC Guidelines," *Notre Dame Law Review* 71 (1996): 965.

185. Spoor, "Go Tell It on the Mountain," 1005.

186. Ibid., 972. This requirement was the result of an amendment to Title VII in 1967. See Spoor, "Go Tell It on the Mountain," 986.

187. "The first federal case to recognize religious harassment under Title VII was Compston v. Borden Inc., 424 F. Supp. 157 (S.D. Ohio 1976). The court reasoned that when an employer engages in activities intended to demean an employee because of his religion, the activities will necessarily alter the conditions of employment. . . . This theory has become widely accepted" (Spoor, "Go Tell It on the Mountain," 973, note 11). "Traditionally, a claim of religious harassment arose when supervisors or co-workers tormented an employee because of his faith. The more common claim of failure to accommodate a religious practice typically arose when employees were forced to work on their Sabbath" (Spoor, "Go Tell It on the Mountain," 975).

188. Ibid., 976.

189. Ibid., 983.

190. Ibid., 1014.

191. *Weiss v. United States*, 595 F. Supp. 1050 (E.D. Va. 1984).

192. Post, "Serpentine Wall," 185.

193. "By resting its decision explicitly on the authority of the lower federal courts and the EEOC, the Court simultaneously ratified 'hostile work environment' doctrine in cases of sexual, racial, religious, and national origin discrimination. Hence the Supreme Court explicitly endorsed the uniformity—and the interdependency—of harassment doctrine under Title VII" (Post, "Serpentine Wall," 187, referring to *Meritor Savings Bank, FSB v. Vinson*). In reference to *Harris v. Forklift Systems, Inc.*, Post says that "the decision of the Supreme Court in Harris is even more significant because it explicitly reaffirmed the uniformity of harassment law under Title VII. The Court concluded that 'the very fact that the discriminatory conduct was so severe or pervasive that it created a work environment abusive to employees because of their race, gender, religion or national origin offends Title VII's broad rule of workplace equality'" (Post, "Serpentine Wall," 189).

194. There is disagreement about whether this is so. See Dunkum, "Where to Draw the Line": "in some cases, the EEOC went too far in its proposal and, in other cases, the criticisms raised were unfounded overreactions" (Dunkum, "Where to Draw the Line," 994–995). Dunkum argues that the EEOC went beyond existing case law in some areas.

195. Post, "Serpentine Wall," 189.

196. See Post, "Serpentine Wall." In describing the critics of the 1993 EEOC *Guidelines*, he says that "congressional critics decried efforts to vindicate the antidiscrimination principle of Title VII at the expense of the First Amendment, characterizing religious harassment doctrine as incompatible with the principle of religious liberty" (Post, "Serpentine Wall," 179).

197. Spoor, "Go Tell It on the Mountain," 1005, note 196, summarizing an argument by Laura S. Underkuffler in her "Discrimination on the Basis of Religion: An Examination of Attempted Value Neutrality in Employment," *William & Mary Law Review* 30 (1989): 610.

198. For arguments that sexual harassment does conflict with the First Amendment, see Kingsley R. Browne, "Title VII as Censorship: Hostile-Environment Harassment and the First Amendment," *Ohio State Law Journal* 52 (1991): 481–550; Eugene Volokh, "Freedom of Speech and Workplace Harassment," *UCLA Law Review* 39 (1992): 1791–1872; and Eugene Volokh, "What Speech Does 'Hostile Work Environment' Harassment Law Restrict?" *Georgetown Law Journal* 85 (1997): 627–648. For arguments that it need not, see Sangree, "Title VII Prohibitions."

199. Post, "Serpentine Wall," 198–200.

200. See 42 *U.S.C.* 2000e-2(e) (1994).

201. Dunkum, "Where to Draw the Line," 960.

202. Americans with Disabilities Act of 1991 (42 *U.S.C.* 12101–12213 (Supp. III 1991)).

203. Ravitch, "Beyond Reasonable Accommodation," 1475.

204. "Proposed Rules," 51269.

205. "The hostile work environment cause of action has been applied in the sex, race, religion, and national origin contexts. Thus, the cause of action is not limited to one protected class; it could apply to any class protected by a statute that prohibits discrimination in the terms and conditions of employment. The language and construction of the ADA, as well as the EEOC Proposed Guidelines, demonstrate the appropriateness of such a cause of action in the context of disability discrimination" (Ravitch, "Beyond Reasonable Accommodation," 1483–1484).

206. Ibid., 1480.

207. *U.S. Code*, 29, secs. 701–797b (1988 & Supps. I—IV 1989–1992). The Rehabilitation Act "only provides protection if the claimant is employed by the federal government, is a government contractor, or receives federal funding" (Ravitch, "Beyond Reasonable Accommodation," 1490).

208. See, for example, *Gillespie v. Derwinski*, 790 F. Supp. 1032 (E.D. Wash. 1991), *Johnson v. Shalala*, 991 F.2d 126 (4th Cir. 1993), and *Doe v. Board of County Commissioners*, 815 F. Supp. 1448 (S.D. Fla. 1992).

209. Ravitch, "Beyond Reasonable Accommodation," 1493–1494.

210. "[E]mployers have a duty to reasonably accommodate the religious practices of employees under Title VII. See *Ansonia Bd. of Educ. v. Philbrook*, 479 U.S. 60 (1986) (discussing the requirement of section 701(j) of Title VII regarding an employer's obligation to accommodate the religious observances of employees). The duty to reasonably accommodate a disabled employee is unique in that such accommodation is required to enable the employee to perform his or her job. The accommodation of religious observances by an employer does not enable that employee to perform the job; it simply acknowledges that employees have a right to observe their religious beliefs without being discriminated against in employment to the extent that such observance does not impose an undue hardship on the employer" (Ravitch, "Beyond Reasonable Accommodation," 1509, note 161).

211. *U.S. Code*, vol. 29, sec. 621 (1988).

212. Vigil, "Expanding the Hostile Environment Theory," 568.

213. Ibid., 591–592.

214. Ibid., 577.

215. Vigil discusses three federal court cases "that have applied the hostile environment theory to age discrimination" ("Expanding the Hostile Environ-

ment Theory," 568): *Drez v. E. R. Squibb & Sons, Inc.*, 674 F. Supp. 1432 (D. Kan. 1987), *Spence v. Maryland Casualty Co.*, 995 F.2d 1147 (2d Cir. 1993), and *Eggleston v. South Bend Community School Corp.*, 858 F. Supp. 841 (N.D. Ind. 1994) (pp. 586–588).

216. Vigil, "Expanding the Hostile Environment Theory," 605.

217. Dunkum, "Where to Draw the Line," 954. From "Religion in the Workplace," *Cleveland Plain Dealer*, November 19, 1994.

Chapter 7

1. *Davis v. Monroe County Board of Education* (97–843). Argued January 12, 1999–Decided May 24, 1999. Justice Kennedy dissenting.

2. See Vicki Schultz, "Reconceptualizing Sexual Harassment," *Yale Law Journal* 107 (1998): 1696–1699.

3. Catharine A. MacKinnon, *Sexual Harassment of Working Women: A Case of Sex Discrimination* (New Haven: Yale University Press, 1979), 1.

4. Ibid., 105.

5. Ibid., 174.

6. See Ellen Frankel Paul, "Bared Buttocks and Federal Cases," *Society* 28, no. 4 (1991): 6; and Kingsley R. Browne, "An Evolutionary Perspective on Sexual Harassment: Seeking Roots in Biology Rather Than Ideology," *Journal of Contemporary Legal Issues* 8 (1997): 65. Paul says that quid pro quo harassment is *analogous* to extortion. She does not think it is sex discrimination. I am quite sure that Browne does not consider quid pro quo sexual harassment to be sex discrimination; however, I am not sure just how he does understand it. He does think that it involves sex and power, and he suggests that it is extortion.

7. Browne, "Evolutionary Perspective," 66–67. Browne cites *Hall v. Gus Construction Co.*, 842 F.2d 1010 (8th Cir. 1988), as an example.

8. "Any professor who trades grades for sex and uses this power as a forceful tool of seduction deserves to face charges. The same would be true if he traded grades for a thousand dollars. . ." (Katie Roiphe, *The Morning After: Sex, Fear, and Feminism* [Boston: Little, Brown, 1993], 104).

9. "The clarity of the definition of sexual harassment as a 'hostile work environment' depends on a universal code of conduct, a shared idea of acceptable behavior that we just don't have. Something that makes one person feel uncomfortable may make another person feel great" (Roiphe, *Morning After*, 91).

10. "We can regulate the work environment. We must have equal opportunity and sexual harassment guidelines, but you cannot legislate relationships" (Camille Paglia, "The Rape Debate, Continued," in *Sex, Art, and American Culture* [New York: Vintage, 1992], 68).

11. Camille Paglia, "The Strange Case of Clarence Thomas and Anita Hill," in *Sex, Art, and American Culture* (New York: Vintage, 1992), 46–48.

12. Paul, "Bared Buttocks," 7.

13. Linda LeMoncheck and Mane Hajdin, *Sexual Harassment: A Debate* (Lanham, Maryland: Rowman & Littlefield, 1997), 127.

14. Schultz "Reconceptualizing Sexual Harassment."

15. Ibid., 1691.

16. Ibid., 1755.

17. Ibid., 1760.

18. "Unlike my account, Franke's analysis does not directly highlight the competence-undermining function of sexual forms of hostile work environment

harassment. Instead, she focuses on the fact that such sexualized conduct enforces gender-based stereotypes. . . . As her examples reveal, however, sexuality is an effective tool for reinforcing prescribed gender roles in some work settings precisely because male workers can use sexual conduct to undermine women's competence and, hence, mark them as inferior workers not fit to hold more highly rewarded jobs" (Schultz, "Reconceptualizing Sexual Harassment," 1766–1767, note 441).

19. Ibid., 1796.

20. See, for example, John C. Hughes and Larry May, "Sexual Harassment," *Social Theory and Practice* 6 (1980): 249–280.

21. Catharine A. MacKinnon, "Sexual Harassment: Its First Decade in Court," in *Feminism Unmodified* (Cambridge: Harvard University Press, 1987), 254, note 17.

22. *Bakke v. University of California Regents*, 438 U.S., 265 (1978). I thank Professor Sidney Gendin for this point.

23. Ronald Dworkin, "The Rights of Allan Bakke, " in *Ethics in Action: An Anthology*, ed. Hugh LaFollette (Cambridge, Mass.: Blackwell, 1997), 448.

24. Larry May and John C. Hughes, "Is Sexual Harassment Coercive?" in *Sexual Harassment: Confrontations and Decisions*, ed. Edmund Wall (Buffalo, New York: Prometheus Books, 1992), 61–68.

25. LeMoncheck and Hajdin, *Sexual Harassment*, 126.

26. *Tomkins v. Public Service Electric & Gas*, 422 F. Supp. 553 (D.C. N.J. 1976), 556.

27. Hughes and May, "*Sexual Harassment*," 267–268.

28. Anita M. Superson, "A Feminist Definition of Sexual Harassment," *Journal of Social Philosophy* 24, no. 1 (1993): 52.

29. May and Hughes, "Is Sexual Harassment Coercive," 64.

30. *Harris v. Forklift Systems, Inc.*, Justice Ginsberg concurring, 372.

31. Schultz, "Reconceptualizing Sexual Harassment," 1800.

32. Ibid., 1794.

BIBLIOGRAPHY

20/20: "The Speech Police: Is Sexual Speech Sexual Harassment?" ABC Television broadcast, May 12, 1995. Available in LEXIS, News Library, Script File.

Abdel-Gawad, Jehan A. "Kiddie Sex Harassment: How Title IX Could Level the Playing Field without Leveling the Playground." *Arizona Law Review* 39 (1997): 727–768.

Abrams, Kathryn. "The Pursuit of Social and Political Equality: Complex Claimants and Reductive Moral Judgments: New Patterns in the Search for Equality." *University of Pittsburgh Law Review* 57 (1996): 337–362.

———. "The Reasonable Woman: Sense and Sensibility in Sexual Harassment Law." *Dissent*, Winter 1995, 48–54.

———. "Title VII and the Complex Female Subject." *Michigan Law Review* 92 (1994): 2479–2540.

Aeberhard-Hodges, Jane. "Sexual Harassment in Employment: Recent Judicial and Arbitral Trends." *International Labour Review* 125, no. 5 (1996): 499–533.

Adams, Carole Elizabeth. *Women Clerks in Wilhelmine Germany*. New York: Cambridge University Press, 1988.

Adler, Robert S., and Ellen R. Peirce. "The Legal, Ethical, and Social Implications of the 'Reasonable Woman' Standard in Sexual Harassment Cases." *Fordham Law Review* 61 (1993): 773–827.

Aggarwal, Arjun P. *Sexual Harassment in the Workplace*. 2nd ed. Toronto: Butterworths, 1992.

Allen, Prudence. *The Concept of Woman: The Aristotelian Revolution, 750 BC–AD1250*. Grand Rapids, Mich.: Eerdmans, 1997.

American Association of University Women. *Hostile Hallways: The AAUW Survey on Sexual Harassment in American Schools*. Washington, D.C.: American Association of University Women, 1993.

Anagol-McGinn, Padma. "Sexual Harassment in India: A Case Study of Eve-teasing in Historical Perspective." In *Rethinking Sexual Harassment*, edited by Clare Brant and Yun Lee Too, 220–234. London: Pluto Press, 1994.

Arbery, Walter Christopher. "Individual Rights and the Powers of Government: Note: A Step Backward for Equality Principles: The 'Reasonable Woman'

Standard in Title VII Hostile Work Environment Sexual Harassment Claims." *Georgia Law Review* 27 (1993): 503–553.

Arvey, Richard D., and Marcie A. Cavanaugh. "Using Surveys to Assess the Prevalence of Sexual Harassment: Some Methodological Problems." *Journal of Social Issues* 51, no. 1 (1995): 39–53.

Ashraf, Saba. "The Reasonableness of the 'Reasonable Woman' Standard: An Evaluation of Its Use in Hostile Environment Sexual Harassment Claims under Title VII of the Civil Rights Act." *Hofstra Law Review* 21 (1992): 483–504.

Backhouse, Constance, and Leah Cohen. *Sexual Harassment on the Job*. Englewood Cliffs, New Jersey: Prentice-Hall, 1982.

Baird, Carol L., Nora L. Bensko, Paul A. Bell, Wayne Viney, and William Douglas Woody. "Gender Influence on Perceptions of Hostile Environment Sexual Harassment." *Psychological Reports* 77 (1995): 79–82.

Baker, Carrie N. "Proposed Title IX Guidelines on Sex Based Harassment of Students." *Emory Law Journal* 43 (1994): 271–319.

———. "Sexual Extortion: Criminalizing Quid Pro Quo Sexual Harassment." *Law and Inequality Journal* 13 (1994): 213–251.

Bernardin, Liesa L. "Does the Reasonable Woman Exist and Does She Have Any Place in Hostile Environment Sexual Harassment Claims under Title VII after Harris?" *Florida Law Review* 46 (1994): 291–322.

Bernstein, Anita. "Law, Culture, and Harassment." *University of Pennsylvania Law Review* 142 (1994): 1227–1331.

Blewett, Mary H. *We Will Rise in Our Might: Workingwomen's Voices from Nineteenth-Century New England*. Ithaca: Cornell University Press, 1991.

Bond, M. "Division 27 Sexual Harassment Survey: Definition, Impact, Environmental Context." *Community Psychologist* 21 (1988): 7–10.

Bowman, Cynthia Grant. "Street Harassment and the Informal Ghettoization of Women." *Harvard Law Review* 106, no. 3 (1993): 517–580.

Brenneman, Deborah S. "From a Woman's Point of View: The Use of the Reasonable Woman Standard in Sexual Harassment Cases." *University of Cincinnati* 60 (1992): 1281–1306.

Browne, Kingsley. "Biology, Equality, and the Law: The Legal Significance of Biological Sex Differences." *Southwestern Law Journal* 38 (1984): 617–702.

———. "An Evolutionary Perspective on Sexual Harassment: Seeking Roots in Biology Rather Than Ideology." *Journal of Contemporary Legal Issues* 8 (1997): 5–77.

———. "Title VII as Censorship: Hostile-Environment Harassment and the First Amendment." *Ohio State Law Journal* 52 (1991): 481–550.

Bukoffsky, Sylvia Hermann. "School District Liability for Student-Inflicted Sexual Harassment: School Administrators Learn a Lesson under Title IX." *Wayne Law Review* 42 (1995): 171–193.

Bularzik, Mary. "Sexual Harassment at the Workplace: Historical Notes." *Radical America* 12 (1978): 25–43.

Bully, Amy A., and Margaret Whitley. *Women's Work*. London: Methuen, 1894.

Buss, David M. *The Evolution of Desire: Strategies of Human Mating*. New York: Basic Books, 1994.

Campbell, Helen. *Prisoners of Poverty: Women Wage-Workers, Their Trades and Their Lives*. 1887. Reprint, New York: Garrett Press, 1970.

Carter, Victoria A. "Working on Dignity: EC Initiatives on Sexual Harassment in the Workplace." *Journal of International Law and Business* 12 (1992): 431–453.

Chamallas, Martha. "Consent, Equality, and the Legal Control of Sexual Conduct." *Southern California Law Review* 61 (1988): 777–861.

————. "Feminist Constructions of Objectivity: Multiple Perspectives in Sexual and Racial Harassment Litigation." *Texas Journal of Women and Legislation* 1 (1992): 95–142.

Chan, Anja Angelica. *Women and Sexual Harassment: A Practical Guide to the Legal Protections of Title VII and the Hostile Environment Claim.* New York: Haworth Press, 1994.

Childers, Jolynn. "Is There a Place for a Reasonable Woman in the Law? A Discussion of Recent Developments in Hostile Environment Sexual Harassment." *Duke Law Journal* 42 (1993): 854–904.

Chrisman, Robert, and Robert L. Allen, eds. *Court of Appeal: The Black Community Speaks Out on the Racial and Sexual Politics of Clarence Thomas vs. Anita Hill.* New York: Ballantine Books, 1992.

Christensen, F. M. "'Sexual Harassment' Must Be Eliminated." *Public Affairs Quarterly* 8, no. 1 (1994): 1–17.

Clark, Anna. *Women's Silence, Men's Violence: Sexual Assault in England 1770–1845.* London: Pandora, 1987.

Clatterbaugh, Kenneth. *Contemporary Perspectives on Masculinity: Men, Women, and Politics in Modern Society.* Boulder, Colorado: Westview Press, 1990.

Cohen, Lloyd R. "Sexual Harassment and the Law." *Society* 28, no. 4 (1991): 8–13.

Cole, E. K., ed. *Sexual Harassment on Campus: A Legal Compendium.* Washington, D.C.: National Association of College and University Attorneys, 1990.

Cole, Elisa Kircher. "Recent Developments in Sexual Harassment." *Journal of College and University Law* 13, no. 3 (1986): 267–284.

Coleman, Phyllis. "Sex in Power Dependency Relationships: Taking Unfair Advantage of the 'Fair' Sex." *Albany Law Review* 53 (1988): 95–141.

Colker, Ruth. "Whores, Fags, Dumb-Ass Women, Surly Blacks, and Competent Heterosexual White Men: The Sexual and Racial Morality Underlying Anti-Discrimination Doctrine." *Yale Journal of Law and Feminism* 7 (1995): 195–225.

Compa, Lance, and Tashia Hinchliffe-Darricarrere. "Doing Business in China and Latin America: Developments in Comparative and International Labor Law: Enforcing International Labor Rights through Corporate Codes of Conduct." *Columbia Journal of Transnational Law* 33 (1995): 663–689.

Connolly, Walter B., Jr., and Alison Marshall. "Sexual Harassment of University or College Students by Faculty Members." *Journal of College and University Law* 15, no. 4 (1989): 381–403.

Cornell, Drucilla. *The Imaginary Domain: Abortion, Pornography, and Sexual Harassment.* New York: Routledge, 1995.

Crenshaw, Kimberle. "Demarginalizing the Intersection of Race and Sex: A Black Feminist Critique of Antidiscrimination Doctrine, Feminist Theory, and Antiracist Politics." *University of Chicago Legal Forum* 139 (1989): 139–67.

Crichton, Michael. *Disclosure.* New York: Knopf, 1994.

Crouch, Margaret A. "Campus Consensual Relationship Policies." In *Globalism and the Obsolescence of the State,* edited by Yeager Hudson, 317–343. Lewiston, New York: Edwin Mellen Press, 1999.

————. "The Coherence of Sexual Harassment Law: The Problem of Same-Sex Harassment," presented at the Michigan Academy of Sciences and Letters, March 1999.

Dank, Barry M. "Campus Romances and Consenting Adults." *Chronicle of Higher Education* 29 (June 1994): B4.

Davis, Angela. *Women, Race, and Class.* New York: Random House, 1982.

Davis, Nancy "Ann." "Sexual Harassment in the University." In *Morality, Responsibility, and the University: Studies in Academic Ethics*, edited by Steven M. Cahn, 150–176. Philadelphia: Temple University Press, 1990.

DeBruin, Debra A. "Identifying Sexual Harassment: The Reasonable Woman Standard." In *Violence against Women: Philosophical Perspectives*, edited by Stanley G. French, Wanda Teays, and Laura M. Purdy, 107–122. Ithaca, New York: Cornell University Press, 1998.

DeChiara, Peter. "The Need for Universities to Have Rules on Consensual Sexual Relationships between Faculty Members and Students." *Columbia Journal of Law and Social Policy* 21 (1988): 137–162.

DeFour, Darlene C. "The Interface of Racism and Sexism on College Campuses." In *Sexual Harassment on College Campuses: Abusing the Ivory Power*, edited by Michele A. Paludi, 49–55. Albany: State University of New York Press, 1996.

del Rey Guanter, Salvador. "Employee Privacy in Spanish Labor Relations." *Comparative Labor Law Journal* 17 (1995): 122–138.

Department of Education. Office for Civil Rights. "Sexual Harassment Guidance: Harassment of Students by School Employees, Other Students, or Third Parties." *Federal Register* 62, no. 49 (March 13, 1997): 12033–12051.

Di Domenico, Timothy E. "Silva v. University of New Hampshire: The Precarious Balance between Student Hostile Environment Claims and Academic Freedom." *St. John's Law Review* 69 (1995): 609–632.

Dine, Janet, and Bob Watt. "Sexual Harassment: Moving Away from Discrimination." *Modern Law Review* 58 (1995): 343–363.

Dunkum, Betty L. "Where to Draw the Line: Handling Religious Harassment Issues in the Wake of the Failed EEOC Guidelines." *Notre Dame Law Review* 71 (1996): 953–989.

Dworkin, Ronald. "The Rights of Allan Bakke." In *Ethics in Action: An Anthology*, edited by Hugh LaFollette, 443–450. Cambridge, Massachusetts: Blackwell, 1997.

Dworkin, Terry Morehead, and Ellen R. Peirce. "Is Religious Harassment 'More Equal'?" *Seton Hall Law Review* 26 (1995): 44–91.

Dziech, Billie Wright, and Linda Weiner. *The Lecherous Professor: Sexual Harassment on Campus.* 2nd ed. Champaign: University of Illinois Press, 1992.

———. *The Lecherous Professor: Sexual Harassment on Campus.* Boston: Beacon Press, 1984.

Earle, Beverley H., and Gerald A. Madek. "An International Perspective on Sexual Harassment Law." *Law and Inequality* 12 (1993): 43–91.

Eason, Yla. "When the Boss Wants Sex." In *Feminist Frameworks: Alternative Accounts of the Relations between Women and Men*, edited by Alison M. Jaggar and Paula S. Rothenberg, 44–49. New York: McGraw-Hill, 1993.

Ellis, Judy T. "Sexual Harassment and Race: A Legal Analysis of Discrimination." *Journal of Legislation* 8, no. 1 (1981): 30–45.

Engels, Friedrich. *The Conditions of the Working Class in England.* Palo Alto: Stanford University Press, 1968.

Epstein, Richard A. *Forbidden Grounds: The Case against Employment Discrimination Laws.* Cambridge: Harvard University Press, 1992.

Eskenazi, Martin, and David Gallen, eds. *Sexual Harassment: Know Your Rights!* New York: Carroll & Graf, 1992.

Estrich, Susan. "Sex at Work." *Stanford Law Review* 43 (1991): 813–861.

Farley, Lin. *Sexual Shakedown: The Sexual Harassment of Women on the Job*. New York: McGraw-Hill, 1978.

Farrell, Warren. *The Myth of Male Power: Why Men Are the Disposable Sex*. New York: Simon & Schuster, 1993.

Feary, Vaughana Macy. "Sexual Harassment: Why the Corporate World Still Doesn't 'Get It,'" *Journal of Business Ethics* 13 (1994): 649–662.

"Female Kyoto University Graduates Report Sexual Harassment." *Japan Weekly Monitor*, November 18, 1996.

Fitzgerald, Louise F. "Sexual Harassment: The Definition and Measurement of a Construct." In *Sexual Harassment on College Campuses*, edited by Michele A. Paludi, 25–47. Albany: State University of New York Press, 1996.

Fitzgerald, Louise F., and Matthew Hesson-McInnis. "The Dimensions of Sexual Harassment: A Structural Analysis." *Journal of Vocational Behavior* 35 (1989): 309–326.

Fitzgerald, Louise F., Lauren M. Weitzman, Yael Gold, and Mimi Ormerod. "Academic Harassment: Sex and Denial in Scholarly Garb." *Psychology of Women Quarterly* 12 (1988): 329–340.

Fitzgerald, Louise F., Sandra L. Shullman, Nancy Bailey, Margaret Richards, Janice Swecker, Yael Gold, Mimi Ormerod, and Laren Weitzman. "The Incidence and Dimensions of Sexual Harassment in Academia and the Workplace." *Journal of Vocational Behavior* 32 (1988): 152–175.

Foner, Philip S. *Women and the Labor Movement: From World War I to the Present*. New York: Free Press, 1980.

Foucault, Michel. *The History of Sexuality*, vol. 1: *An Introduction*. Translated by Robert Hurley. New York: Vintage Books, 1978.

"France: Law against Sexual Harassment." *International Labour Review* 132, no. 1 (1993): 5.

Franke, Katherine M. "The Central Mistake of Sex Discrimination Law: The Disaggregation of Sex from Gender." *University of Pennsylvania Law Review* 144 (1995): 1–99.

———. "What's Wrong with Sexual Harassment?" *Stanford Law Review* 49, no. 4 (1997): 691–772.

Friedan, Betty. *The Feminine Mystique*. New York: Dell, 1974.

Frye, Marilyn. "The Possibility of Feminist Theory." In *Feminist Frameworks: Alternative Theoretical Accounts of the Relations between Women and Men*, edited by Alison M. Jaggar and Paula S. Rothenberg, 103–112. 3rd ed. New York: McGraw-Hill, 1993.

Gallop, Jane. *Feminist Accused of Sexual Harassment*. Durham: Duke University Press, 1997.

———. "The Lecherous Professor." *Differences: A Journal of Feminist Cultural Studies* 7 (1995): 1–14.

Gamble, Barbara S., ed. *Sex Discrimination Handbook*. Washington, D.C.: Bureau of National Affairs, 1992.

Gerard, Jules B. "The First Amendment in a Hostile Environment: A Primer on Free Speech and Sexual Harassment." *Notre Dame Law Review* 68 (1993): 1003–1035.

Giddings, Paula. *When and Where I Enter: The Impact of Black Women on Race and Sex in America*. New York: Bantam Books, 1984.

Gilmore, David D. *Manhood in the Making: Cultural Concepts of Masculinity*. New Haven: Yale University Press, 1990.

Glaser, Robert D., and Joseph S. Thorpe. "Unethical Intimacy: A Survey of Contact and Advances between Psychology Educators and Female Graduate Students." *American Psychologist* 41 (1986): 43–51.

Gorney, Cynthia. "Teaching Johnny the Appropriate Way to Flirt." *New York Times Magazine*, June 13, 1999, 42–7, 67, 73, 80, 82–3.

Govier, Trudy. *A Practical Study of Argument.* 2nd ed. Belmont, California: Wadsworth, 1988.

Gowan, Mary A., and Raymond A. Zimmerman. "Impact of Ethnicity, Gender, and Previous Experience on Juror Judgments in Sexual Harassment Cases." *Journal of Applied Social Psychology* 26, no. 7 (1996): 596–617.

Gregory, Robert J. "You Can Call Me a 'Bitch' Just Don't Use the 'N-Word': Some Thoughts on *Galloway v. General Motors Service Parts Operations* and *Rodgers v. Western-Southern Life Insurance Co."* *DePaul Law Review* 46 (1997): 741–777.

Grimsely, Kirstin Downey. "Mitsubishi Settles for $34 Million." *Washington Post,* June 12, 1998, A01.

Gross, Kara L. "Toward Gender Equality and Understanding: Recognizing that Same-Sex Sexual Harassment Is Sex Discrimination." *Brooklyn Law Review* 62 (1996): 1165–1215.

Gutek, B. A., B. Morasch, and A. G. Cohen. "Interpreting Social-Sexual Behavior in a Work Setting." *Journal of Vocational Behavior* 22 (1983): 30–48.

Gutek, Barbara A. *Sex and the Workplace: The Impact of Sexual Behavior and Harassment on Women, Men, and Organizations.* San Francisco: Jossey-Bass, 1985.

Gutek, Barbara A., and Maureen O'Conner. "The Empirical Basis for the Reasonable Woman Standard." *Journal of Social Issues* 51 (1995): 151–66.

Hager, Mark McLaughlin. "Harassment As a Tort: Why Title VII Hostile Environment Liability Should Be Curtailed." *Connecticut Law Review* 30, no. 2 (1998): 375–439.

Harding, Sandra. *The Science Question in Feminism.* Ithaca, New York: Cornell University Press, 1986.

———. *Whose Science? Whose Knowledge? Thinking from Women's Lives.* Ithaca, New York: Cornell University Press, 1991.

Harris, Angela P. "Race and Essentialism in Feminist Legal Theory." *Stanford Law Review* 42 (1990): 581–616.

Hayashi, Hiroko. "Women's Rights as International Human Rights: Sexual Harassment in the Workplace and Equal Employment Legislation." *St. John's Law Review* 69 (1995): 37–60.

Hearn, J., and W. Parkin. *'Sex' at 'Work': The Power and Paradox of Organisation and Sexuality.* New York: St. Martin's, 1987.

Hebert, L. Camille. "Sexual Harassment Is Gender Harassment." *Kansas Law Review* 43 (1995): 565–607.

Henken, Jill W. "Hostile Environment Claims of Sexual Harassment: The Continuing Expansion of Sexual Harassment Law." *Villanova Law Review* 34, no. 6 (1989): 1243–1264.

Hessler, Richard M. *Social Research Methods.* St. Paul, Minn.: West, 1992.

Hill, Anita Faye, and Emma Coleman Jordan, eds. *Race, Gender, and Power in America: The Legacy of the Hill-Thomas Hearings.* New York: Oxford University Press, 1995.

Hoffman, Frances L. "Sexual Harassment in Academia: Feminist Theory and Institutional Practice." *Harvard Educational Review* 56, no. 2 (1986): 105–21.

Hoff-Wilson, Joan. *Law, Gender, and Injustice: A Legal History of U.S. Women.* New York: New York University Press, 1991.

Honderich, Ted, ed. *The Oxford Companion to Philosophy*. New York: Oxford University Press, 1995.

hooks, bell. *Feminist Theory: From Margin to Center*. Boston: South End Press, 1984.

Hughes, John C., and Larry May. "Is Sexual Harassment Coercive?" In *Moral Rights in the Work Place*, edited by Gertrude Ezorsky, 65–68. Albany: State University of New York Press, 1987.

———. "Sexual Harassment." *Social Theory and Practice* 6 (1980): 249–280.

Hustoles, Thomas P. "Consensual Relations Issues in Higher Education." In *Sexual Harassment on Campus: A Legal Compendium*, edited by E. K. Cole, 251–255. Washington, D.C.: National Association of College and University Attorneys, 1990.

International Labour Organization. "Combating Sexual Harassment." *Conditions of Work Digest* 11, no. 1 (1992).

"Japan Adopts Action Plan on Sexual Discrimination." *Reuters North American Wire*, December 13, 1996.

"Japan Firms Have No Sex Harassment Countermeasures." *Reuters World Service*, December 12, 1996.

Jones, Jacqueline. *Labor of Love, Labor of Sorrow: Black Women and Work and the Family, from Slavery to the Present*. New York: Vintage Books, 1985.

Joyce, Amy. "Companies Insuring Selves against Discrimination Suits." *Washington Post*, May 17, 1998, financial section.

Juliano, A. C. "Did She Ask for It?: The 'Unwelcome' Requirement in Sexual Harassment Cases." *Cornell Law Review* 77 (1992): 1558–1592.

Keller, Elisabeth A. "Consensual Amorous Relationships between Faculty and Students: Policy Implications and the Constitutional Right to Privacy." In *Sexual Harassment on Campus: A Legal Compendium*, edited by Joan Van Tol, 80–88. Washington, D.C.: National Association of College and University Attorneys, 1987.

Kelly, Joseph M., and Bob Watt. "Damages in Sex Harassment Cases: A Comparative Study of American, Canadian, and British Law." *New York Law School Journal of International and Comparative Law* 16 (1996): 79–134.

Kitcher, Philip. *Vaulting Ambition: Sociobiology and the Quest for Human Nature*. Cambridge: MIT Press, 1985.

Korda, Michael. *Male Chauvinism! How It Works*. New York: Random House, 1973.

Kymlicka, Will. "Liberalism." In *The Oxford Companion to Philosophy*, edited by Ted Honderich, 483–485. New York: Oxford University Press, 1995.

LeMoncheck, Linda, and Mane Hajdin. *Sexual Harassment: A Debate*. Lanham, Maryland: Rowman & Littlefield, 1997.

Lengnick-Hall, Mark L. "Sexual Harassment Research: A Methodological Critique." *Personnel Psychology* 48, no. 4 (1995): 290–308.

Lerner, Gerda, ed. *Black Women in White America: A Documentary History*. New York: Pantheon Books, 1972.

Lindemann, Barbara, and David D. Kadue. *Sexual Harassment in Employment Law*. Washington, D.C.: Bureau of National Affairs, 1992.

Lipper, Nicolle R. "Sexual Harassment in the Workplace: A Comparative Study of Great Britain and the United States." *Comparative Labor Law Journal* 13 (1992): 293–342.

Lippman, Thomas W. "State Dept. Seeks Gains For Women." *Washington Post*, March 25, 1997.

Locke, John. *An Essay concerning Human Understanding*. Oxford: Clarendon Press, 1975.

Lorde, Audre. *Sister Outsider*. Trumansburg, New York: Crossing Press, 1984.

Lugones, Maria. "Playfulness, 'World'-Traveling, and Loving Perception." *Hypatia* 2, no. 2 (1987): 3–19

MacKinnon, Catharine A. *Feminism Unmodified: Discourses on Life and Law*. Cambridge: Harvard University Press, 1987.

———. *Only Words*. Cambridge: Harvard University Press, 1993.

———. *Sexual Harassment of Working Women: A Case of Sex Discrimination*. New Haven: Yale University Press, 1979.

———. *Toward a Feminist Theory of the State*. Cambridge: Harvard University Press, 1989.

Mansnerus, Laura. "Colleges Break Up Dangerous Liaisons." *New York Times*, April 7, 1991.

Mappes, Thomas A., and Jane S. Zembaty, eds. *Social Ethics: Morality and Social Policy*. 4th ed. New York: McGraw-Hill, 1992.

Maule, Frances. *She Strives to Conquer: Business Behavior, Opportunities, and Job Requirements for Women*. New York: Funk & Wagnalls, 1935.

May, Larry, and John C. Hughes. "Is Sexual Harassment Coercive?" In *Sexual Harassment: Confrontations and Decisions*, edited by Edmund Wall, 61–68. Buffalo, New York: Prometheus Books, 1992.

Mead, Margaret. "A Proposal: We Need Taboos on Sex at Work." *Redbook*, April 1978, 31.

Monnin, Paul N. "Proving Welcomeness: The Admissibility of Evidence of Sexual History in Sexual Harassment Claims after the 1994 Amendments to Federal Rule of Evidence 412." *Vanderbilt Law Review* 48 (1995): 1155–1213.

Moore, Brooke Noel, and Richard Parker. *Critical Thinking*. 4th ed. Mountain View, California: Mayfield, 1995.

Morrison, Toni, ed. *Race-ing Justice, En-gendering Power: Essays on Anita Hill, Clarence Thomas, and the Construction of Social Reality*. New York: Pantheon Books, 1992.

Mundiya, Tariq. "Book Review: Conditions of Work Digest: Combating Sexual Harassment at Work." *Comparative Labor Law Journal* 15 (1993): 119–126.

Murphy, Jeffrie, and Jules Coleman. *The Philosophy of Law: An Introduction to Jurisprudence*. Totowa, New Jersey: Rowman & Allanheld, 1984.

Nathan, Maud. *The Story of an Epoch-Making Movement*. Garden City, New York: Doubleday, Page, 1926.

"No Bliss from Boy's Kiss," *Washington Post*, September 25, 1996.

Note. "Sexual Harassment Claims of Abusive Work Environment under Title VII." *Harvard Law Review* 97 (1984): 1449–1467.

Olsen, Jack. *The Girls in the Office*. New York: Simon & Schuster, 1972.

Ontiveros, Maria L. "Fictionalizing Harassment—Disclosing the Truth." *Michigan Law Review* 93 (1995): 1373–1400.

"Over 90% of Firms Lack Steps on Sexual Harassment." *Japan Economic Newswire*, December 12, 1996.

Padgitt, S. C., and J. S. Padgitt. "Cognitive Structure of Sexual Harassment: Implications of University Policy." *Journal of College Student Personnel* (January 1986): 34–39.

Paglia, Camille. *Sex, Art, and American Culture*. New York: Vintage Books, 1992.

———. *Vamps and Tramps*. New York: Vintage Books, 1994.

Paludi, Michele A., ed. *Sexual Harassment on College Campuses: Abusing the Ivory Power*. Albany: State University of New York Press, 1996.

Paludi, Michele A., and Richard Barickman. *Academic and Workplace Sexual Harassment: A Resource Manual.* Albany: State University of New York Press, 1991.

Paul, Ellen Frankel. "Bared Buttocks and Federal Cases." *Society* 28, no. 4 (1991): 4–7.

———. "Sexual Harassment as Sex Discrimination: A Defective Paradigm." *Yale Law and Policy Review* 8, no. 2 (1990): 333–365.

Pellicciotti, Joseph M. "Workplace Sexual Harassment Law in Canada and The United States: A Comparative Study of the Doctrinal Development concerning the Nature of Actionable Sexual Harassment." *Pace International Law Review* 8 (1996): 339–397.

Petrocelli, William, and Barbara Kate Repa. *Sexual Harassment on the Job.* Berkeley, California: Nolo Press, 1992.

Pinker, Steven. "Why They Kill Their Newborns." *New York Times Magazine,* November 2, 1997, 52–54.

Pollack, Kenneth L. "Current Issues in Sexual Harassment Law." *Vanderbilt Law Review* 48 (1995): 1009–1018.

Pomeroy, Sarah B. *Goddesses, Whores, Wives, and Slaves: Women in Classical Antiquity.* New York: Shocken, 1975.

Pope, K., H. Levenson, and L. Schover. "Sexual Intimacy in Psychology Training: Results and Implications of a National Survey." *American Psychologist* 34, no. 3 (1979): 682–689.

Popovich, Paula M., DeeAnn N. Gehlauf, Jeffrey A. Jolton, Jill M. Somers, and Rhonda M. Godinho. "Perceptions of Sexual Harassment as a Function of Sex of Rater and Incident Form and Consequence." *Sex Roles* 27, nos. 11/12 (1992): 609–625.

Popovich, P. M., B. J. Licata, D. Nokovich, T. Martelli, and S. Zoloty. "Assessing the Incidence and Perceptions of Sexual Harassment Behaviors among American Undergraduates." *Journal of Psychology* 120 (1986): 387–396.

Post, Russell S. "The Serpentine Wall and the Serpent's Tongue: Rethinking the Religious Harassment Debate." *Virginia Law Review* 83 (1997): 177–206.

Postrel, Virginia I. "Persecution Complex." *Reason,* August 26/September 1994, 4, 6.

"Proposed Rules." *Federal Register* 58, no. 189 (October 1, 1993).

Putnam, Hilary. *Reason, Truth, and History.* Cambridge: Cambridge University Press, 1981.

Ravitch, Frank. "Beyond Reasonable Accommodation: The Availability and Structure of a Cause of Action for Workplace Harassment under the Americans with Disabilities Act." *Cardozo Law Review* 15 (1994): 1475–1522.

Reilly, M. E., B. Lott, and S. M. Gallogy. "Sexual Harassment of University Students." *Sex Roles* 15 (1986): 333–358.

Rhode, Deborah L. *Justice and Gender: Sex Discrimination and the Law.* Cambridge: Harvard University Press, 1989.

Richards, Janet Radcliffe. *The Skeptical Feminist.* London: Routledge & Kegan Paul, 1980.

Richardson, Dorothy. *The Long Day: The True Story of a New York Working Girl as Told by Herself.* New York: The Century Co., 1905.

Riggs, Robert O., Patricia H. Murrell, and JoAnne C. Cutting. *Sexual Harassment in Higher Education: From Conflict to Community.* Washington, D.C.: ASHE-ERIC Higher Education Report 93–2, 1993.

Roberts, Barry S., and Richard A. Mann. "Sexual Harassment in the Workplace: A Primer." *Akron Law Review* 29 (1996): 269–289.

Robinson, W., and P. Reid. "Sexual Intimacies in Psychology Revisited." *Professional Psychology: Research and Practice* 16, no. 4 (1985): 512–20.

Roiphe, Katie. *The Morning After: Sex, Fear, and Feminism.* Boston: Little, Brown, 1993.

Romano, Carlin. Review of *Only Words*, by Catharine A. MacKinnon. *Nation*, November 15, 1993, 563–570.

Root, Michael. *Philosophy of Social Science: The Methods, Ideals, and Politics of Social Inquiry.* Cambridge, Massachusetts: Blackwell, 1993.

Roth, Stefanie H. "Sex Discrimination 101: Developing a Title IX Analysis for Sexual Harassment in Education." *Journal of Law and Education* 23, no. 4 (1994): 459–521.

"Rough Traders of Wall Street." *Guardian Weekly*, May 3, 1998, 22.

Rubenstein, Michael. "Dealing with Sexual Harassment at Work: The Experience of Industrialized Countries." *Conditions of Work Digest* 11, no. 1 (1992): 7–19.

———. *The Dignity of Women at Work: A Report on the Problem of Sexual Harassment in the Member States of the European Communities.* Luxembourg: Commission of the European Communities, Office for Official Publications of the European Communities, 1988.

Rubenstein, Michael, and Ineke M. de Vries. *How to Combat Sexual Harassment at Work: A Guide to Implementing the European Commission Code of Practice.* Luxembourg: Commission of the European Communities, Office for Official Publications of the European Communities, 1993.

Safran, Claire. "How Do You Handle Sex on the Job?" *Redbook*, January 1976, 74–75.

———. "What Men Do to Women on the Job: A Shocking Look at Sexual Harassment." *Redbook*, November 1976, 149, 217–224.

Sangree, Suzanne. "Title VII Prohibitions against Hostile Environment Sexual Harassment and the First Amendment: No Collision in Sight." *Rutgers Law Review* 47 (1995): 461–561.

Schafer, Judith K. "Open and Notorious Concubinage." In *Black Women in American History: From Colonial Times through the Nineteenth Century*, vol. 4, edited by Darlene Hines, 1192–1194. Brooklyn: Carlson, 1990.

Schlafly, Phyllis. "Feminist Assault on Reasonableness." *Phyllis Schlafly Report* 30, no. 5 (December 1996).

———. "Feminist Hypocrisy and Double Standards." *Phyllis Schlafly Report* 31, no. 10 (May 1998).

———. "President Clinton is Embarrassed," www.eagleforum.org/column/dec96/96–12–26.html.

Schneider, Ronna Greff. "Sexual Harassment and Higher Education." *Texas Law Review* 65 (1987): 525–83.

Schultz, Vicki. "Reconceptualizing Sexual Harassment." *Yale Law Journal* 107 (1998): 1696–1805.

———. "Sex Is the Least of It: Let's Focus Harassment Law on Work, Not Sex." *Nation*, May 25, 1998, 11–15.

Segrave, Kerry. *The Sexual Harassment of Women in the Workplace, 1600–1993.* Jefferson, North Carolina: McFarland, 1994.

Shenon, Philip. "Command Decision: Army Blames Its Leadership for Sex Harassment." *Ann Arbor News*, September 12, 1997.

Sherer, Monica L. "No Longer Just Child's Play: School Liability under Title IX for Peer Sexual Harassment." *University of Pennsylvania Law Review* 141 (1993): 2119–2158.

Shimbun, Yomiuri. "Beefing Up Sexual Harassment Policies." *Daily Yomiuri*, May 8, 1996, p. 9.

Shively, Tanya Martinez. "Sexual Harassment in the European Union: King Rex Meets Potiphar's Wife." *Louisiana Law Review* 55 (1995): 1087–1148.

Silverman, Dierdre. "Sexual Harassment: Working Women's Dilemma." *Quest* 3 (1976–77): 13–24.

Skaine, Rosemarie. *Power and Gender: Issues in Sexual Dominance and Harassment.* Jefferson, North Carolina: McFarland, 1996.

Small, Mary Jo, and Julia Mears. "To Draft a More Perfect Policy: The Development of the University of Iowa's Sexual Harassment Policy." In *Sexual Harassment on Campus: A Legal Compendium*, edited by Joan Van Tol, 135–149. Washington, D.C.: National Association of College and University Attorneys, 1988.

Smart, Carol. *Law, Crime, and Sexuality: Essays in Feminism.* London: Sage Publications, 1995.

Smuts, Robert W. *Women and Work in America.* New York: Columbia University Press, 1959.

Solomon, Robert C. "The Virtue of (Erotic) Love." In *The Philosophy of (Erotic) Love*, edited by Robert C. Solomon and Kathleen M. Higgins, 492–518. Manhattanville: University Press of Kansas, 1991.

Sommers, Christina Hoff. *Who Stole Feminism? How Women Have Betrayed Women.* New York: Simon & Schuster, 1994.

"Spain Revises 147-year-old Penal Code." *Reuters North American Wire*, November 8, 1995.

Spelman, Elizabeth V. *Inessential Woman: Problems of Exclusion in Feminist Thought.* Boston: Beacon Press, 1988.

Spoor, Julia. "Go Tell It on the Mountain, but Keep It Out of the Office: Religious Harassment in the Workplace." *Valparaiso University Law Review* 31 (1997): 971–1016.

Stanovich, Keith E. *How to Think Straight about Psychology.* 5th ed. New York: Longman, 1998.

Stewart, James B. "Coming Out at Chrysler." *New Yorker*, July 21, 1997, 38–49.

Stites, M. Cynara. "University Consensual Relationship Policies." In *Sexual Harassment on College Campuses: Abusing the Ivory Power*, edited by Michele A. Paludi, 153–175. Albany: State University of New York Press, 1996.

———. "What's Wrong with Faculty-Student Consensual Sexual Relationships?" In *Sexual Harassment on College Campuses: Abusing the Ivory Power*, edited by Michele A. Paludi, 115–139. Albany: State University of New York Press, 1996.

Strossen, Nadine. *Defending Pornography.* New York: Anchor, 1996.

Superson, Anita M. "A Feminist Definition of Sexual Harassment." *Journal of Social Philosophy* 24, no. 1 (1993): 46–64.

Swisher, Karin L., ed. *Sexual Harassment.* San Diego, California: Greenhaven Press, 1992.

Tangri, Sandra S., Martha R. Burt, and Leanor B. Johnson. "Sexual Harassment at Work: Three Explanatory Models." *Journal of Social Issues* 38, no. 4 (1982): 33–54.

Tata, Jasmine. "The Structure and Phenomenon of Sexual Harassment: Impact of Category of Sexually Harassing Behavior, Gender, and Hierarchical Level." *Journal of Applied Social Psychology* 23 (1993): 199–211.

Tead, Ordway. *Instincts in Industry: A Study of Working-Class Psychology.* 1918. Reprint. New York: Arno & New York Times, 1969.

Terpstra, David E., and Susan E. Cook. "Complaint Characteristics and Reported

Behaviors and Consequences Associated with Formal Sexual Harassment Charges." *Personnel Psychology* 38 (1985): 559–574.

Thacker, Rebecca A., and Stephen F. Gohmann. "Male/Female Differences in Perceptions and Effects of Hostile Environment Sexual Harassment: 'Reasonable Assumptions'?" *Public Personnel Management* 22, no. 3 (1993): 461–472.

Thorpe, Joshua F. "Gender-Based Harassment and the Hostile Work Environment." *Duke Law Journal* (1990): 1361–1397.

Till, Frank. J. *Sexual Harassment: A Report on the Sexual Harassment of Students.* Washington, D.C.: U.S. Dept. of Education, 1980.

Tong, Rosemarie. *Feminist Thought: A Comprehensive Introduction.* Boulder, Colorado: Westview Press, 1989.

———. *Women, Sex, and the Law.* Totowa, New Jersey: Rowman & Littlefield, 1984.

Trigg, Roger. *Understanding Social Science: A Philosophical Introduction to the Social Sciences.* Oxford: Basil Blackwell, 1985.

Trusted, Jennifer. *Inquiry and Understanding: An Introduction to Explanation in the Physical and Human Sciences.* London: MacMillan, 1987.

Tuana, Nancy. "Sexual Harassment in Academe: Issues of Power and Coercion." In *Sexual Harassment: Confrontations and Decisions,* edited by Edmund Wall, 49–60. Buffalo, New York: Prometheus Books, 1992.

"U.K.: Why Business Is in Two Minds over Europe." *Aberdeen Press and Journal,* May 14, 1997.

"UN Committee on Elimination of Discrimination against Women Concludes Seventeenth Session at HQ." *M2 Presswire,* July 29, 1997.

Unikel, Robert. "'Reasonable' Doubts: A Critique of the Reasonable Woman Standard in American Jurisprudence." *Northwestern University Law Review* 87 (1992): 326–375.

United nations. *The Nairobi Forward-Looking Strategies for the Advancement of Women.* Adopted by the World Conference to Review and Appraise the Achievements of the United Nations Decade for Women: Equality, Development and Peace, Nairobi, Kenya, 15–26 July 1985.

U.S. Congress. Senate. Committee on Labor and Human Relations. *Sex Discrimination in the Workplace: Hearing before the Committee on Labor and Human Resources.* 97th Cong., 1st sess. 1981.

U.S. Merit Systems Protection Board. *Sexual Harassment in the Federal Workplace: Trends, Progress, Continuing Challenges.* Washington, D.C.: U.S. Government Printing Office, 1995.

———. *Sexual Harassment in the Federal Government: An Update.* Washington, D.C.: U.S. Government Printing Office, 1988.

———. *Sexual Harassment in the Federal Workplace: Is It a Problem?* Washington, D.C.: U.S. Government Printing Office, 1981.

Vaux, Alan. "Paradigmatic Assumptions in Sexual Harassment Research: Being Guided without Being Misled." *Journal of Vocational Behavior* 42 (1993): 116–135.

Vhay, Michael D. "The Harms of Asking: Towards a Comprehensive Treatment of Sexual Harassment." *University of Chicago Law Review* 55 (1988): 328–362.

Vigil, Julie. "Expanding the Hostile Environment Theory to Cover Age Discrimination: How Far Is Too Far?" *Pepperdine Law Review* 23 (1996): 565–606.

Volokh, Eugene. "Freedom of Speech and Workplace Harassment." *UCLA Law Review* 39 (1992): 1791–1872.

———. "What Speech Does 'Hostile Work Environment' Harassment Law Restrict?" *Georgetown Law Journal* 85 (1997): 627–648.

Wall, Edmund. "The Definition of Sexual Harassment." In *Sexual Harassment: Confrontations and Decisions*, edited by Edmund Wall, 69–85. Buffalo, New York: Prometheus Books, 1992.

Wall, Edmund, ed. *Sexual Harassment: Confrontations and Decisions*. Buffalo, New York: Prometheus Books, 1992.

Wartenberg, Thomas E. *The Forms of Power: From Domination to Transformation*. Philadelphia: Temple University Press, 1990.

Watts, Barbara. "Legal Issues." In *Sexual Harassment on College Campuses: Abusing the Ivory Power*, edited by Michele A. Paludi, 9–24. Albany: State University of New York Press, 1996.

Weeks, Elaine Lunsford, Jacqueline M. Boles, Albeno P. Garbin, and John Blount. "The Transformation of Sexual Harassment from a Private Trouble into a Public Issue." *Sociological Inquiry* 56, no. 4 (1986): 432–455.

Wei, Virginia W. "Asian Women and Employment Discrimination: Using Intersectionality Theory to Address Title VII Claims Based on Combined Factors of Race, Gender, and National Origin." *Boston College Law Review* 37 (1996): 771–812.

Weiss, Philip. "Don't Even Think About It." *New York Times Magazine*, May 3, 1998, 43–47, 58–60, 68, 81.

West, Robin. *Narrative, Authority, and Law*. Ann Arbor: University of Michigan Press, 1993.

White, David. "Spain Overhauls Penal Code." *Financial Times* (London), November 9, 1995, 3.

Widor, Aimee L. "Fact or Fiction?: Role-Reversal Sexual Harassment in the Modern Workplace." *University of Pittsburgh Law Review* 58 (1996): 225–254.

Will, George. "Sex in Sacramento." *Newsweek*, April 3, 1995, 76.

Williams, Patricia J. "A Rare Case Study of Muleheadedness and Men." In *Race-ing Justice, En-gendering Power*, edited by Toni Morrison, 159–171. New York: Pantheon Books, 1992.

Wilson, E.O. *On Human Nature*. Cambridge: Harvard University Press, 1978.

Winks, Patricia L. "Legal Implications of Sexual Contact between Teacher and Student." *Journal of Law and Education* 11, no. 4 (1982): 437–477.

Winston, Judith A. "Mirror, Mirror on the Wall: Title VII, Section 1981, and the Intersection of Race and Gender in the Civil Rights Act of 1990." *California Law Review* 79 (1991): 775–805.

Wittgenstein, Ludwig. *Philosophical Investigations*. Translated by G. E. M. Anscombe. 3rd ed. New York: Macmillan, 1968.

Wolf, Naomi. *Fire with Fire: The New Female Power and How It Will Change the 21st Century*. New York: Random House, 1993.

Wolff, Leon. "Eastern Twists on Western Concepts: Equality Jurisprudence and Sexual Harassment In Japan." *Pacific Rim Law & Policy Journal* 5 (1996): 509–535.

"Women's Groups, Unions Press for Sexual Harassment Ban." *Japan Weekly Monitor*, August 25, 1996.

Wood, Julia T. "Saying It Makes It So: The Discursive Construction of Sexual Harassment." In *Conceptualizing Sexual Harassment as Discursive Practice*, edited by Shereen G. Bingham. Westport, Connecticut: Praeger, 1994.

Woodhouse, Susan Perissinotto. "Same-Gender Sexual Harassment: Is It Sex Discrimination under Title VII?" *Santa Clara Law Review* 36 (1996): 1147–1186.

Young, Sherry. "Getting to Yes: The Case against Banning Consensual Relationships in Higher Education." *American University Journal of Gender and Law* 4 (Spring 1996): 269–302.

Zalk, Sue Rosenberg, Judith Dederich, and Michele A. Paludi. "Women Students' Assessment of Consensual Relationships with Their Professors: Ivory Power Reconsidered." In *Sexual Harassment on Campus: A Legal Compendium*, edited by E. K. Cole, 103–133. Washington, D.C.: National Association of College and University Attorneys, 1990.

Zimmer, Michael J., Charles A. Sullivan, Richard F. Richards, and Deborah A. Calloway. *Cases and Materials on Employment Discrimination*. 3rd edition. New York: Little, Brown, 1994.

INDEX

Abrams, Kathryn, 146, 164, 192, 198
abuse of power
  and the definition of sexual
    harassment, 4, 5, 231
  and discrimination law, 177
  and empirical research, 116
  and the liberal perspective, 164,
    224
  and quid pro quo sexual harass-
    ment, 181, 223, 228
  and sexual harassment torts, 183
  and the sociocultural perspective
    35, 151
  and the United Nations classifica-
    tion of sexual harassment, 90
academic sexual harassment, 69–84
  of kindergarten through twelfth
    grade students, 3, 117–121
  of college and university students,
    104, 105–107, 108–109,
    115–117
  See also peer harassment.
African Americans, sexual harassment of, 6, 26, 39, 50, 117–121,
  197
Age Discrimination in Employment
  Act of 1988, 219–220
age, harassment on the basis of, 206,
  219–220
Alexander v. Yale University, 70–71

American Association of University
  Women (AAUW) survey,
  117–121
Americans with Disabilities Act of
  1991, 218–219
arguments linking sexual harassment and sex discrimination. *See*
  differential treatment argument;
  sex stereotype argument; sexual
  desire argument
Arvey, Richard D., and Marcie A.
  Cavanaugh, 103–104

Baker, Carrie, 74–75, 76
*Bakke v. University of California
  Regents,* 226
Barnes v. Costle, 41–43, 47–48, 53,
  70, 155
Barnes v. Train, 39, 40, 41, 47, 83
because of sex. *See* sex-based
Bernstein, Anita, 184–185
bias in empirical research on sexual
  harassment
  in reports of respondents,
    104–105
  of researchers, 105–107
  in samples, 103–104
bisexual harasser, 43–46, 179,
  229–230, 246 n. 60
Bork, Robert, 38, 246 n. 60